determine age-appropriate...
our books in four categories: EVERYONE,
TEEN, TEEN + and MATURE. For the TEEN,
TEEN + and MATURE categories, we include
additional, specific descriptions to assist con-
sumers in determining if the book is age
appropriate. (Our MATURE books are shipped
shrink-wrapped with a Parental Advisory
sticker affixed to the wrapper.)

EVERYONE

**Titles with this rating are appropriate
for all age readers. They contain no
offensive material. They may contain
mild violence and/or some comic
mischief.**

TEEN

**Titles with this rating are appropriate
for a teen audience and older. They
may contain some violent content,
language, and/or suggestive themes.**

**TEEN
PLUS**

Titles with this rating are appropriate
for an audience of 16 and older.
They may contain partial nudity, mild
language and intense violence.

...re appropriate
... They may con-
...udity, sex and
...r older readers.

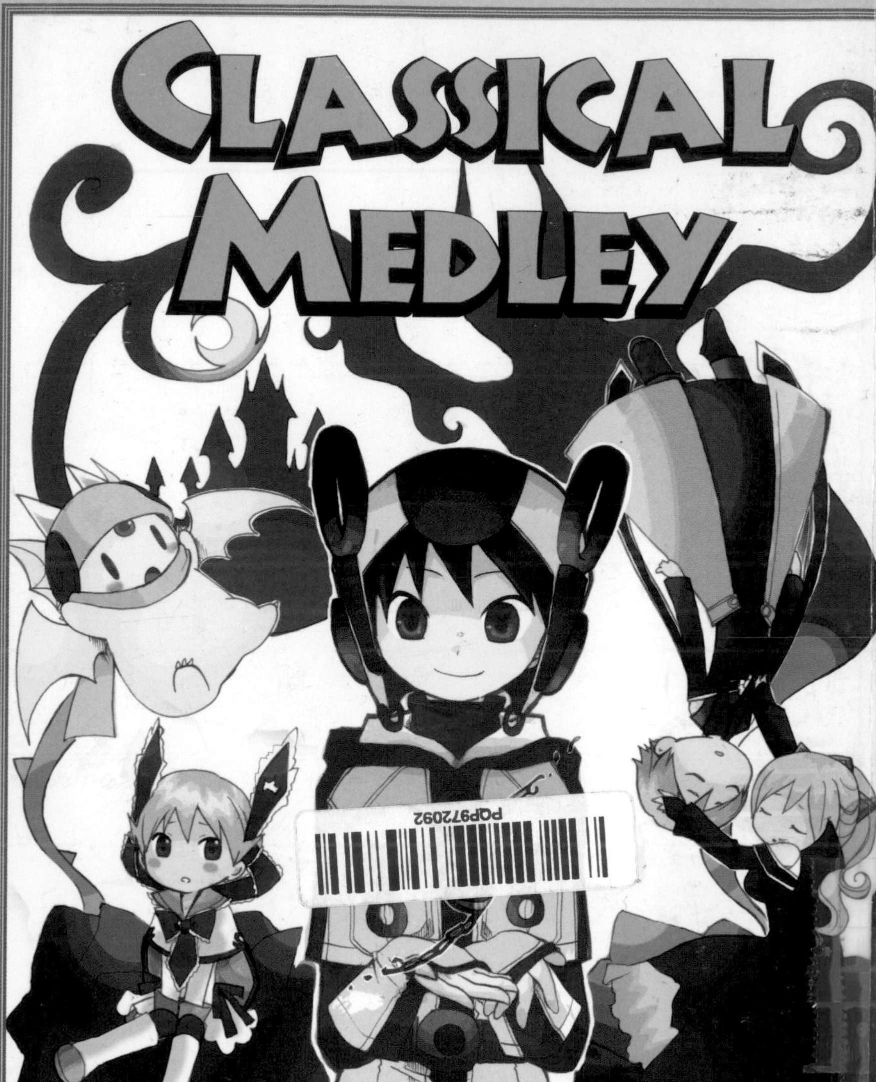
CLASSICAL MEDLEY
1
Sanae Kana

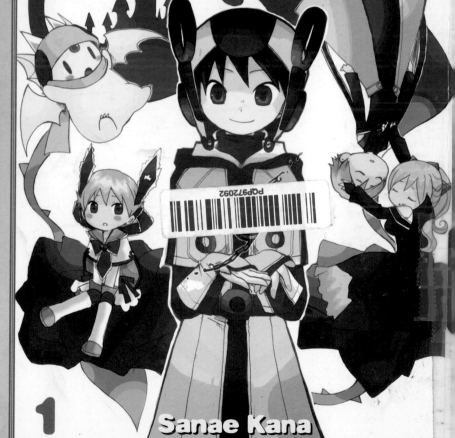

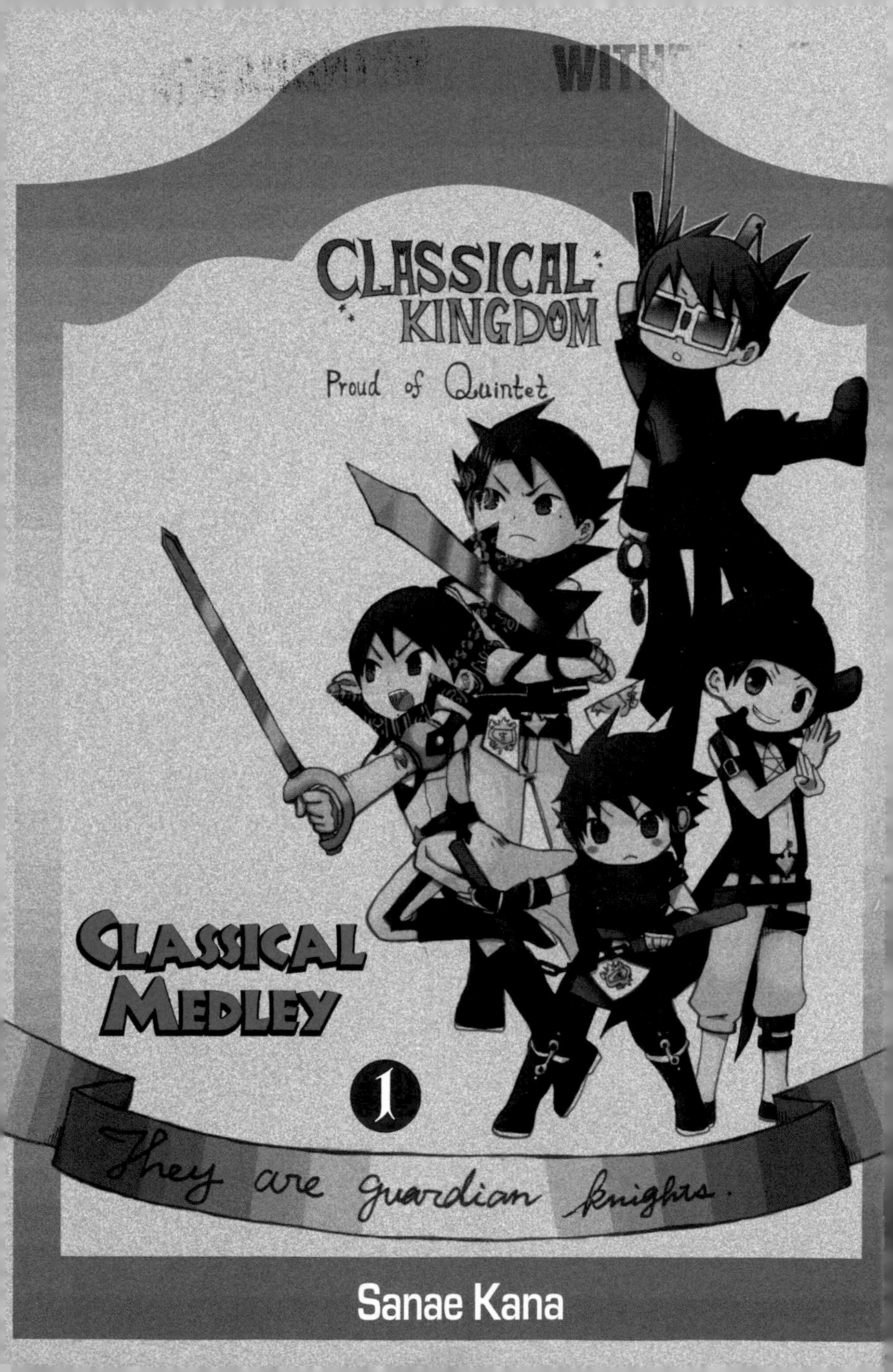

CLASSICAL KINGDOM
Proud of Quintet
CLASSICAL MEDLEY
1
They are guardian knights.
Sanae Kana

CONTENTS

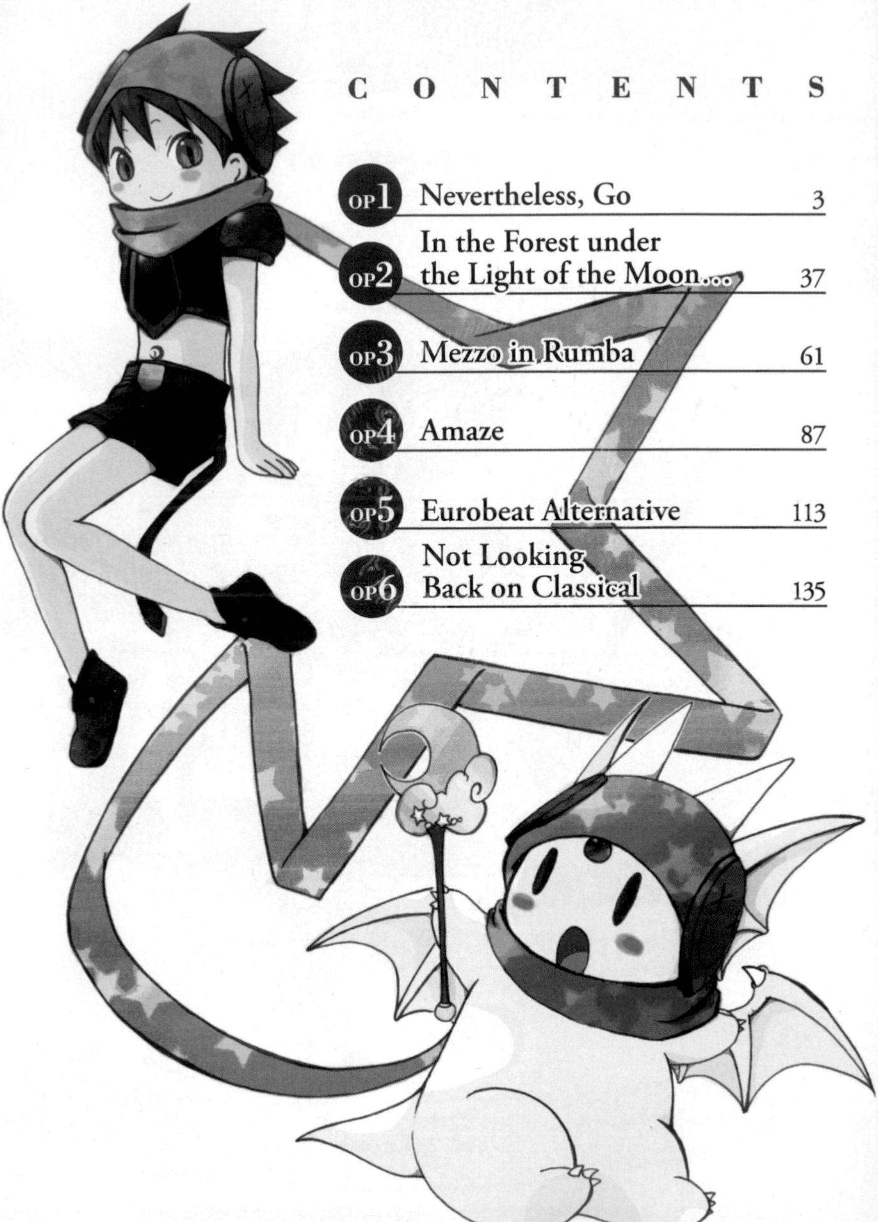

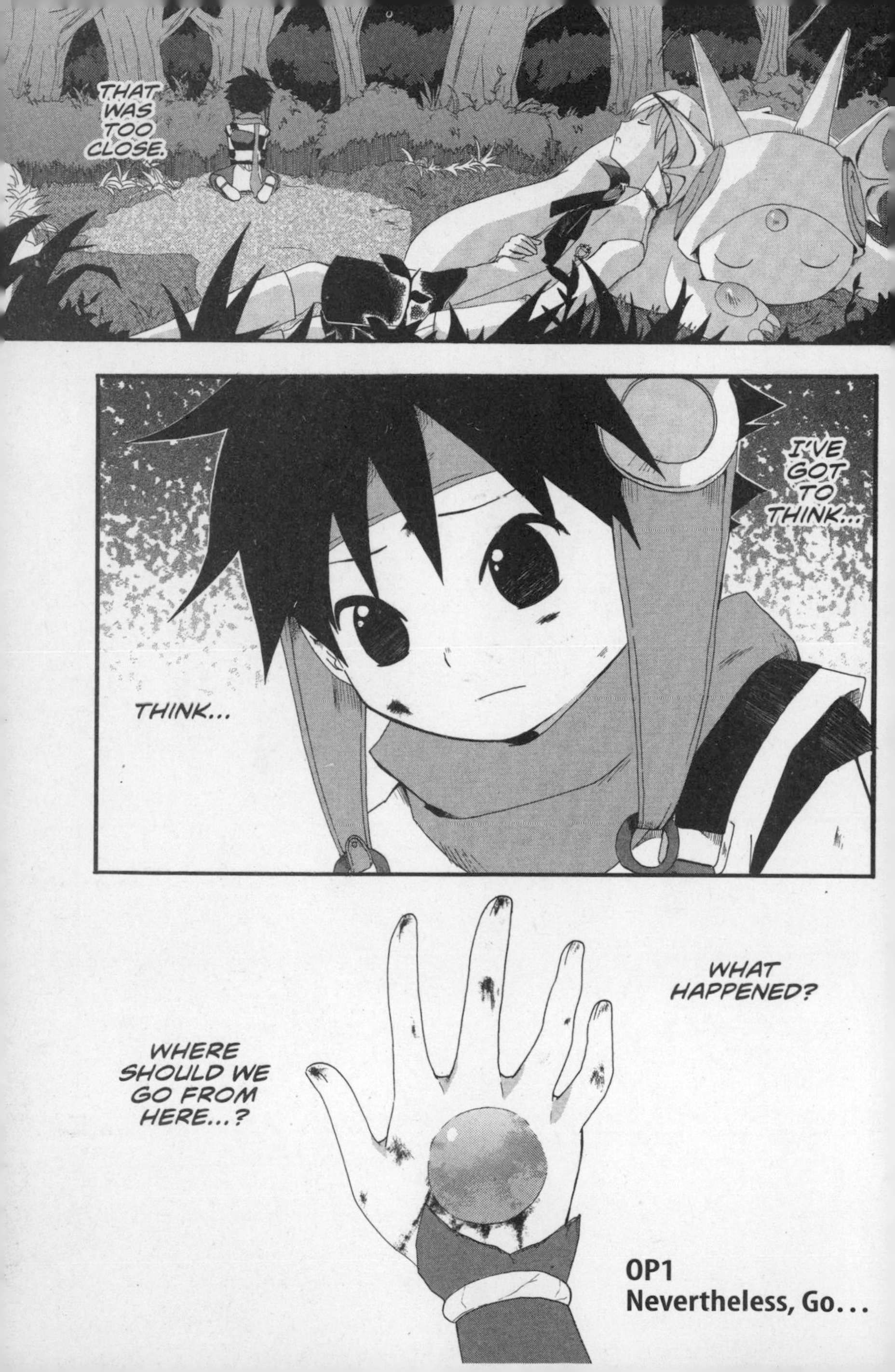
THAT WAS TOO CLOSE.
I'VE GOT TO THINK...
THINK...
WHAT HAPPENED?
WHERE SHOULD WE GO FROM HERE...?

OP1 Nevertheless, Go...

OP1: Nevertheless, Go

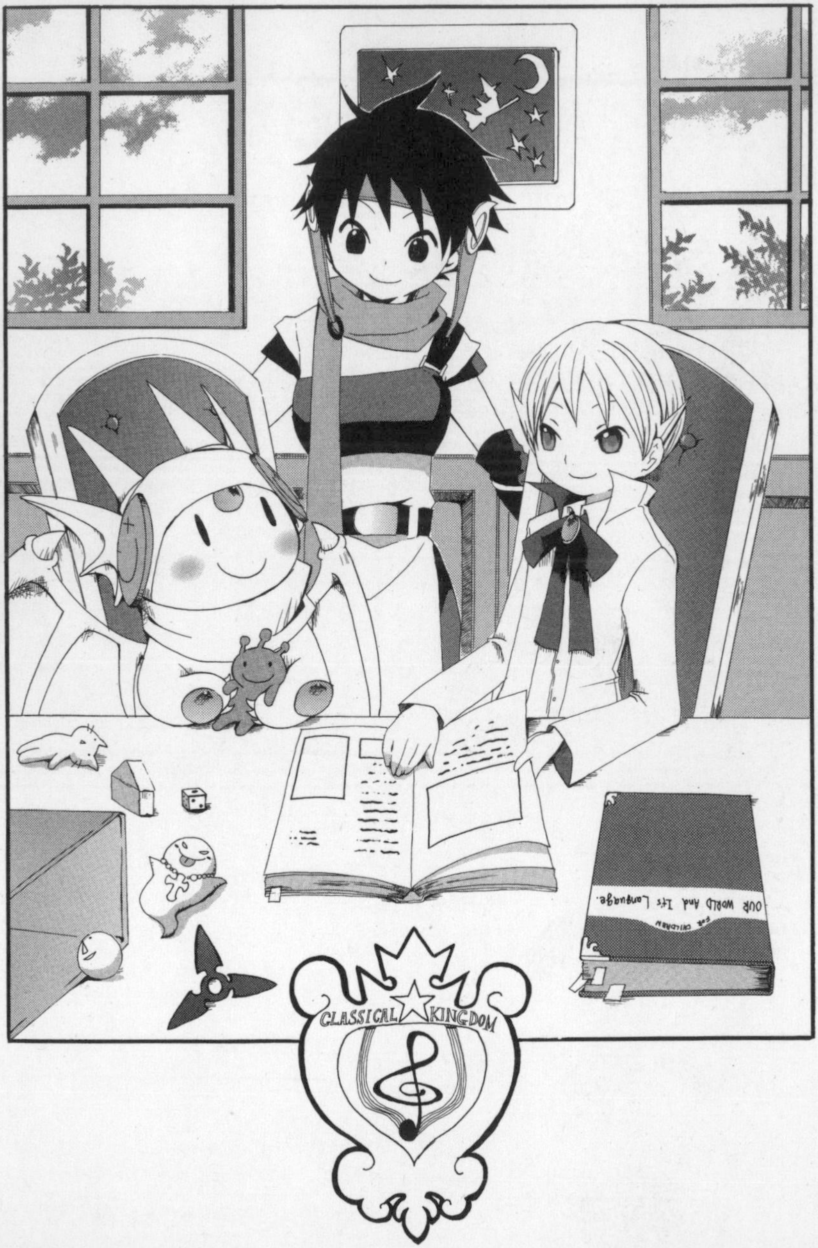
OUR WORLD And It's Language.
CLASSICAL KINGDOM

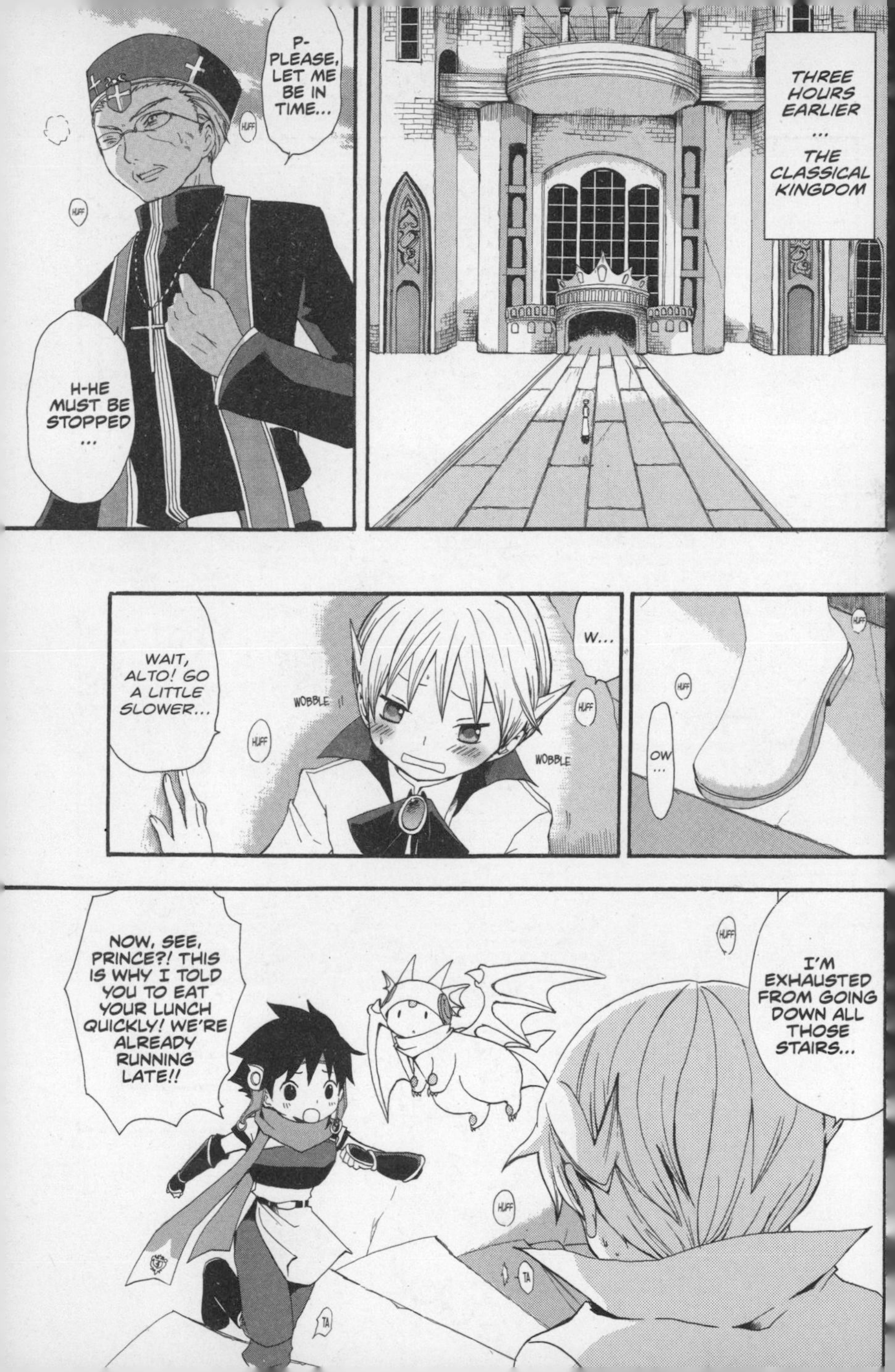
THREE HOURS EARLIER ... THE CLASSICAL KINGDOM
P-PLEASE, LET ME BE IN TIME...
HUFF
HUFF
H-HE MUST BE STOPPED ...
HUFF
HUFF
OW ...
W...
HUFF
WOBBLE
WOBBLE
WAIT, ALTO! GO A LITTLE SLOWER...
HUFF
HUFF
I'M EXHAUSTED FROM GOING DOWN ALL THOSE STAIRS...
NOW, SEE, PRINCE?! THIS IS WHY I TOLD YOU TO EAT YOUR LUNCH QUICKLY! WE'RE ALREADY RUNNING LATE!!
HUFF
TA
TA

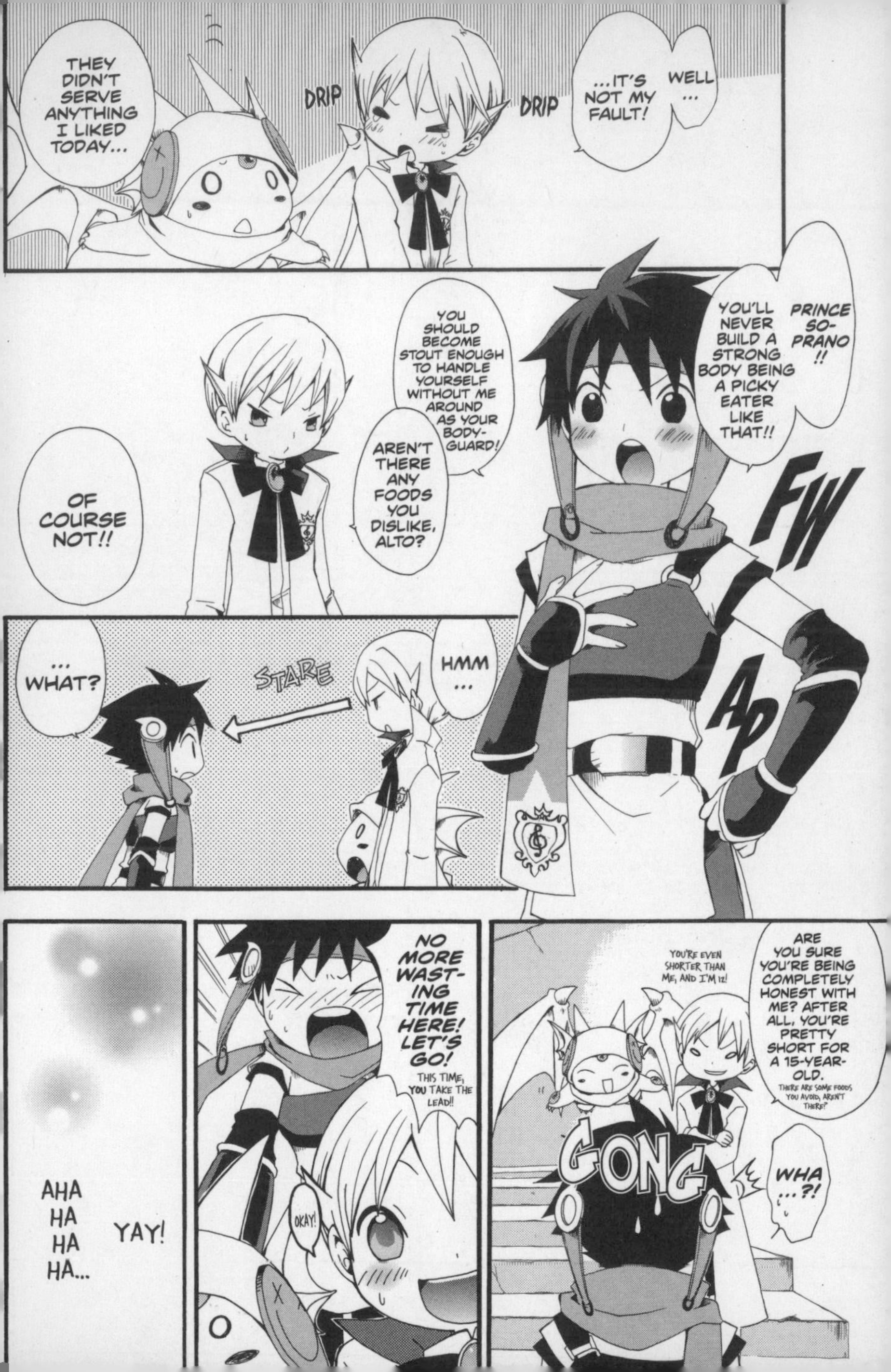
WELL ...
...IT'S NOT MY FAULT!
DRIP
DRIP
THEY DIDN'T SERVE ANYTHING I LIKED TODAY...
PRINCE SO-PRANO!!
YOU'LL NEVER BUILD A STRONG BODY BEING A PICKY EATER LIKE THAT!!
FWAP
YOU SHOULD BECOME STOUT ENOUGH TO HANDLE YOURSELF WITHOUT ME AROUND AS YOUR BODY-GUARD!
AREN'T THERE ANY FOODS YOU DISLIKE, ALTO?
OF COURSE NOT!!
HMM ...
STARE
... WHAT?
ARE YOU SURE YOU'RE BEING COMPLETELY HONEST WITH ME? AFTER ALL, YOU'RE PRETTY SHORT FOR A 15-YEAR-OLD.
YOU'RE EVEN SHORTER THAN ME, AND I'M 12!
THERE ARE SOME FOODS YOU AVOID, AREN'T THERE?
GONG
WHA ...?!
NO MORE WASTING TIME HERE! LET'S GO!
THIS TIME, YOU TAKE THE LEAD!!
OKAY!
YAY!
AHA HA HA HA...

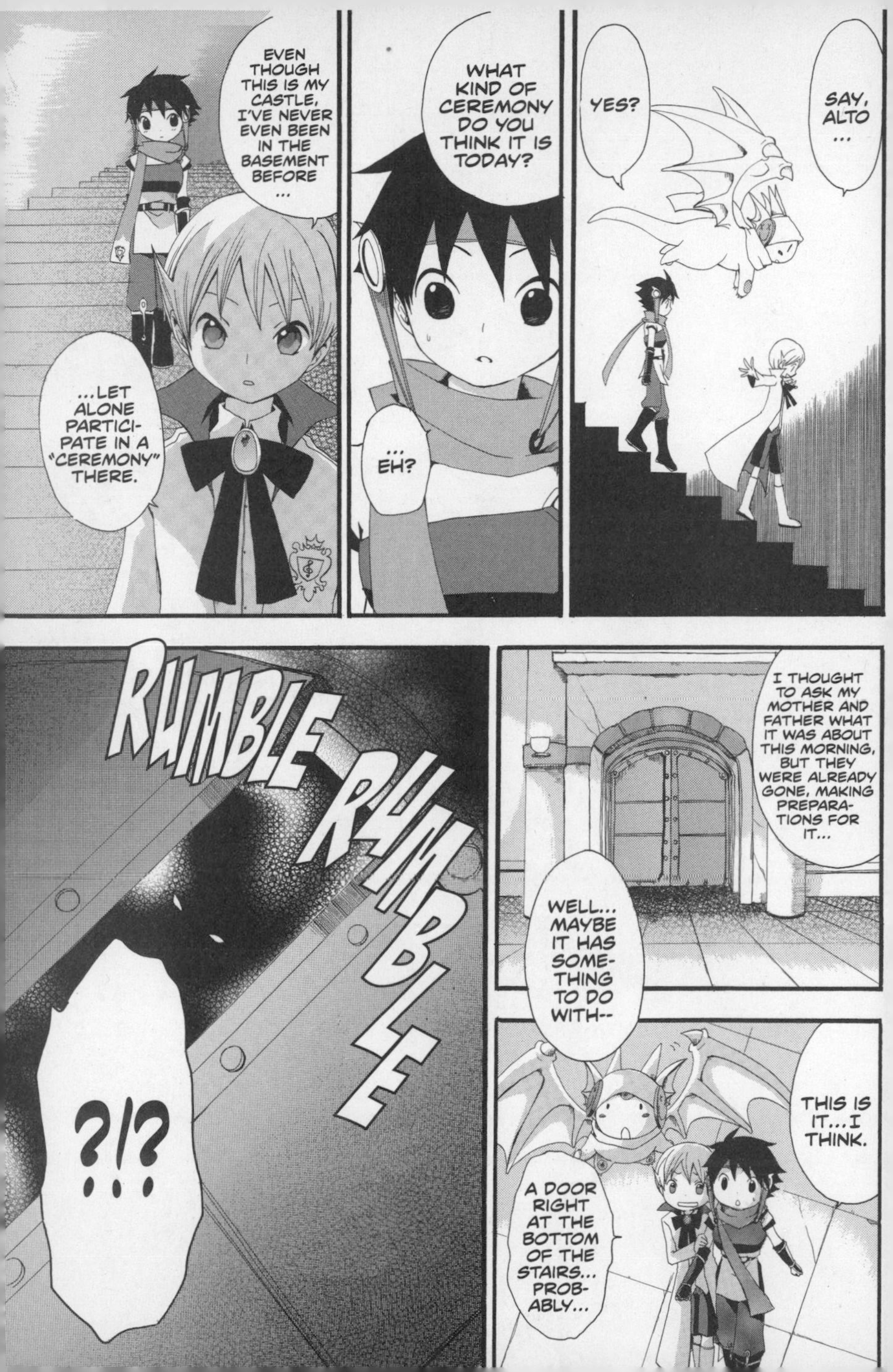
SAY, ALTO...
YES?
WHAT KIND OF CEREMONY DO YOU THINK IT IS TODAY?
...EH?
EVEN THOUGH THIS IS MY CASTLE, I'VE NEVER EVEN BEEN IN THE BASEMENT BEFORE...
...LET ALONE PARTICIPATE IN A "CEREMONY" THERE.
I THOUGHT TO ASK MY MOTHER AND FATHER WHAT IT WAS ABOUT THIS MORNING, BUT THEY WERE ALREADY GONE, MAKING PREPARATIONS FOR IT...
WELL... MAYBE IT HAS SOMETHING TO DO WITH--
THIS IS IT... I THINK.
A DOOR RIGHT AT THE BOTTOM OF THE STAIRS... PROBABLY...
RUMBLE
RUMBLE
?!?

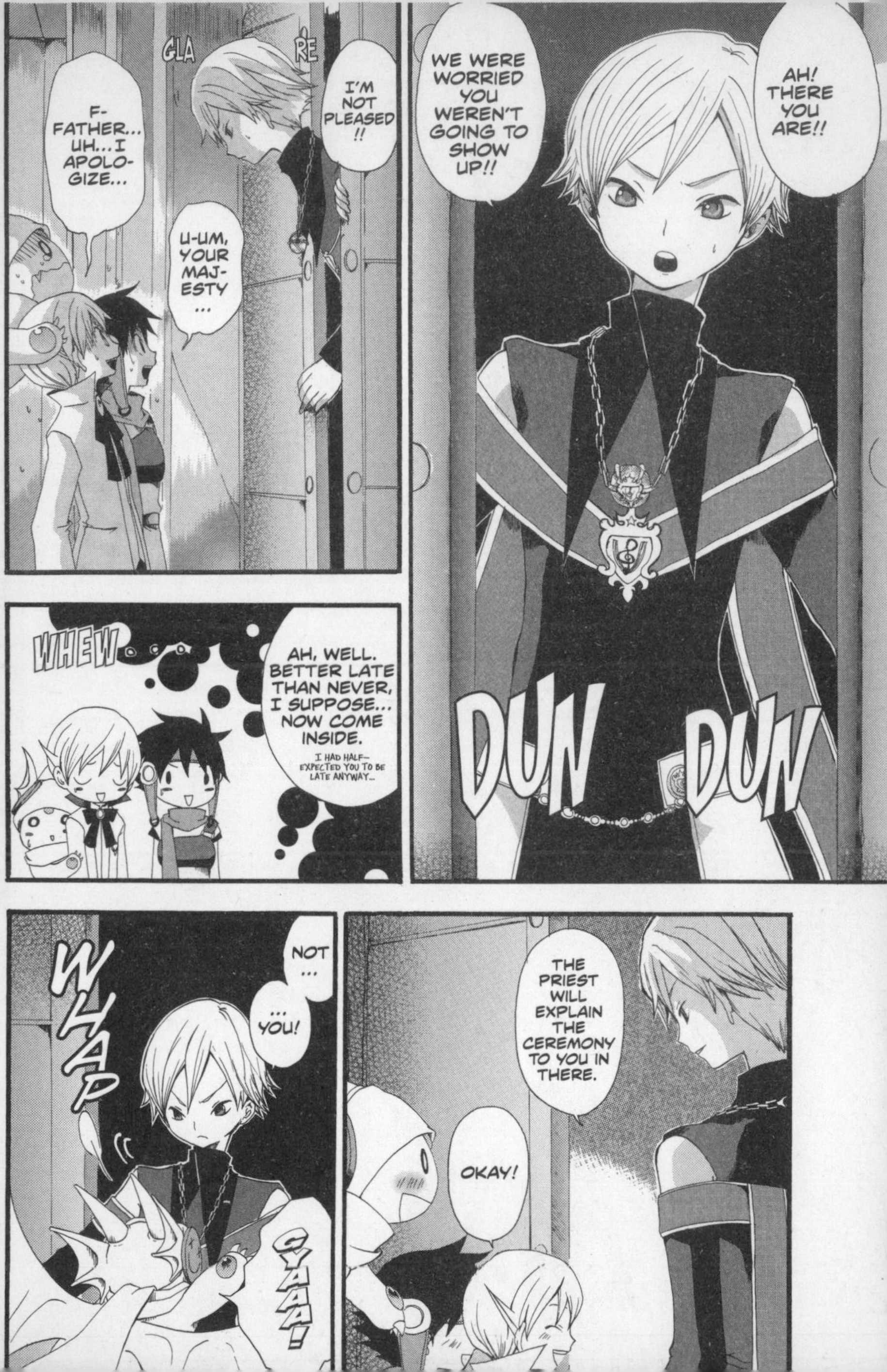
AH! THERE YOU ARE!!
WE WERE WORRIED YOU WEREN'T GOING TO SHOW UP!!
DUN
DUN
GLA
RE
I'M NOT PLEASED!!
F-FATHER... UH...I APOLOGIZE...
U-UM, YOUR MAJESTY...
AH, WELL. BETTER LATE THAN NEVER, I SUPPOSE... NOW COME INSIDE.
I HAD HALF-EXPECTED YOU TO BE LATE ANYWAY...
WHEW
THE PRIEST WILL EXPLAIN THE CEREMONY TO YOU IN THERE.
OKAY!
NOT...
...YOU!
WHAP
GYAAA!

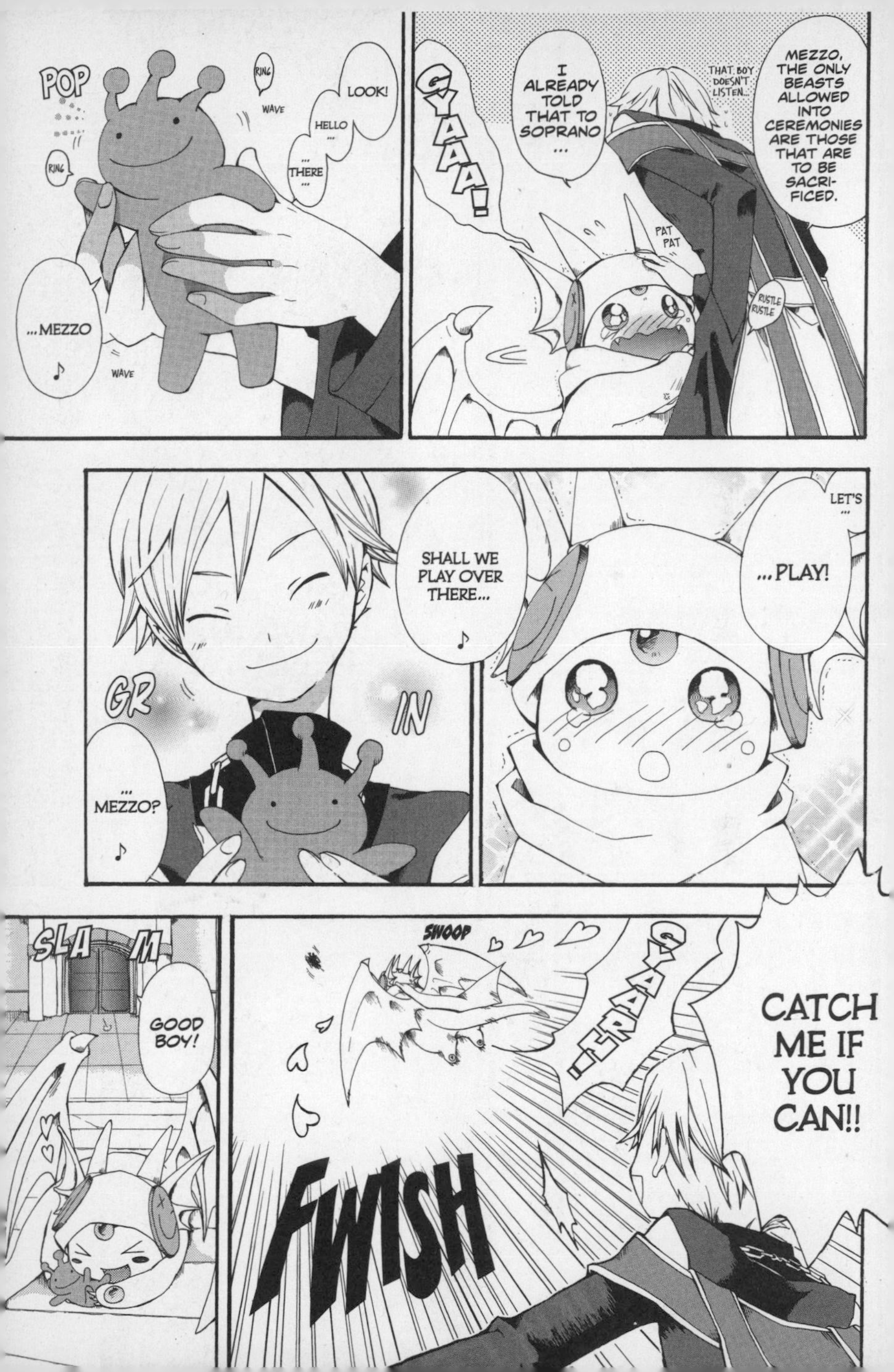

MEZZO, THE ONLY BEASTS ALLOWED INTO CEREMONIES ARE THOSE THAT ARE TO BE SACRIFICED.
THAT BOY DOESN'T LISTEN...
I ALREADY TOLD THAT TO SOPRANO...
GYAAA!
PAT PAT
RUSTLE RUSTLE
LOOK!
RING
HELLO...
...THERE...
POP
WAVE
RING
...MEZZO ♪
WAVE
LET'S...
...PLAY!
SHALL WE PLAY OVER THERE... ♪
GR
IN
...MEZZO? ♪
CATCH ME IF YOU CAN!!
GYAAA...!
SWOOP
FWISH
SLAM
GOOD BOY!

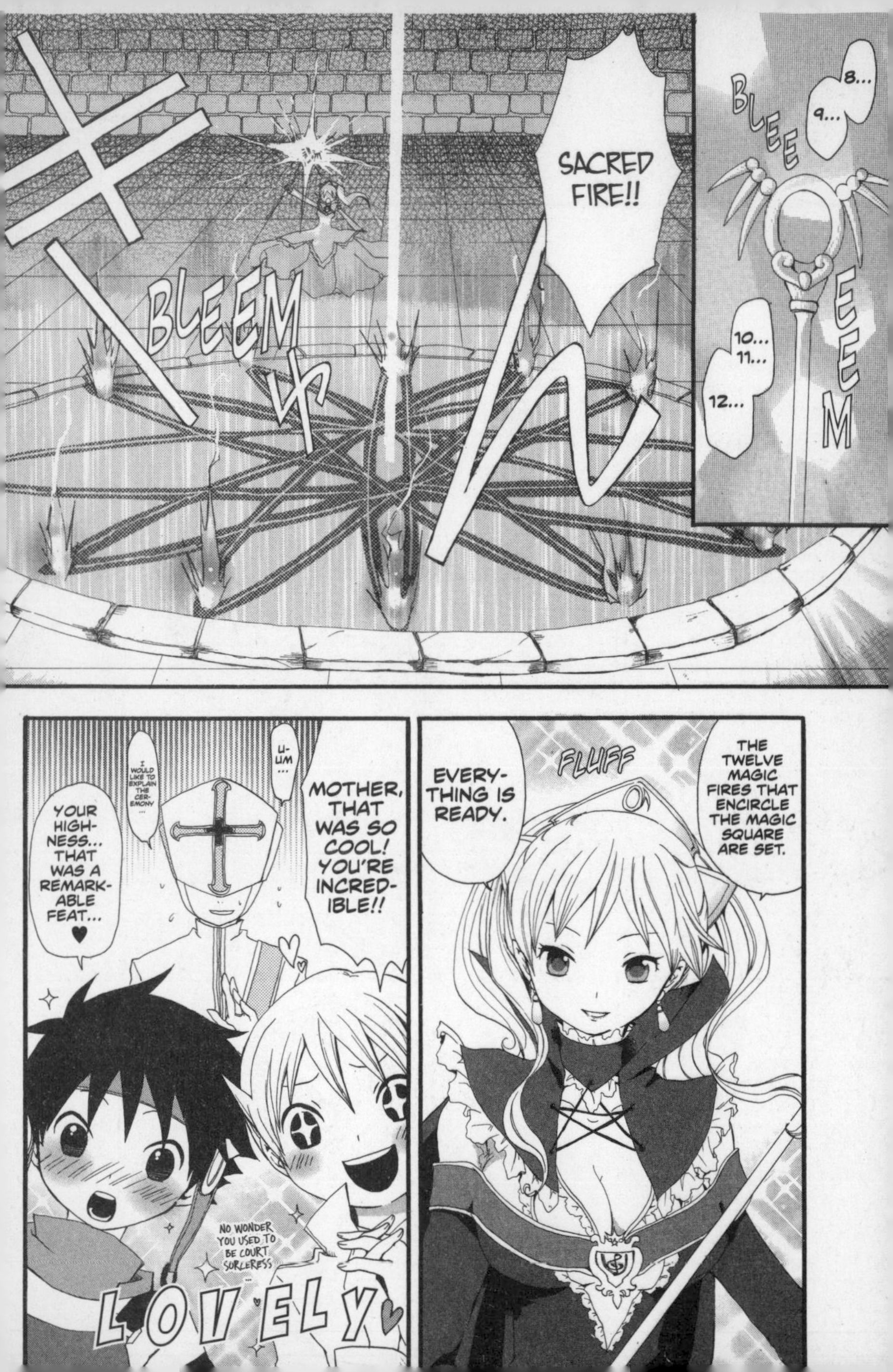
8...
9...
BLEEEEEM
10...
11...
12...
SACRED FIRE!!
BLEEM
THE TWELVE MAGIC FIRES THAT ENCIRCLE THE MAGIC SQUARE ARE SET.
FLUFF
EVERY-THING IS READY.
U-UM...
MOTHER, THAT WAS SO COOL! YOU'RE INCRED-IBLE!!
I WOULD LIKE TO EXPLAIN THE CER-EMONY...
YOUR HIGH-NESS... THAT WAS A REMARK-ABLE FEAT...♥
NO WONDER YOU USED TO BE COURT SORCERESS...
LOVELY♥

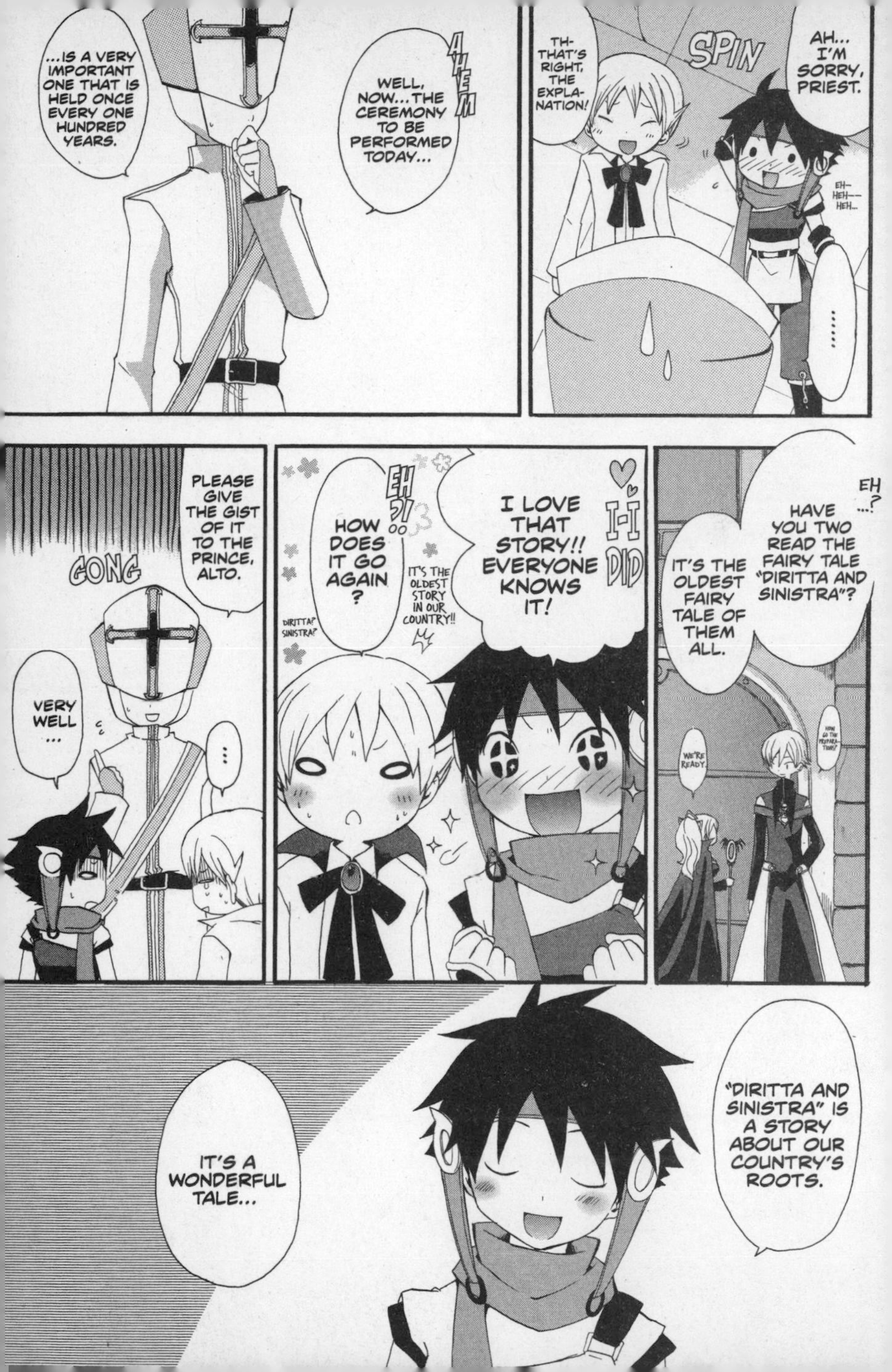
AH... I'M SORRY, PRIEST.
SPIN
TH-THAT'S RIGHT, THE EXPLANATION!
EH-HEH--HEH...
......
AHEM
WELL, NOW...THE CEREMONY TO BE PERFORMED TODAY...
...IS A VERY IMPORTANT ONE THAT IS HELD ONCE EVERY ONE HUNDRED YEARS.
EH ...?
HAVE YOU TWO READ THE FAIRY TALE "DIRITTA AND SINISTRA"?
IT'S THE OLDEST FAIRY TALE OF THEM ALL.
HOW GO THE PREPARATIONS?
WE'RE READY.
I-I DID
I LOVE THAT STORY!! EVERYONE KNOWS IT!
IT'S THE OLDEST STORY IN OUR COUNTRY!!
EH?!
HOW DOES IT GO AGAIN?
DIRITTA? SINISTRA?
PLEASE GIVE THE GIST OF IT TO THE PRINCE, ALTO.
GONG
...
VERY WELL...
"DIRITTA AND SINISTRA" IS A STORY ABOUT OUR COUNTRY'S ROOTS.
IT'S A WONDERFUL TALE...

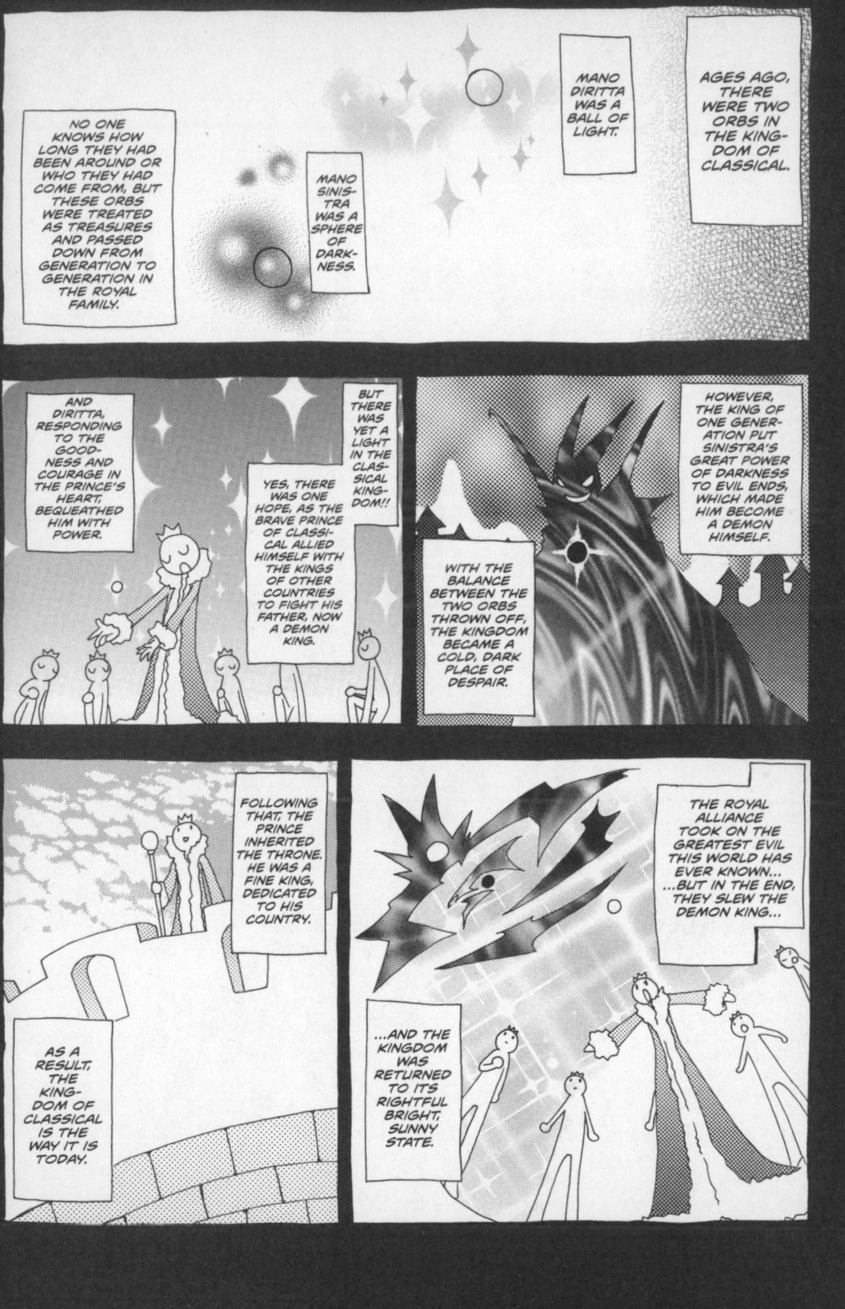
AGES AGO, THERE WERE TWO ORBS IN THE KINGDOM OF CLASSICAL.
MANO DIRITTA WAS A BALL OF LIGHT.
MANO SINISTRA WAS A SPHERE OF DARKNESS.
NO ONE KNOWS HOW LONG THEY HAD BEEN AROUND OR WHO THEY HAD COME FROM, BUT THESE ORBS WERE TREATED AS TREASURES AND PASSED DOWN FROM GENERATION TO GENERATION IN THE ROYAL FAMILY.
HOWEVER, THE KING OF ONE GENERATION PUT SINISTRA'S GREAT POWER OF DARKNESS TO EVIL ENDS, WHICH MADE HIM BECOME A DEMON HIMSELF.
WITH THE BALANCE BETWEEN THE TWO ORBS THROWN OFF, THE KINGDOM BECAME A COLD, DARK PLACE OF DESPAIR.
BUT THERE WAS YET A LIGHT IN THE CLASSICAL KINGDOM!!
YES, THERE WAS ONE HOPE, AS THE BRAVE PRINCE OF CLASSICAL ALLIED HIMSELF WITH THE KINGS OF OTHER COUNTRIES TO FIGHT HIS FATHER, NOW A DEMON KING.
AND DIRITTA, RESPONDING TO THE GOODNESS AND COURAGE IN THE PRINCE'S HEART, BEQUEATHED HIM WITH POWER.
THE ROYAL ALLIANCE TOOK ON THE GREATEST EVIL THIS WORLD HAS EVER KNOWN... ...BUT IN THE END, THEY SLEW THE DEMON KING...
...AND THE KINGDOM WAS RETURNED TO ITS RIGHTFUL BRIGHT, SUNNY STATE.
FOLLOWING THAT, THE PRINCE INHERITED THE THRONE. HE WAS A FINE KING, DEDICATED TO HIS COUNTRY.
AS A RESULT, THE KINGDOM OF CLASSICAL IS THE WAY IT IS TODAY.

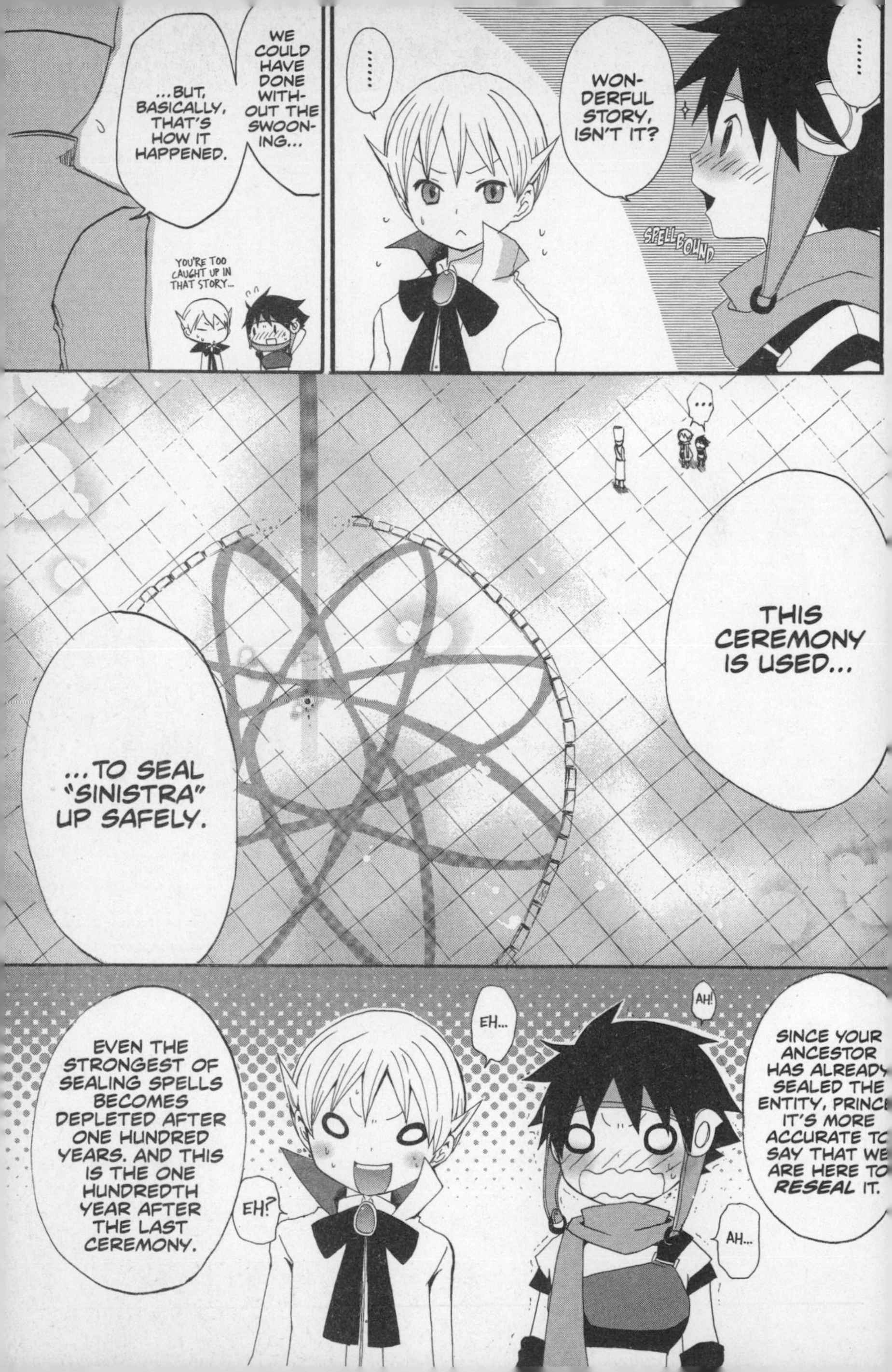
......
WONDERFUL STORY, ISN'T IT?
SPELLBOUND
......
WE COULD HAVE DONE WITHOUT THE SWOONING...
...BUT, BASICALLY, THAT'S HOW IT HAPPENED.
YOU'RE TOO CAUGHT UP IN THAT STORY...
...
THIS CEREMONY IS USED...
...TO SEAL "SINISTRA" UP SAFELY.
AH!
SINCE YOUR ANCESTOR HAS ALREADY SEALED THE ENTITY, PRINCE, IT'S MORE ACCURATE TO SAY THAT WE ARE HERE TO *RESEAL* IT.
EH...
AH...
EVEN THE STRONGEST OF SEALING SPELLS BECOMES DEPLETED AFTER ONE HUNDRED YEARS. AND THIS IS THE ONE HUNDREDTH YEAR AFTER THE LAST CEREMONY.
EH?

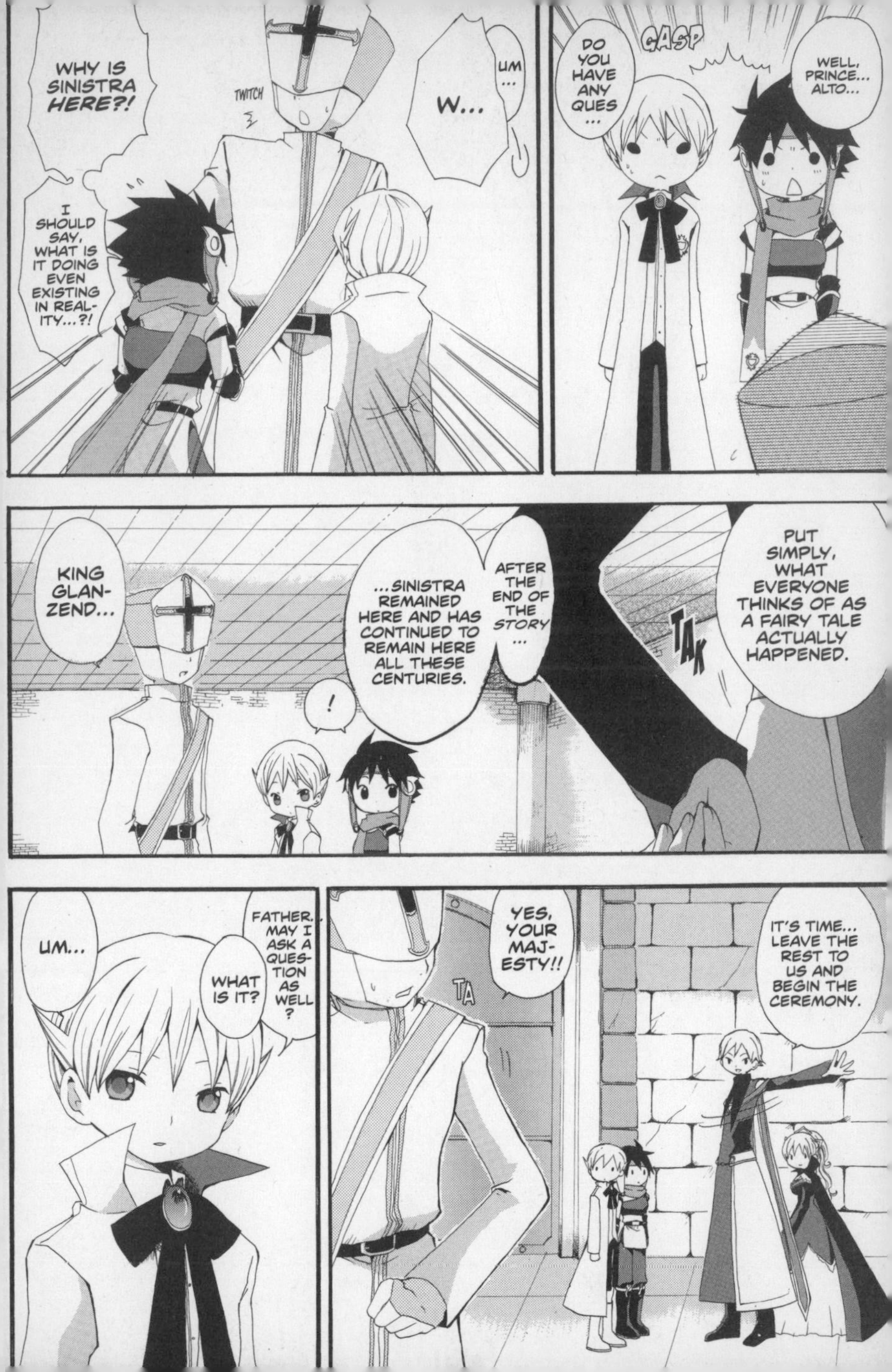
WELL, PRINCE... ALTO...
GASP
DO YOU HAVE ANY QUES...
UM ...
W...
TWITCH
WHY IS SINISTRA *HERE?!*
I SHOULD SAY, WHAT IS IT DOING EVEN EXISTING IN REAL-ITY...?!
PUT SIMPLY, WHAT EVERYONE THINKS OF AS A FAIRY TALE ACTUALLY HAPPENED.
TAK
AFTER THE END OF THE *STORY* ...
...SINISTRA REMAINED HERE AND HAS CONTINUED TO REMAIN HERE ALL THESE CENTURIES.
!
KING GLAN-ZEND...
IT'S TIME... LEAVE THE REST TO US AND BEGIN THE CEREMONY.
YES, YOUR MAJ-ESTY!!
TA
FATHER, MAY I ASK A QUES-TION AS WELL?
WHAT IS IT?
UM...

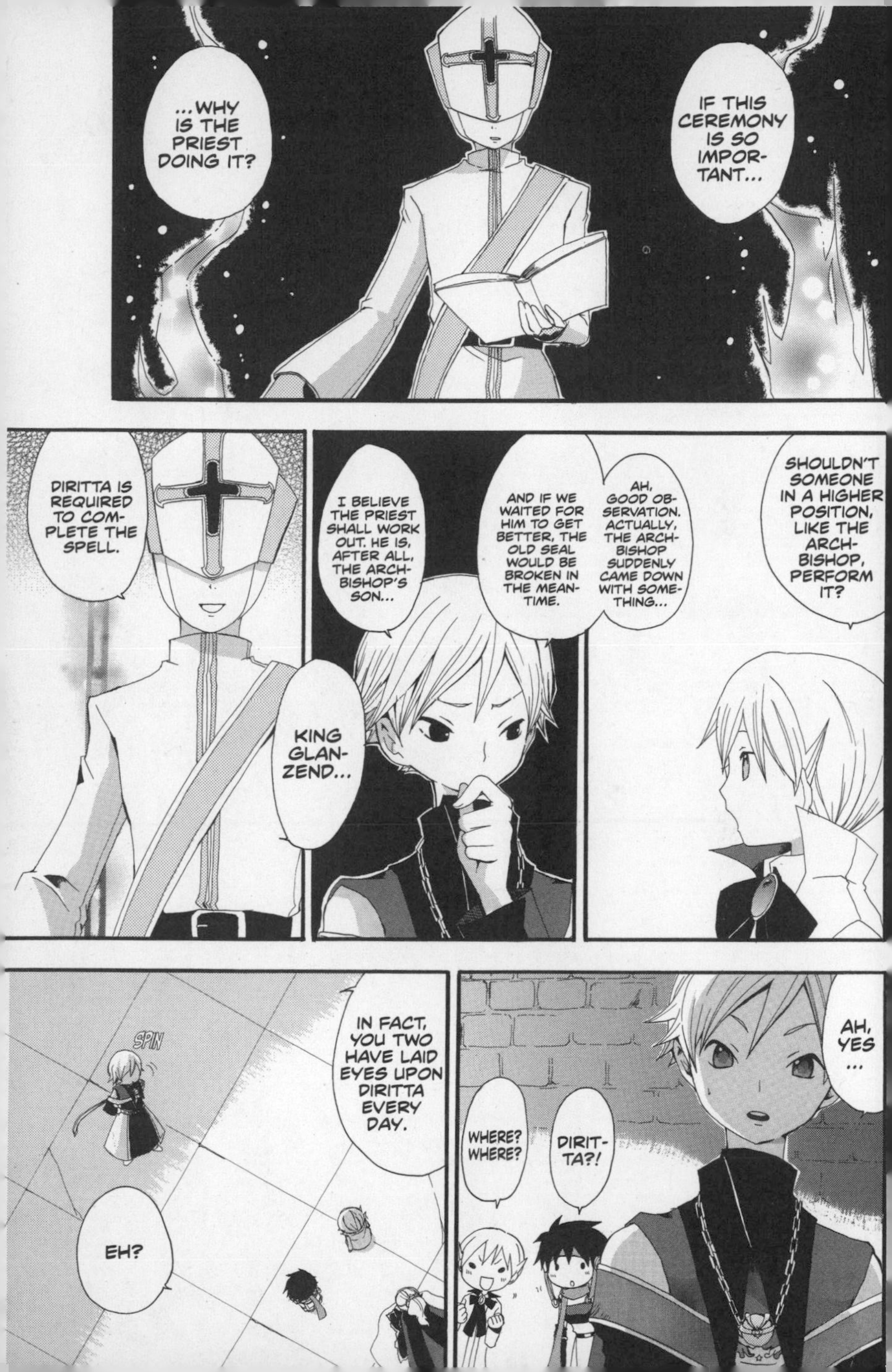
IF THIS CEREMONY IS SO IMPORTANT...
...WHY IS THE PRIEST DOING IT?
SHOULDN'T SOMEONE IN A HIGHER POSITION, LIKE THE ARCHBISHOP, PERFORM IT?
AH, GOOD OBSERVATION. ACTUALLY, THE ARCHBISHOP SUDDENLY CAME DOWN WITH SOMETHING...
AND IF WE WAITED FOR HIM TO GET BETTER, THE OLD SEAL WOULD BE BROKEN IN THE MEANTIME.
I BELIEVE THE PRIEST SHALL WORK OUT. HE IS, AFTER ALL, THE ARCHBISHOP'S SON...
KING GLANZEND...
DIRITTA IS REQUIRED TO COMPLETE THE SPELL.
AH, YES...
DIRITTA?!
WHERE? WHERE?
IN FACT, YOU TWO HAVE LAID EYES UPON DIRITTA EVERY DAY.
SPIN
EH?

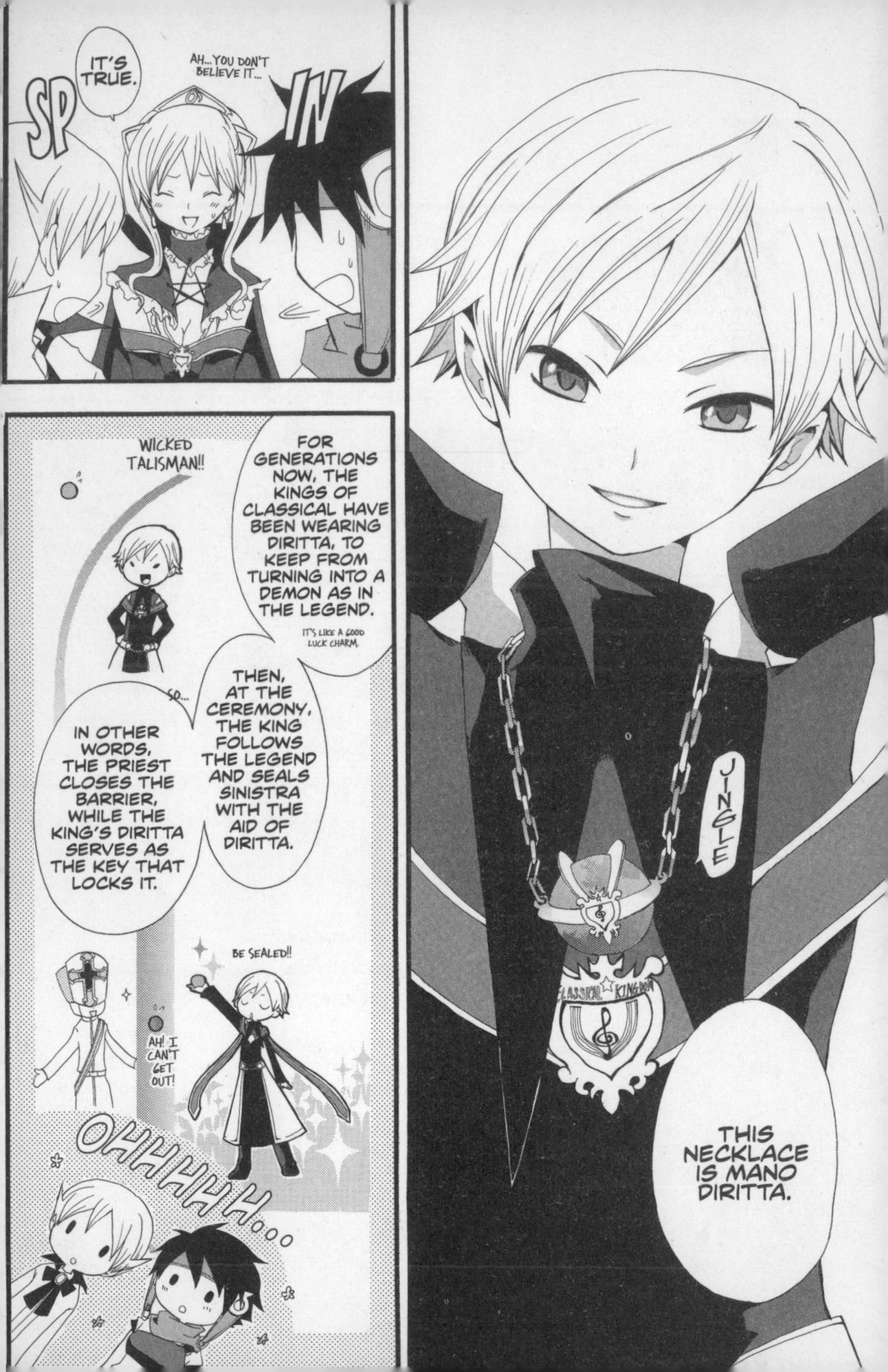
JINGLE
THIS NECKLACE IS MANO DIRITTA.
AH...YOU DON'T BELIEVE IT...
IN
IT'S TRUE.
SP
FOR GENERATIONS NOW, THE KINGS OF CLASSICAL HAVE BEEN WEARING DIRITTA, TO KEEP FROM TURNING INTO A DEMON AS IN THE LEGEND.
WICKED TALISMAN!!
IT'S LIKE A GOOD LUCK CHARM.
THEN, AT THE CEREMONY, THE KING FOLLOWS THE LEGEND AND SEALS SINISTRA WITH THE AID OF DIRITTA.
SO...
IN OTHER WORDS, THE PRIEST CLOSES THE BARRIER, WHILE THE KING'S DIRITTA SERVES AS THE KEY THAT LOCKS IT.
BE SEALED!!
AH! I CAN'T GET OUT!
OHHHHHH...

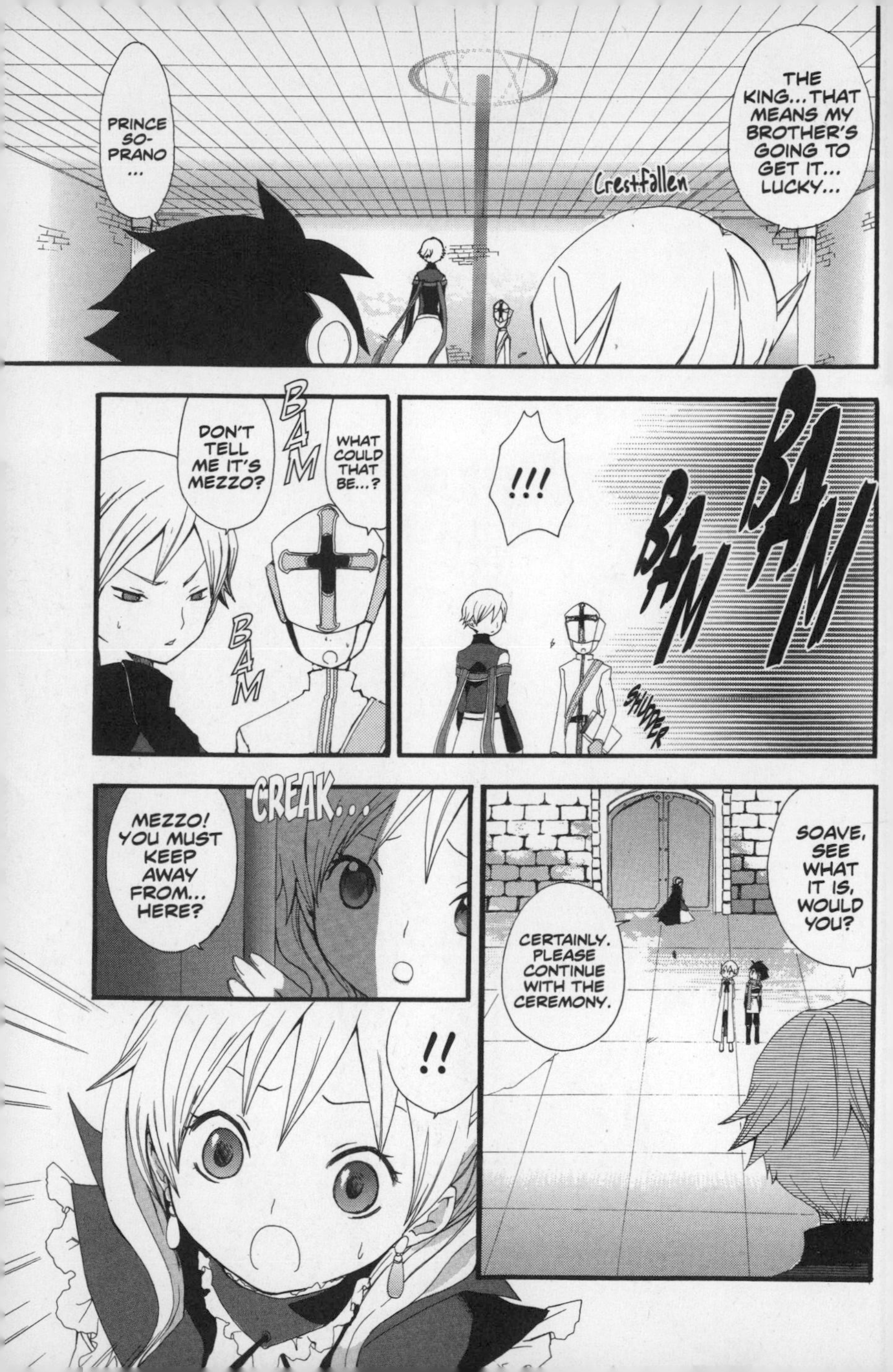

THE KING...THAT MEANS MY BROTHER'S GOING TO GET IT... LUCKY...
Crestfallen
PRINCE SO-PRANO ...
BAM BAM
BAM BAM
SHUDDER
!!!
WHAT COULD THAT BE...?
BAM
DON'T TELL ME IT'S MEZZO?
BAM
SOAVE, SEE WHAT IT IS, WOULD YOU?
CERTAINLY. PLEASE CONTINUE WITH THE CEREMONY.
CREAK...
MEZZO! YOU MUST KEEP AWAY FROM... HERE?
!!

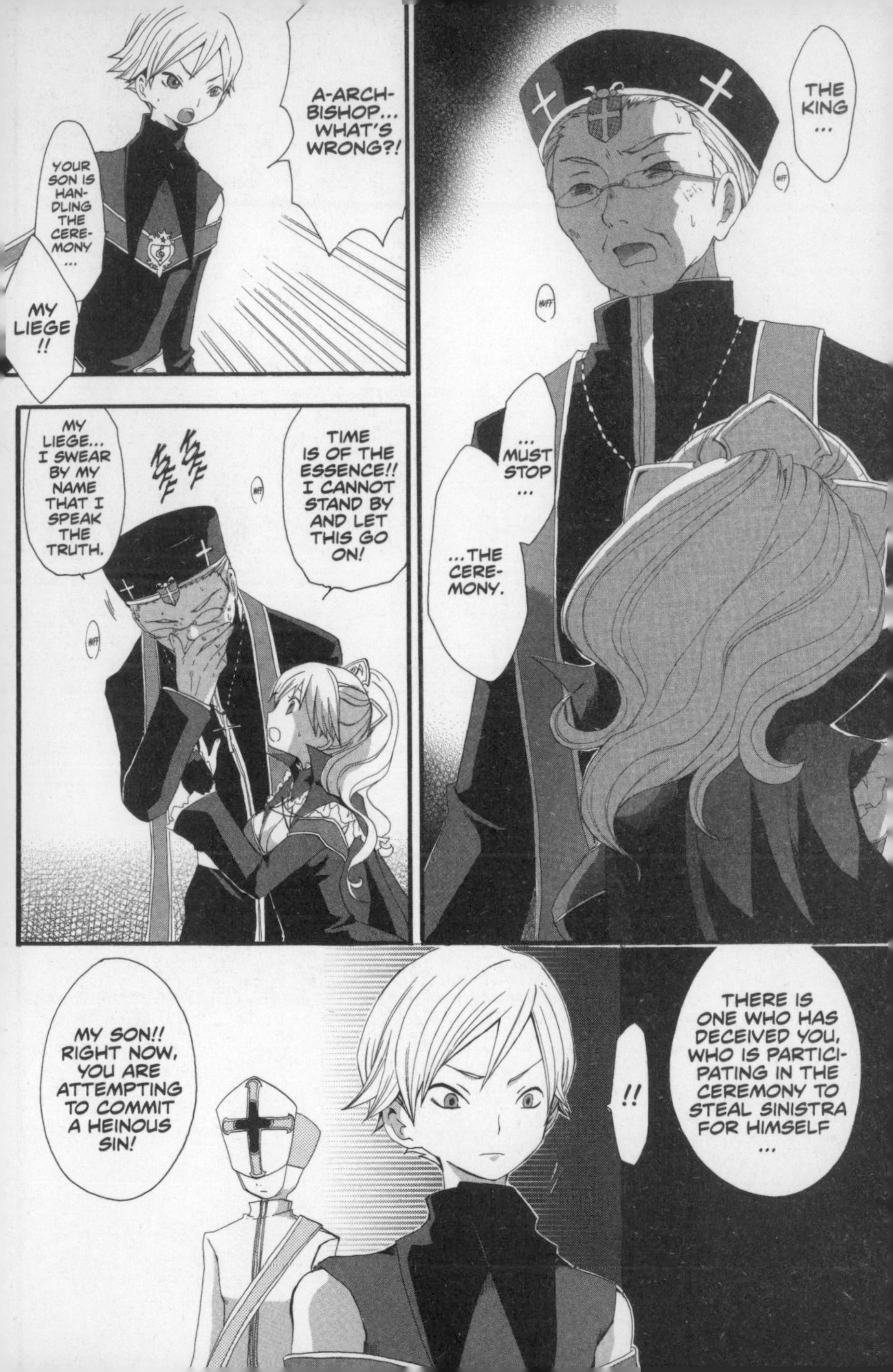
THE KING ...
... MUST STOP ...
...THE CEREMONY.
A-ARCHBISHOP... WHAT'S WRONG?!
YOUR SON IS HANDLING THE CEREMONY ...
MY LIEGE !!
TIME IS OF THE ESSENCE!! I CANNOT STAND BY AND LET THIS GO ON!
MY LIEGE... I SWEAR BY MY NAME THAT I SPEAK THE TRUTH.
THERE IS ONE WHO HAS DECEIVED YOU, WHO IS PARTICIPATING IN THE CEREMONY TO STEAL SINISTRA FOR HIMSELF ...
!!
MY SON!! RIGHT NOW, YOU ARE ATTEMPTING TO COMMIT A HEINOUS SIN!

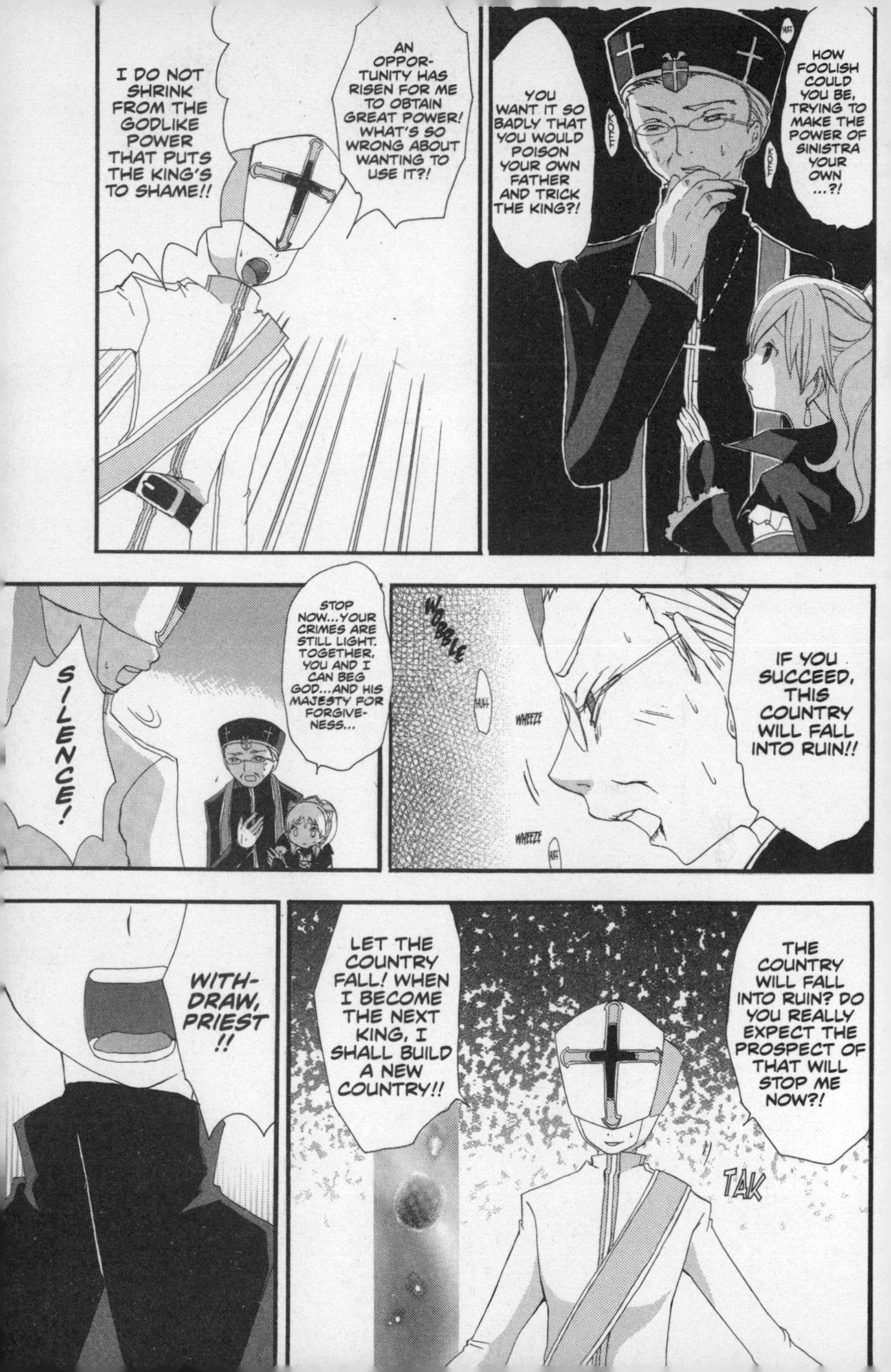
HUFF
HOW FOOLISH COULD YOU BE, TRYING TO MAKE THE POWER OF SINISTRA YOUR OWN ...?!
KOFF
KOFF
YOU WANT IT SO BADLY THAT YOU WOULD POISON YOUR OWN FATHER AND TRICK THE KING?!
AN OPPOR-TUNITY HAS RISEN FOR ME TO OBTAIN GREAT POWER! WHAT'S SO WRONG ABOUT WANTING TO USE IT?!
I DO NOT SHRINK FROM THE GODLIKE POWER THAT PUTS THE KING'S TO SHAME!!
IF YOU SUCCEED, THIS COUNTRY WILL FALL INTO RUIN!!
WOBBLE
HUFF
WHEEZE
WHEEZE
HUFF
STOP NOW...YOUR CRIMES ARE STILL LIGHT. TOGETHER, YOU AND I CAN BEG GOD...AND HIS MAJESTY FOR FORGIVE-NESS...
SILENCE!
THE COUNTRY WILL FALL INTO RUIN? DO YOU REALLY EXPECT THE PROSPECT OF THAT WILL STOP ME NOW?!
LET THE COUNTRY FALL! WHEN I BECOME THE NEXT KING, I SHALL BUILD A NEW COUNTRY!!
TAK
WITH-DRAW, PRIEST!!

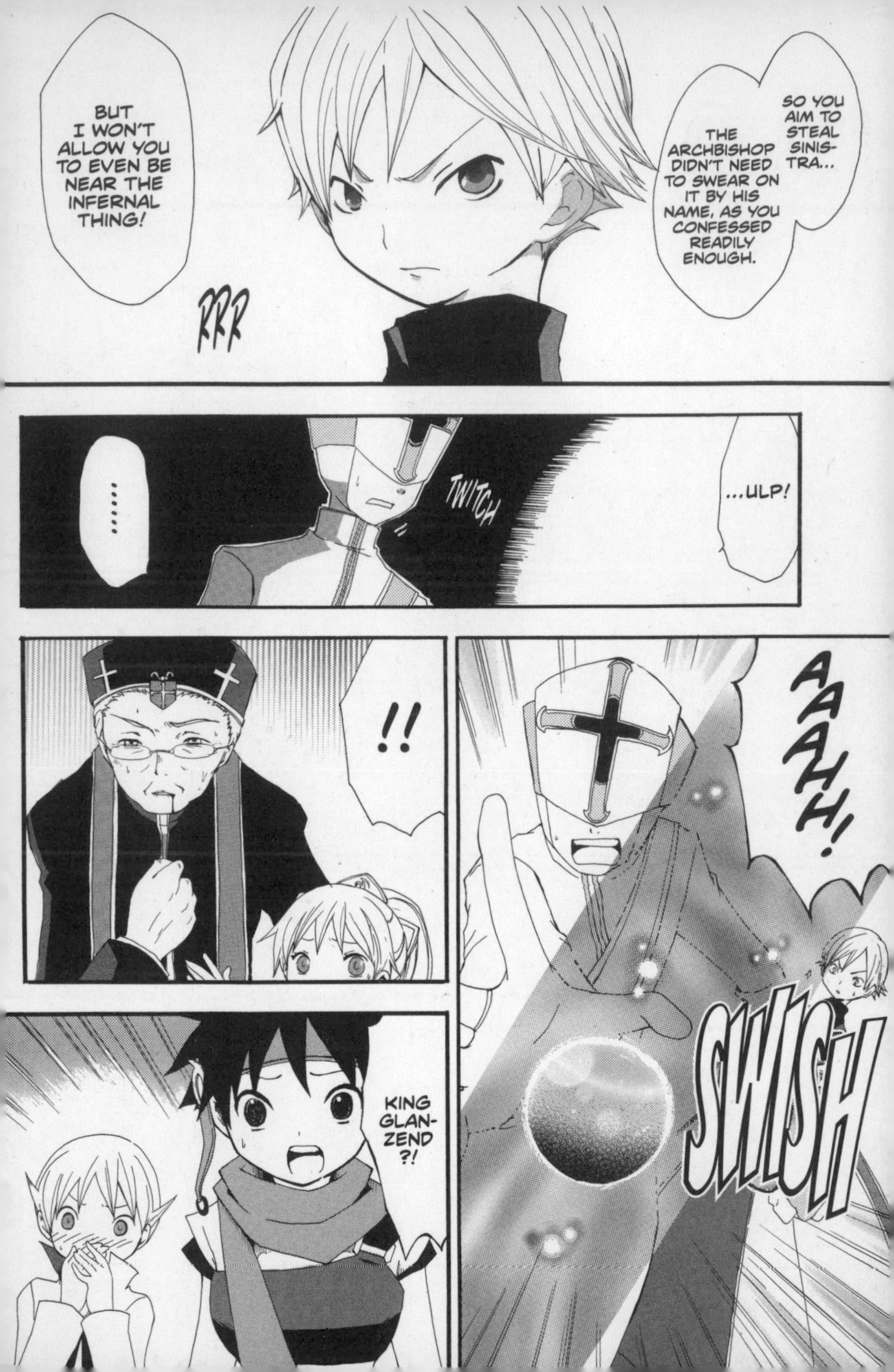
SO YOU AIM TO STEAL SINIS-TRA...
THE ARCHBISHOP DIDN'T NEED TO SWEAR ON IT BY HIS NAME, AS YOU CONFESSED READILY ENOUGH.
BUT I WON'T ALLOW YOU TO EVEN BE NEAR THE INFERNAL THING!
RRR
...ULP!
TWITCH
......
AAAAHH!
SWISH
!!
KING GLAN-ZEND ?!

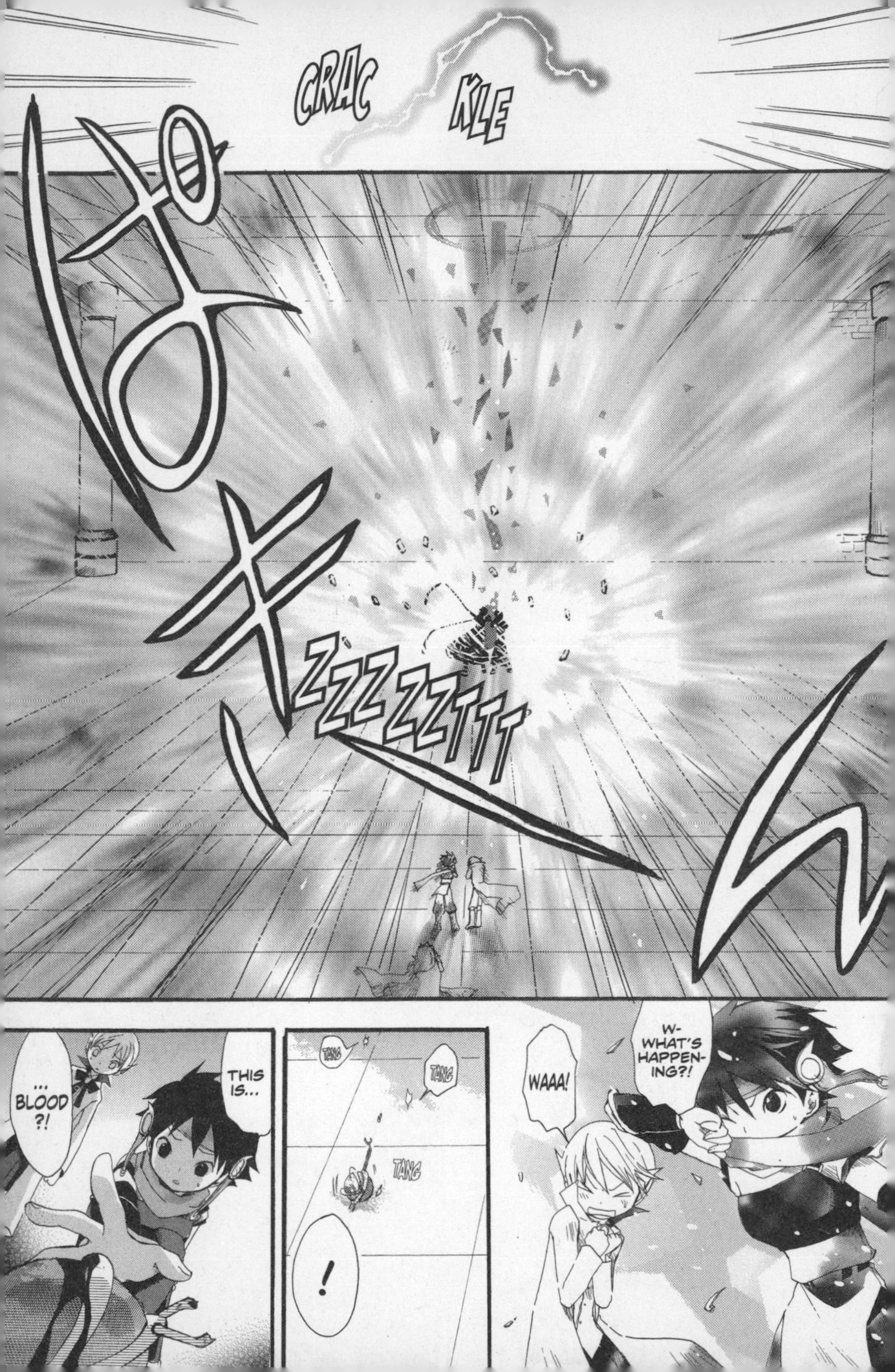
CRAC KLE
ZZZZZTTT
W-WHAT'S HAPPENING?!
WAAA!
TANG
TANG
TANG
!
THIS IS...
...BLOOD?!

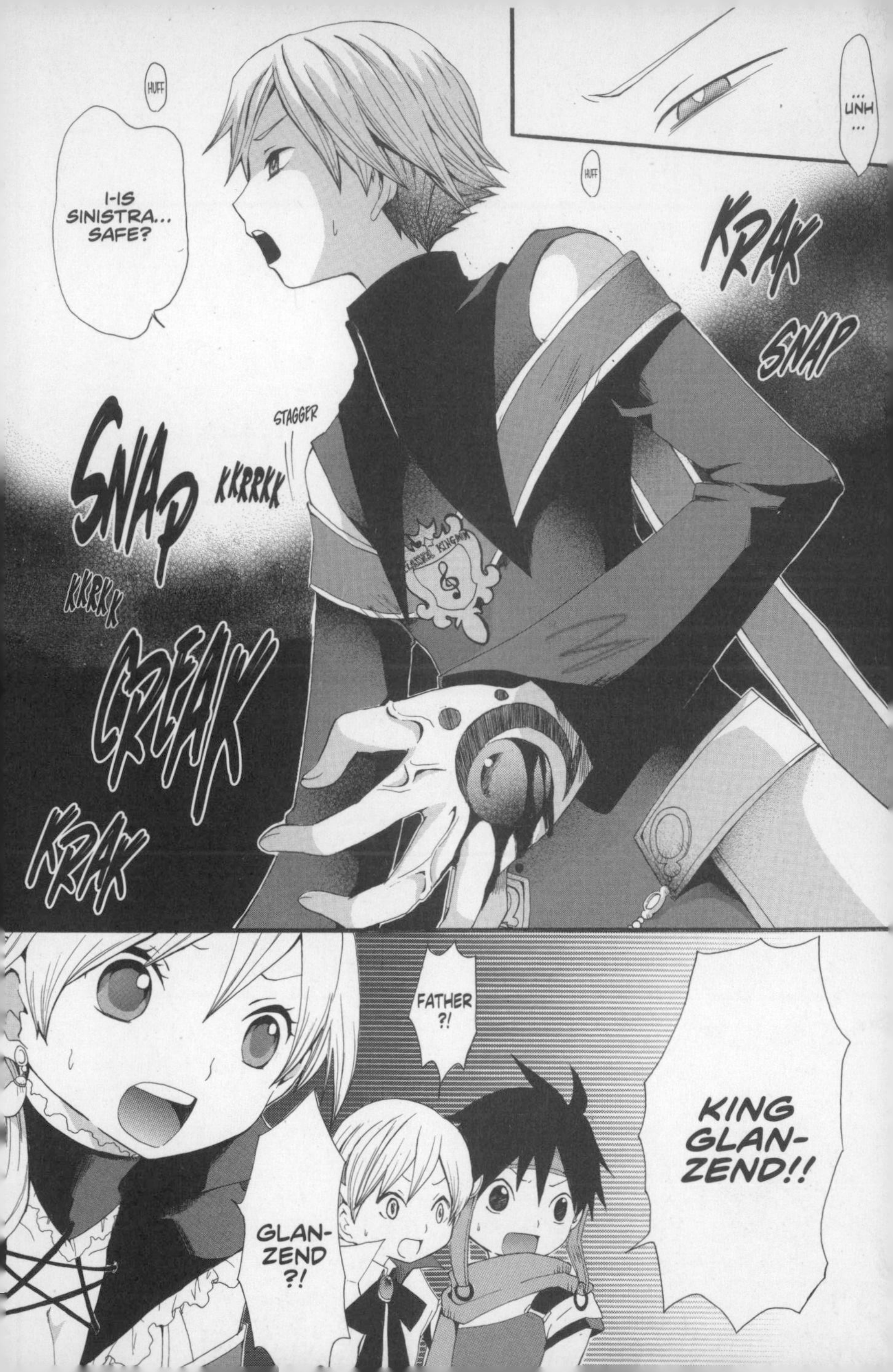
...UNH...
HUFF
HUFF
I-IS SINISTRA... SAFE?
KRAK
SNAP
STAGGER
SNAP
KKRRKK
KKRKK
CREAK
KRAK
KING GLAN-ZEND!!
FATHER?!
GLAN-ZEND?!

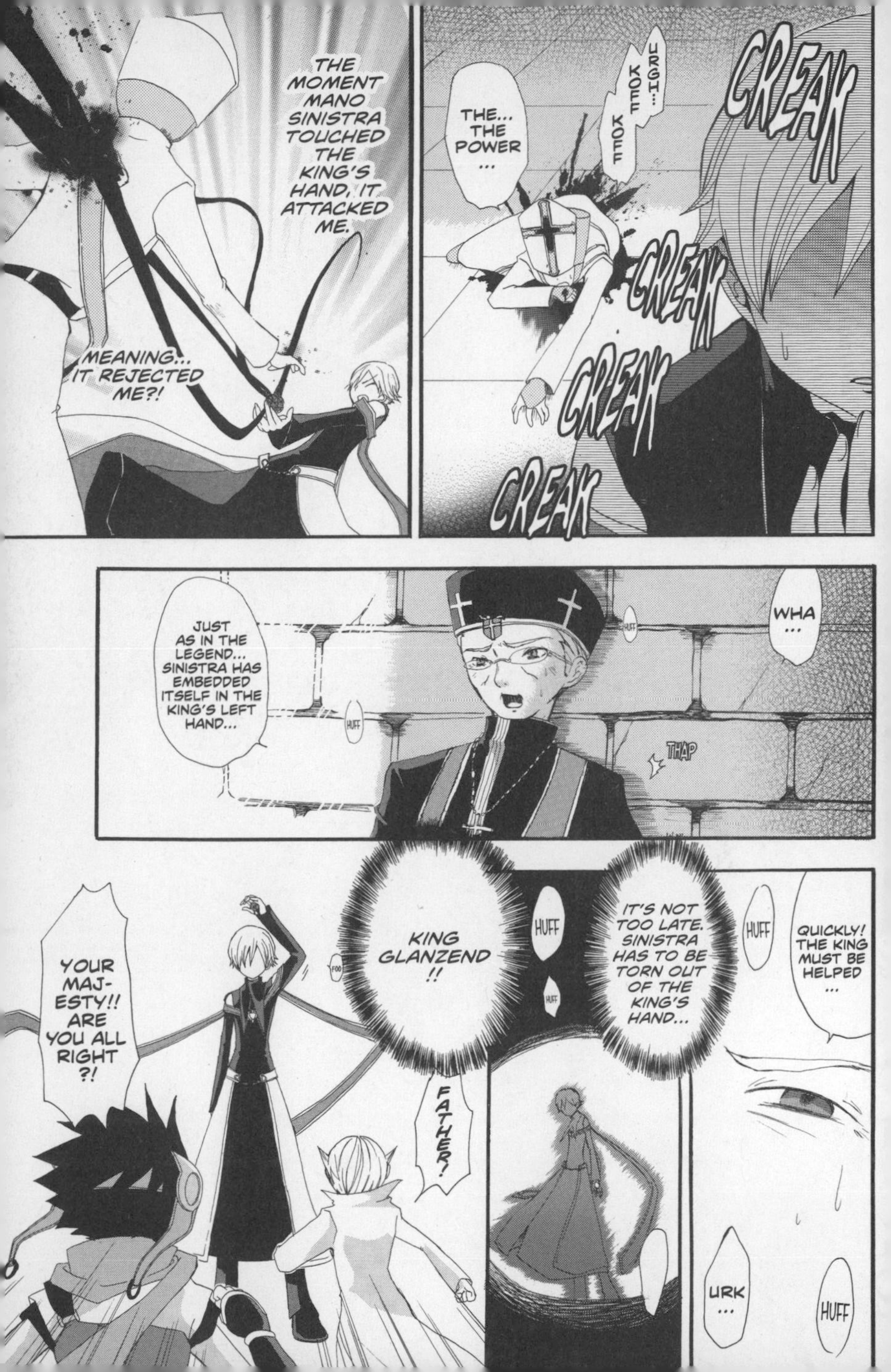
CREAK
URGH... KOFF KOFF
THE... THE POWER...
CREAK
CREAK
CREAK
THE MOMENT MANO SINISTRA TOUCHED THE KING'S HAND, IT ATTACKED ME.
MEANING... IT REJECTED ME?!
WHA...
HUFF
JUST AS IN THE LEGEND... SINISTRA HAS EMBEDDED ITSELF IN THE KING'S LEFT HAND...
HUFF
THAP
QUICKLY! THE KING MUST BE HELPED...
HUFF
URK...
HUFF
IT'S NOT TOO LATE. SINISTRA HAS TO BE TORN OUT OF THE KING'S HAND...
HUFF
HUFF
KING GLANZEND!!
FATHER?!
FOO
YOUR MAJESTY!! ARE YOU ALL RIGHT?!

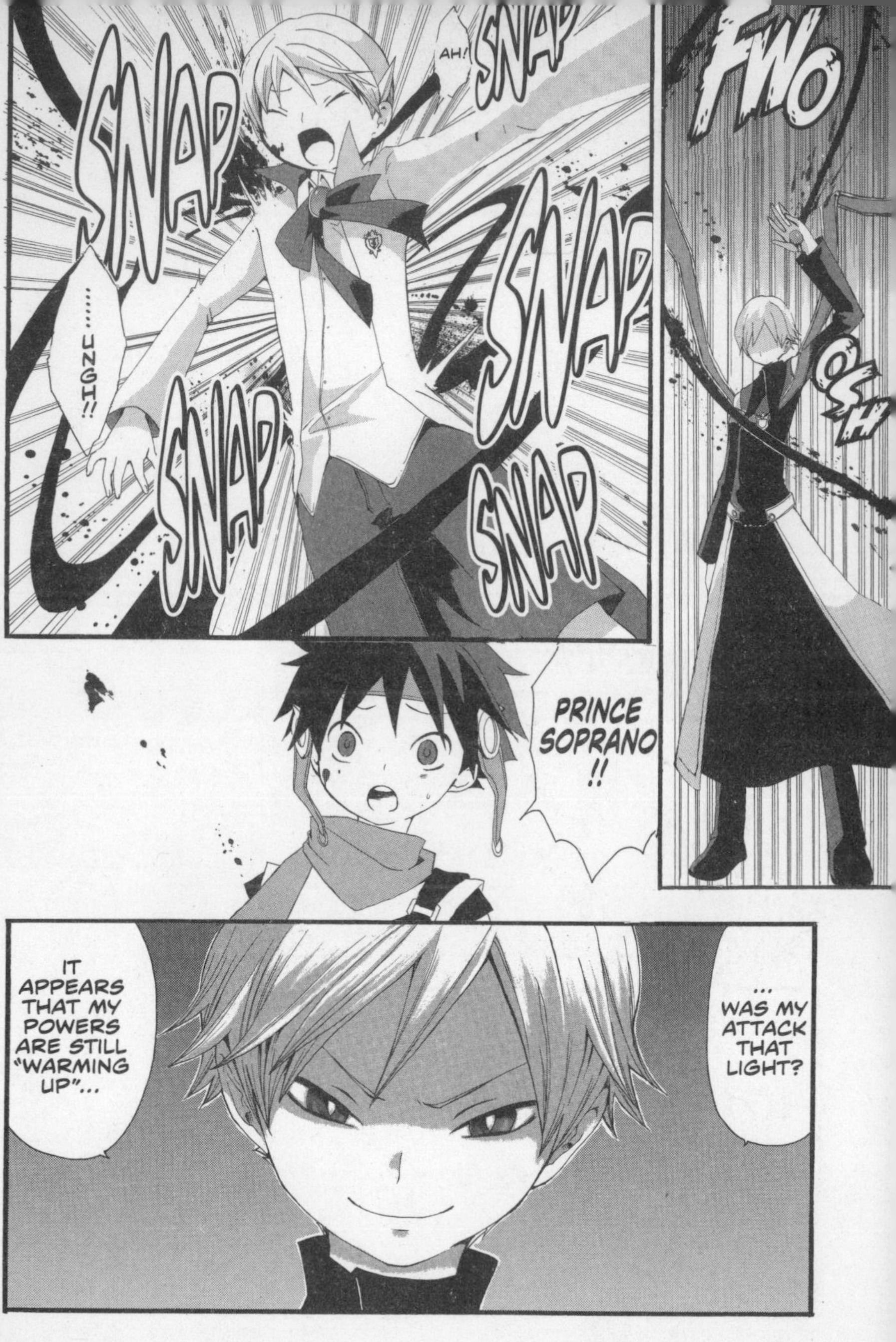
FWO
OSH
AH!
SNAP
SNAP
SNAP
SNAP
SNAP
SNAP
......UNGH!!
PRINCE SOPRANO!!
...WAS MY ATTACK THAT LIGHT?
IT APPEARS THAT MY POWERS ARE STILL "WARMING UP"...

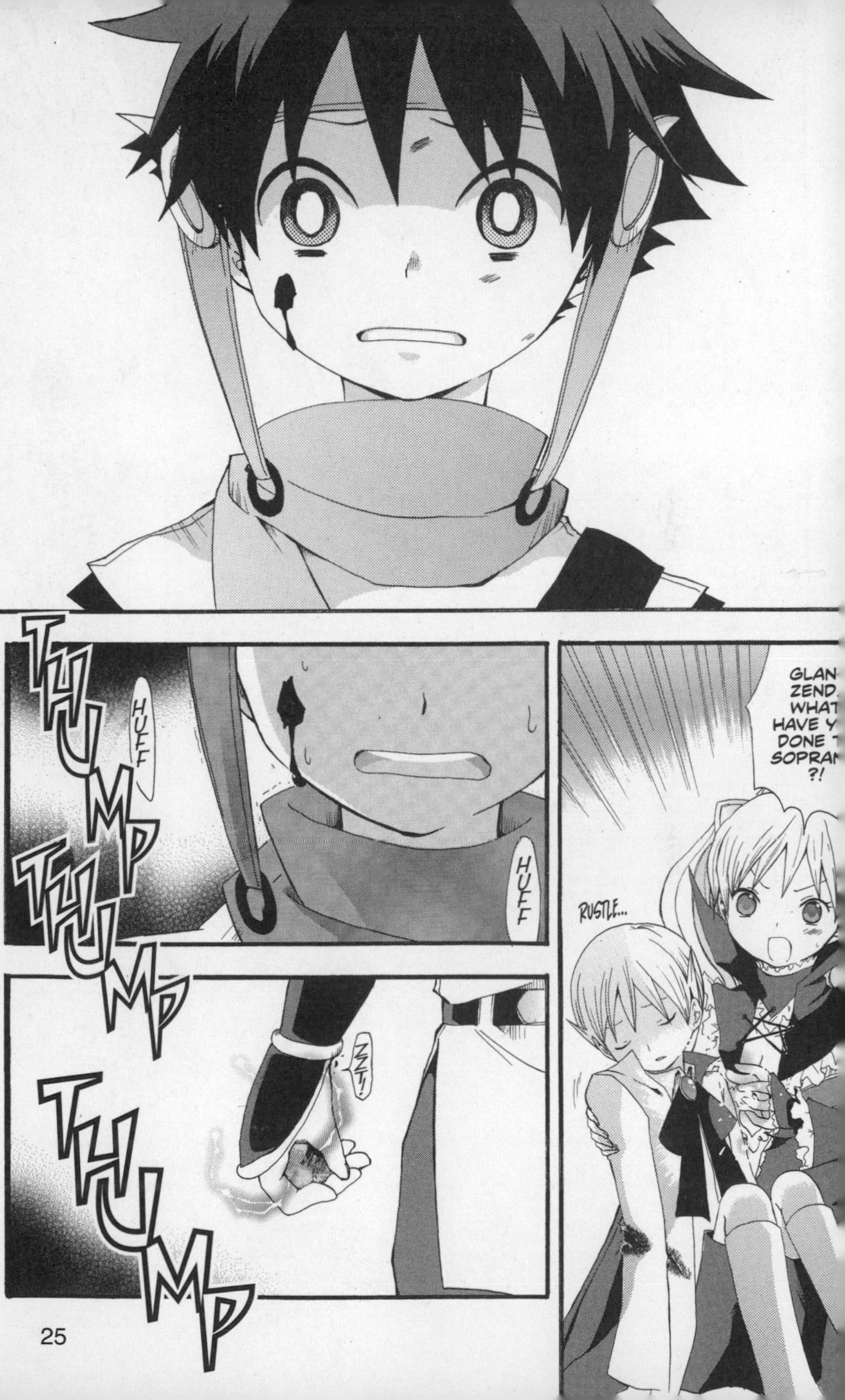
GLAN-ZEND... WHAT HAVE Y DONE T SOPRAN ?!
RUSTLE...
HUFF
HUFF
THUMP
THUMP
ZZT!
THUMP

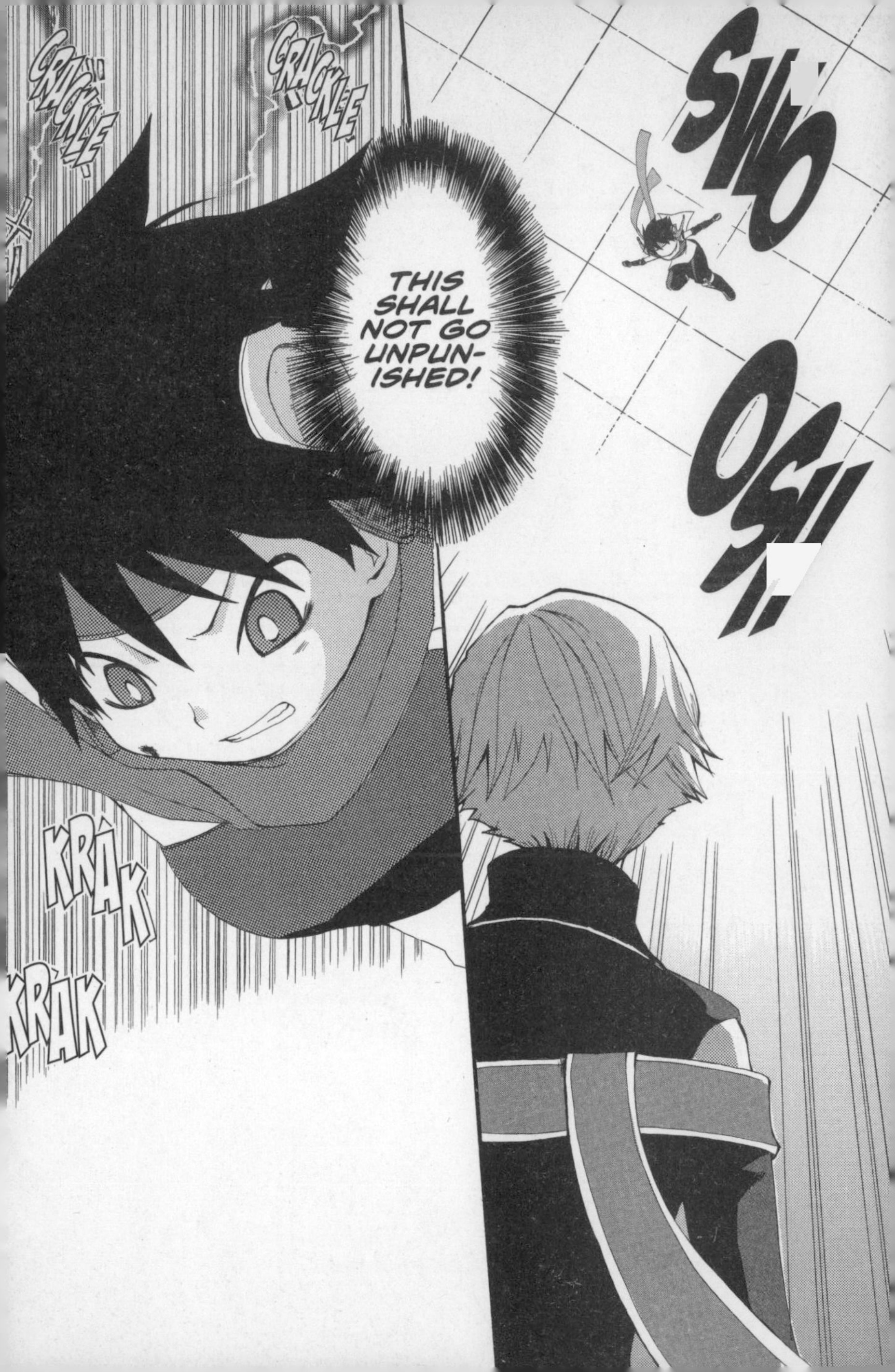
SWOOOSH!!
CRACKLE
CRACKLE
THIS SHALL NOT GO UNPUN-ISHED!
KRAK
KRAK

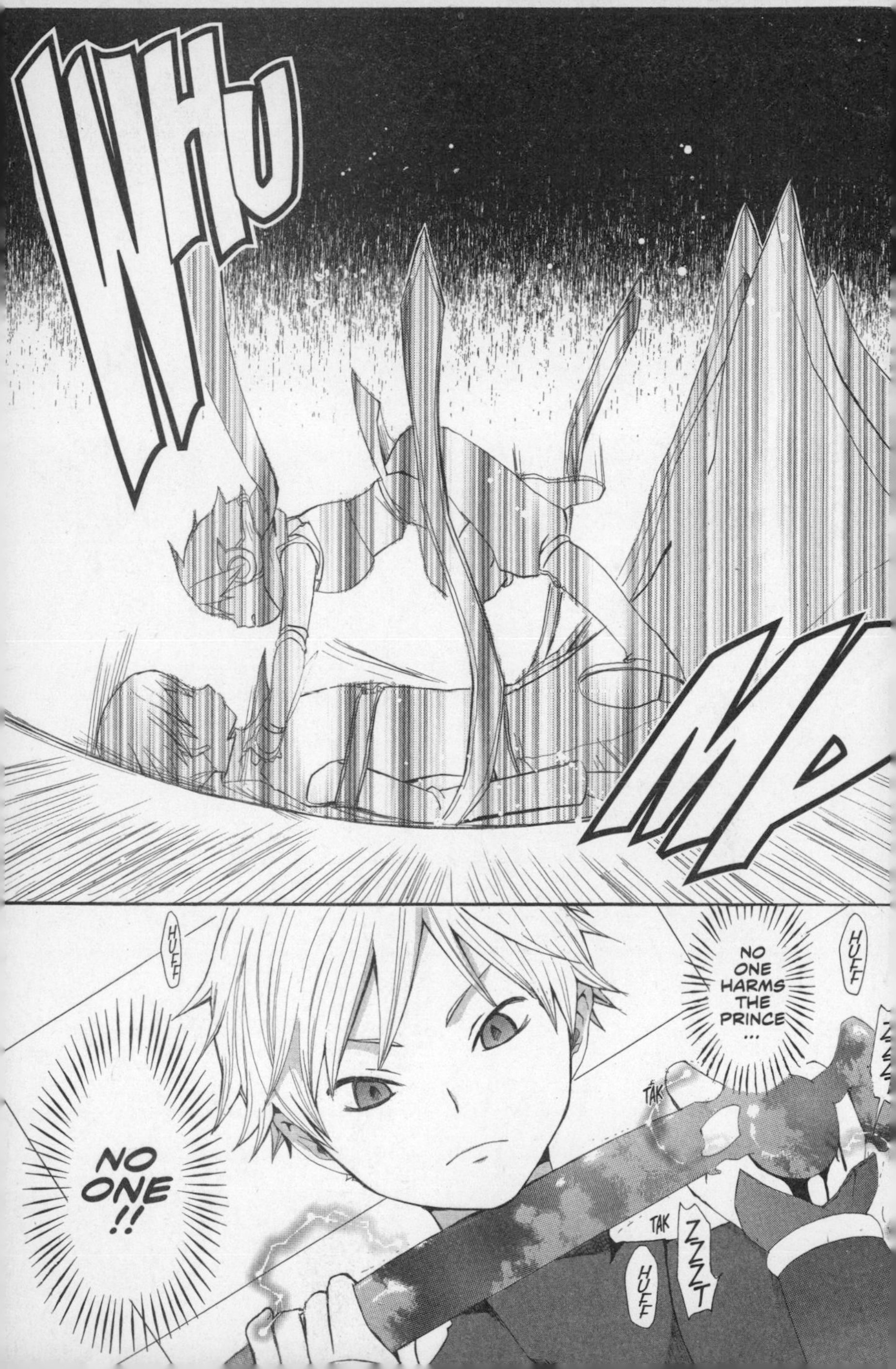
WHUMP
HUFF
NO ONE HARMS THE PRINCE...
TAK
TAK
ZZZT
HUFF
HUFF
NO ONE!!

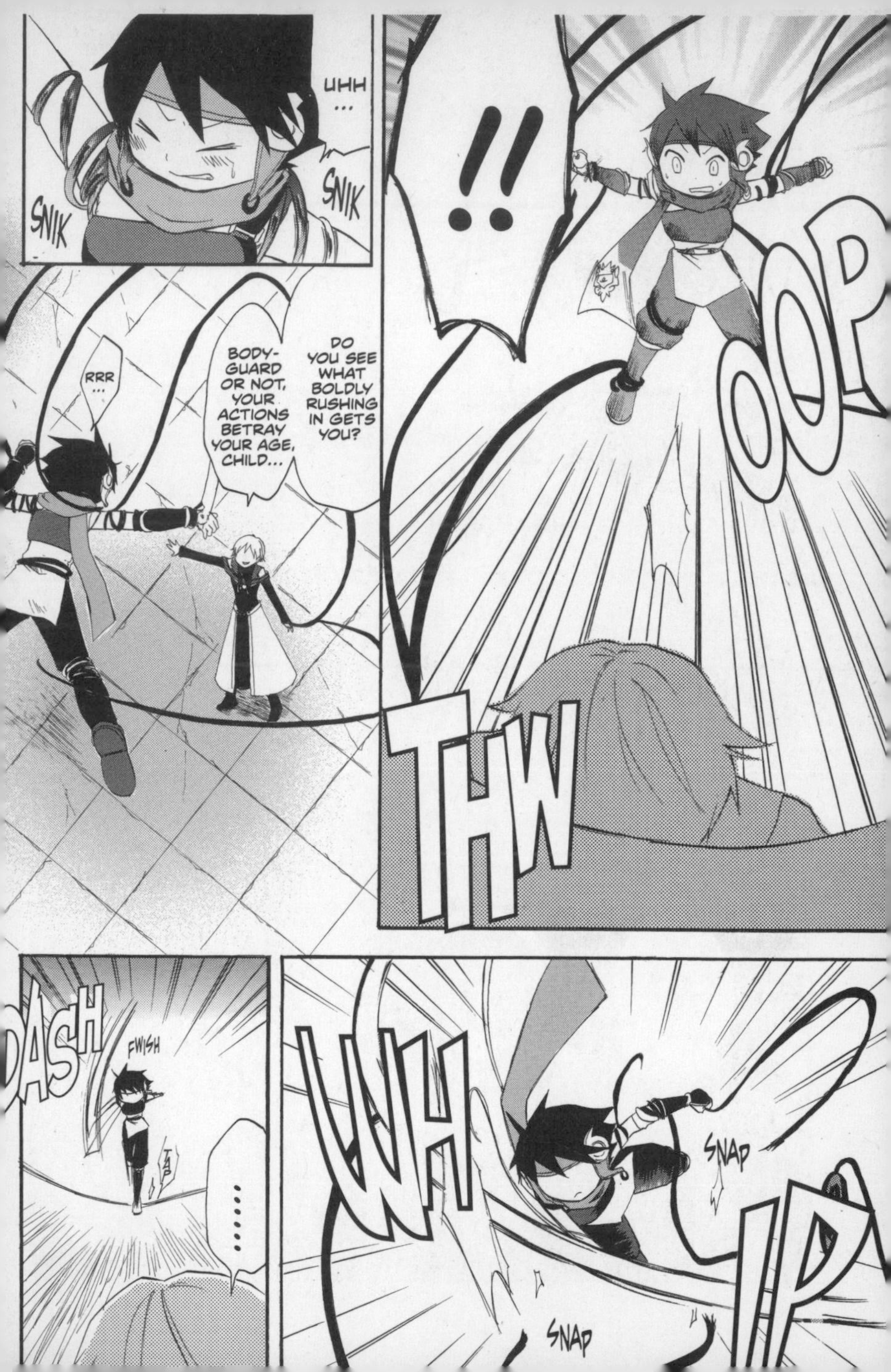
!!
OOP
THW
UHH...
SNIK
SNIK
DO YOU SEE WHAT BOLDLY RUSHING IN GETS YOU?
BODY-GUARD OR NOT, YOUR ACTIONS BETRAY YOUR AGE, CHILD...
RRR...
WH
IP
SNAP
SNAP
DASH
FWISH
TAP
......

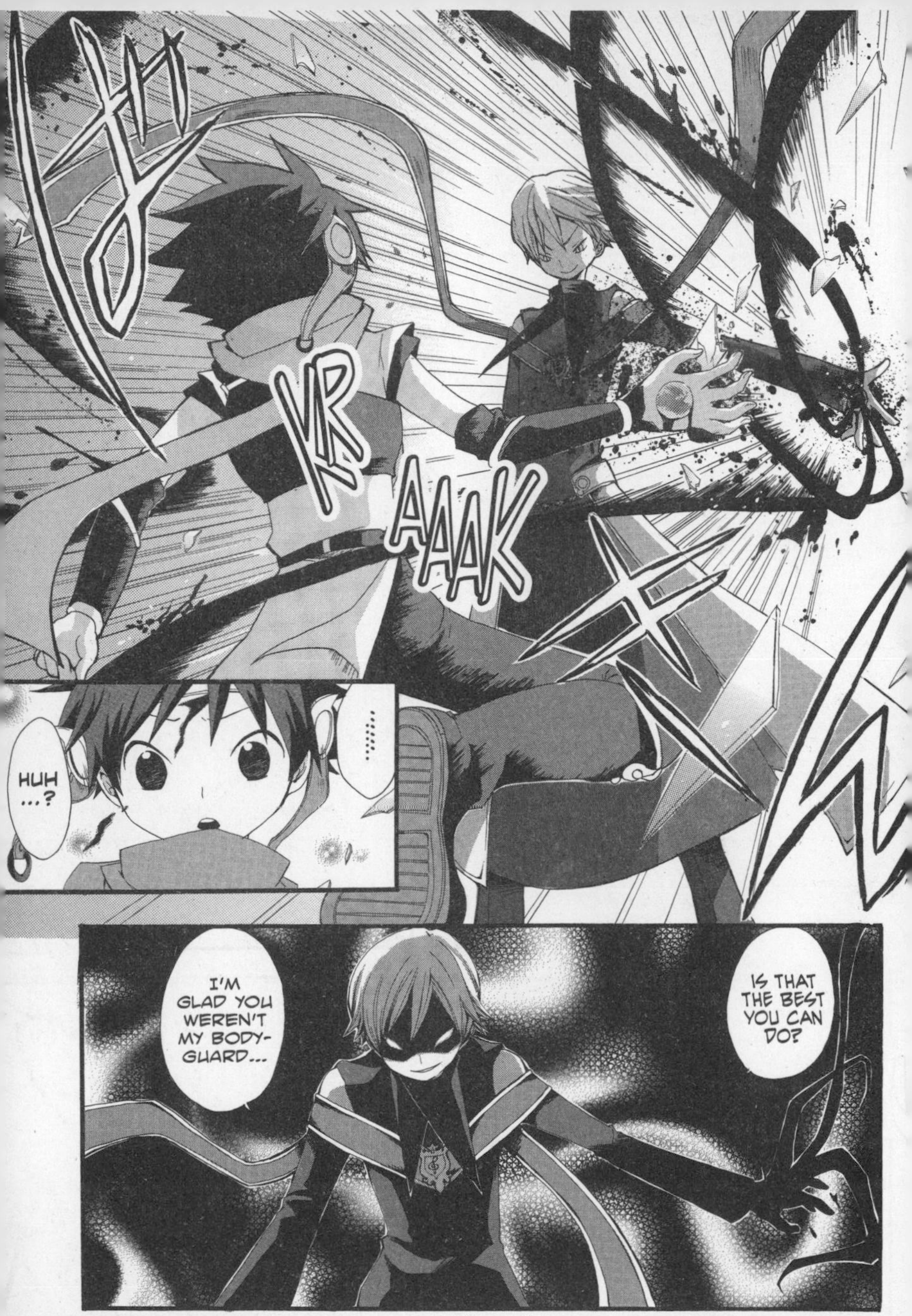
KR
AAAK
......
HUH ...?
IS THAT THE BEST YOU CAN DO?
I'M GLAD YOU WEREN'T MY BODY-GUARD...

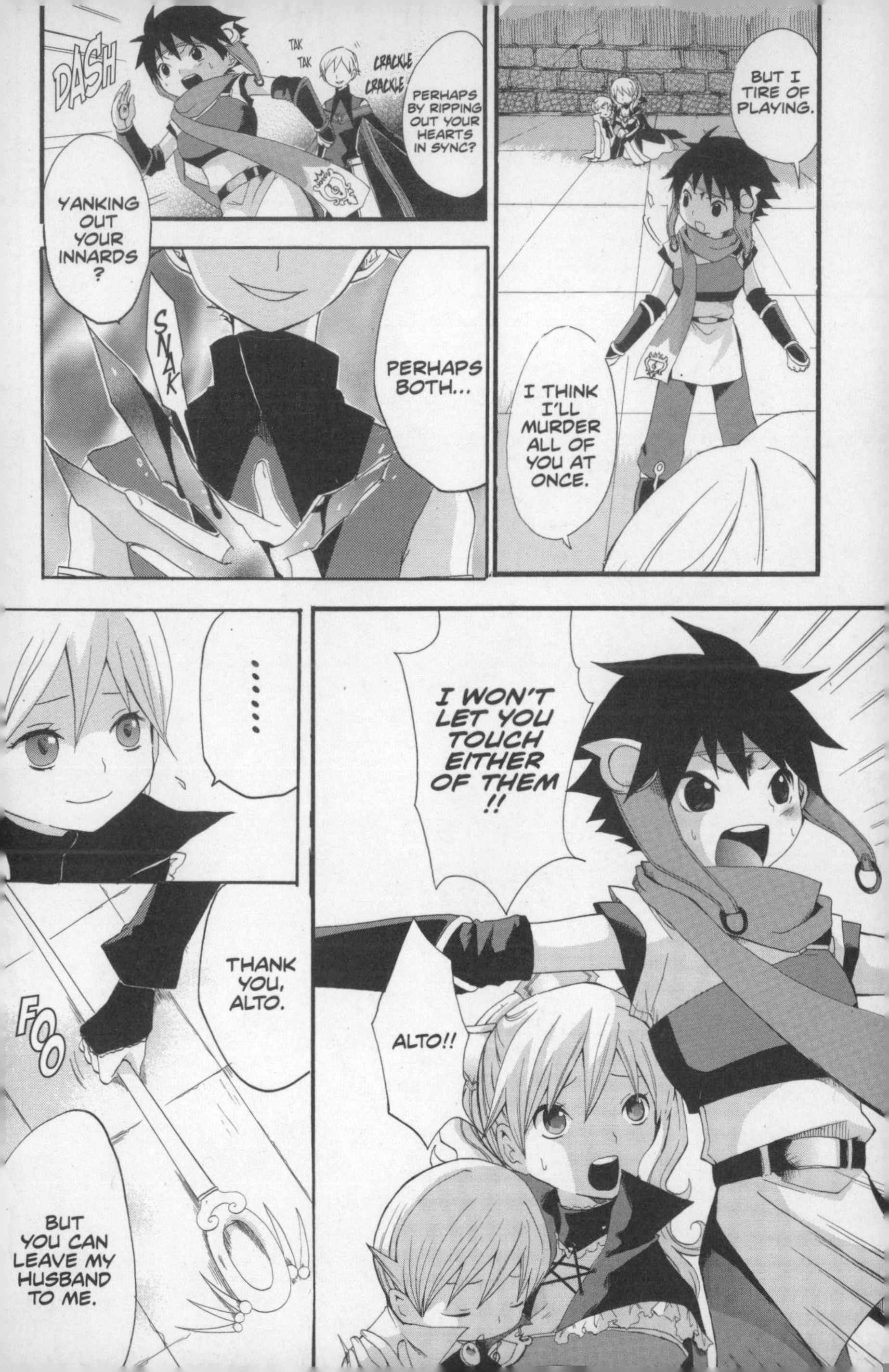
BUT I TIRE OF PLAYING.
I THINK I'LL MURDER ALL OF YOU AT ONCE.
CRACKLE CRACKLE
TAK TAK
PERHAPS BY RIPPING OUT YOUR HEARTS IN SYNC?
DASH
YANKING OUT YOUR INNARDS?
PERHAPS BOTH...
SNAK
I WON'T LET YOU TOUCH EITHER OF THEM!!
ALTO!!
......
THANK YOU, ALTO.
FOO
BUT YOU CAN LEAVE MY HUSBAND TO ME.

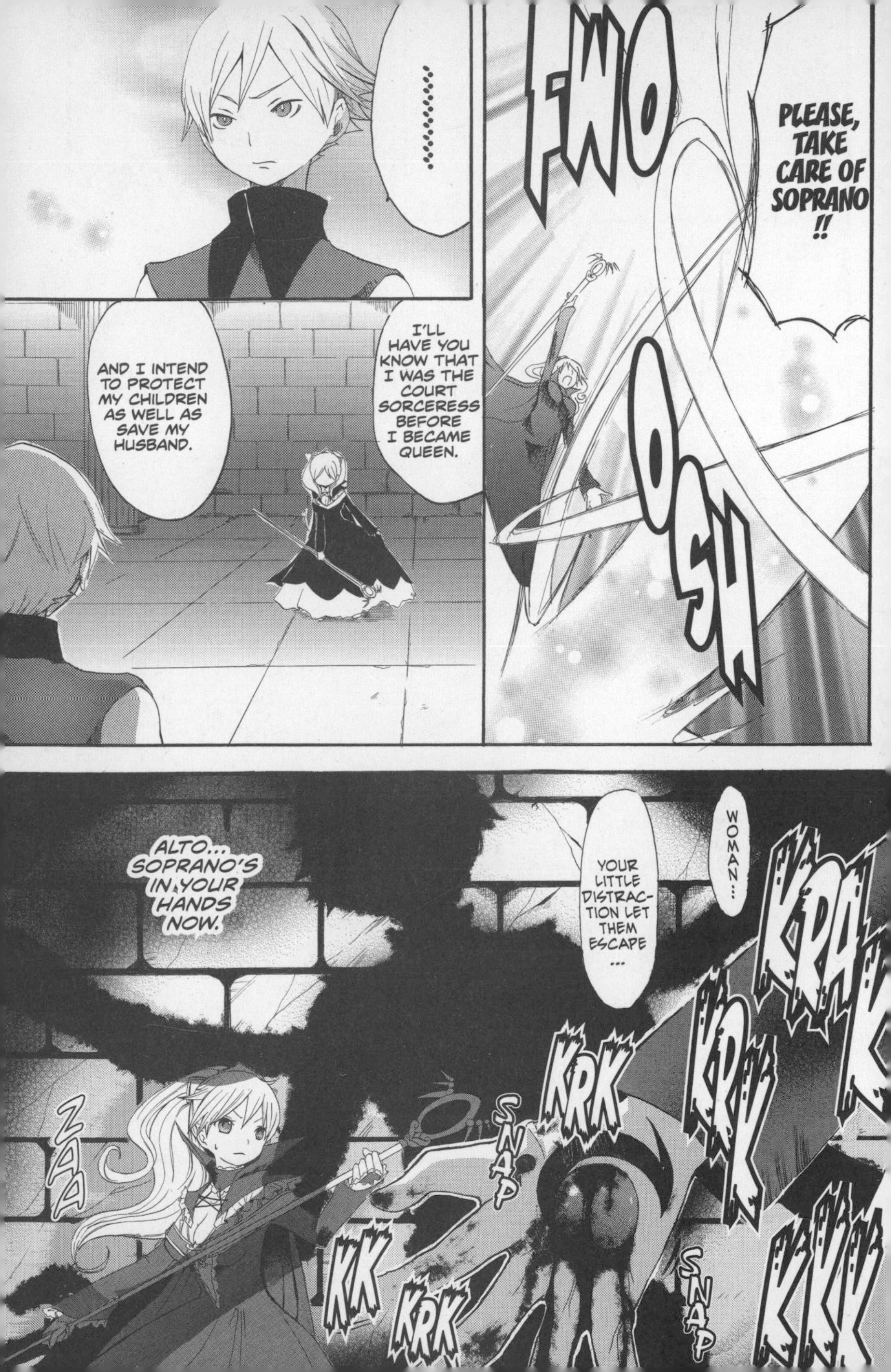
FWOOSH
PLEASE, TAKE CARE OF SOPRANO!!
......
I'LL HAVE YOU KNOW THAT I WAS THE COURT SORCERESS BEFORE I BECAME QUEEN.
AND I INTEND TO PROTECT MY CHILDREN AS WELL AS SAVE MY HUSBAND.
KRAK
WOMAN...
YOUR LITTLE DISTRACTION LET THEM ESCAPE...
ALTO... SOPRANO'S IN YOUR HANDS NOW.
KRK
KRK
SNAP
SNAP
KKK
KK
KRK
ZAA

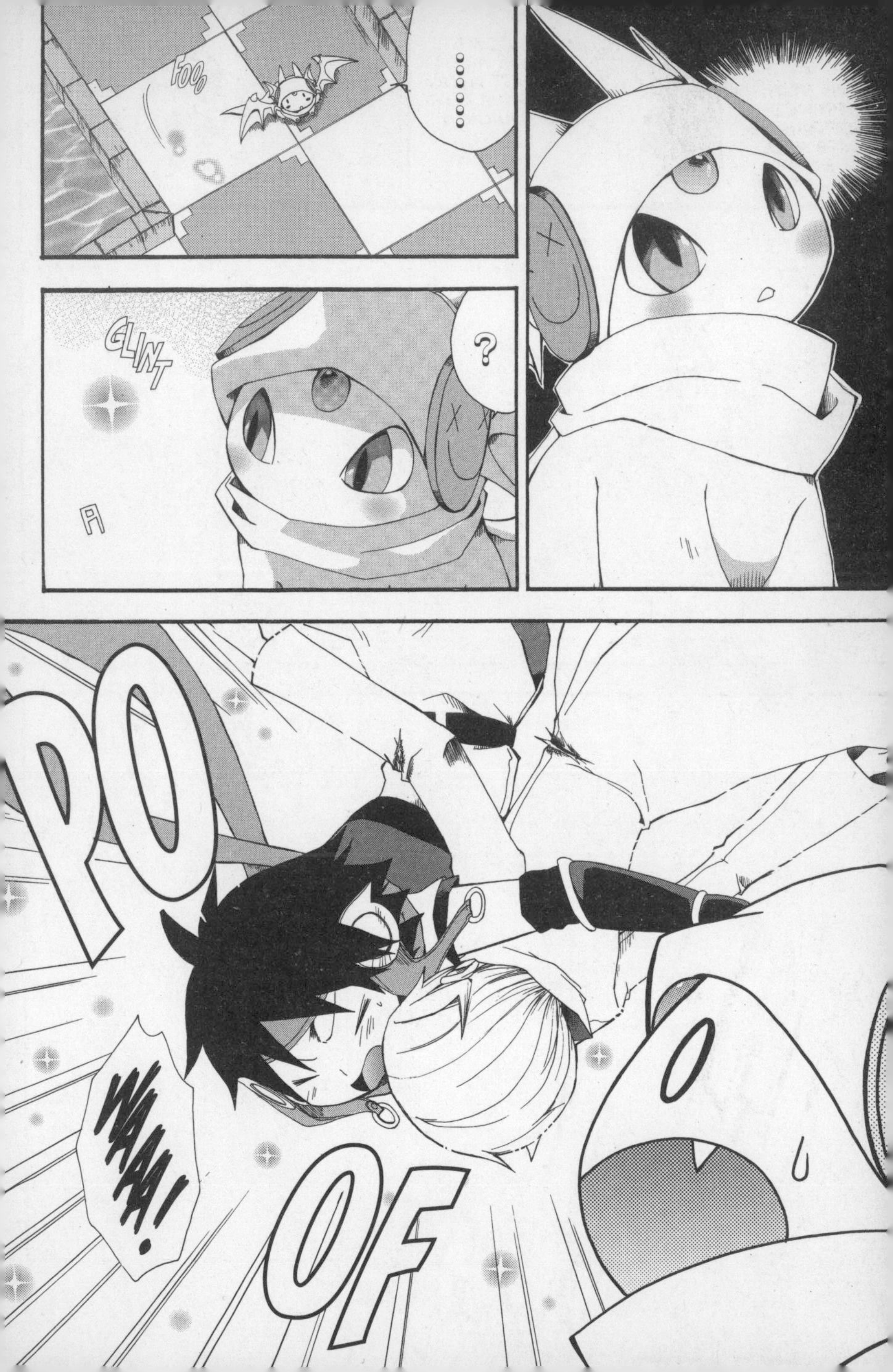

....
FOOO
?
GLINT
A
POOF
WHAAA!

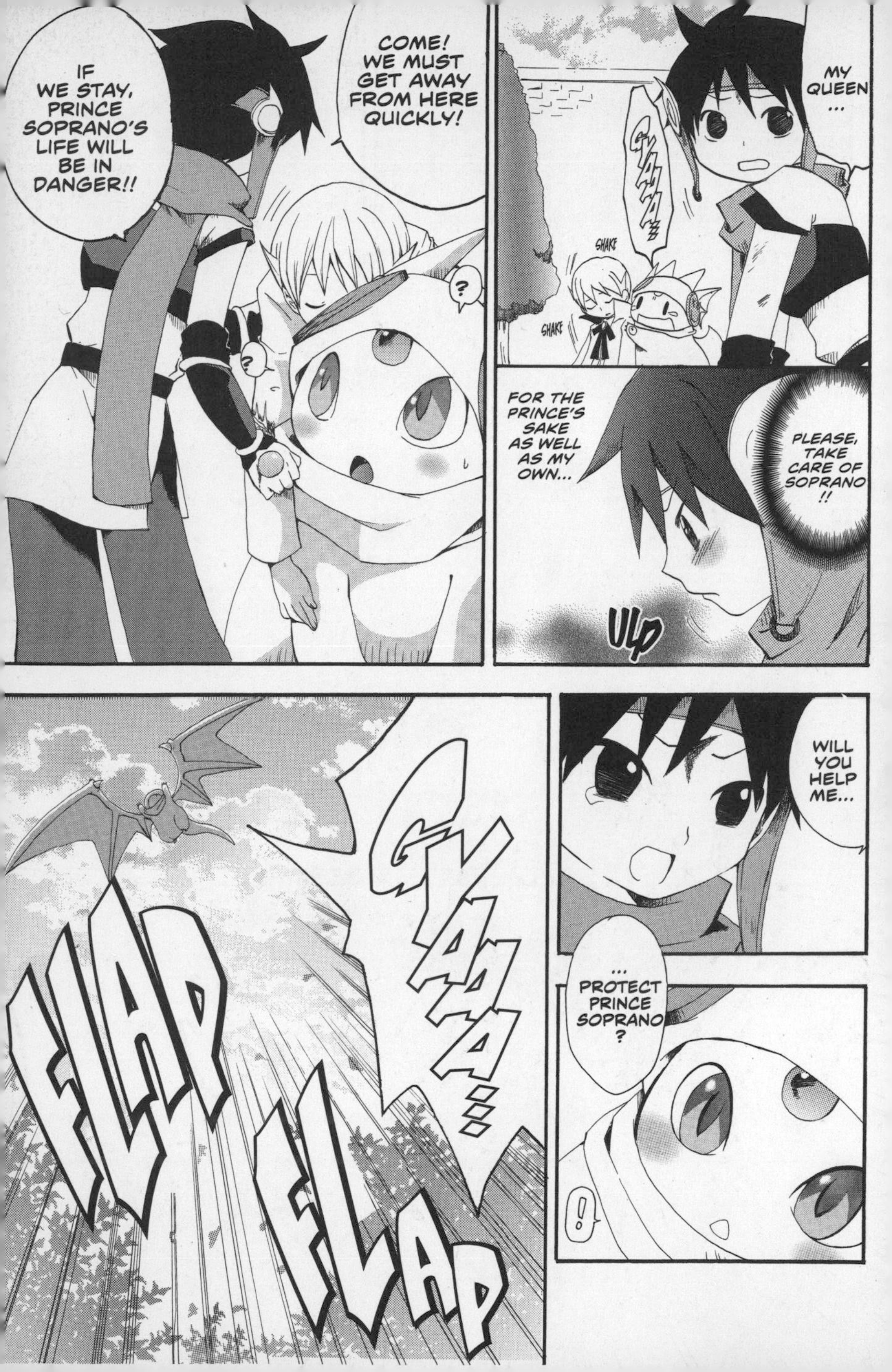
MY QUEEN ...
GYAAA
SHAKE
SHAKE
PLEASE, TAKE CARE OF SOPRANO !!
FOR THE PRINCE'S SAKE AS WELL AS MY OWN...
ULP
COME! WE MUST GET AWAY FROM HERE QUICKLY!
IF WE STAY, PRINCE SOPRANO'S LIFE WILL BE IN DANGER!!
?
?
WILL YOU HELP ME...
... PROTECT PRINCE SOPRANO ?
!
GYAAA...
FLAP
FLAP

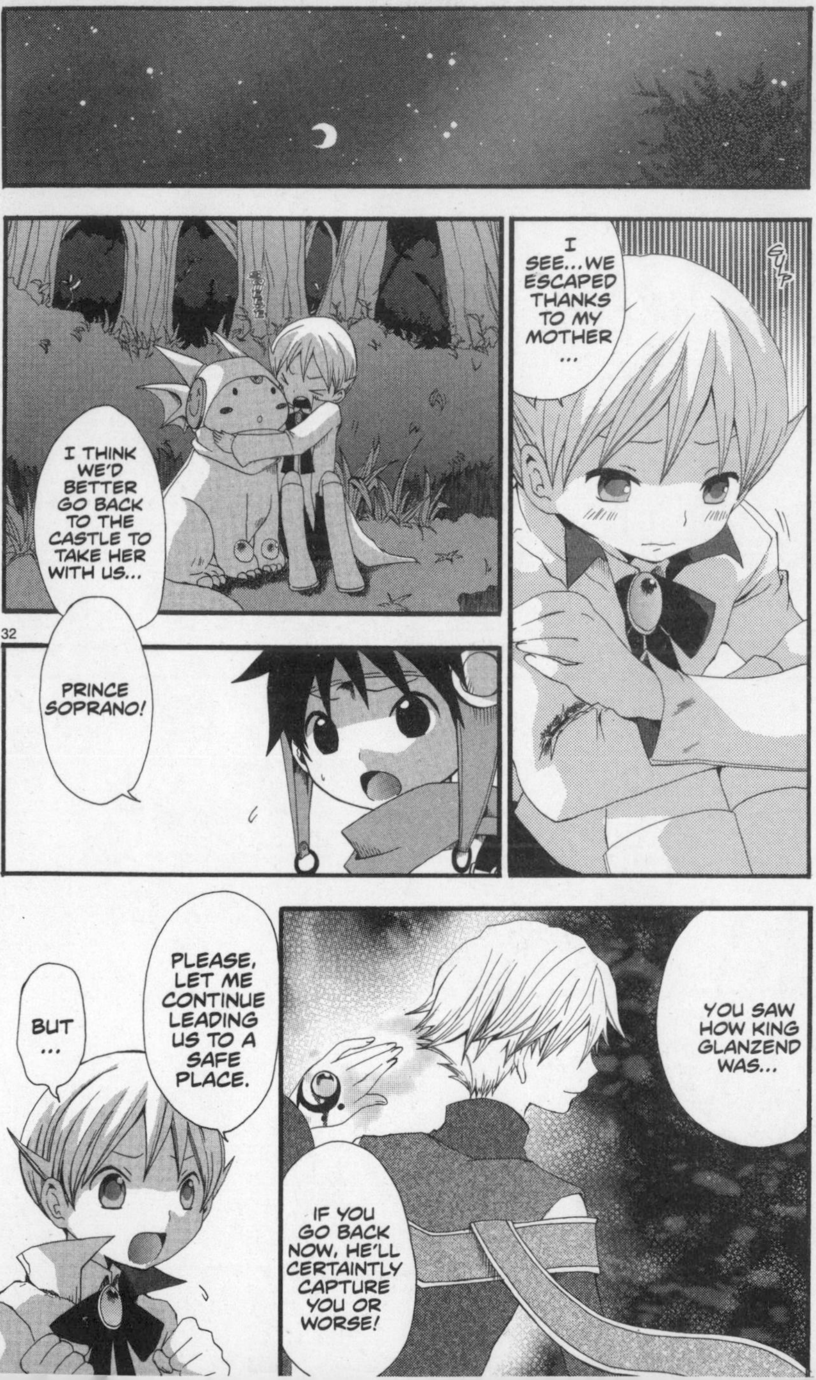
I SEE...WE ESCAPED THANKS TO MY MOTHER ...
GULP
I THINK WE'D BETTER GO BACK TO THE CASTLE TO TAKE HER WITH US...
PRINCE SOPRANO!
YOU SAW HOW KING GLANZEND WAS...
IF YOU GO BACK NOW, HE'LL CERTAINLY CAPTURE YOU OR WORSE!
PLEASE, LET ME CONTINUE LEADING US TO A SAFE PLACE.
BUT ...

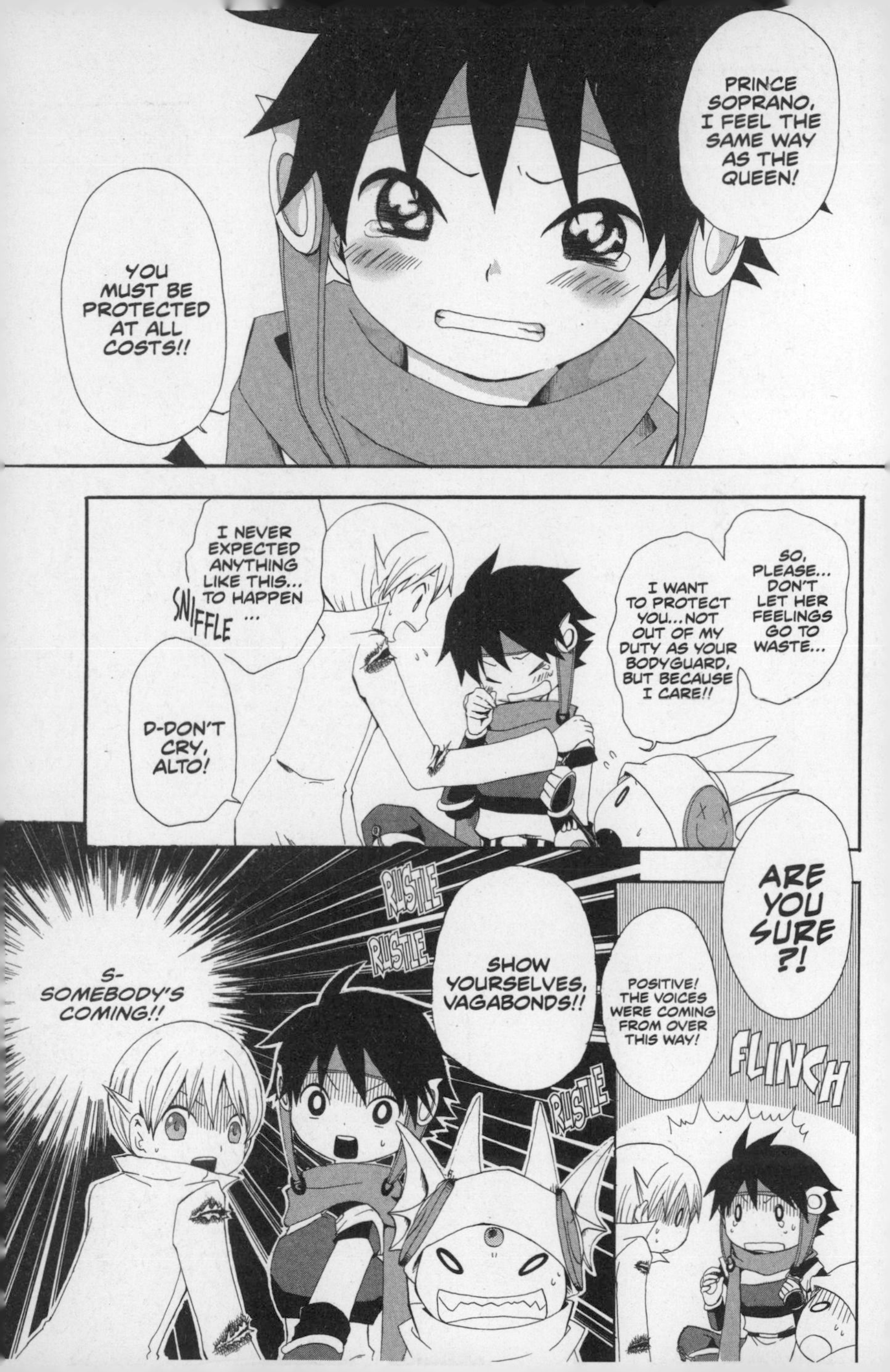
PRINCE SOPRANO, I FEEL THE SAME WAY AS THE QUEEN!
YOU MUST BE PROTECTED AT ALL COSTS!!
SO, PLEASE... DON'T LET HER FEELINGS GO TO WASTE...
I WANT TO PROTECT YOU...NOT OUT OF MY DUTY AS YOUR BODYGUARD, BUT BECAUSE I CARE!!
I NEVER EXPECTED ANYTHING LIKE THIS... TO HAPPEN ...
SNIFFLE
D-DON'T CRY, ALTO!
ARE YOU SURE ?!
POSITIVE! THE VOICES WERE COMING FROM OVER THIS WAY!
FLINCH
RUSTLE
RUSTLE
SHOW YOURSELVES, VAGABONDS!!
RUSTLE
S-SOMEBODY'S COMING!!

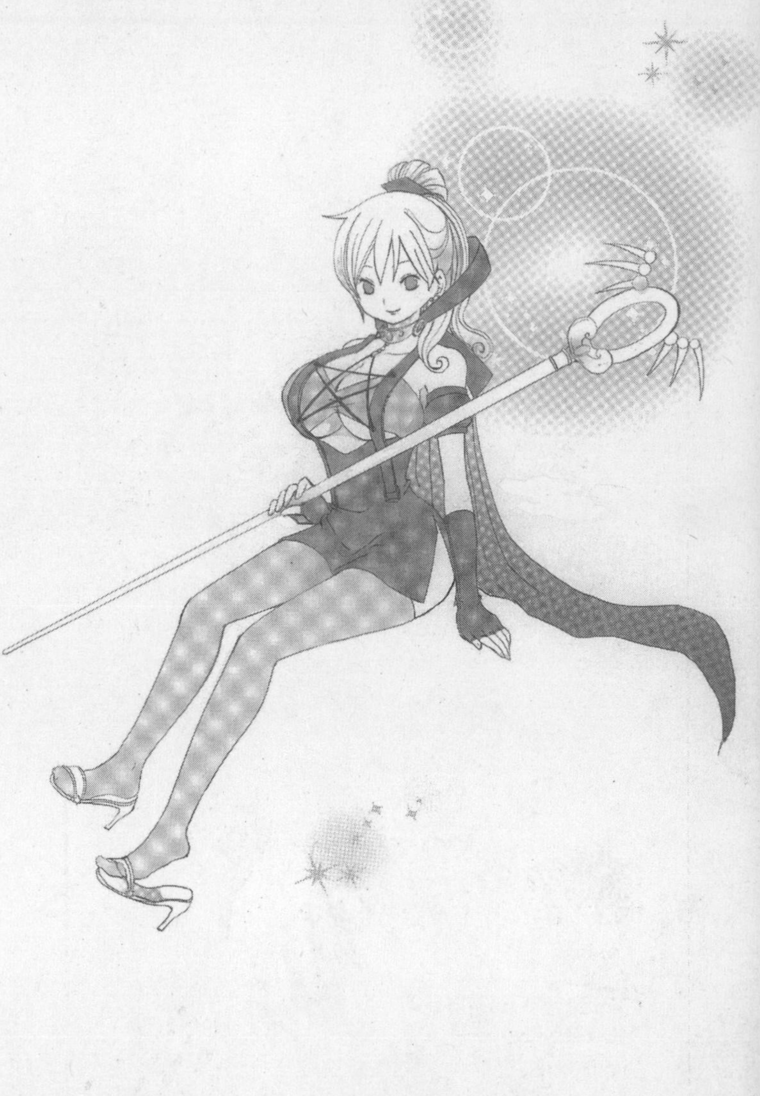

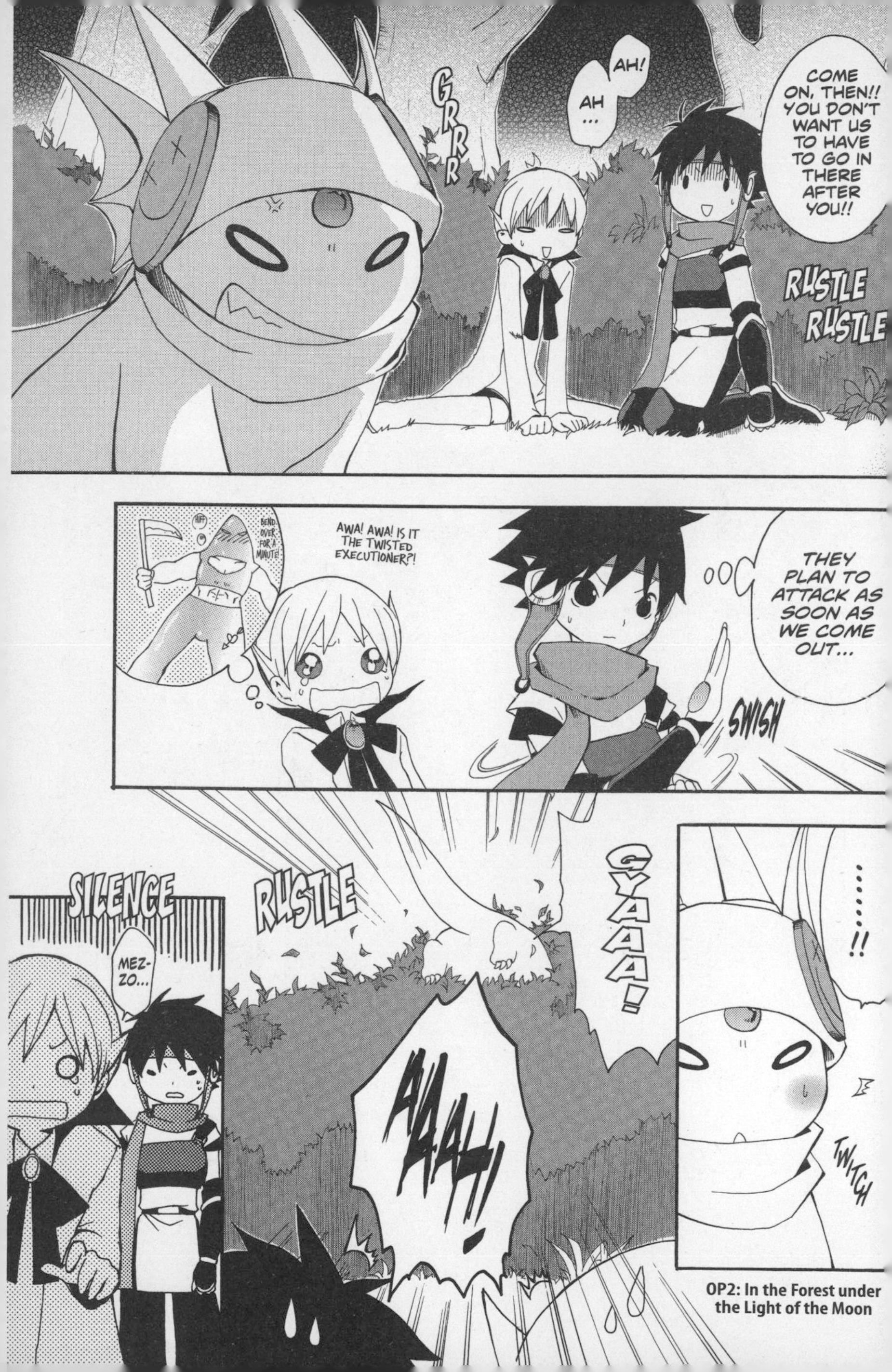
COME ON, THEN!! YOU DON'T WANT US TO HAVE TO GO IN THERE AFTER YOU!!
AH!
AH ...
GRRR
RUSTLE RUSTLE
THEY PLAN TO ATTACK AS SOON AS WE COME OUT...
SWISH
AWA! AWA! IS IT THE TWISTED EXECUTIONER?!
HUFF
BEND OVER FOR A MINUTE!
......!!
TWITCH
GYAAA!
RUSTLE
AAAAH!!
SILENCE
MEZ-ZO...

OP2: In the Forest under the Light of the Moon

OP2: In the Forest under the Light of the Moon

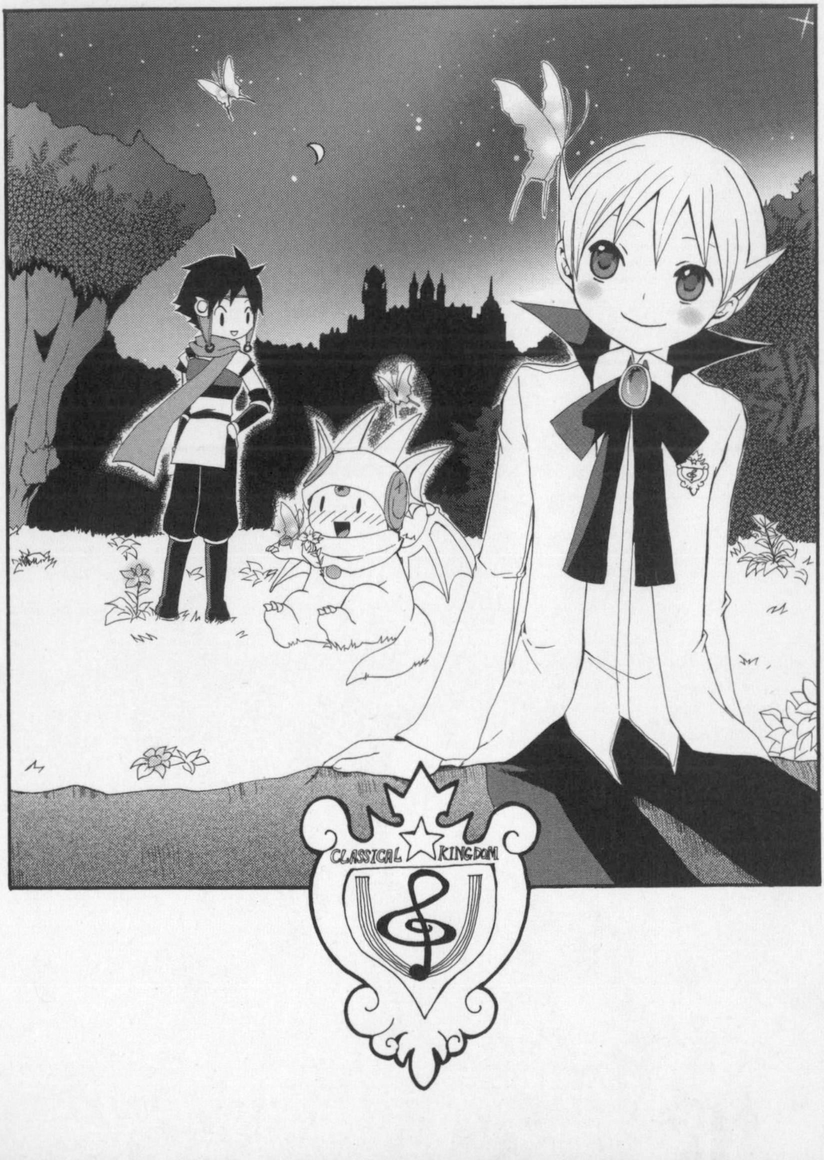
CLASSICAL KINGDOM

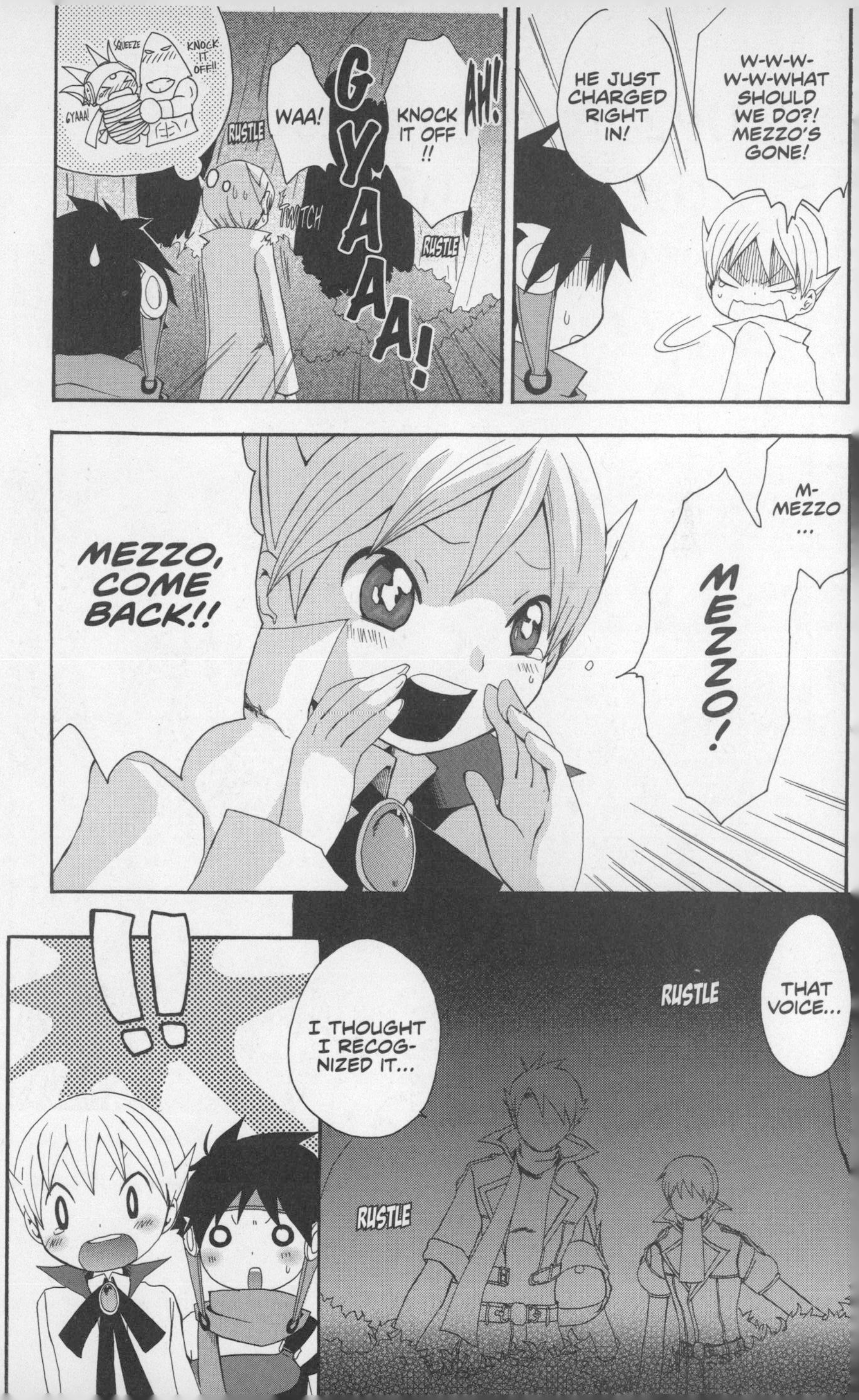
W-W-W-W-W-WHAT SHOULD WE DO?! MEZZO'S GONE!
HE JUST CHARGED RIGHT IN!
AH!
KNOCK IT OFF !!
GYAAA!
WAA!
RUSTLE
KNOCK IT OFF!!
SQUEEZE
GYAAA!
TWITCH
RUSTLE
M-MEZZO...
MEZZO!
MEZZO, COME BACK!!
THAT VOICE...
RUSTLE
I THOUGHT I RECOG-NIZED IT...
RUSTLE
!!

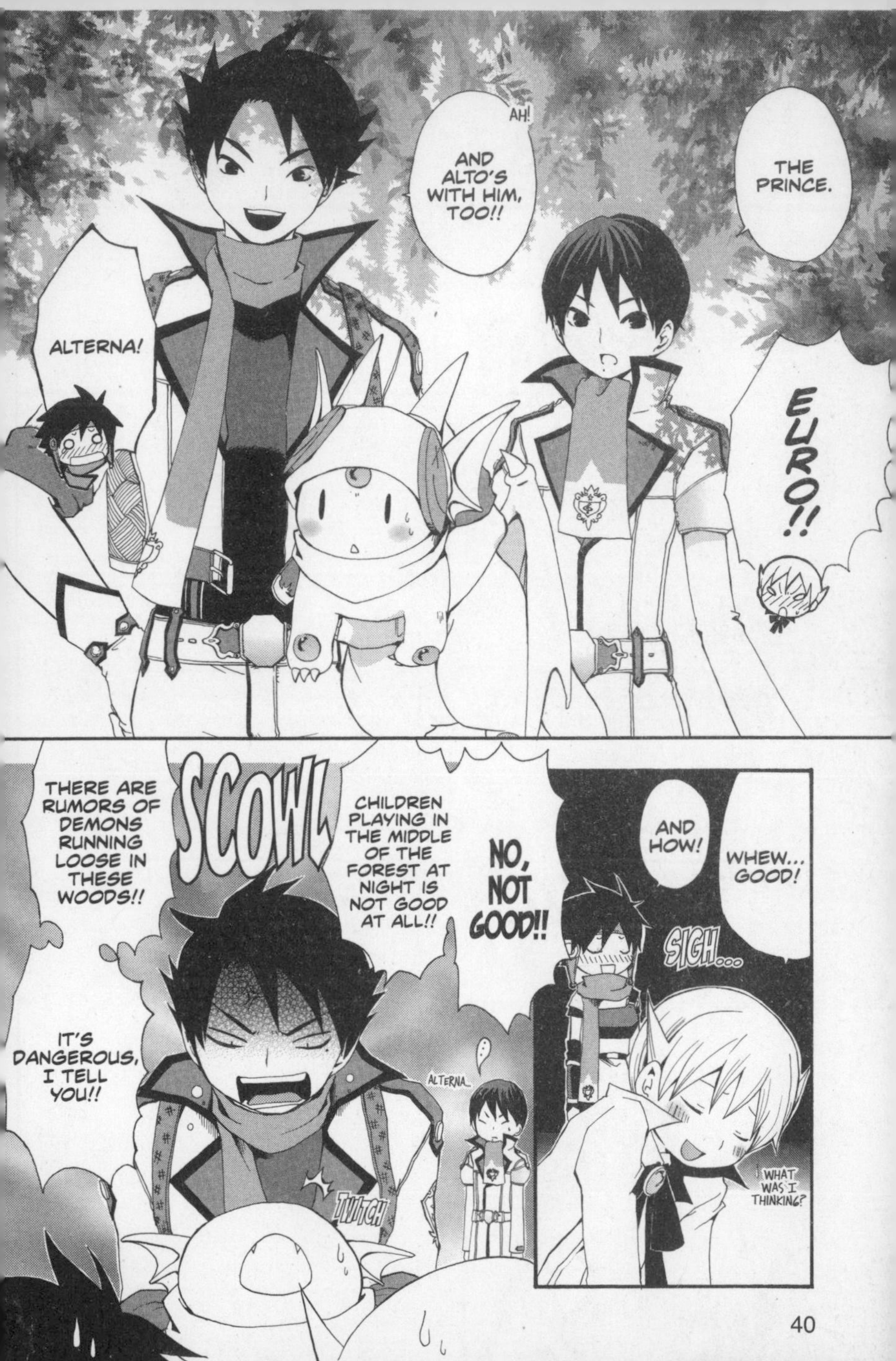
THE PRINCE.
EURO!!
AH!
AND ALTO'S WITH HIM, TOO!!
ALTERNA!
WHEW... GOOD!
AND HOW!
SIGH...
WHAT WAS I THINKING?
NO, NOT GOOD!!
CHILDREN PLAYING IN THE MIDDLE OF THE FOREST AT NIGHT IS NOT GOOD AT ALL!!
SCOWL
THERE ARE RUMORS OF DEMONS RUNNING LOOSE IN THESE WOODS!!
ALTERNA...
IT'S DANGEROUS, I TELL YOU!!
TWITCH

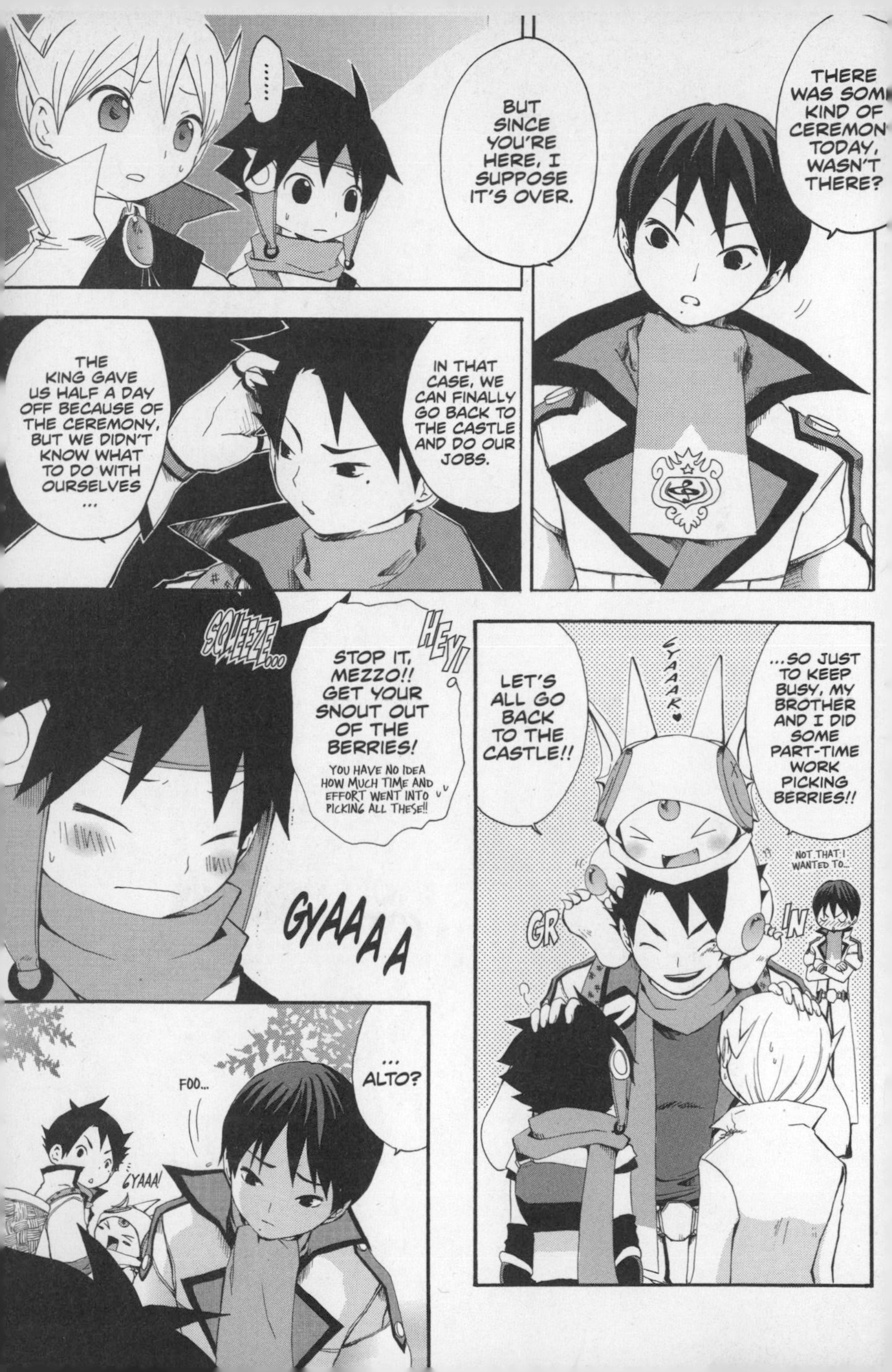
THERE WAS SOM KIND OF CEREMON TODAY, WASN'T THERE?
BUT SINCE YOU'RE HERE, I SUPPOSE IT'S OVER.
......
IN THAT CASE, WE CAN FINALLY GO BACK TO THE CASTLE AND DO OUR JOBS.
THE KING GAVE US HALF A DAY OFF BECAUSE OF THE CEREMONY, BUT WE DIDN'T KNOW WHAT TO DO WITH OURSELVES ...
...SO JUST TO KEEP BUSY, MY BROTHER AND I DID SOME PART-TIME WORK PICKING BERRIES!!
GYAAAK♥
LET'S ALL GO BACK TO THE CASTLE!!
NOT THAT I WANTED TO...
N
GR
HEY!
STOP IT, MEZZO!! GET YOUR SNOUT OUT OF THE BERRIES!
YOU HAVE NO IDEA HOW MUCH TIME AND EFFORT WENT INTO PICKING ALL THESE!!
SQUEEZE...
GYAAAAA
... ALTO?
FOO...
GYAAA!

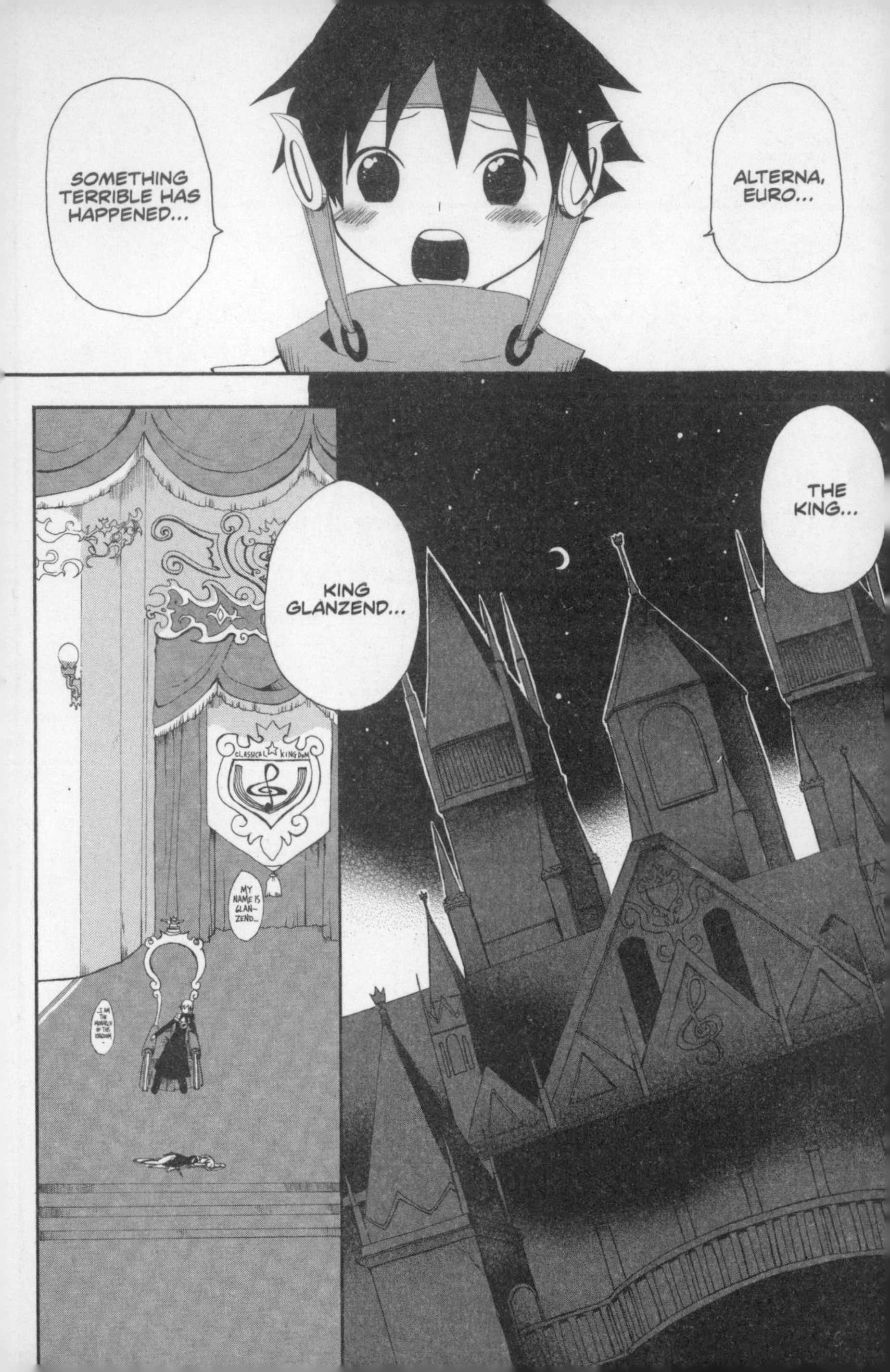
ALTERNA, EURO...
SOMETHING TERRIBLE HAS HAPPENED...
THE KING...
KING GLANZEND...
CLASSICAL KINGDOM
MY NAME IS GLAN-ZEND...
...I AM THE MONARCH OF THIS KINGDOM...

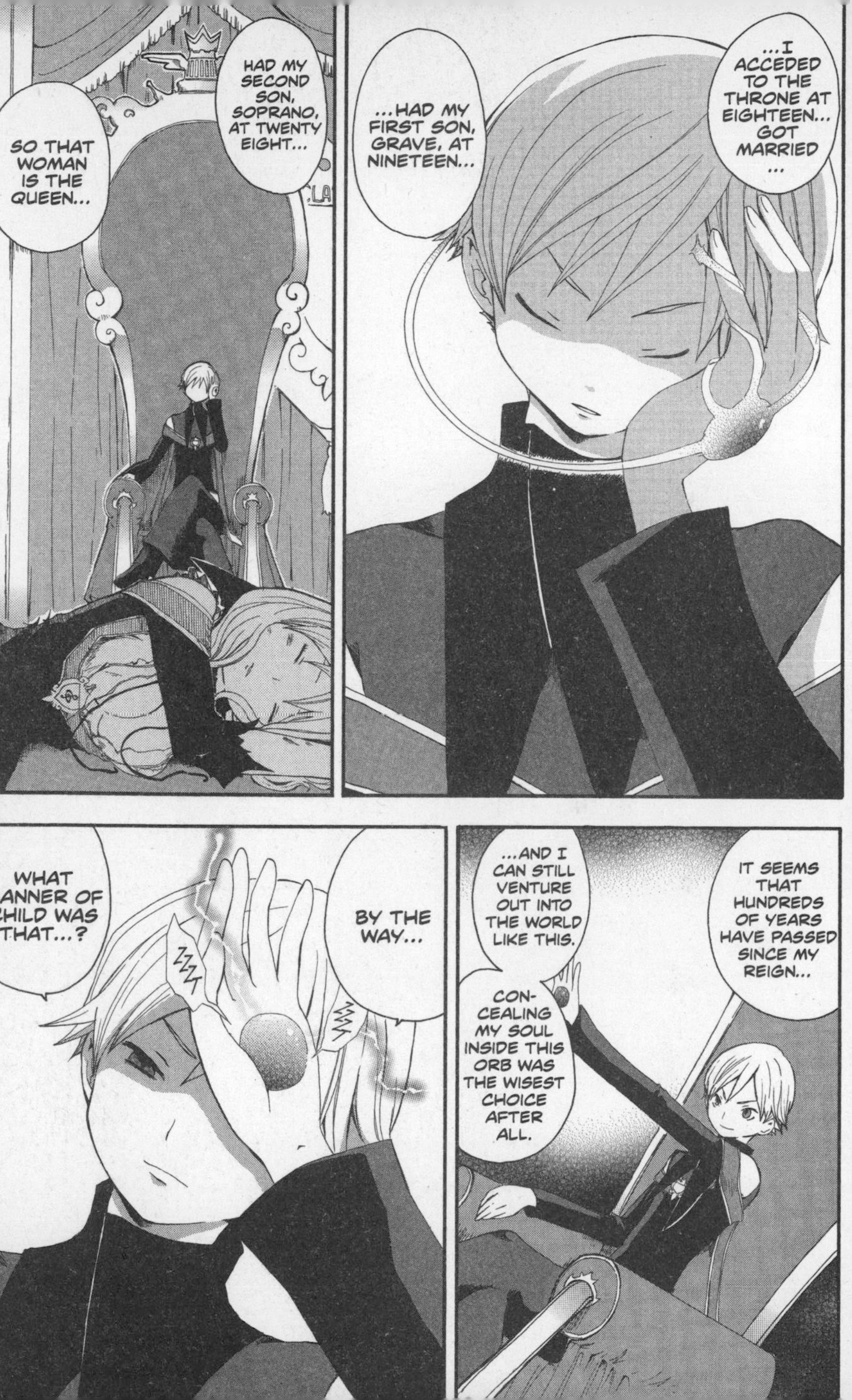
...I ACCEDED TO THE THRONE AT EIGHTEEN... GOT MARRIED ...
...HAD MY FIRST SON, GRAVE, AT NINETEEN...
HAD MY SECOND SON, SOPRANO, AT TWENTY EIGHT...
SO THAT WOMAN IS THE QUEEN...
IT SEEMS THAT HUNDREDS OF YEARS HAVE PASSED SINCE MY REIGN...
...AND I CAN STILL VENTURE OUT INTO THE WORLD LIKE THIS.
CONCEALING MY SOUL INSIDE THIS ORB WAS THE WISEST CHOICE AFTER ALL.
BY THE WAY...
ZZZT
ZZZT
WHAT MANNER OF CHILD WAS THAT...?

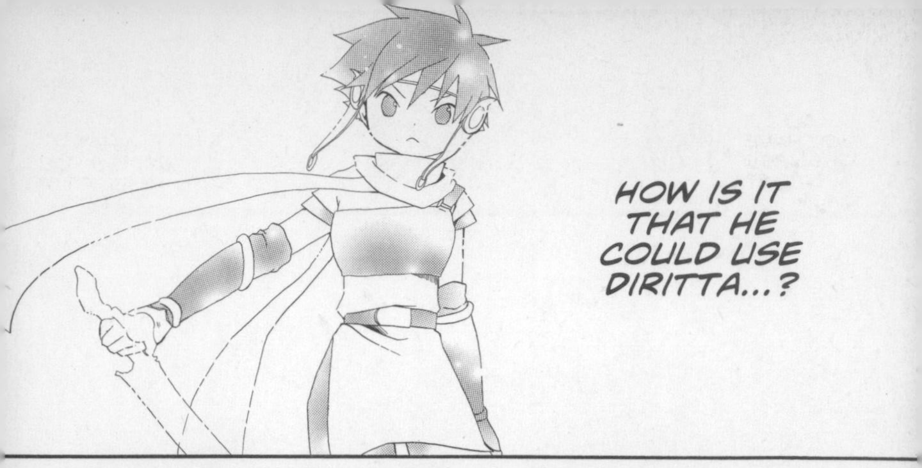
HOW IS IT THAT HE COULD USE DIRITTA...?

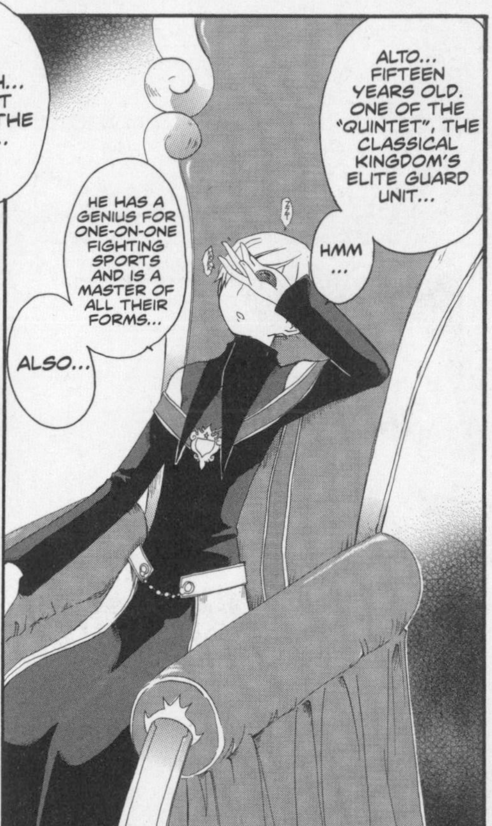
ALTO... FIFTEEN YEARS OLD. ONE OF THE "QUINTET", THE CLASSICAL KINGDOM'S ELITE GUARD UNIT...
HMM...
HE HAS A GENIUS FOR ONE-ON-ONE FIGHTING SPORTS AND IS A MASTER OF ALL THEIR FORMS...
ALSO...

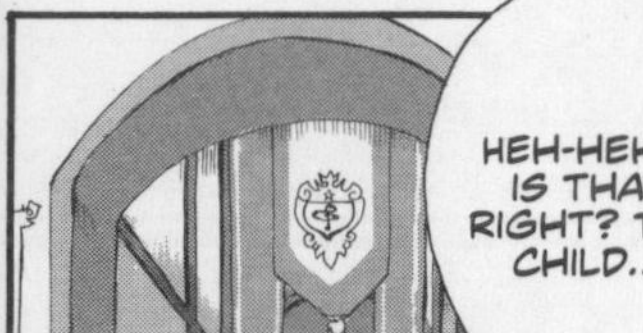
HEH-HEH... IS THAT RIGHT? THE CHILD...
...IS QUITE AMUSING.
TAK
TAK
TAK

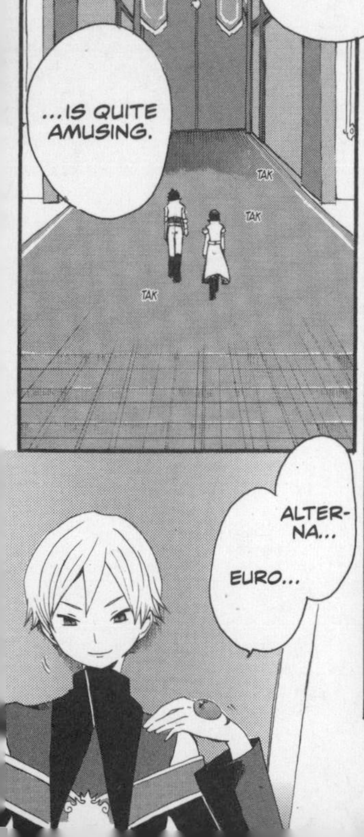
ALTER-NA...
EURO...

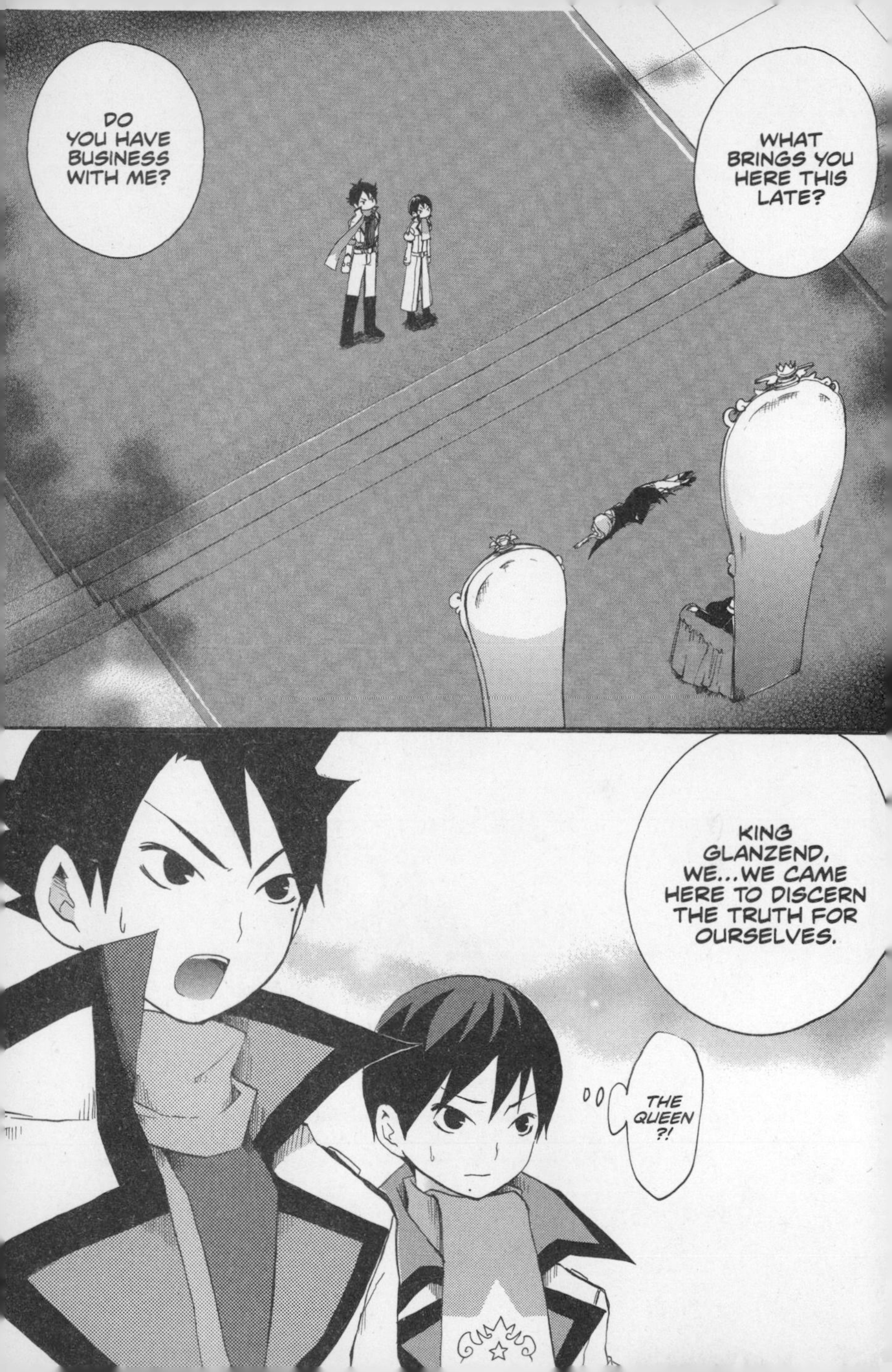
WHAT BRINGS YOU HERE THIS LATE?
DO YOU HAVE BUSINESS WITH ME?
KING GLANZEND, WE...WE CAME HERE TO DISCERN THE TRUTH FOR OURSELVES.
THE QUEEN ?!

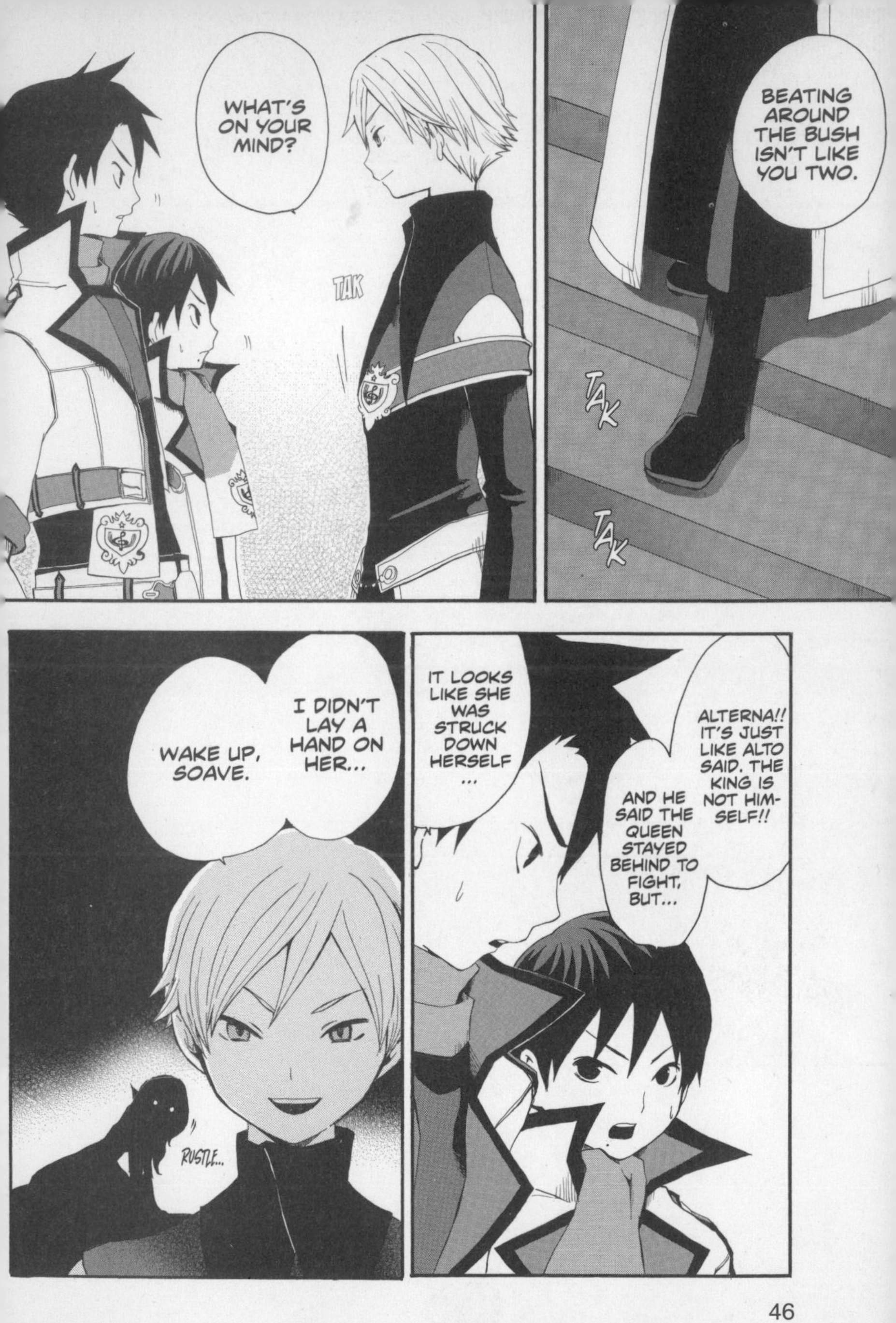

BEATING AROUND THE BUSH ISN'T LIKE YOU TWO.
TAK
TAK
WHAT'S ON YOUR MIND?
TAK
ALTERNA!! IT'S JUST LIKE ALTO SAID. THE KING IS NOT HIM-SELF!!
AND HE SAID THE QUEEN STAYED BEHIND TO FIGHT, BUT...
IT LOOKS LIKE SHE WAS STRUCK DOWN HERSELF...
I DIDN'T LAY A HAND ON HER...
WAKE UP, SOAVE.
RUSTLE...

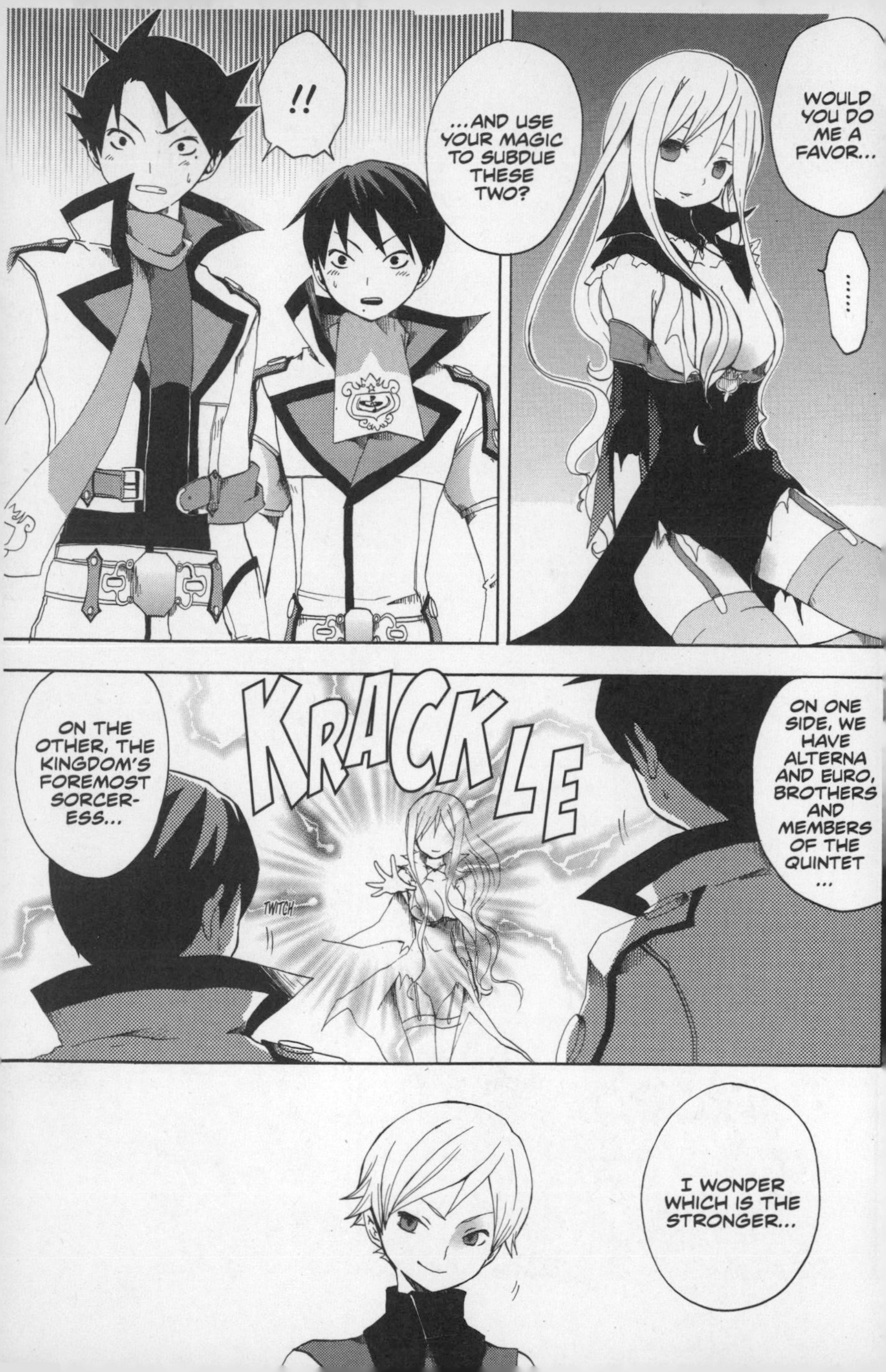
WOULD YOU DO ME A FAVOR...
......
...AND USE YOUR MAGIC TO SUBDUE THESE TWO?
!!
KRACKLE
ON ONE SIDE, WE HAVE ALTERNA AND EURO, BROTHERS AND MEMBERS OF THE QUINTET ...
ON THE OTHER, THE KINGDOM'S FOREMOST SORCERER-ESS...
TWITCH
I WONDER WHICH IS THE STRONGER...

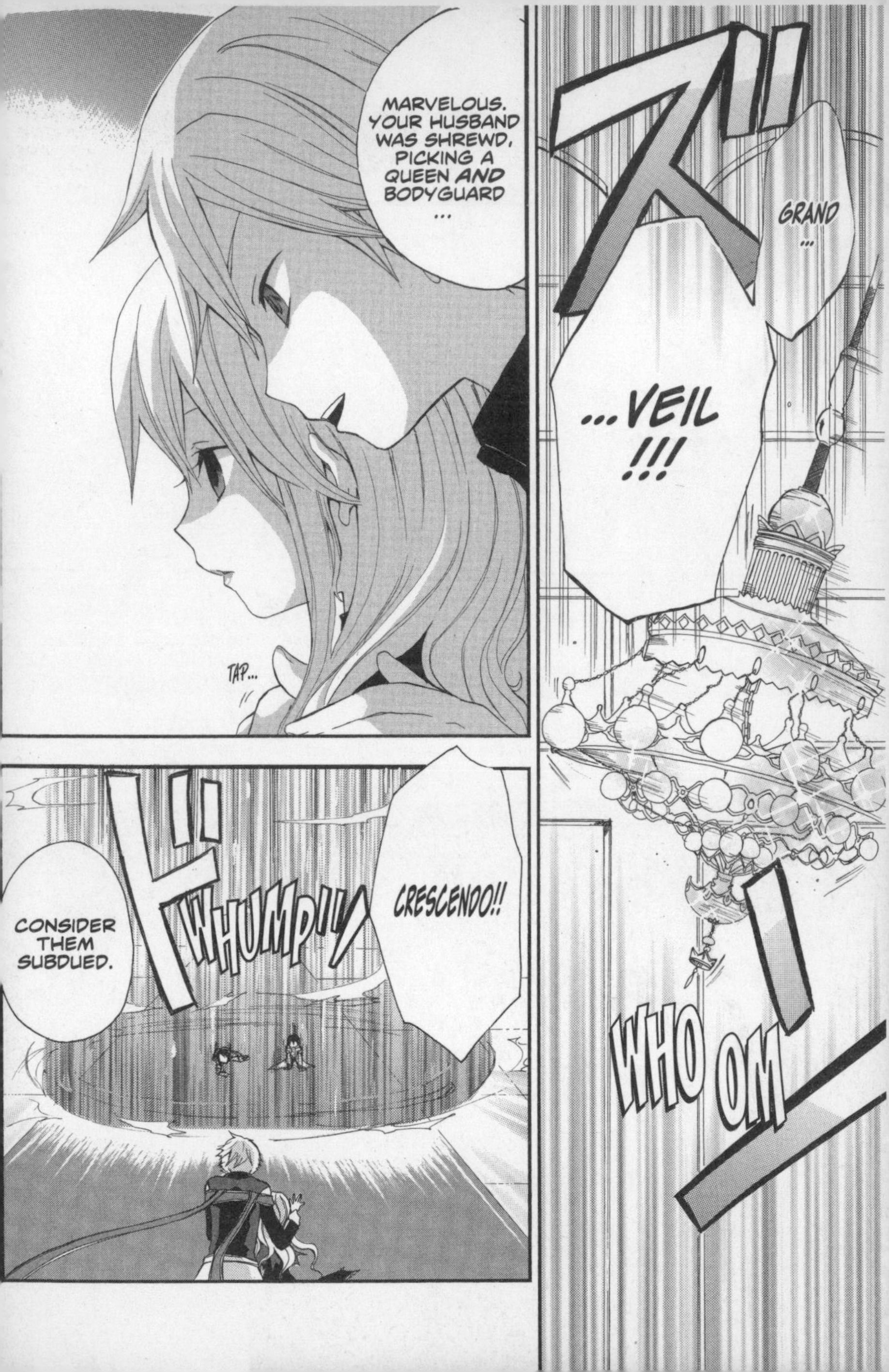
ズ"
GRAND ...
...VEIL !!!
WHO OM
MARVELOUS. YOUR HUSBAND WAS SHREWD, PICKING A QUEEN AND BODYGUARD ...
TAP...
CRESCENDO!!
WHUMP!!
CONSIDER THEM SUBDUED.

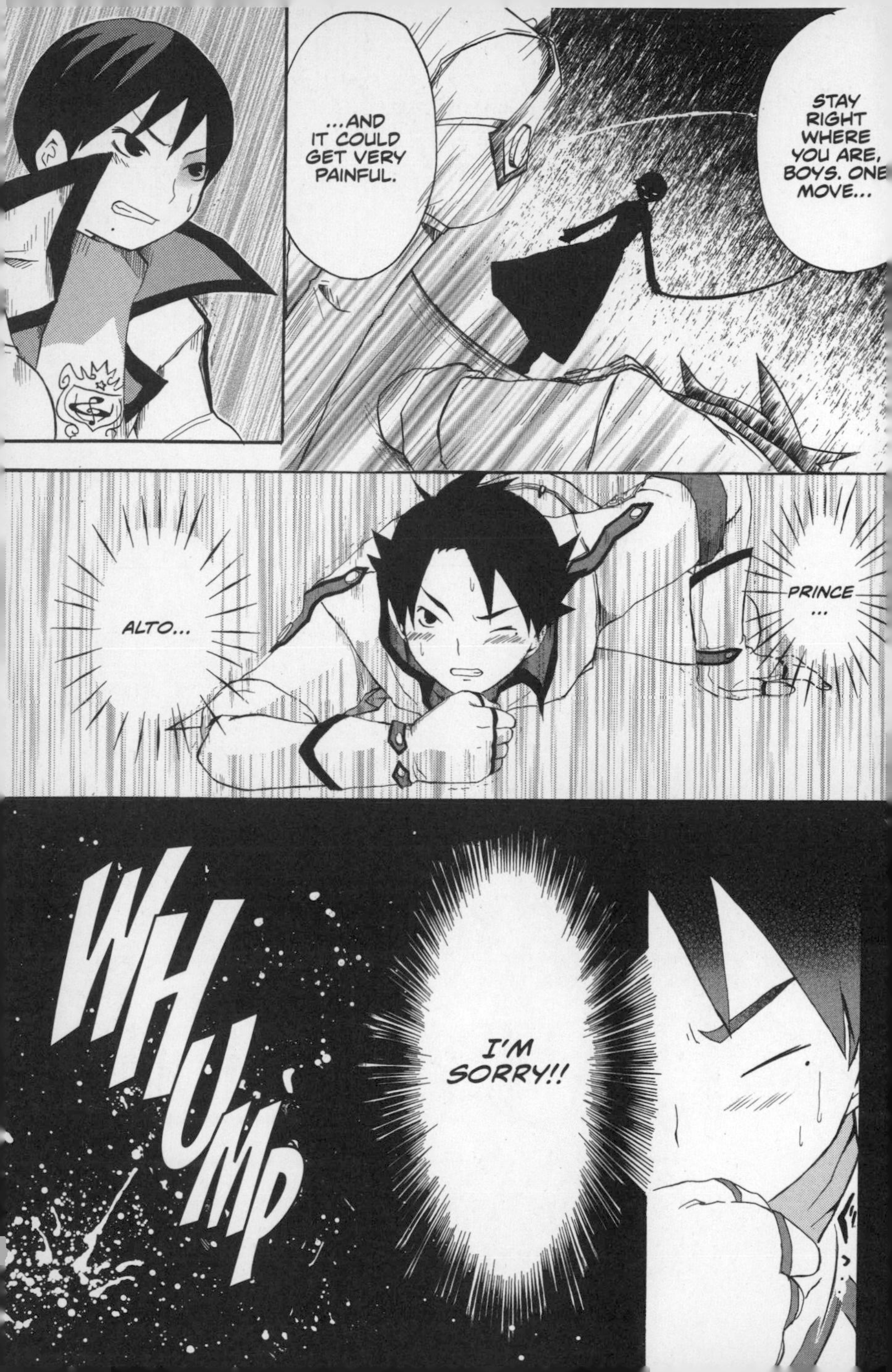

STAY RIGHT WHERE YOU ARE, BOYS. ONE MOVE...
...AND IT COULD GET VERY PAINFUL.
PRINCE...
ALTO...
I'M SORRY!!
WHUMP

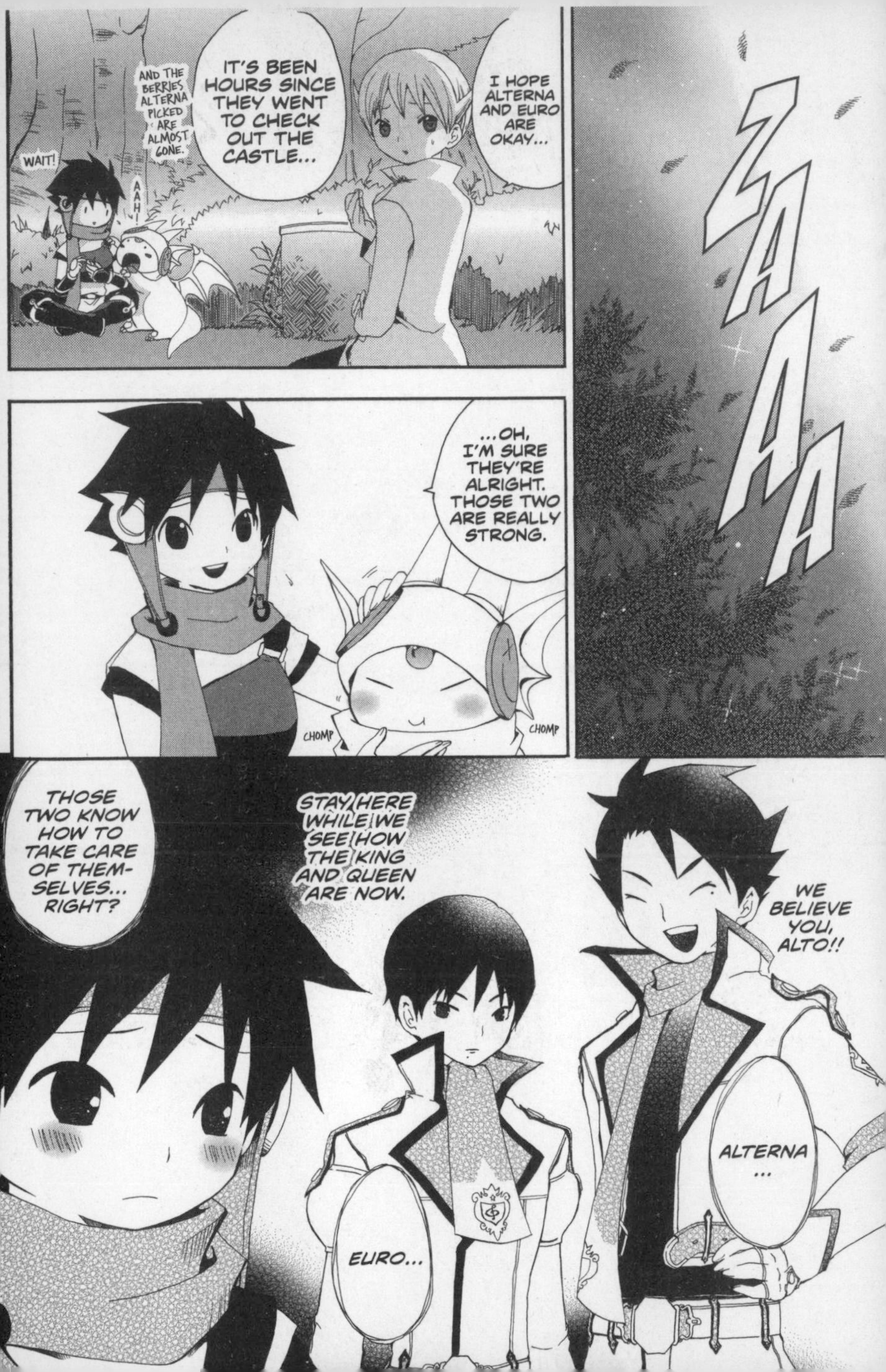
ZAAAA
I HOPE ALTERNA AND EURO ARE OKAY...
IT'S BEEN HOURS SINCE THEY WENT TO CHECK OUT THE CASTLE...
AND THE BERRIES ALTERNA PICKED ARE ALMOST GONE.
AAH!
WAIT!
...OH, I'M SURE THEY'RE ALRIGHT. THOSE TWO ARE REALLY STRONG.
CHOMP
CHOMP
WE BELIEVE YOU, ALTO!!
STAY HERE WHILE WE SEE HOW THE KING AND QUEEN ARE NOW.
THOSE TWO KNOW HOW TO TAKE CARE OF THEM-SELVES... RIGHT?
ALTERNA ...
EURO...

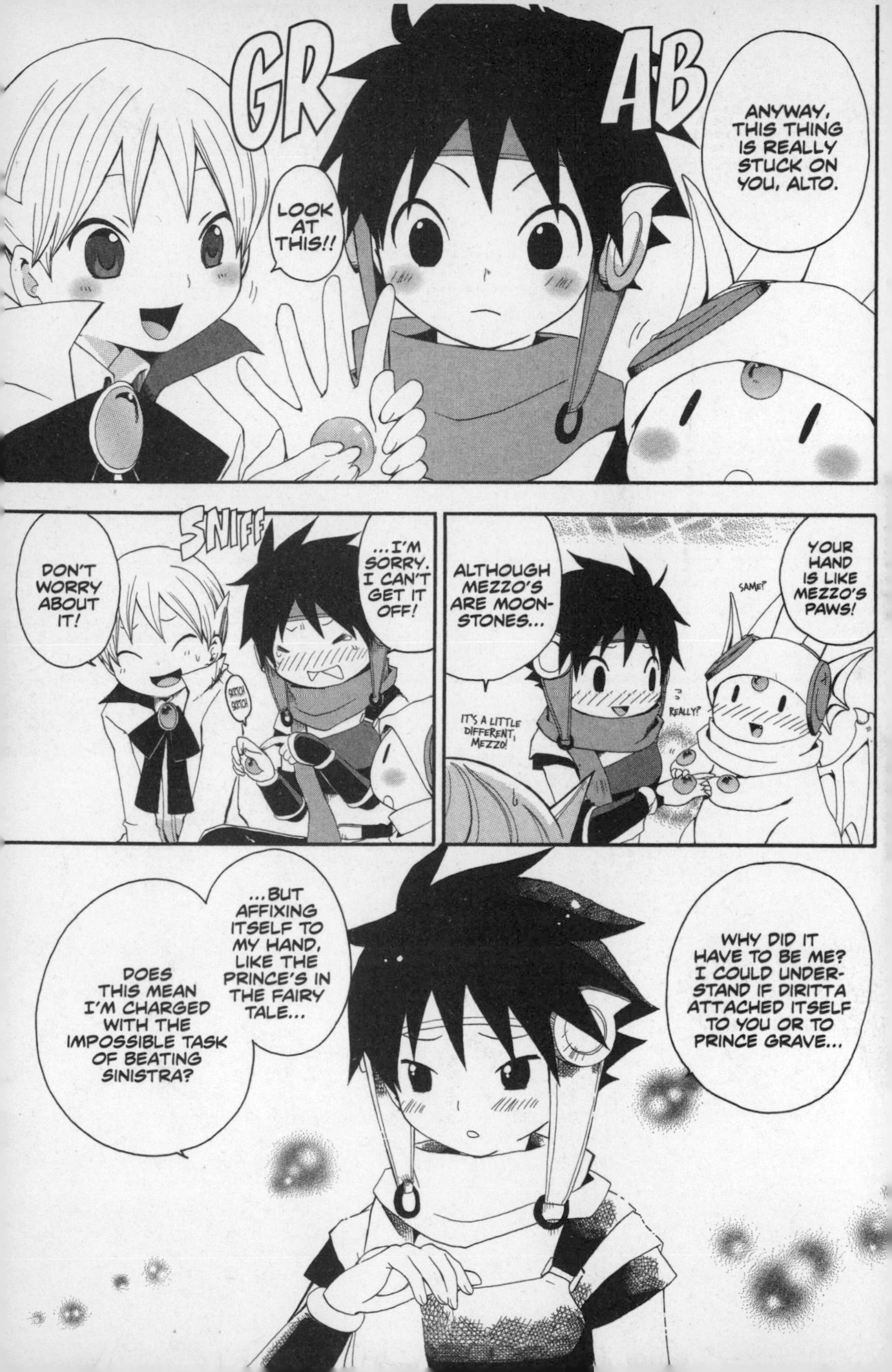
GRAB
ANYWAY, THIS THING IS REALLY STUCK ON YOU, ALTO.
LOOK AT THIS!!
YOUR HAND IS LIKE MEZZO'S PAWS!
SAME?
ALTHOUGH MEZZO'S ARE MOON-STONES...
REALLY?
IT'S A LITTLE DIFFERENT, MEZZO!
...I'M SORRY. I CAN'T GET IT OFF!
SNIFF
DON'T WORRY ABOUT IT!
WHY DID IT HAVE TO BE ME? I COULD UNDER-STAND IF DIRITTA ATTACHED ITSELF TO YOU OR TO PRINCE GRAVE...
...BUT AFFIXING ITSELF TO MY HAND, LIKE THE PRINCE'S IN THE FAIRY TALE...
DOES THIS MEAN I'M CHARGED WITH THE IMPOSSIBLE TASK OF BEATING SINISTRA?

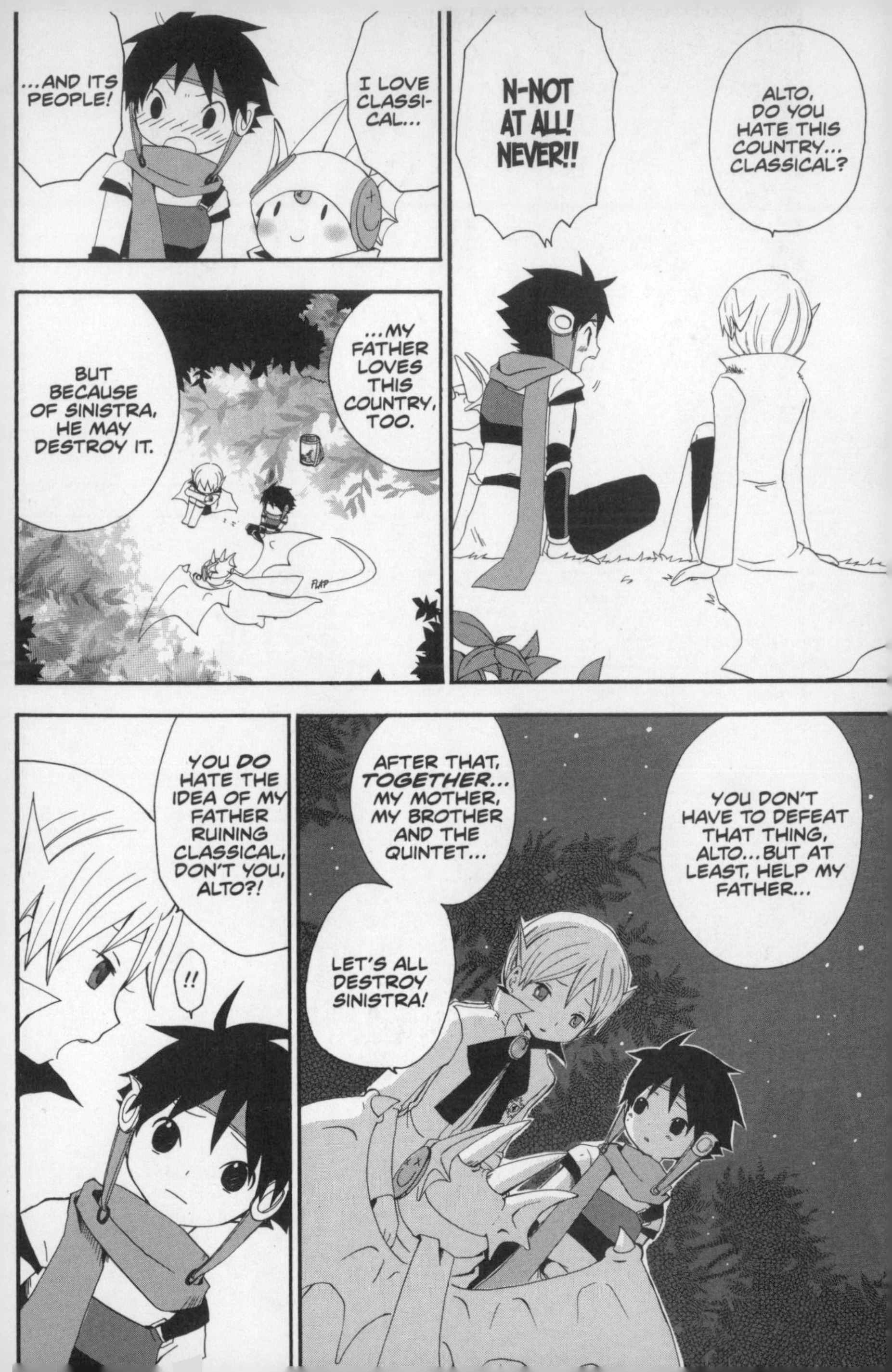
ALTO, DO YOU HATE THIS COUNTRY... CLASSICAL?
N-NOT AT ALL! NEVER!!
I LOVE CLASSICAL...
...AND ITS PEOPLE!
...MY FATHER LOVES THIS COUNTRY, TOO.
BUT BECAUSE OF SINISTRA, HE MAY DESTROY IT.
FLAP
YOU DON'T HAVE TO DEFEAT THAT THING, ALTO...BUT AT LEAST, HELP MY FATHER...
AFTER THAT, *TOGETHER*... MY MOTHER, MY BROTHER AND THE QUINTET...
LET'S ALL DESTROY SINISTRA!
YOU *DO* HATE THE IDEA OF MY FATHER RUINING CLASSICAL, DON'T YOU, ALTO?!
!!

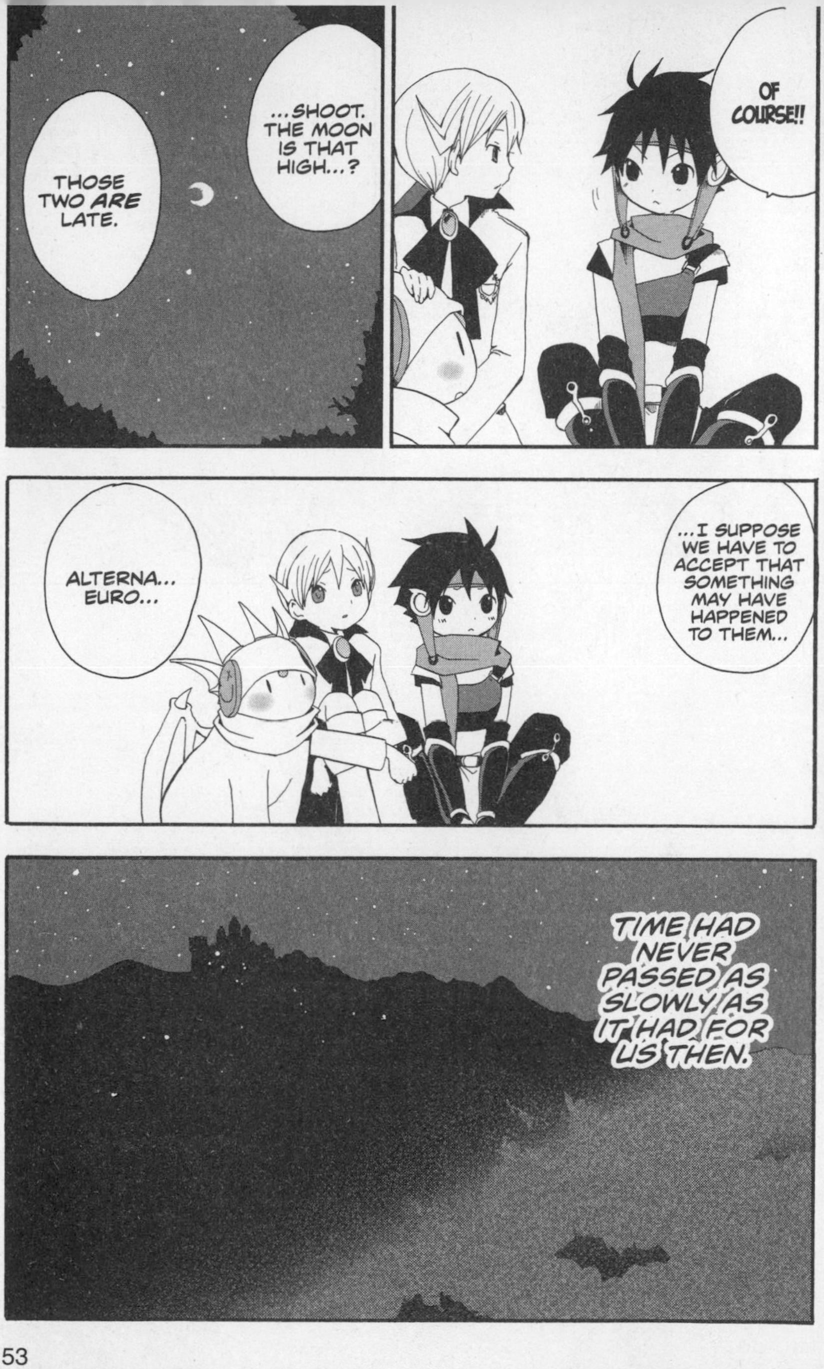
OF COURSE!!
...SHOOT. THE MOON IS THAT HIGH...?
THOSE TWO *ARE* LATE.
...I SUPPOSE WE HAVE TO ACCEPT THAT SOMETHING MAY HAVE HAPPENED TO THEM...
ALTERNA... EURO...
TIME HAD NEVER PASSED AS SLOWLY AS IT HAD FOR US THEN.

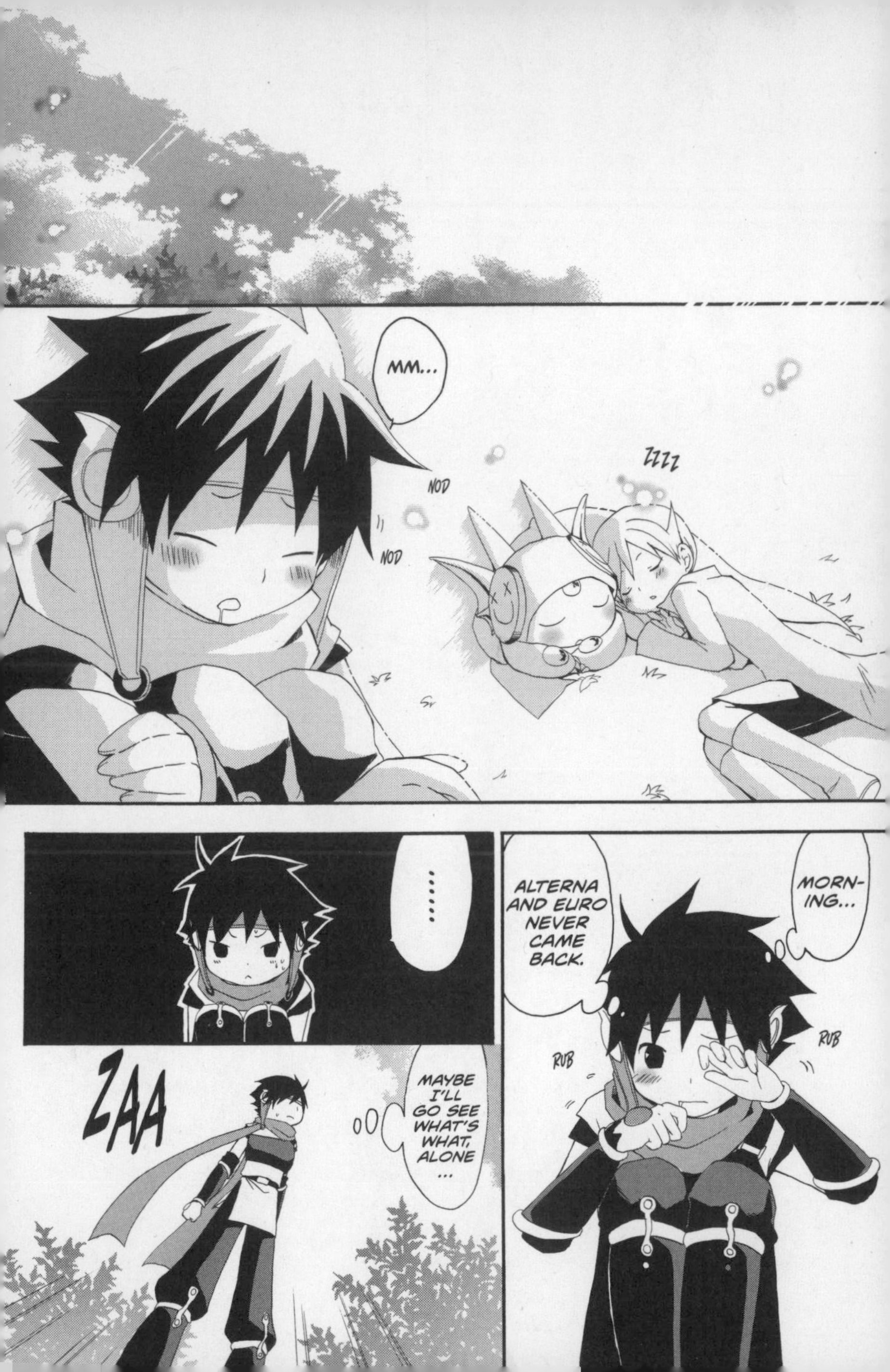
MM...
ZZZZ
NOD
NOD
MORNING...
ALTERNA AND EURO NEVER CAME BACK.
RUB
RUB
......
MAYBE I'LL GO SEE WHAT'S WHAT, ALONE ...
ZAA

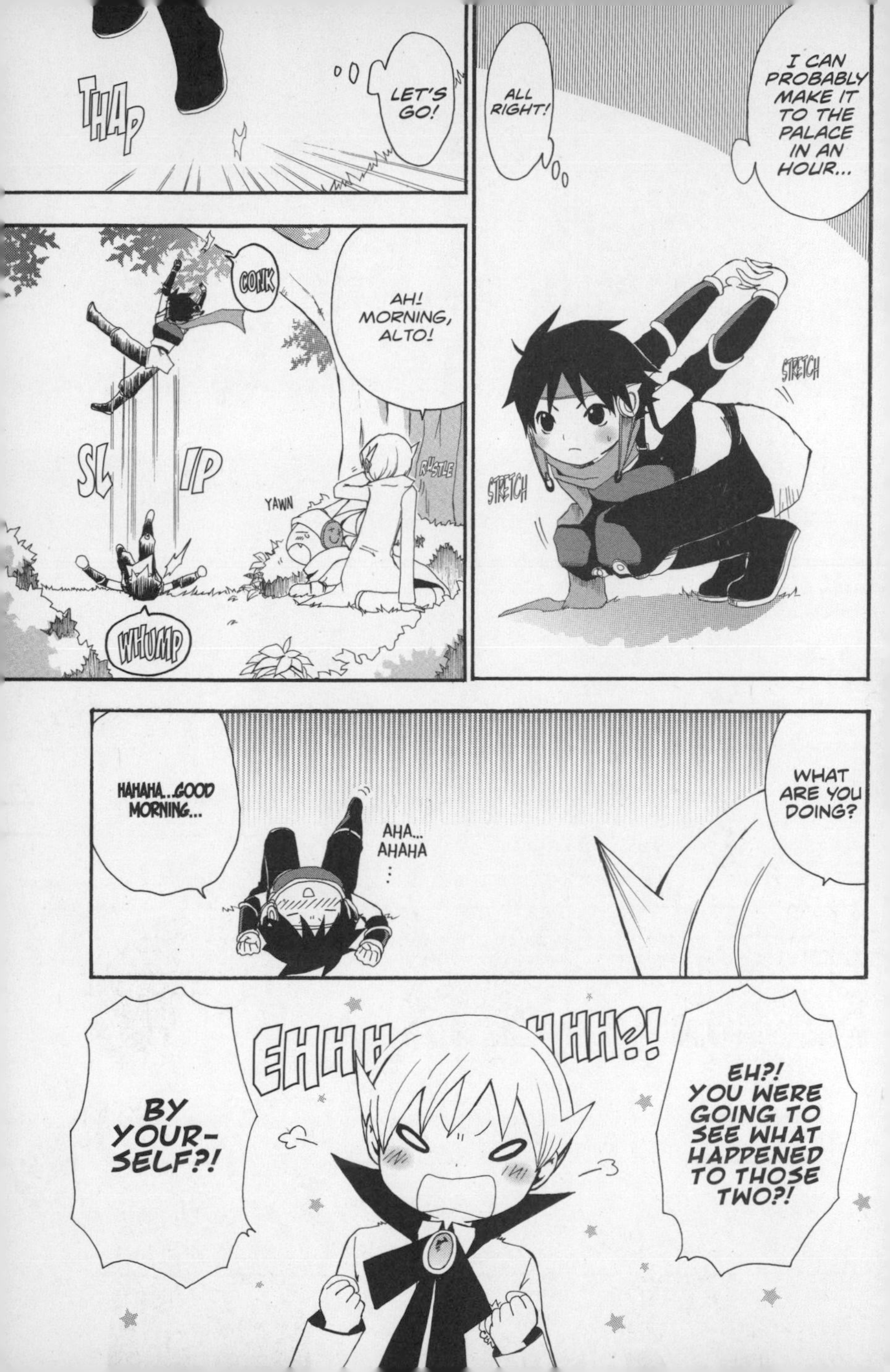
I CAN PROBABLY MAKE IT TO THE PALACE IN AN HOUR...
ALL RIGHT!
STRETCH
STRETCH
LET'S GO!
THAP
AH! MORNING, ALTO!
CONK
RUSTLE
YAWN
SL IP
WHUMP
WHAT ARE YOU DOING?
AHA... AHAHA ...
HAHAHA...GOOD MORNING...
EH?! YOU WERE GOING TO SEE WHAT HAPPENED TO THOSE TWO?!
EHHH HHH?!
BY YOUR-SELF?!

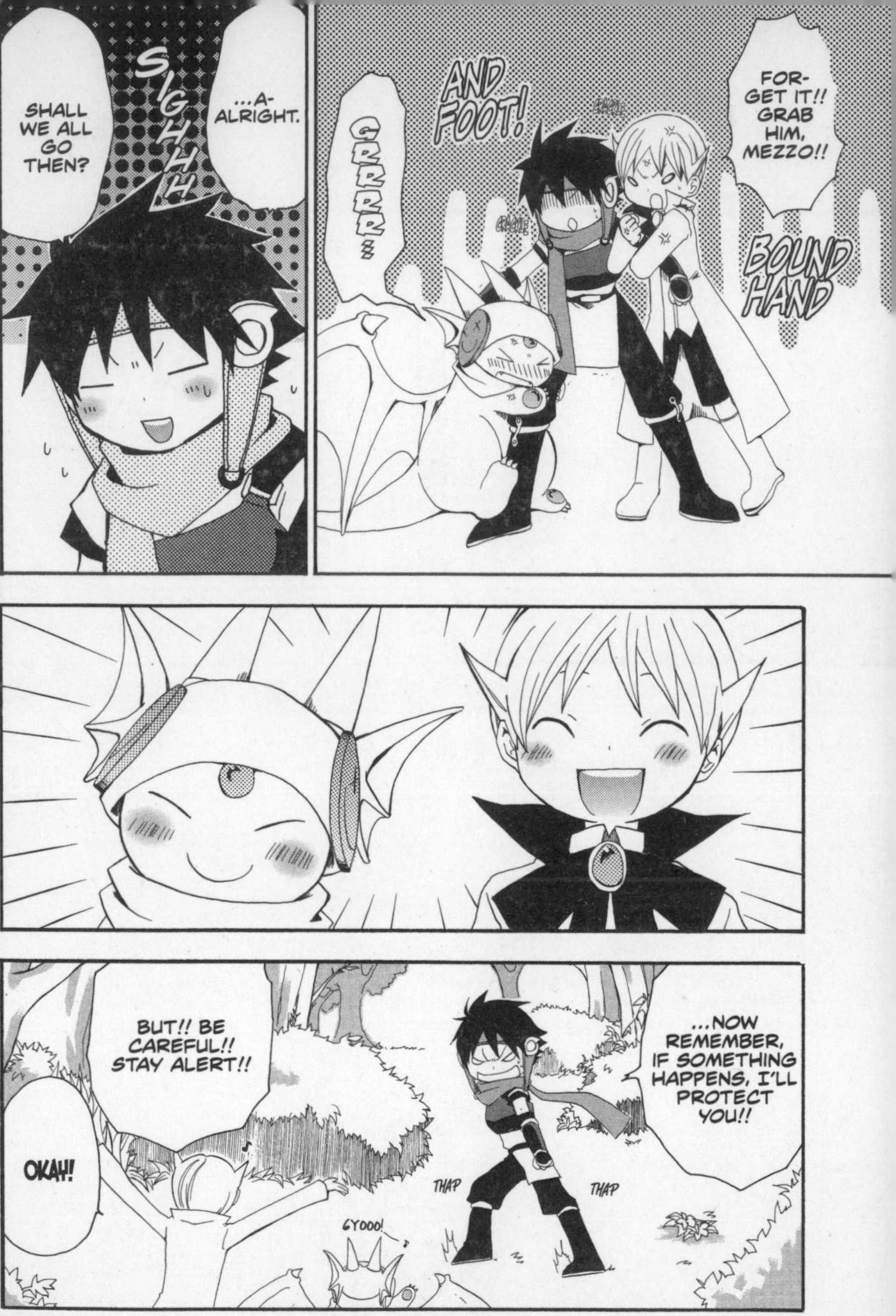
FOR-GET IT!! GRAB HIM, MEZZO!!
BOUND HAND
AND FOOT!
CRACKLE
CRACKLE
GRRRR...
...A-ALRIGHT.
SIGHHH
SHALL WE ALL GO THEN?
...NOW REMEMBER, IF SOMETHING HAPPENS, I'LL PROTECT YOU!!
THAP
THAP
GYOOO!
BUT!! BE CAREFUL!! STAY ALERT!!
OKAY!

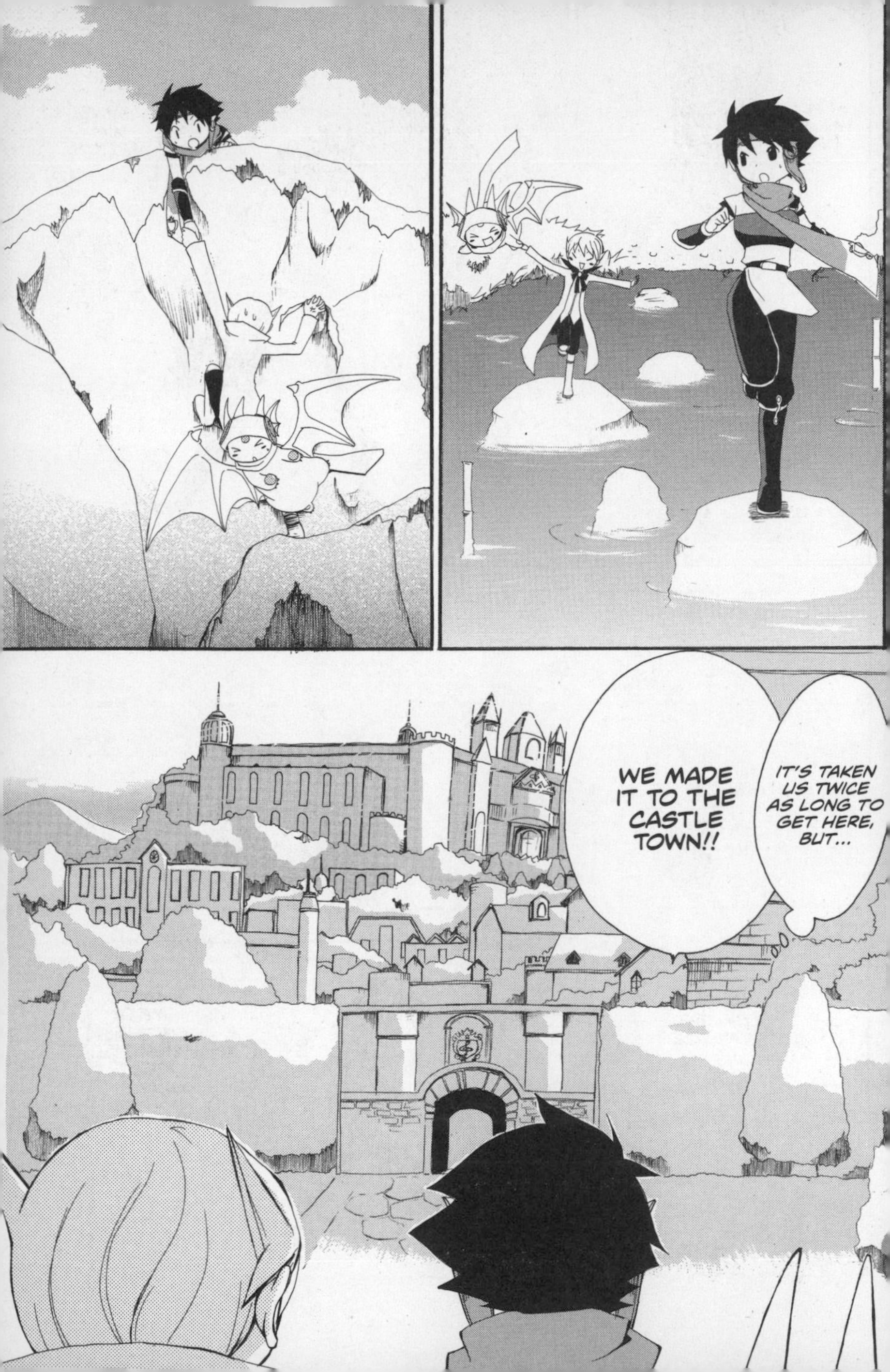
IT'S TAKEN US TWICE AS LONG TO GET HERE, BUT...
WE MADE IT TO THE CASTLE TOWN!!

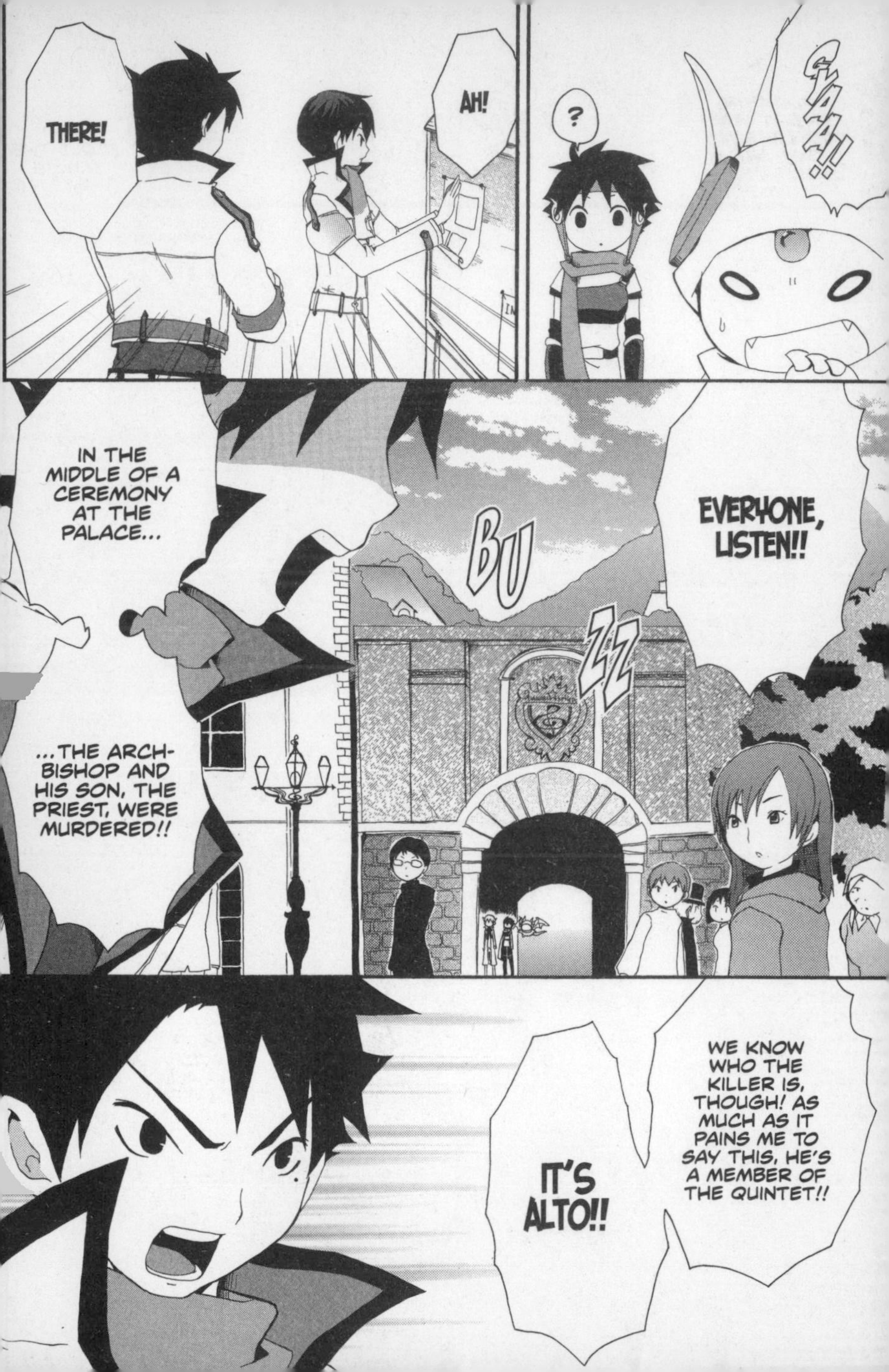
GYAAA!!
?
AH!
THERE!
EVERYONE, LISTEN!!
BUZZ
IN THE MIDDLE OF A CEREMONY AT THE PALACE...
...THE ARCH-BISHOP AND HIS SON, THE PRIEST, WERE MURDERED!!
WE KNOW WHO THE KILLER IS, THOUGH! AS MUCH AS IT PAINS ME TO SAY THIS, HE'S A MEMBER OF THE QUINTET!!
IT'S ALTO!!

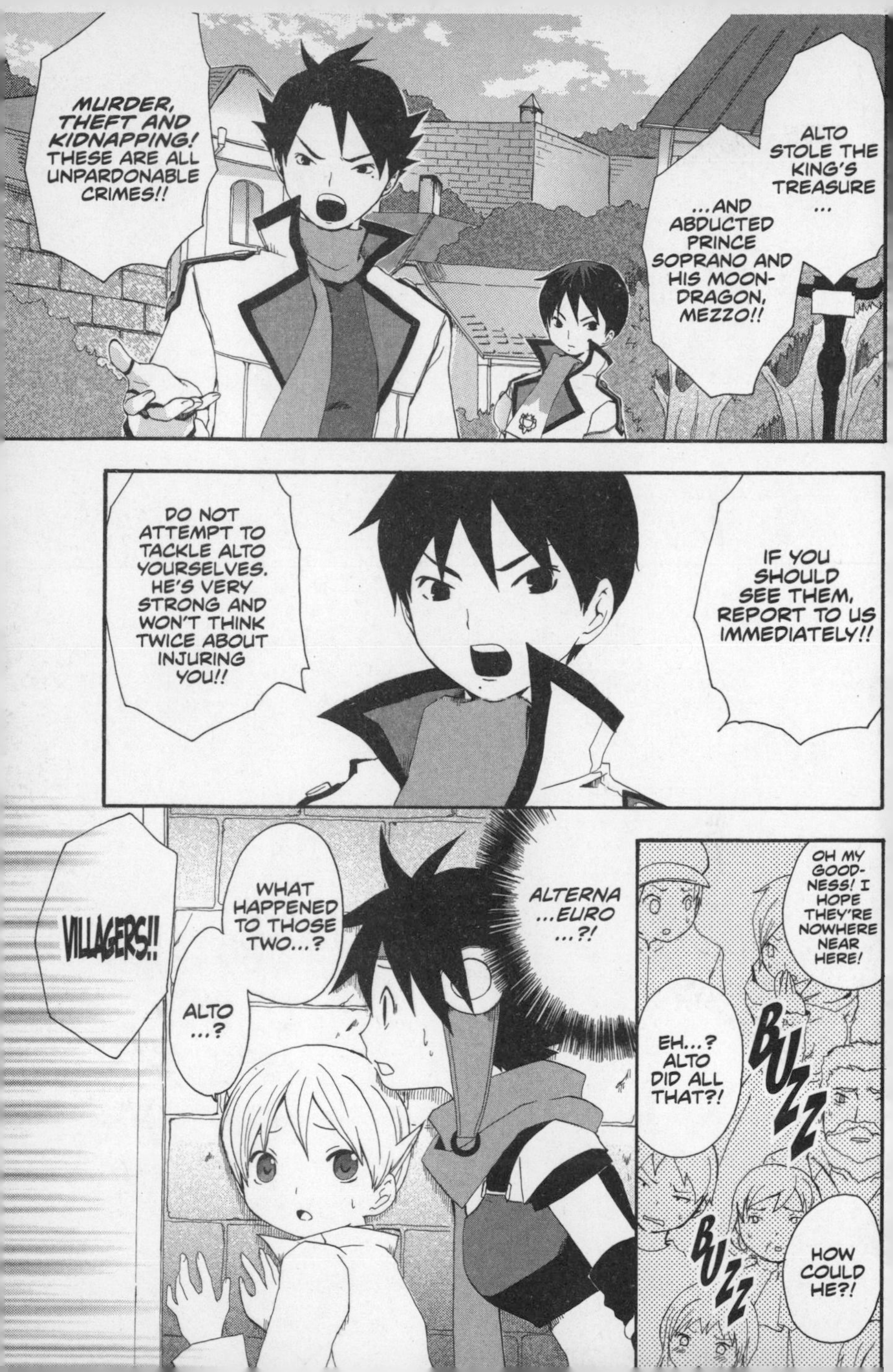
ALTO STOLE THE KING'S TREASURE ...
...AND ABDUCTED PRINCE SOPRANO AND HIS MOON-DRAGON, MEZZO!!
MURDER, THEFT AND KIDNAPPING! THESE ARE ALL UNPARDONABLE CRIMES!!
IF YOU SHOULD SEE THEM, REPORT TO US IMMEDIATELY!!
DO NOT ATTEMPT TO TACKLE ALTO YOURSELVES. HE'S VERY STRONG AND WON'T THINK TWICE ABOUT INJURING YOU!!
OH MY GOOD-NESS! I HOPE THEY'RE NOWHERE NEAR HERE!
EH...? ALTO DID ALL THAT?!
BUZZ
BUZZ
HOW COULD HE?!
ALTERNA ...EURO ...?!
WHAT HAPPENED TO THOSE TWO...?
ALTO ...?
VILLAGERS!!

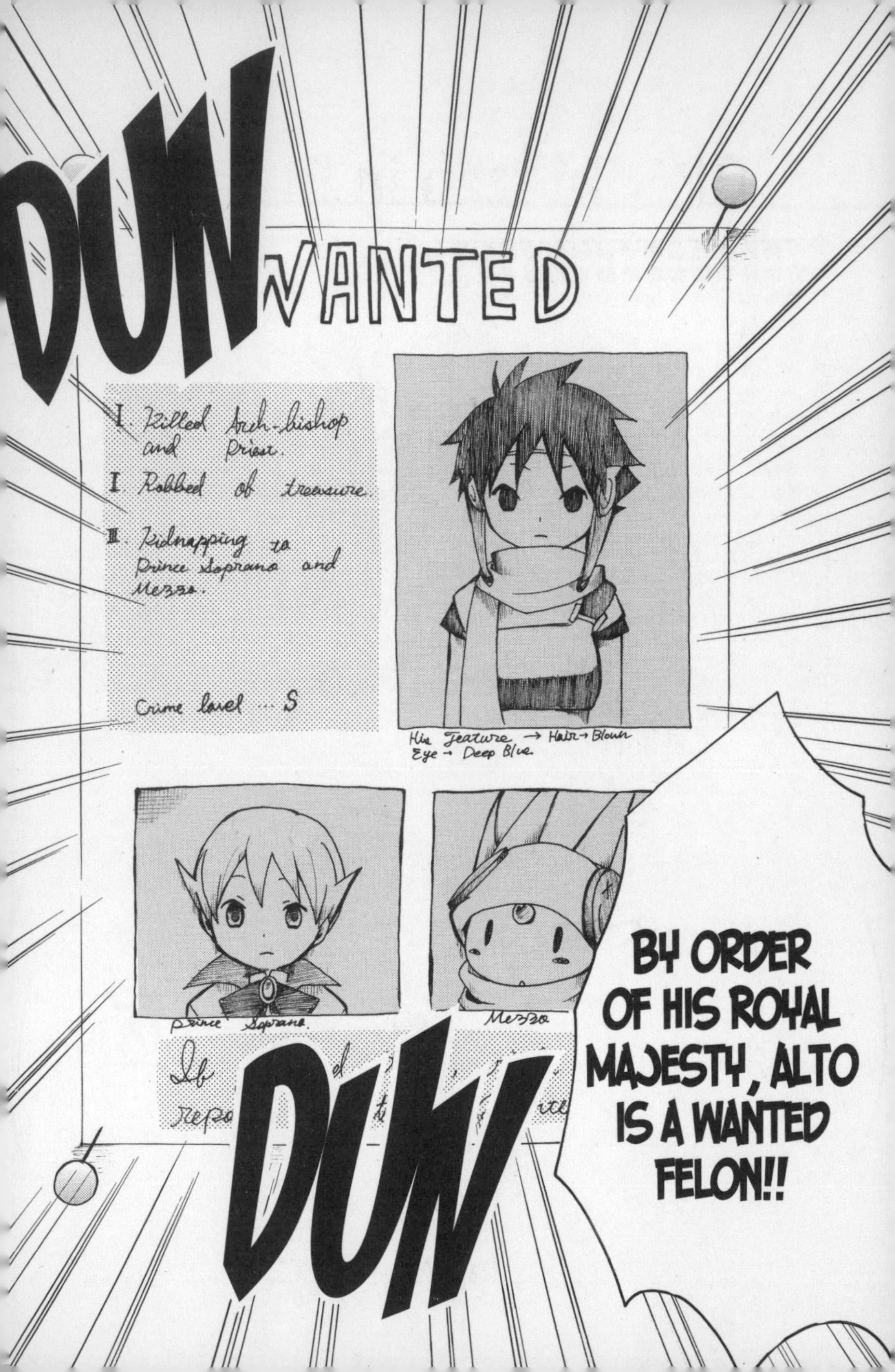
DUN
WANTED
I. Killed Arch-bishop and Priest.
I. Robbed of treasure.
III. Kidnapping to Prince Soprano and Mezzo.
Crime level ... S
His Feature → Hair → Blown
Eye → Deep Blue
Prince Soprano
Mezzo
BY ORDER OF HIS ROYAL MAJESTY, ALTO IS A WANTED FELON!!
DUN

OP3: Mezzo in Rumba

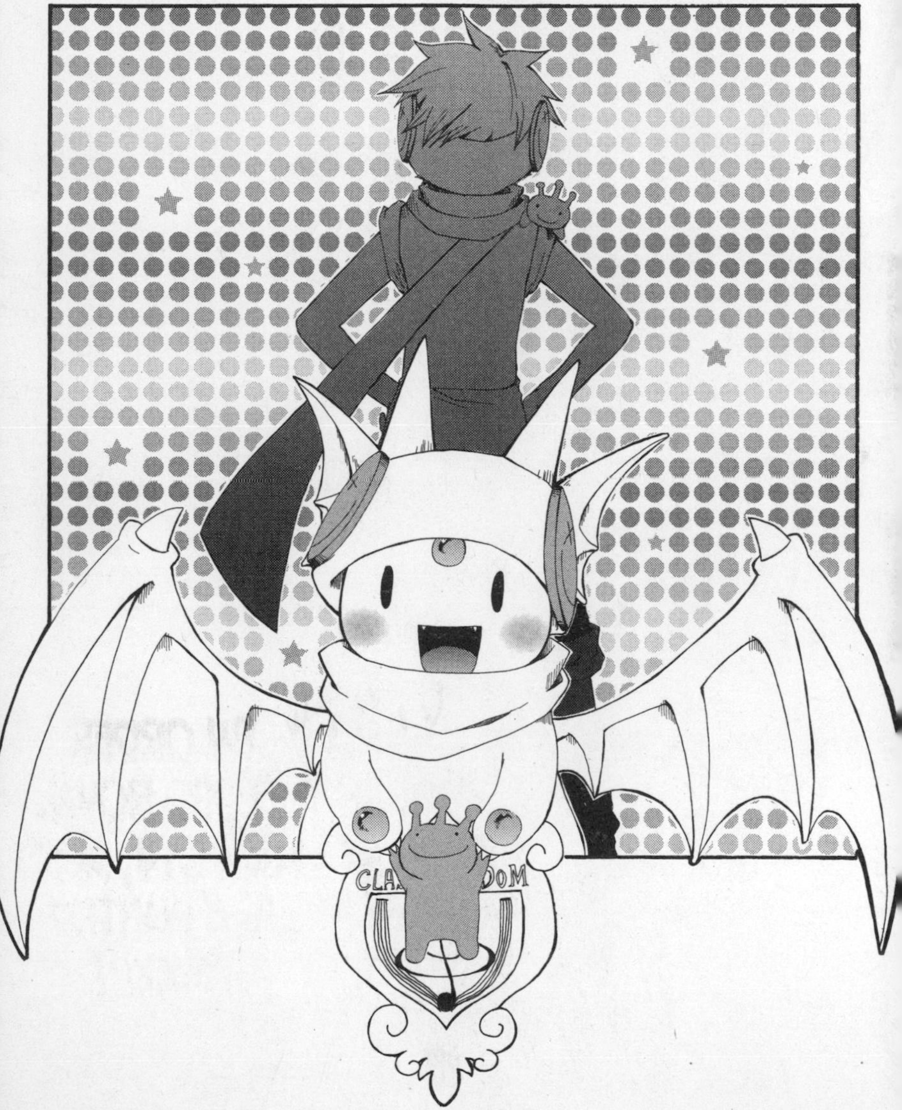

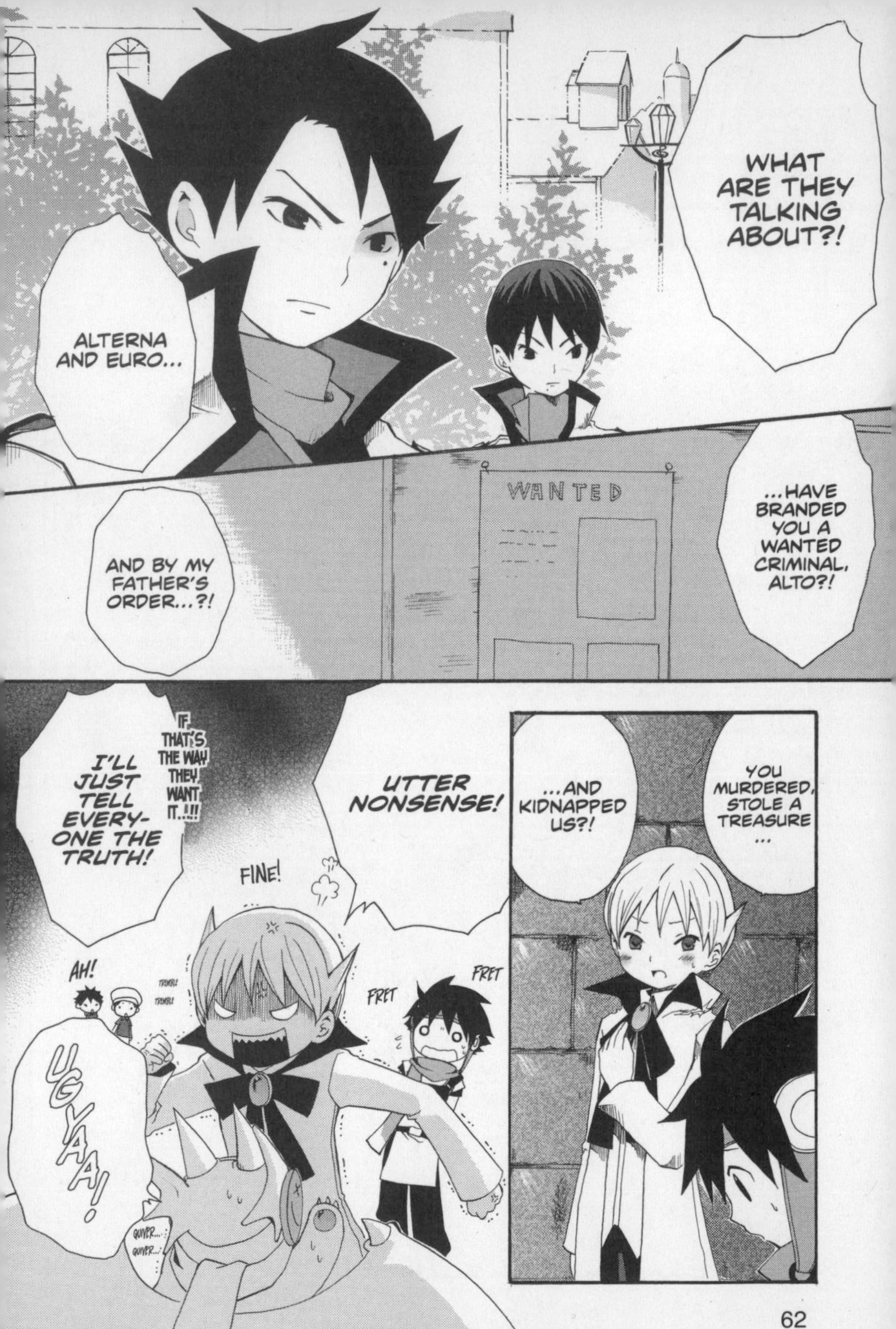
WHAT ARE THEY TALKING ABOUT?!
ALTERNA AND EURO...
...HAVE BRANDED YOU A WANTED CRIMINAL, ALTO?!
WANTED
AND BY MY FATHER'S ORDER...?!
YOU MURDERED, STOLE A TREASURE ...
...AND KIDNAPPED US?!
UTTER NONSENSE!
FINE!
IF THAT'S THE WAY THEY WANT IT..!!!
I'LL JUST TELL EVERY-ONE THE TRUTH!
FRET
FRET
AH!
TREMBLE
TREMBLE
UGYAA!
QUIVER...
QUIVER...

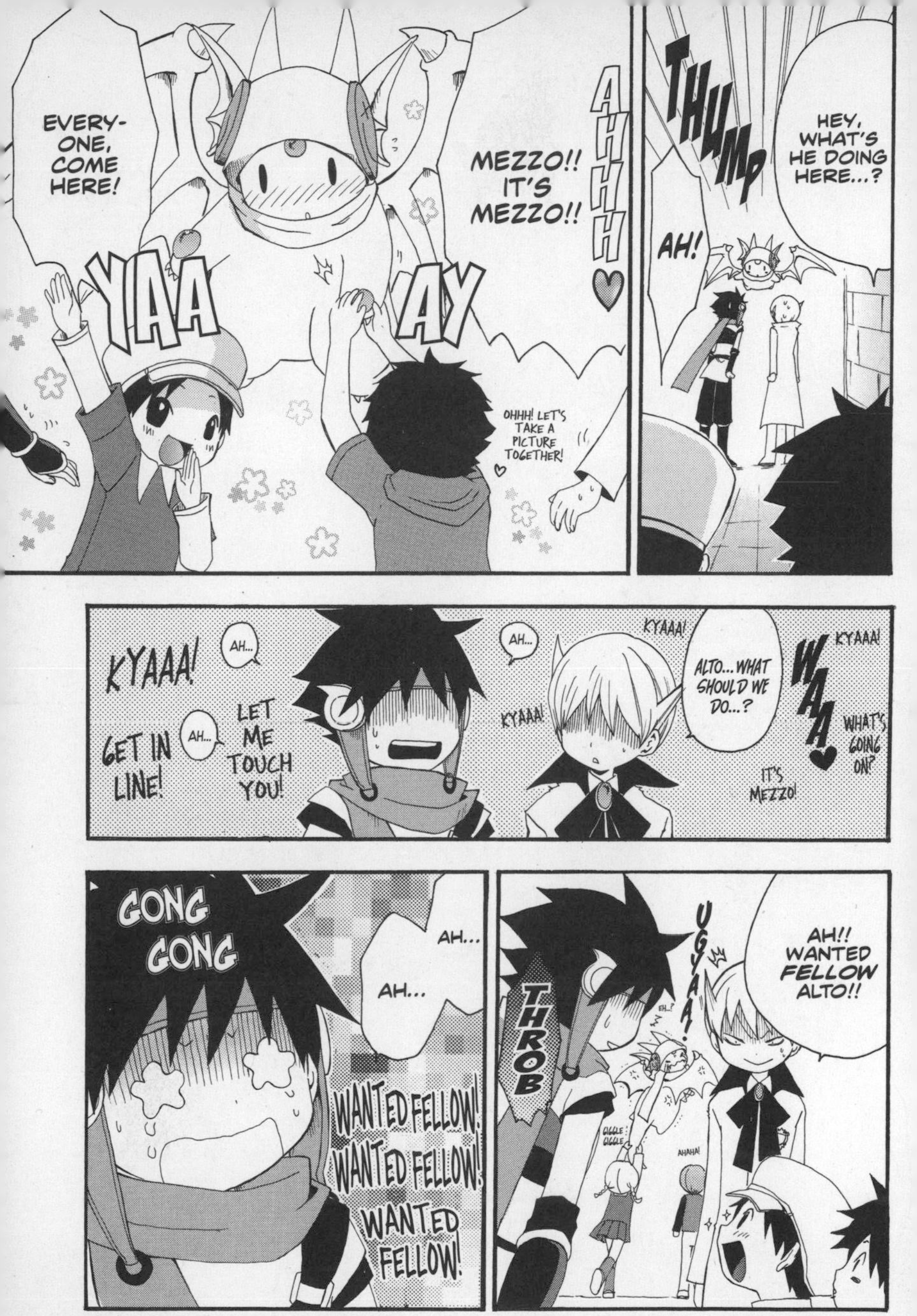
HEY, WHAT'S HE DOING HERE...?
THUMP
AH!
AHHHH♥
MEZZO!! IT'S MEZZO!!
EVERY-ONE, COME HERE!
YAAAY
OHHH! LET'S TAKE A PICTURE TOGETHER!
KYAAA!
WAAA♥
WHAT'S GOING ON?
ALTO... WHAT SHOULD WE DO...?
KYAAA!
IT'S MEZZO!
AH...
KYAAA!
AH...
LET ME TOUCH YOU!
AH...
KYAAA!
GET IN LINE!
AH!! WANTED FELLOW ALTO!!
UGYAA!
EH..?
THROB
GIGGLE GIGGLE
AHAHA!
AH...
AH...
GONG GONG
WANTED FELLOW! WANTED FELLOW! WANTED FELLOW!

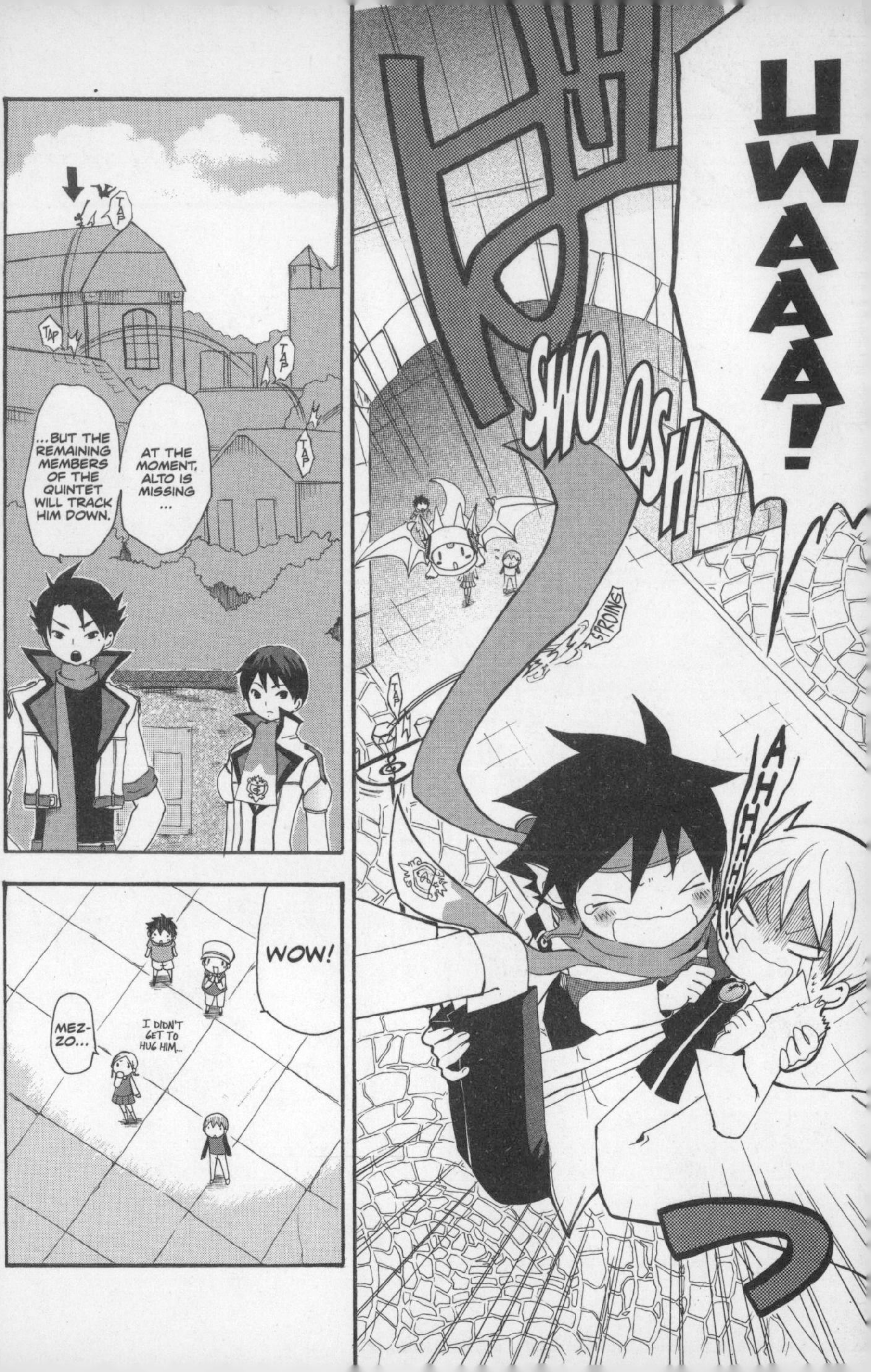
UWAAA!
SWO OSH
AHHHHHH
SPROING
TAP
TAP
TAP
TAP
TAP
AT THE MOMENT, ALTO IS MISSING ...
...BUT THE REMAINING MEMBERS OF THE QUINTET WILL TRACK HIM DOWN.
WOW!
I DIDN'T GET TO HUG HIM...
MEZ-ZO...

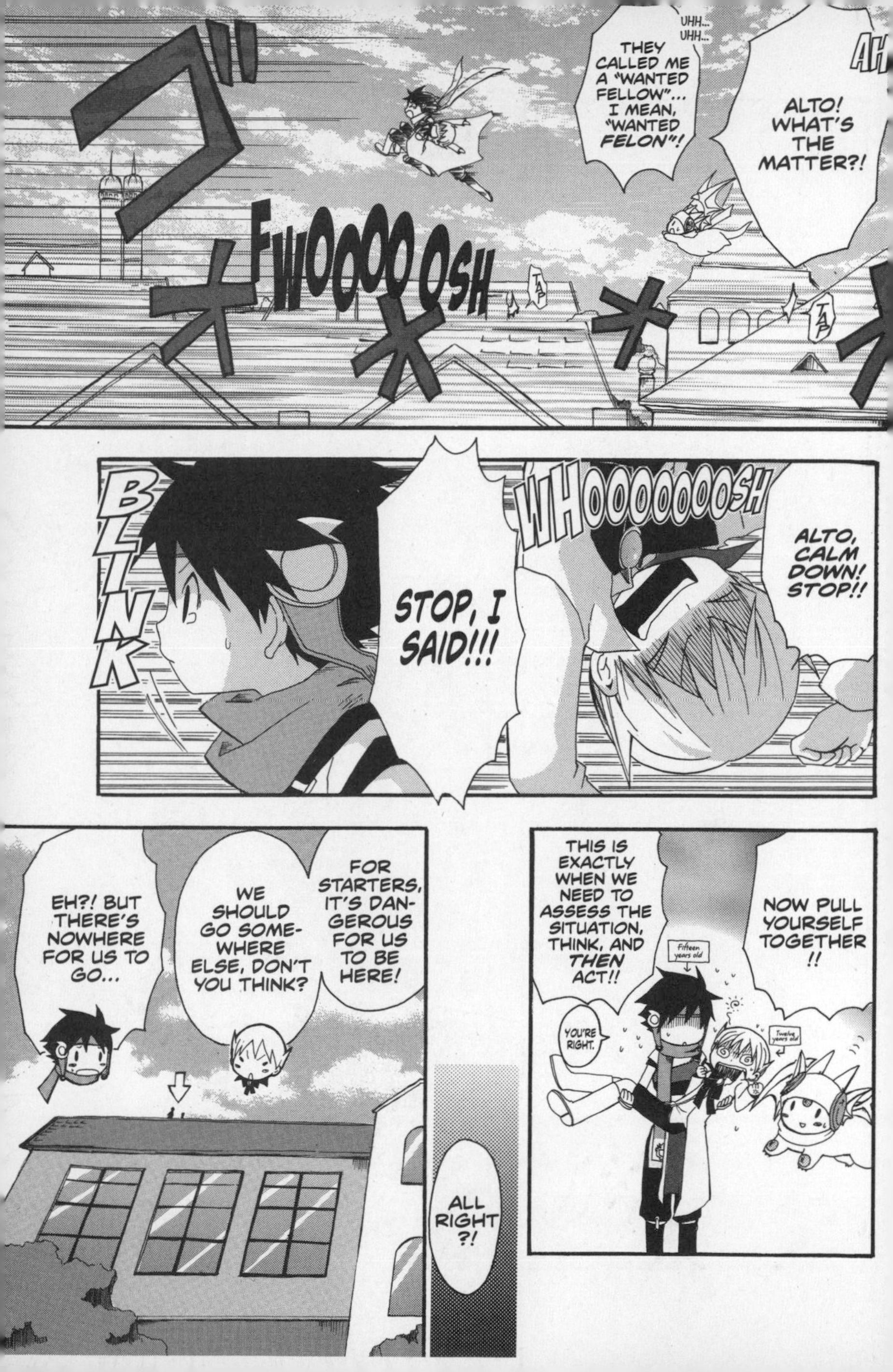
AH
ALTO! WHAT'S THE MATTER?!
UHH... UHH...
THEY CALLED ME A "WANTED FELLOW"... I MEAN, "WANTED FELON"!
FWOOOOOSH
TAP
TAP
ゴ
ALTO, CALM DOWN! STOP!!
WHOOOOOOOSH
STOP, I SAID!!!
BLINK
NOW PULL YOURSELF TOGETHER!!
THIS IS EXACTLY WHEN WE NEED TO ASSESS THE SITUATION, THINK, AND THEN ACT!!
Fifteen years old
Twelve years old
YOU'RE RIGHT.
ALL RIGHT?!
FOR STARTERS, IT'S DANGEROUS FOR US TO BE HERE!
WE SHOULD GO SOMEWHERE ELSE, DON'T YOU THINK?
EH?! BUT THERE'S NOWHERE FOR US TO GO...

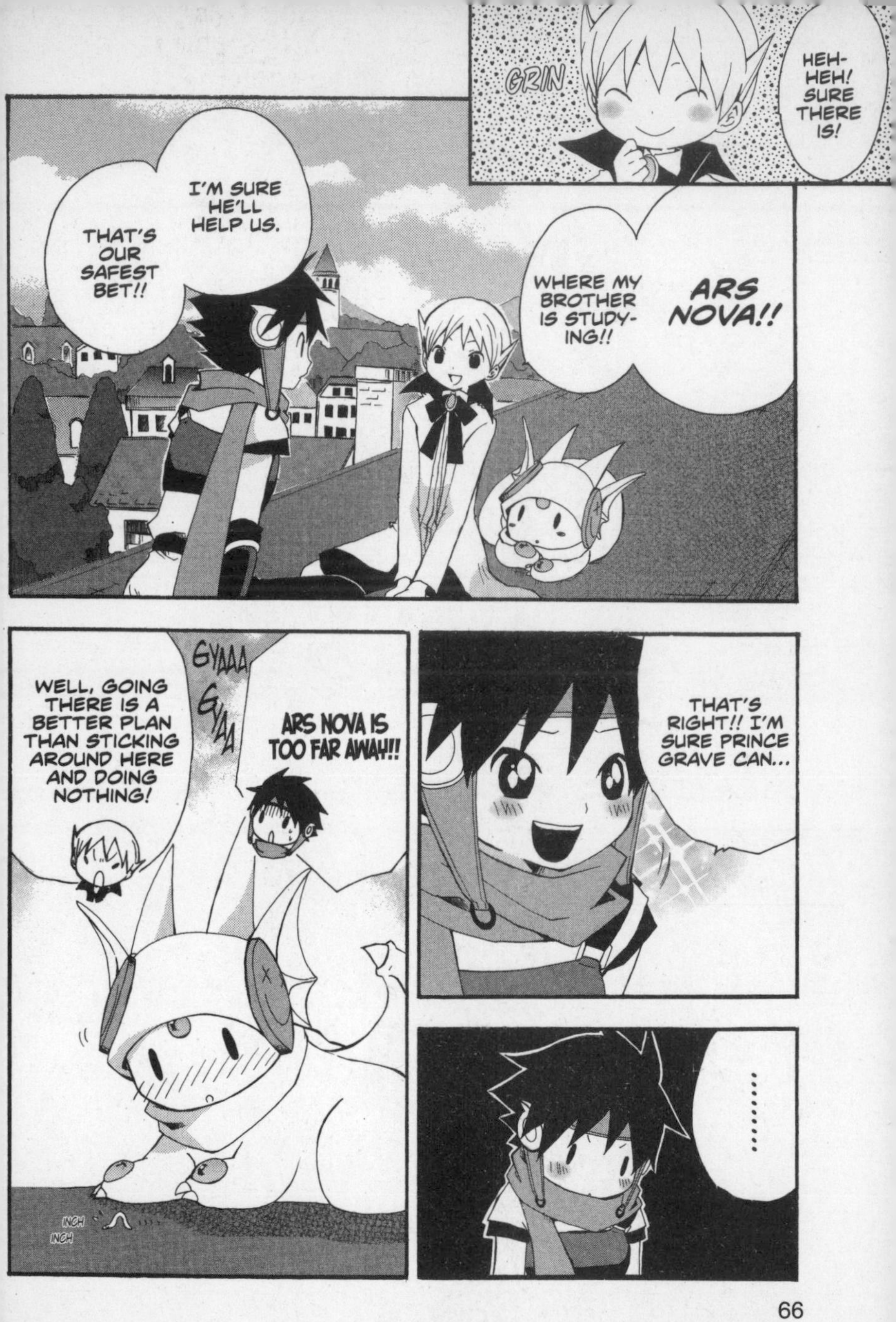
GRIN
HEH-HEH! SURE THERE IS!
ARS NOVA!!
WHERE MY BROTHER IS STUDYING!!
I'M SURE HE'LL HELP US.
THAT'S OUR SAFEST BET!!
THAT'S RIGHT!! I'M SURE PRINCE GRAVE CAN...
......
ARS NOVA IS TOO FAR AWAY!!
GYAAA GYAA
WELL, GOING THERE IS A BETTER PLAN THAN STICKING AROUND HERE AND DOING NOTHING!
INCH INCH

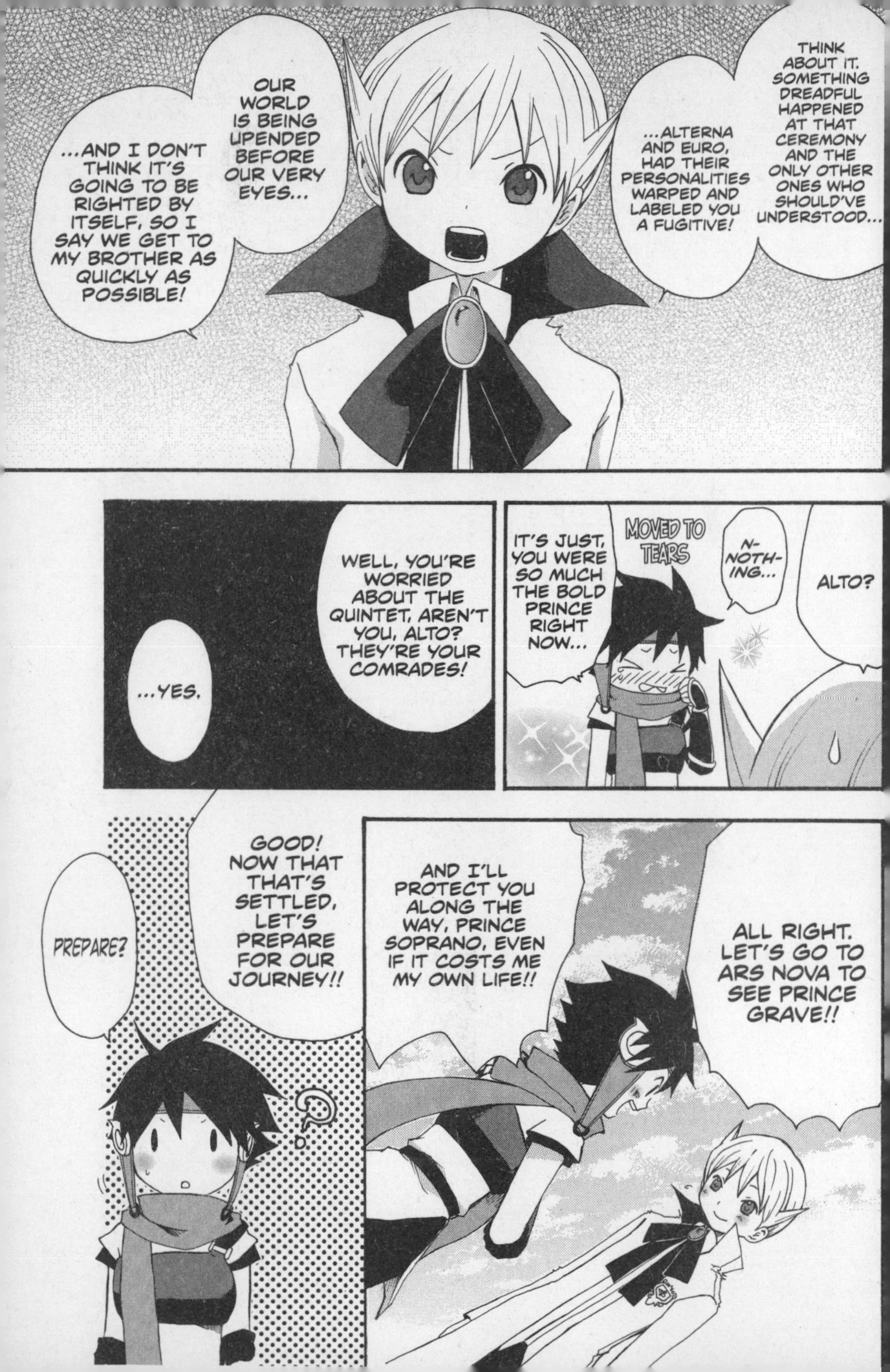
THINK ABOUT IT. SOMETHING DREADFUL HAPPENED AT THAT CEREMONY AND THE ONLY OTHER ONES WHO SHOULD'VE UNDERSTOOD...
...ALTERNA AND EURO, HAD THEIR PERSONALITIES WARPED AND LABELED YOU A FUGITIVE!
OUR WORLD IS BEING UPENDED BEFORE OUR VERY EYES...
...AND I DON'T THINK IT'S GOING TO BE RIGHTED BY ITSELF, SO I SAY WE GET TO MY BROTHER AS QUICKLY AS POSSIBLE!
ALTO?
N-NOTHING...
MOVED TO TEARS
IT'S JUST, YOU WERE SO MUCH THE BOLD PRINCE RIGHT NOW...
WELL, YOU'RE WORRIED ABOUT THE QUINTET, AREN'T YOU, ALTO? THEY'RE YOUR COMRADES!
...YES.
ALL RIGHT. LET'S GO TO ARS NOVA TO SEE PRINCE GRAVE!!
AND I'LL PROTECT YOU ALONG THE WAY, PRINCE SOPRANO, EVEN IF IT COSTS ME MY OWN LIFE!!
GOOD! NOW THAT THAT'S SETTLED, LET'S PREPARE FOR OUR JOURNEY!!
PREPARE?

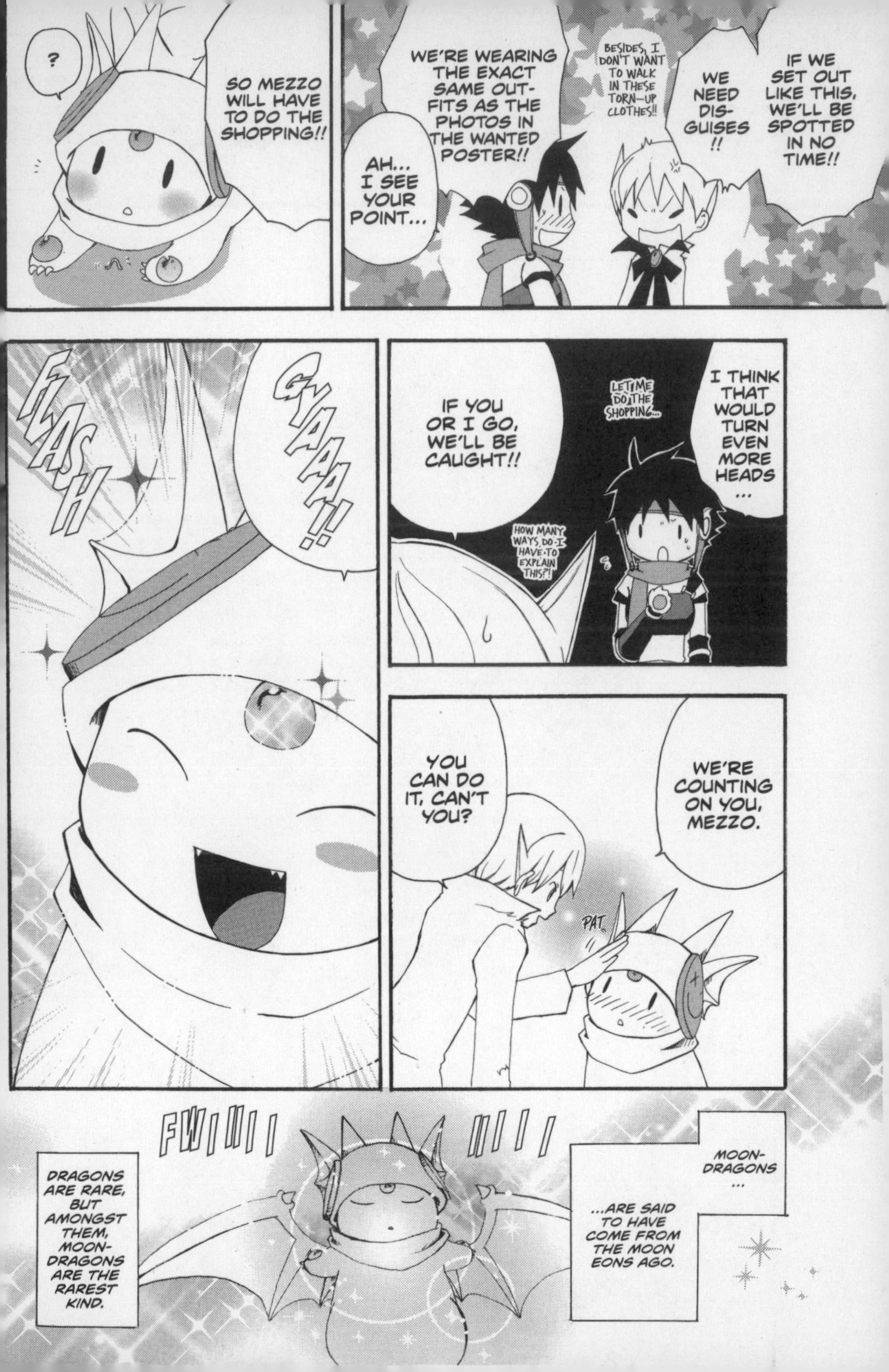
IF WE SET OUT LIKE THIS, WE'LL BE SPOTTED IN NO TIME!!
WE NEED DIS-GUISES!!
BESIDES, I DON'T WANT TO WALK IN THESE TORN-UP CLOTHES!!
WE'RE WEARING THE EXACT SAME OUT-FITS AS THE PHOTOS IN THE WANTED POSTER!!
AH... I SEE YOUR POINT...
SO MEZZO WILL HAVE TO DO THE SHOPPING!!
?
I THINK THAT WOULD TURN EVEN MORE HEADS...
LET ME DO THE SHOPPING...
IF YOU OR I GO, WE'LL BE CAUGHT!!
HOW MANY WAYS DO I HAVE TO EXPLAIN THIS?!
WE'RE COUNTING ON YOU, MEZZO.
YOU CAN DO IT, CAN'T YOU?
PAT
GYAAAA!!
FLASH
MOON-DRAGONS...
...ARE SAID TO HAVE COME FROM THE MOON EONS AGO.
FWIIII IIII
DRAGONS ARE RARE, BUT AMONGST THEM, MOON-DRAGONS ARE THE RAREST KIND.

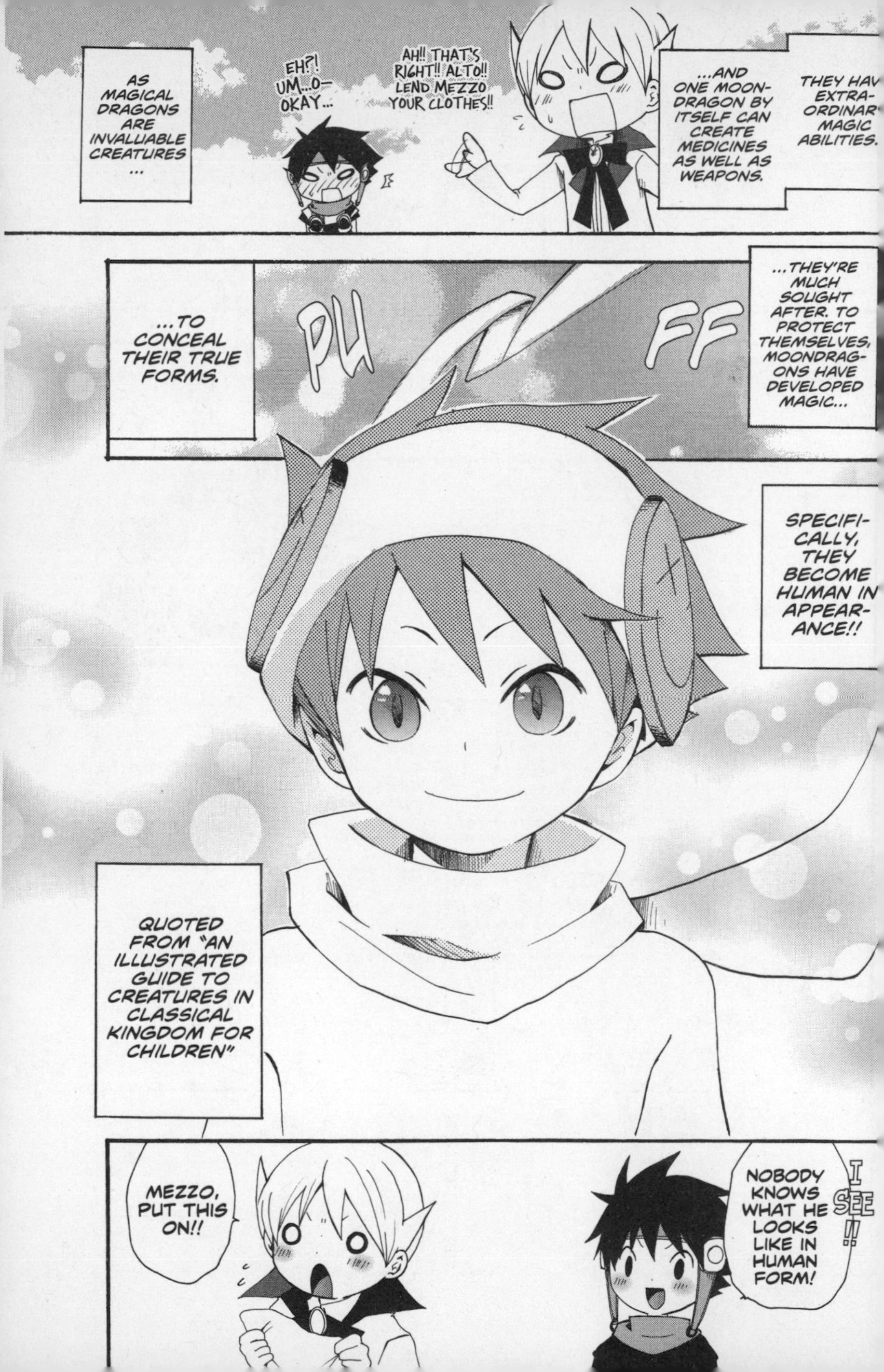
THEY HAV EXTRA-ORDINAR MAGIC ABILITIES.
...AND ONE MOON-DRAGON BY ITSELF CAN CREATE MEDICINES AS WELL AS WEAPONS.
AH!! THAT'S RIGHT!! ALTO!! LEND MEZZO YOUR CLOTHES!!
EH?! UM...O-OKAY...
AS MAGICAL DRAGONS ARE INVALUABLE CREATURES ...
...THEY'RE MUCH SOUGHT AFTER. TO PROTECT THEMSELVES, MOONDRAG-ONS HAVE DEVELOPED MAGIC...
PU FF
...TO CONCEAL THEIR TRUE FORMS.
SPECIFI-CALLY, THEY BECOME HUMAN IN APPEAR-ANCE!!
QUOTED FROM "AN ILLUSTRATED GUIDE TO CREATURES IN CLASSICAL KINGDOM FOR CHILDREN"
I SEE!!
NOBODY KNOWS WHAT HE LOOKS LIKE IN HUMAN FORM!
MEZZO, PUT THIS ON!!

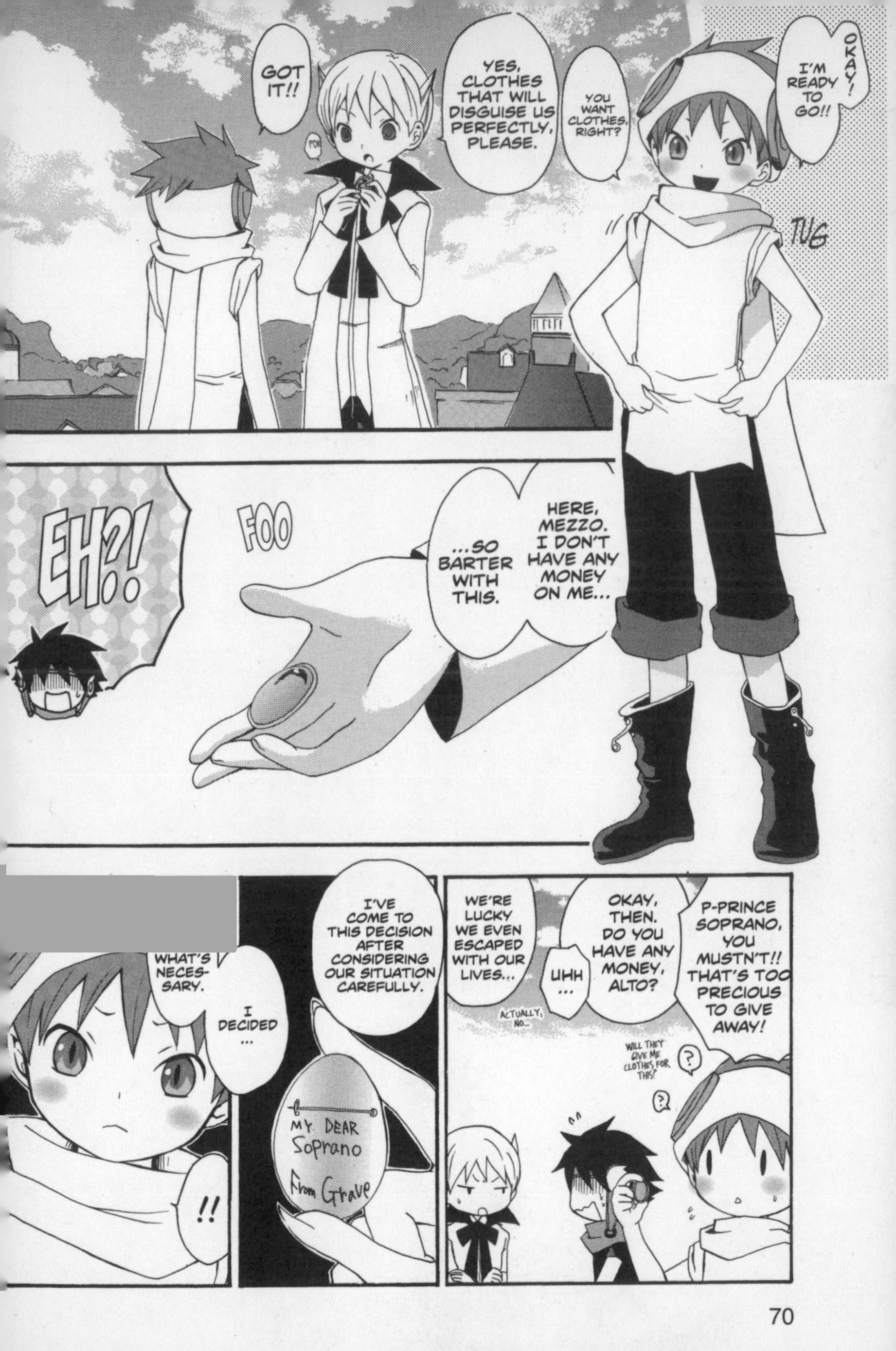
OKAY! I'M READY TO GO!!
TUG
YOU WANT CLOTHES, RIGHT?
YES, CLOTHES THAT WILL DISGUISE US PERFECTLY, PLEASE.
GOT IT!!
HERE, MEZZO. I DON'T HAVE ANY MONEY ON ME...
...SO BARTER WITH THIS.
FOO
EH?!
P-PRINCE SOPRANO, YOU MUSTN'T!! THAT'S TOO PRECIOUS TO GIVE AWAY!
OKAY, THEN. DO YOU HAVE ANY MONEY, ALTO?
UHH...
ACTUALLY, NO...
WE'RE LUCKY WE EVEN ESCAPED WITH OUR LIVES...
WILL THEY GIVE ME CLOTHES FOR THIS?
?
?
I'VE COME TO THIS DECISION AFTER CONSIDERING OUR SITUATION CAREFULLY.
MY DEAR Soprano
From Grave
I DECIDED ...
WHAT'S NECES-SARY.
!!

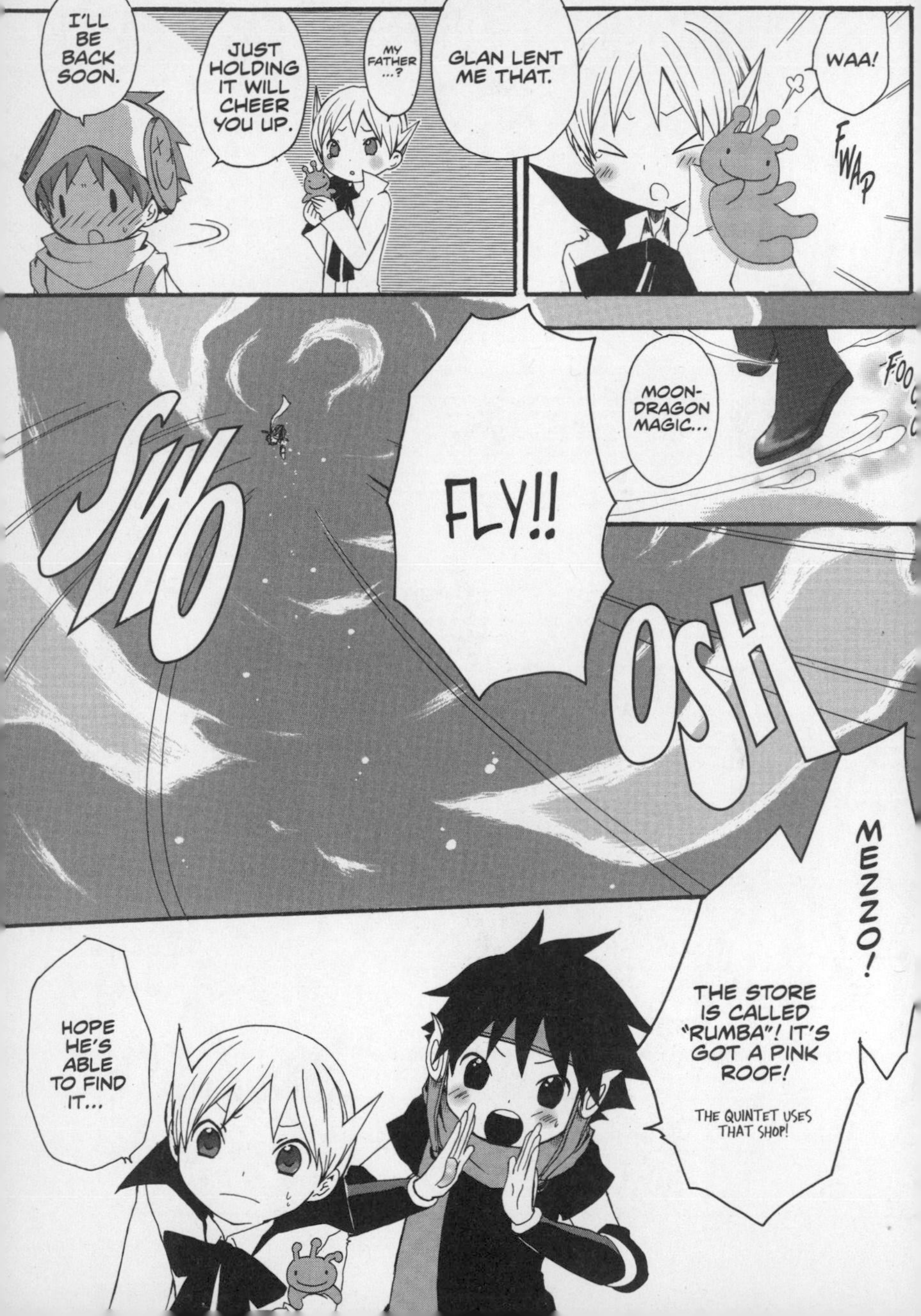
WAA!
FWAP
GLAN LENT ME THAT.
MY FATHER ...?
JUST HOLDING IT WILL CHEER YOU UP.
I'LL BE BACK SOON.
FOO
MOON-DRAGON MAGIC...
FLY!!
SWO
OSH
MEZZO!
THE STORE IS CALLED "RUMBA"! IT'S GOT A PINK ROOF!
THE QUINTET USES THAT SHOP!
HOPE HE'S ABLE TO FIND IT...

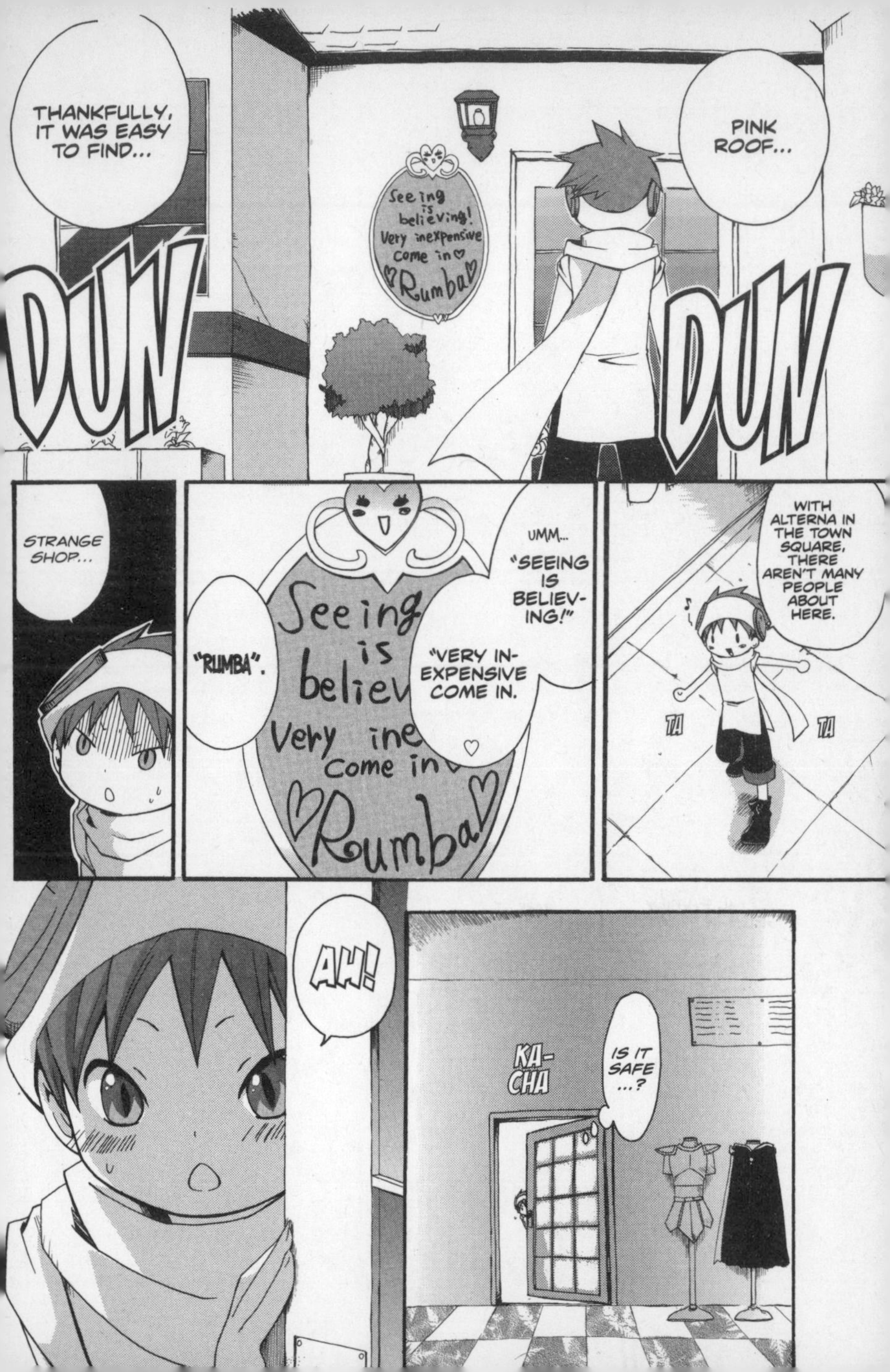
PINK ROOF...
DUN
Seeing is believing! Very inexpensive come in ♡ ♡Rumba♡
THANKFULLY, IT WAS EASY TO FIND...
DUN
WITH ALTERNA IN THE TOWN SQUARE, THERE AREN'T MANY PEOPLE ABOUT HERE.
TA
TA
UMM... "SEEING IS BELIEV-ING!"
"VERY IN-EXPENSIVE COME IN. ♡
"RUMBA".
Seeing is believ Very ine come in ♡ ♡Rumba♡
STRANGE SHOP...
KA-CHA
IS IT SAFE ...?
AH!

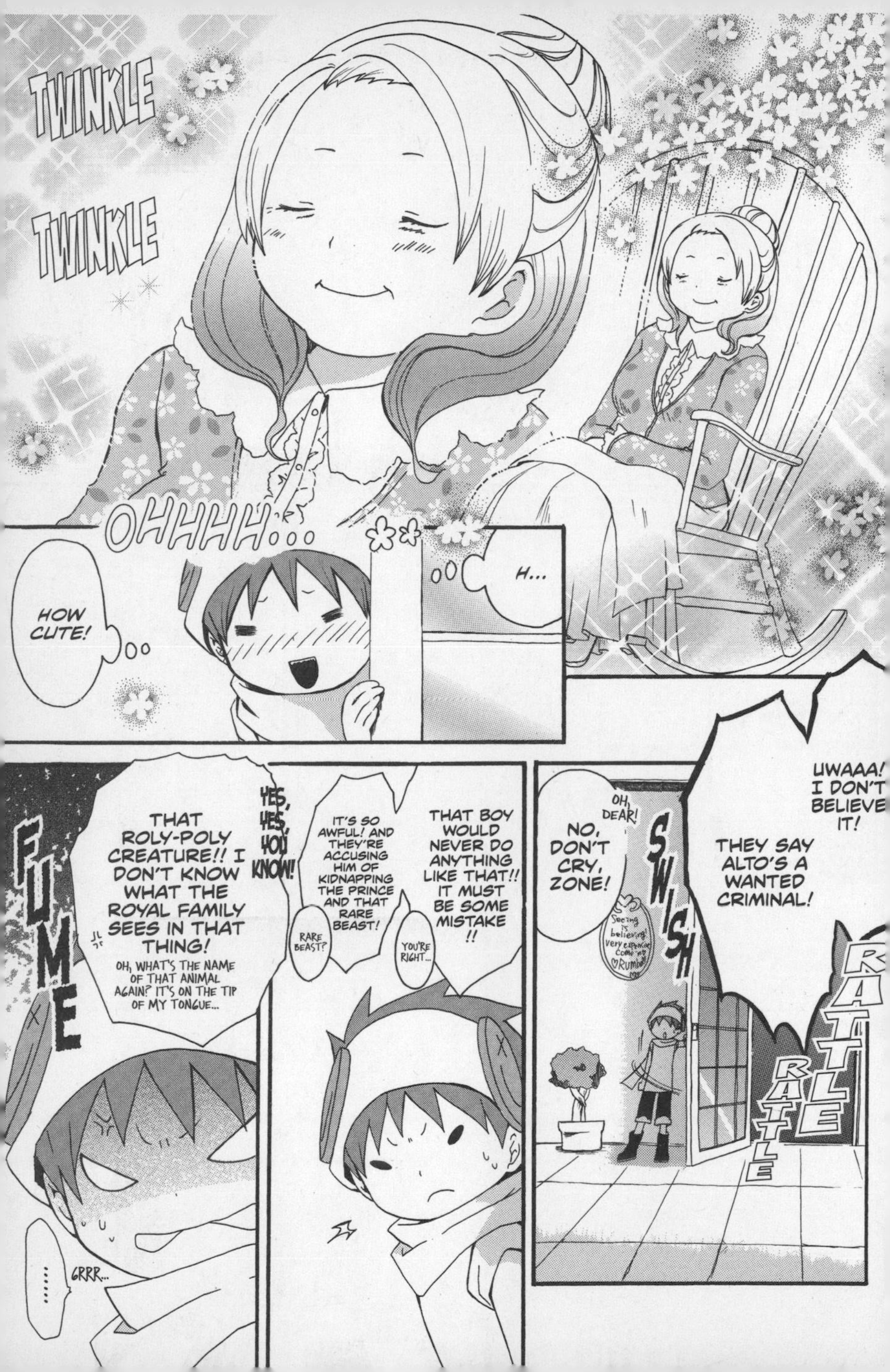
TWINKLE
TWINKLE
H...
OHHHH...
HOW CUTE!
UWAAA! I DON'T BELIEVE IT!
THEY SAY ALTO'S A WANTED CRIMINAL!
RATTLE
RATTLE
RATTLE
SWISH
OH, DEAR!
NO, DON'T CRY, ZONE!
THAT BOY WOULD NEVER DO ANYTHING LIKE THAT!! IT MUST BE SOME MISTAKE!!
IT'S SO AWFUL! AND THEY'RE ACCUSING HIM OF KIDNAPPING THE PRINCE AND THAT RARE BEAST!
YES, YES, YOU KNOW!
YOU'RE RIGHT...
RARE BEAST?
THAT ROLY-POLY CREATURE!! I DON'T KNOW WHAT THE ROYAL FAMILY SEES IN THAT THING!
OH, WHAT'S THE NAME OF THAT ANIMAL AGAIN? IT'S ON THE TIP OF MY TONGUE...
FUME
......
GRRR...

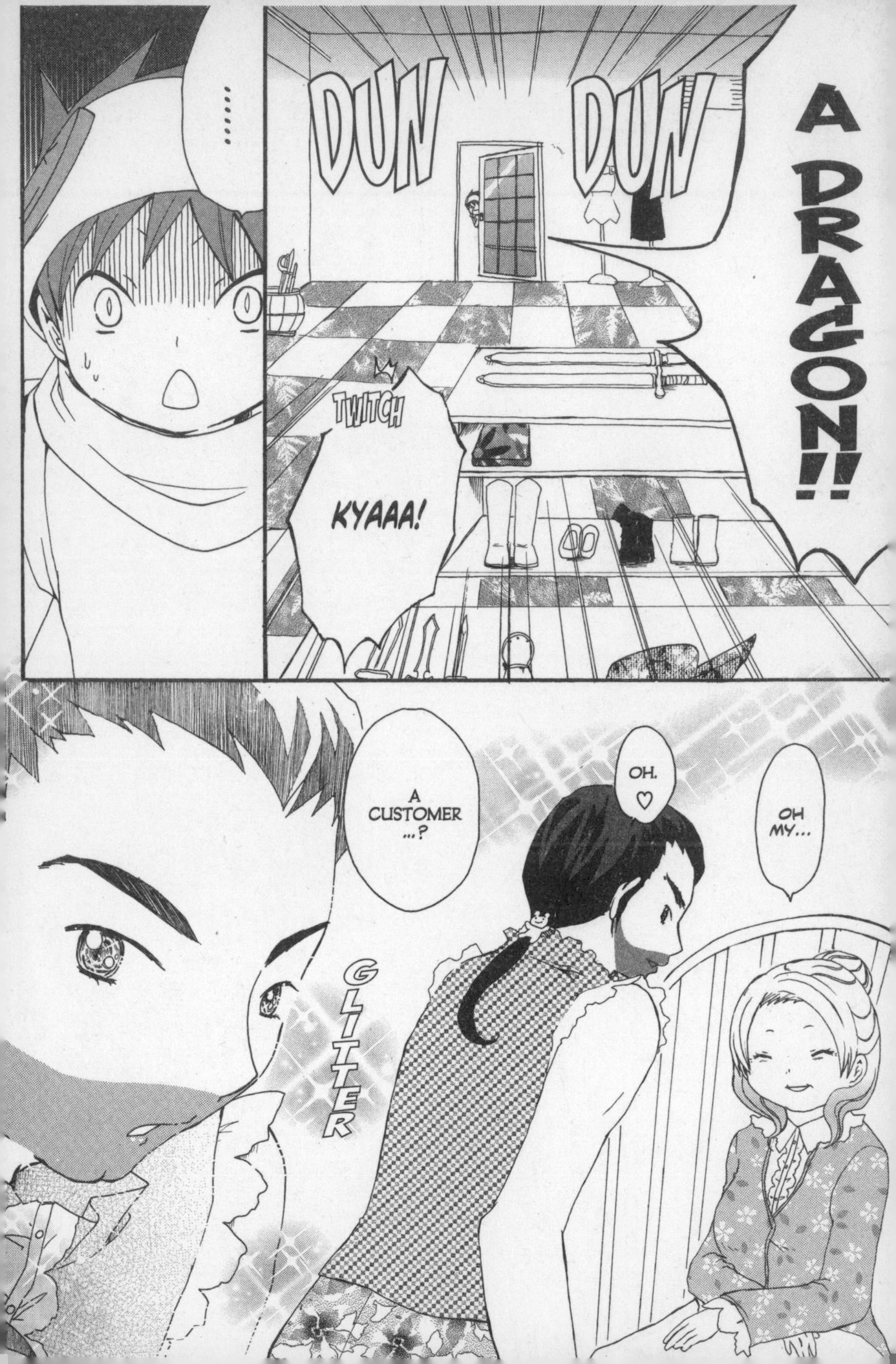
A DRAGON!!
DUN DUN
TWITCH
KYAAA!
......
OH MY...
OH. ♡
A CUSTOMER ...?
GLITTER

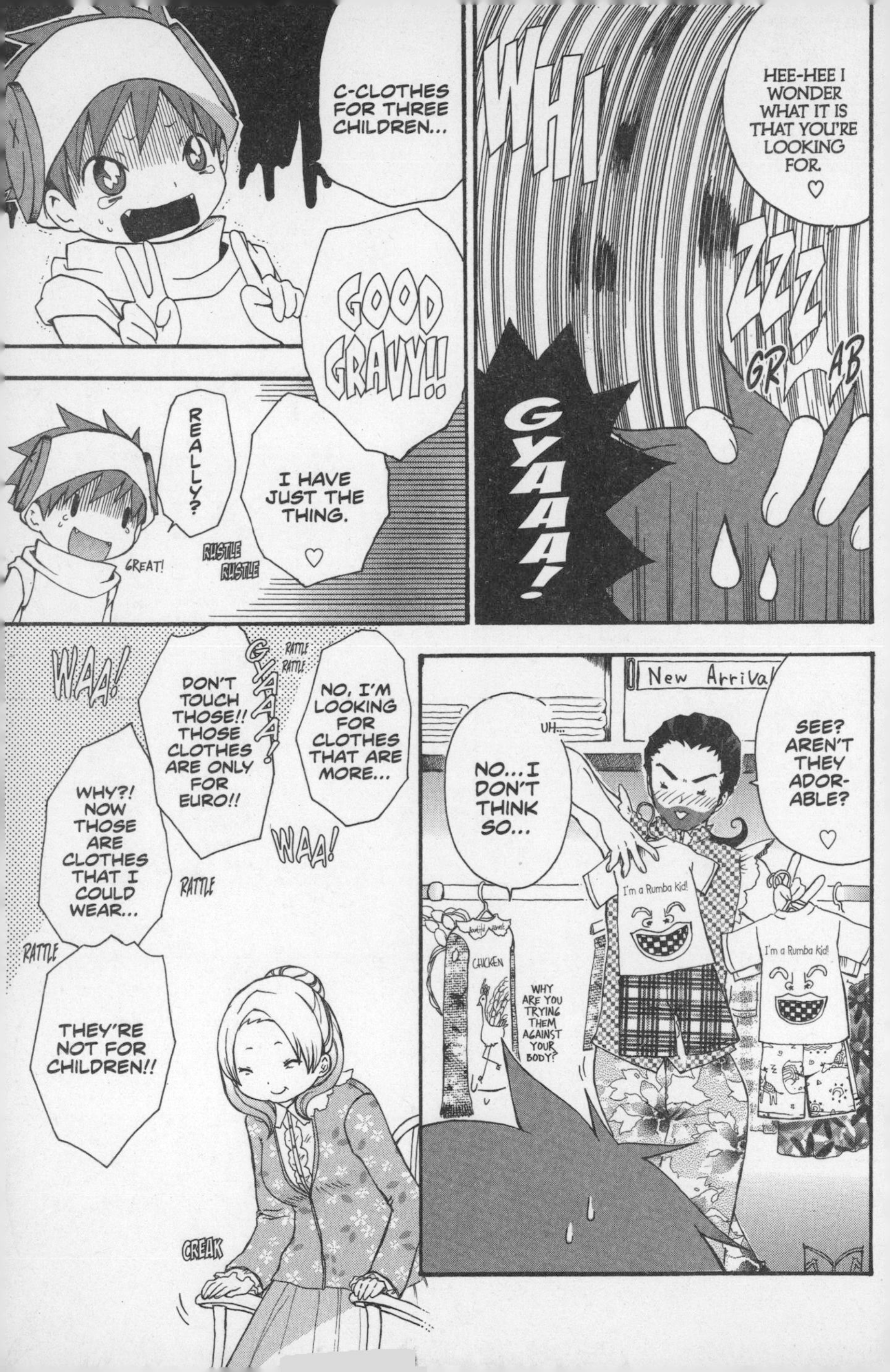
HEE-HEE I WONDER WHAT IT IS THAT YOU'RE LOOKING FOR. ♡
WHI
ZZZ
GRAB
GYAAA!
C-CLOTHES FOR THREE CHILDREN...
GOOD GRAVY!!
I HAVE JUST THE THING. ♡
REALLY?
RUSTLE RUSTLE
GREAT!
SEE? AREN'T THEY ADORABLE? ♡
New Arrival
UH...
NO... I DON'T THINK SO...
I'm a Rumba Kid!
I'm a Rumba Kid!
CHICKEN
WHY ARE YOU TRYING THEM AGAINST YOUR BODY?
NO, I'M LOOKING FOR CLOTHES THAT ARE MORE...
RATTLE RATTLE
GYAAAA!
DON'T TOUCH THOSE!! THOSE CLOTHES ARE ONLY FOR EURO!!
WAA!
WHY?! NOW THOSE ARE CLOTHES THAT I COULD WEAR...
WAA!
RATTLE
RATTLE
THEY'RE NOT FOR CHILDREN!!
CREAK

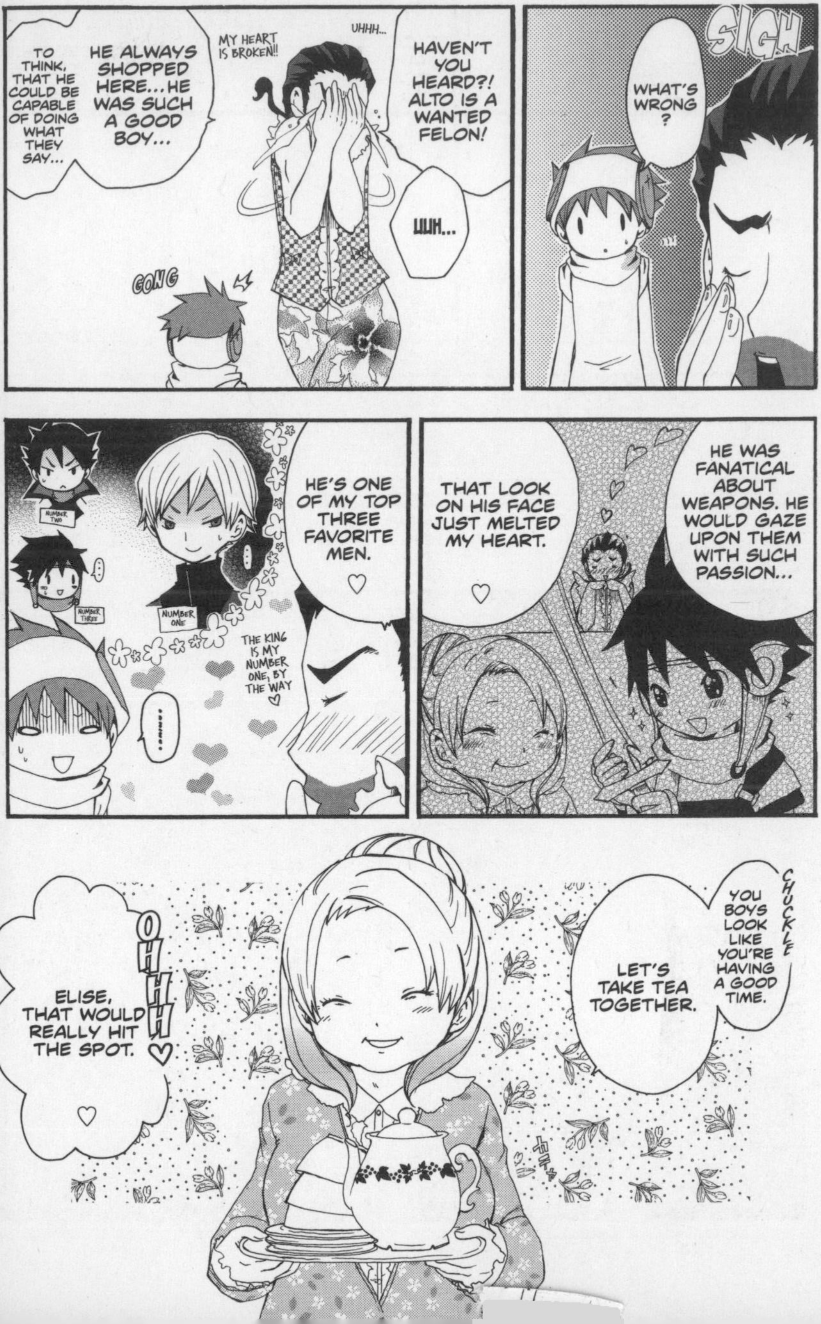
SIGH
WHAT'S WRONG?
HAVEN'T YOU HEARD?! ALTO IS A WANTED FELON!
UHHH...
MY HEART IS BROKEN!!
HE ALWAYS SHOPPED HERE...HE WAS SUCH A GOOD BOY...
TO THINK, THAT HE COULD BE CAPABLE OF DOING WHAT THEY SAY...
UUH...
GONG
HE WAS FANATICAL ABOUT WEAPONS. HE WOULD GAZE UPON THEM WITH SUCH PASSION...
THAT LOOK ON HIS FACE JUST MELTED MY HEART. ♡
HE'S ONE OF MY TOP THREE FAVORITE MEN. ♡
NUMBER ONE
NUMBER TWO
...
NUMBER THREE
THE KING IS MY NUMBER ONE, BY THE WAY ♡
......
CHUCKLE
YOU BOYS LOOK LIKE YOU'RE HAVING A GOOD TIME.
LET'S TAKE TEA TOGETHER.
OHHHH
ELISE, THAT WOULD REALLY HIT THE SPOT. ♡

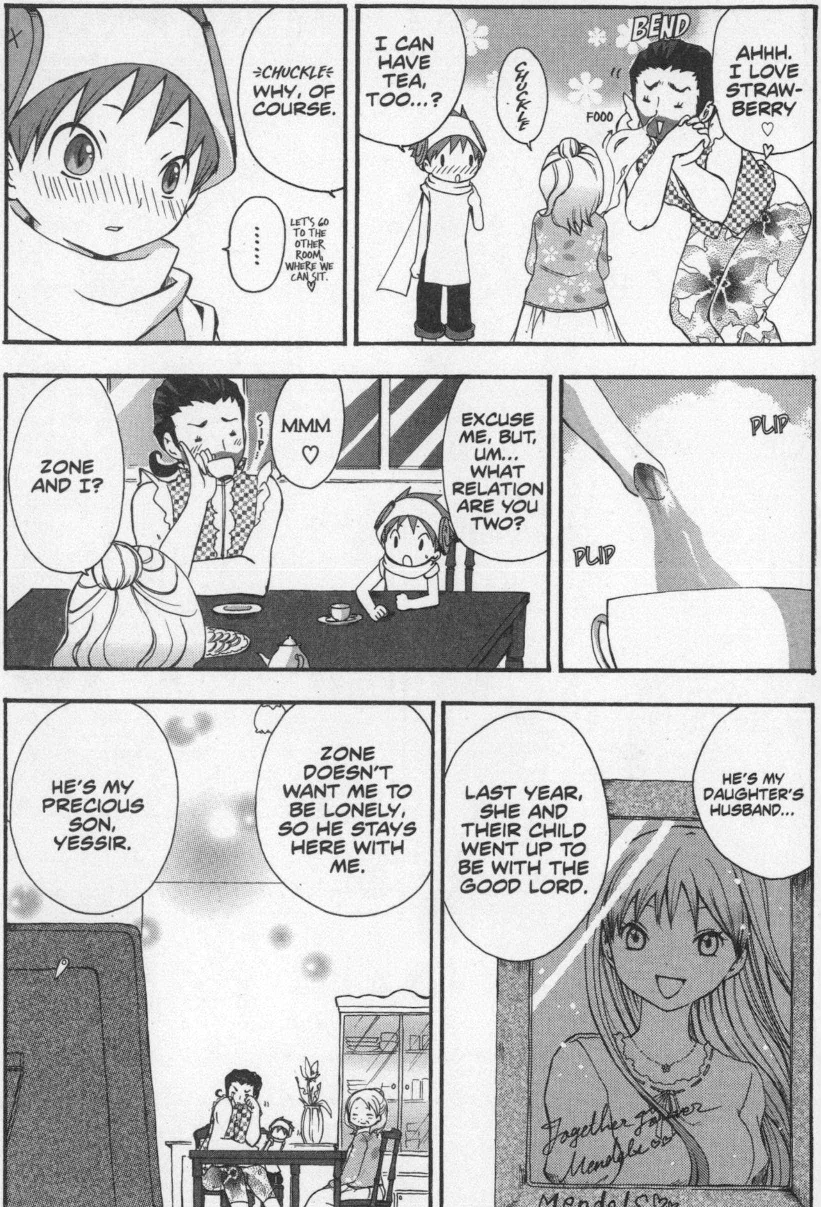

BEND
AHHH. I LOVE STRAWBERRY ♡
FOOO
I CAN HAVE TEA, TOO...?
CHUCKLE
≈CHUCKLE≈ WHY, OF COURSE.
......
LET'S GO TO THE OTHER ROOM, WHERE WE CAN SIT. ♡
PLIP
PLIP
EXCUSE ME, BUT, UM... WHAT RELATION ARE YOU TWO?
MMM ♡
SIP...
ZONE AND I?
HE'S MY DAUGHTER'S HUSBAND...
LAST YEAR, SHE AND THEIR CHILD WENT UP TO BE WITH THE GOOD LORD.
Together Forever
MendelS♡♡
ZONE DOESN'T WANT ME TO BE LONELY, SO HE STAYS HERE WITH ME.
HE'S MY PRECIOUS SON, YESSIR.

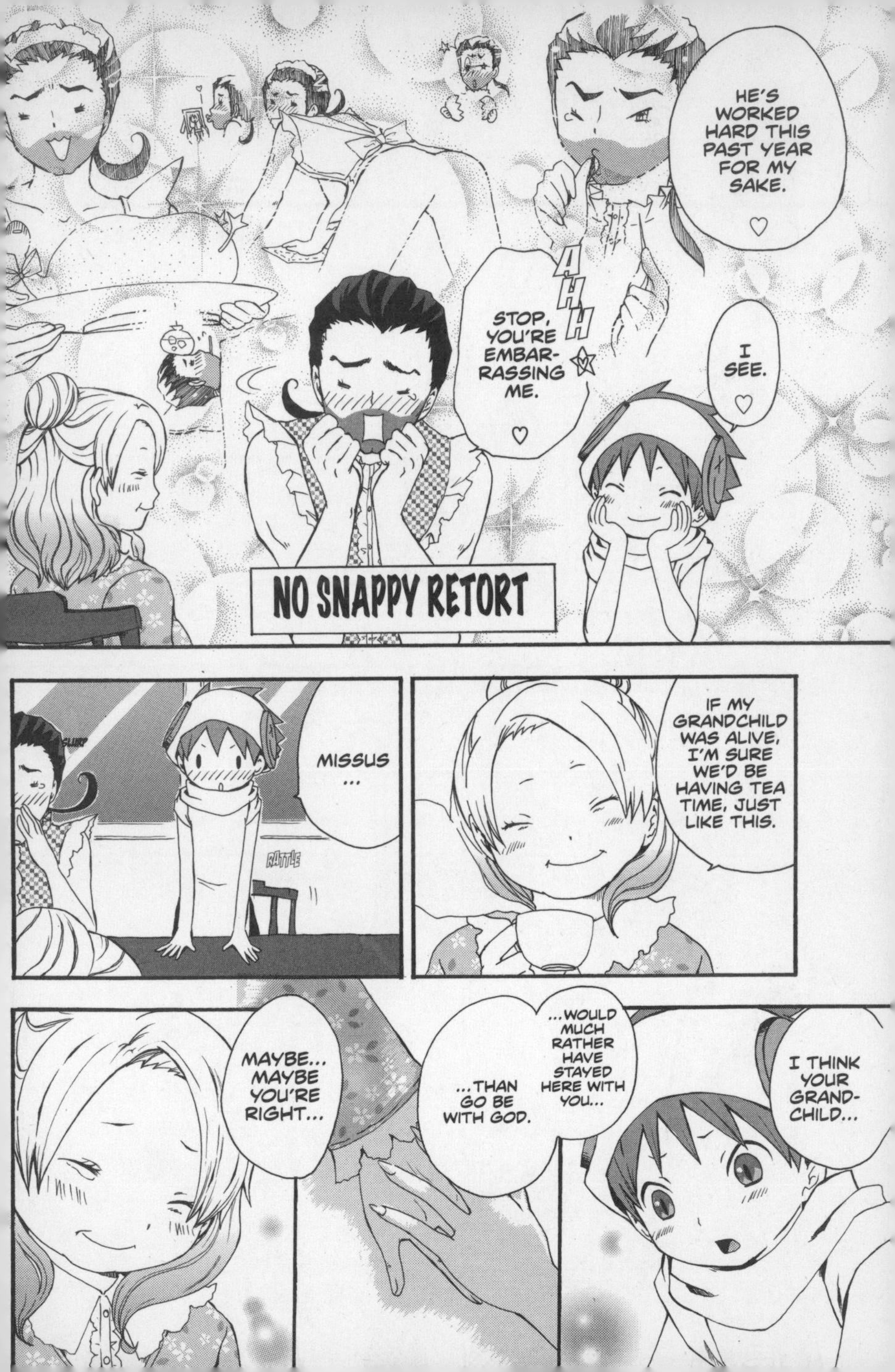

HE'S WORKED HARD THIS PAST YEAR FOR MY SAKE. ♡
I SEE. ♡
AHHH
STOP, YOU'RE EMBARRASSING ME. ♡
NO SNAPPY RETORT
IF MY GRANDCHILD WAS ALIVE, I'M SURE WE'D BE HAVING TEA TIME, JUST LIKE THIS.
MISSUS ...
SLURP
RATTLE
I THINK YOUR GRANDCHILD...
...WOULD MUCH RATHER HAVE STAYED HERE WITH YOU...
...THAN GO BE WITH GOD.
MAYBE... MAYBE YOU'RE RIGHT...

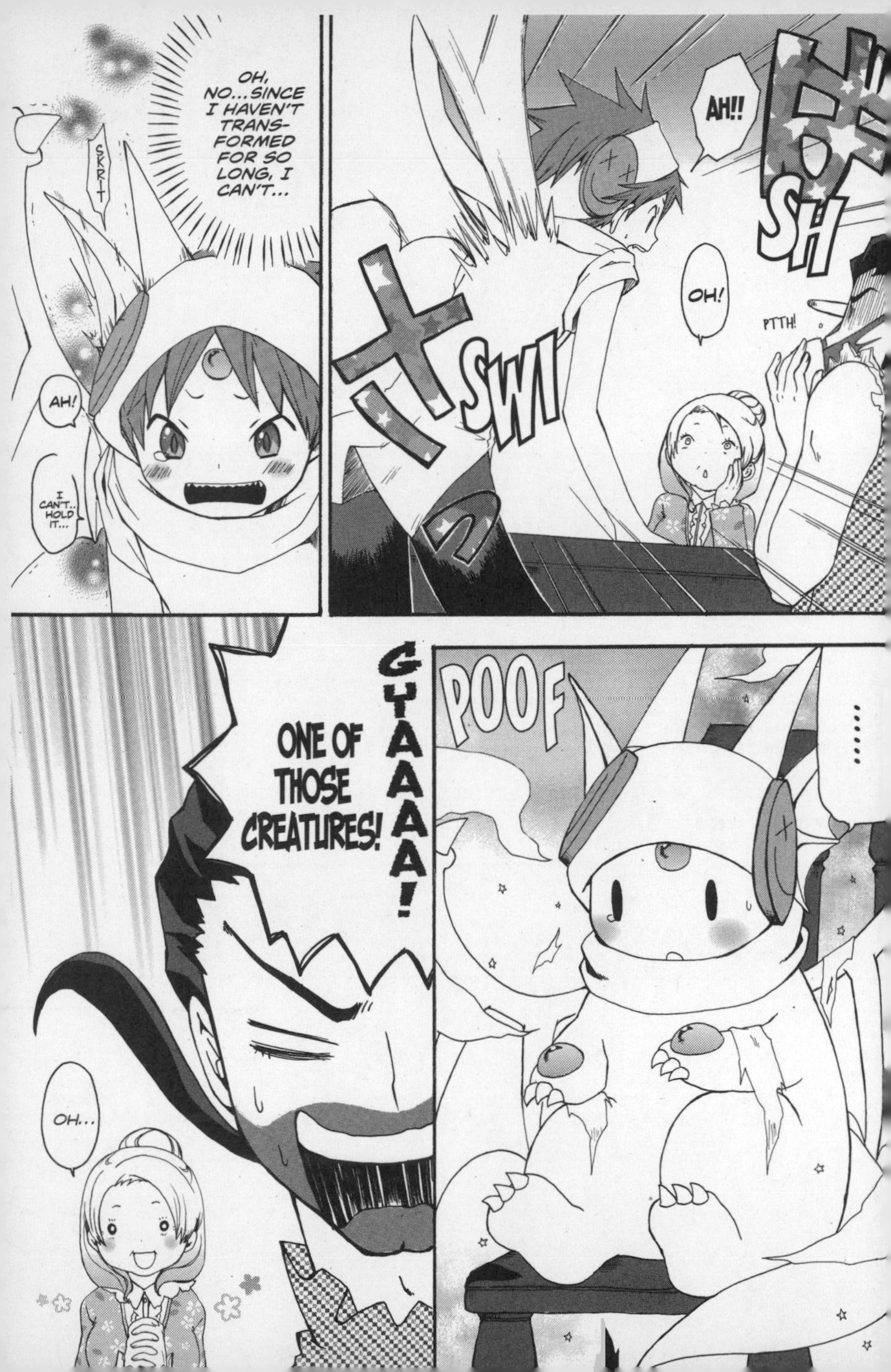
AH!!
SH
OH!
PTTH!
SWI
OH, NO...SINCE I HAVEN'T TRANS-FORMED FOR SO LONG, I CAN'T...
SKRT
AH!
I CAN'T... HOLD IT...
POOF
......
GYAAAAA!
ONE OF THOSE CREATURES!
OH...

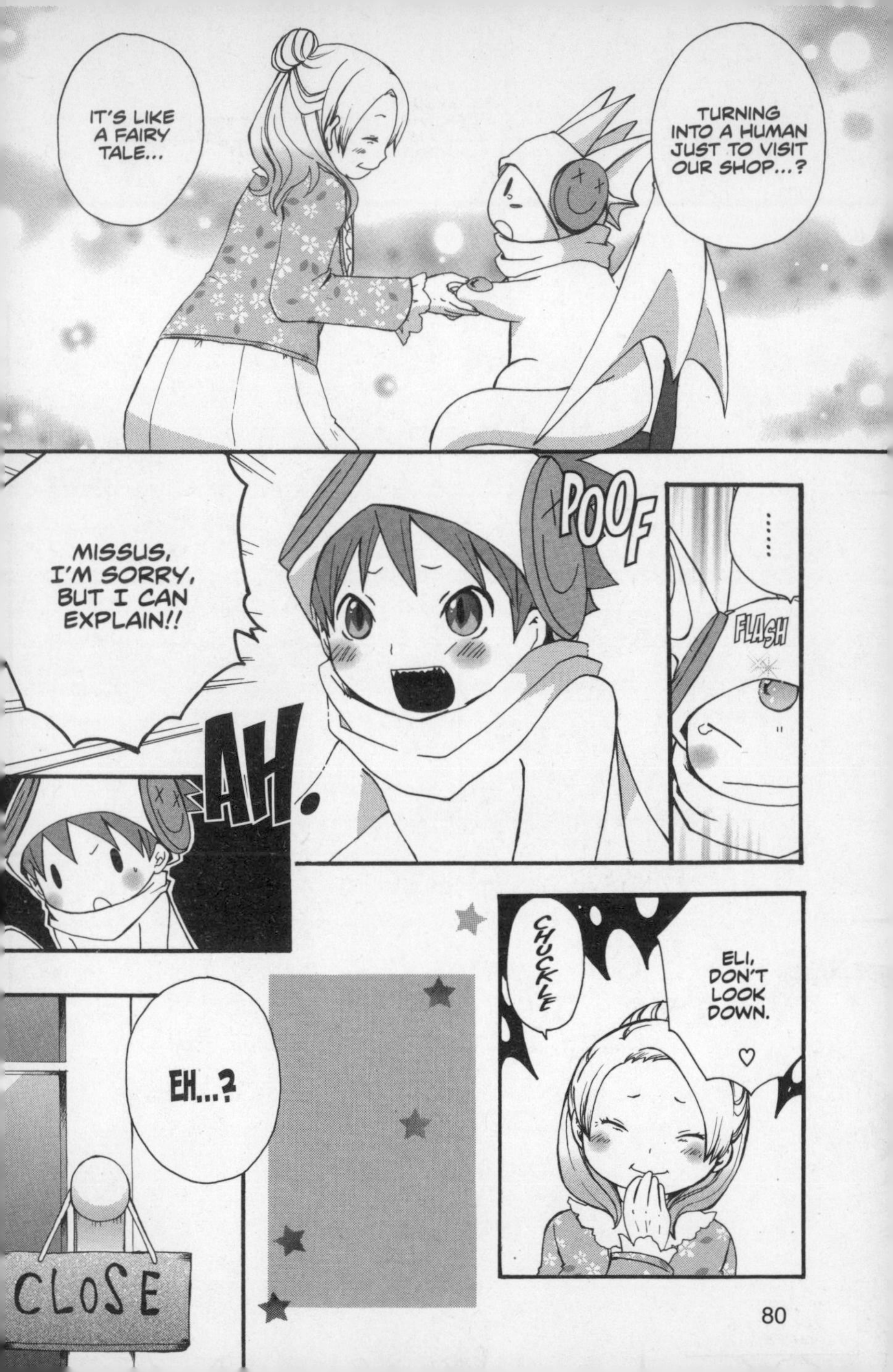
TURNING INTO A HUMAN JUST TO VISIT OUR SHOP...?
IT'S LIKE A FAIRY TALE...
......
FLASH
POOF
MISSUS, I'M SORRY, BUT I CAN EXPLAIN!!
AH
ELI, DON'T LOOK DOWN.
CHUCKLE
EH...?
CLOSE

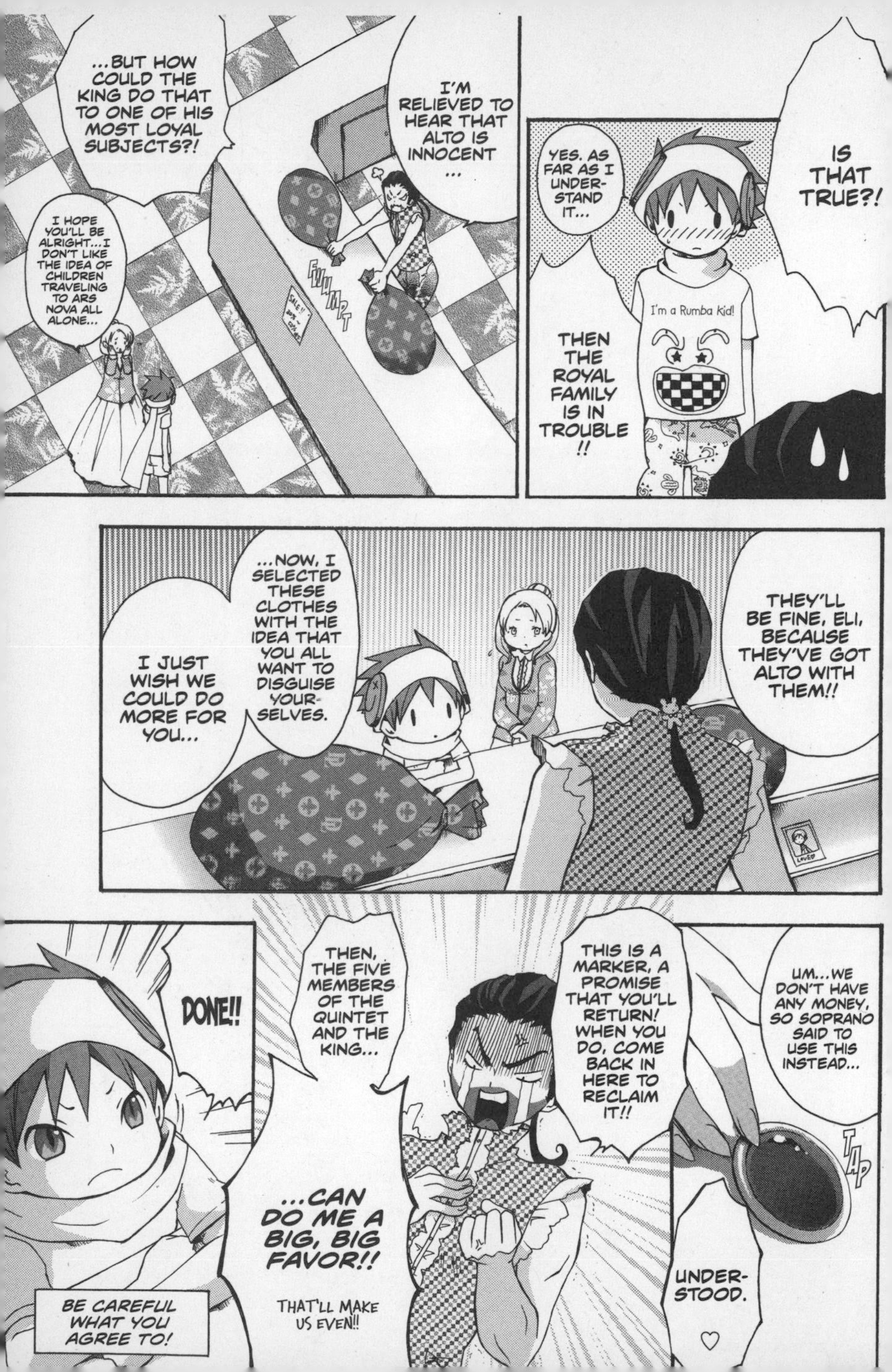
IS THAT TRUE?!
YES. AS FAR AS I UNDERSTAND IT...
I'm a Rumba Kid!
THEN THE ROYAL FAMILY IS IN TROUBLE!!
I'M RELIEVED TO HEAR THAT ALTO IS INNOCENT...
...BUT HOW COULD THE KING DO THAT TO ONE OF HIS MOST LOYAL SUBJECTS?!
FWUMPT
I HOPE YOU'LL BE ALRIGHT...I DON'T LIKE THE IDEA OF CHILDREN TRAVELING TO ARS NOVA ALL ALONE...
THEY'LL BE FINE, ELI, BECAUSE THEY'VE GOT ALTO WITH THEM!!
...NOW, I SELECTED THESE CLOTHES WITH THE IDEA THAT YOU ALL WANT TO DISGUISE YOURSELVES.
I JUST WISH WE COULD DO MORE FOR YOU...
UM...WE DON'T HAVE ANY MONEY, SO SOPRANO SAID TO USE THIS INSTEAD...
TAP
UNDERSTOOD.
THIS IS A MARKER, A PROMISE THAT YOU'LL RETURN! WHEN YOU DO, COME BACK IN HERE TO RECLAIM IT!!
THEN, THE FIVE MEMBERS OF THE QUINTET AND THE KING...
...CAN DO ME A BIG, BIG FAVOR!!
THAT'LL MAKE US EVEN!!
DONE!!
BE CAREFUL WHAT YOU AGREE TO!

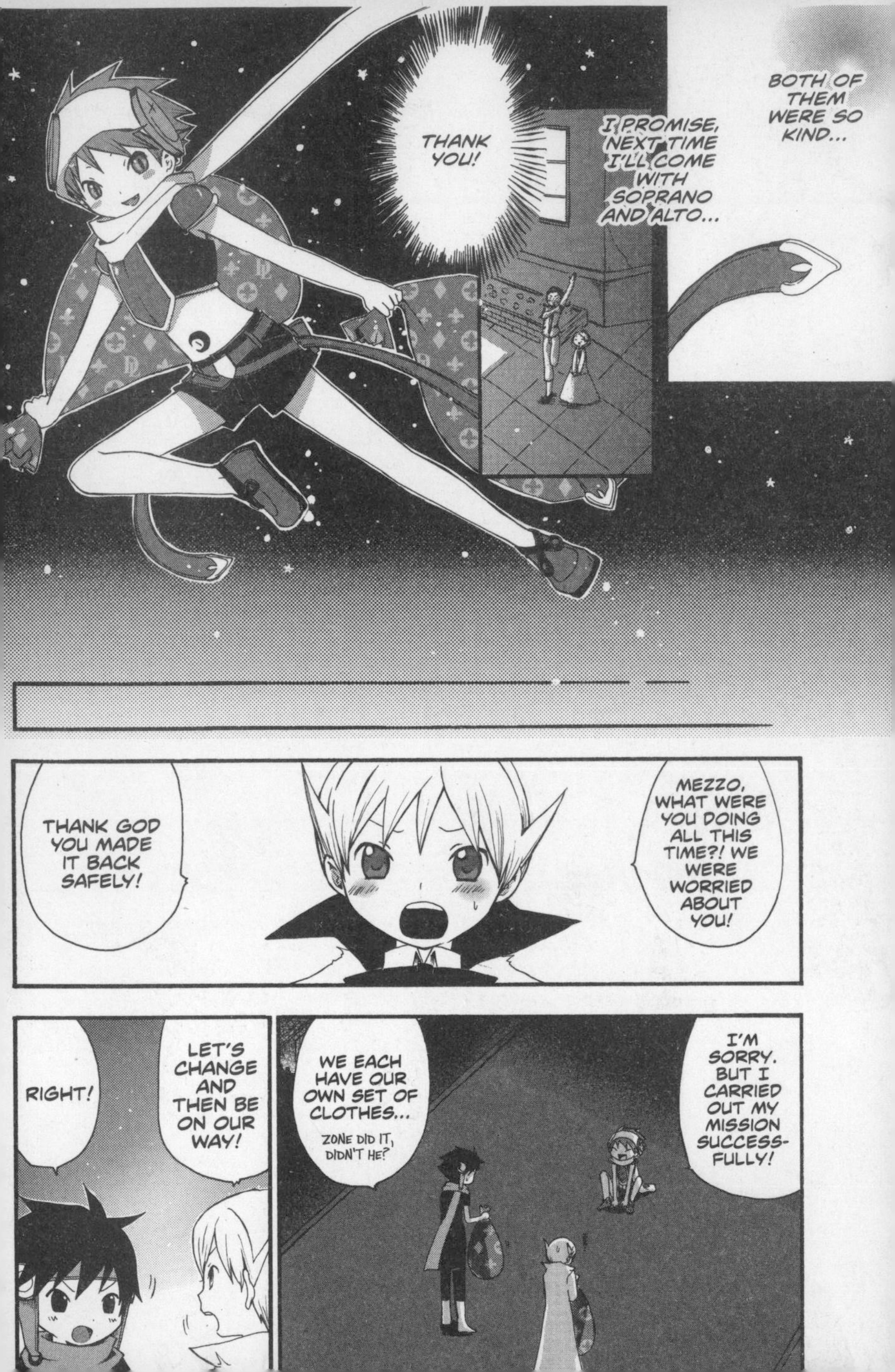
BOTH OF THEM WERE SO KIND...
I PROMISE, NEXT TIME I'LL COME WITH SOPRANO AND ALTO...
THANK YOU!
MEZZO, WHAT WERE YOU DOING ALL THIS TIME?! WE WERE WORRIED ABOUT YOU!
THANK GOD YOU MADE IT BACK SAFELY!
I'M SORRY. BUT I CARRIED OUT MY MISSION SUCCESS-FULLY!
WE EACH HAVE OUR OWN SET OF CLOTHES...
ZONE DID IT, DIDN'T HE?
LET'S CHANGE AND THEN BE ON OUR WAY!
RIGHT!

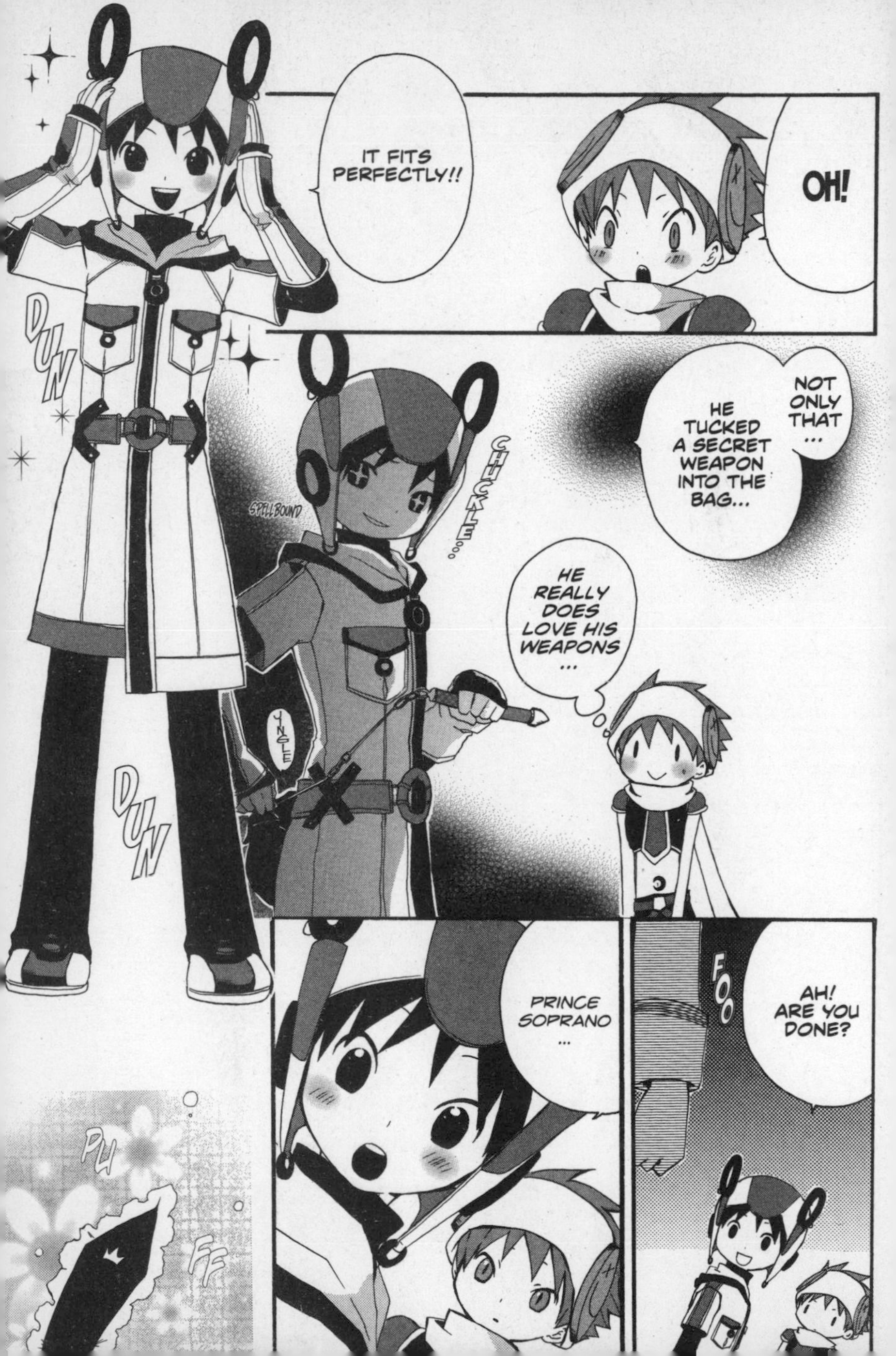
OH!
IT FITS PERFECTLY!!
DUN
DUN
NOT ONLY THAT ...
HE TUCKED A SECRET WEAPON INTO THE BAG...
CHUCKLE
SPELLBOUND
JINGLE
HE REALLY DOES LOVE HIS WEAPONS ...
FOO
AH! ARE YOU DONE?
PRINCE SOPRANO ...
PU
FF

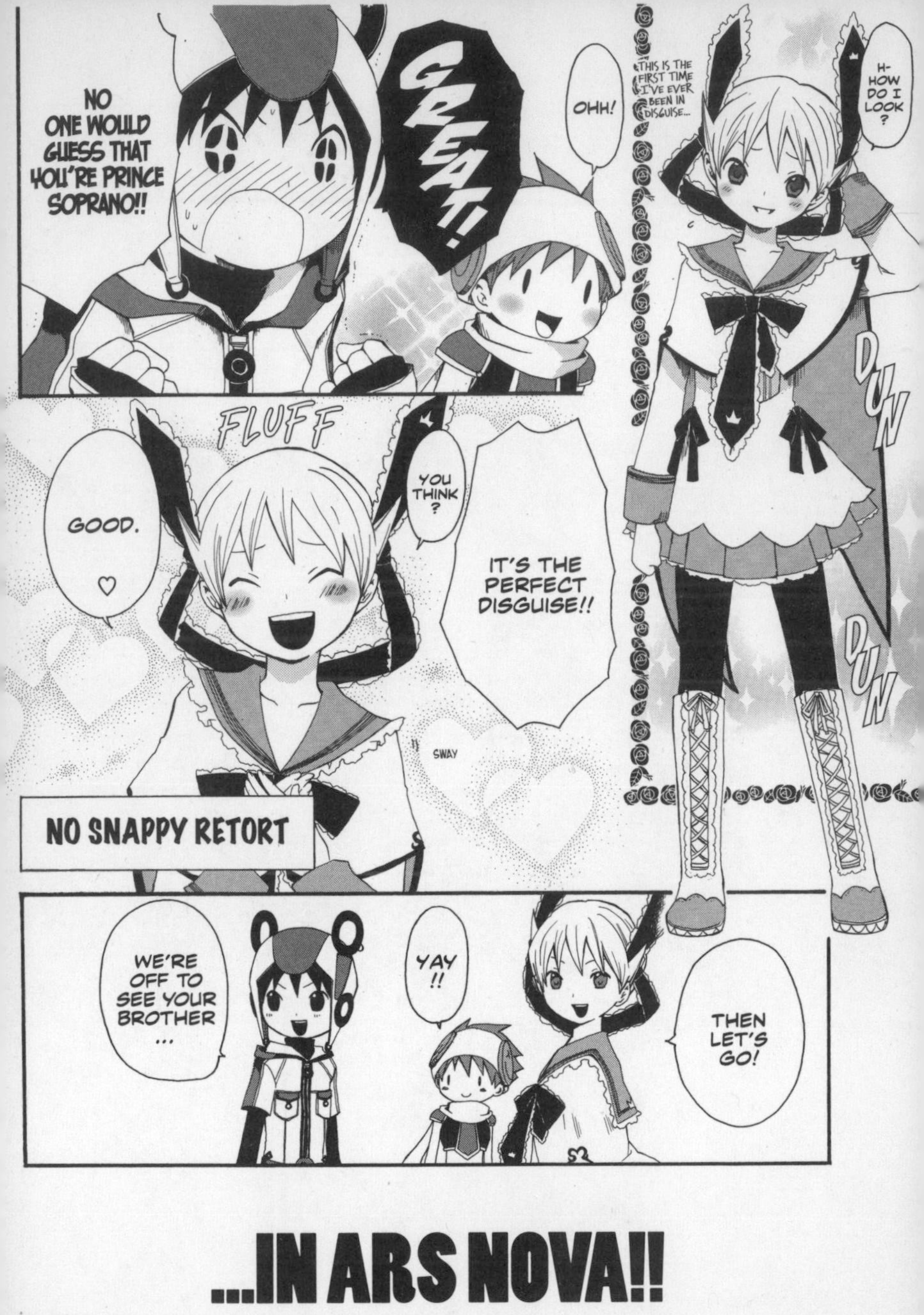
H-HOW DO I LOOK?
THIS IS THE FIRST TIME I'VE EVER BEEN IN DISGUISE...
DUN
DUN
OHH!
GREAT!!
NO ONE WOULD GUESS THAT YOU'RE PRINCE SOPRANO!!
IT'S THE PERFECT DISGUISE!!
YOU THINK?
FLUFF
GOOD. ♡
SWAY
NO SNAPPY RETORT
THEN LET'S GO!
YAY!!
WE'RE OFF TO SEE YOUR BROTHER...

...IN ARS NOVA!!

Classical Medley

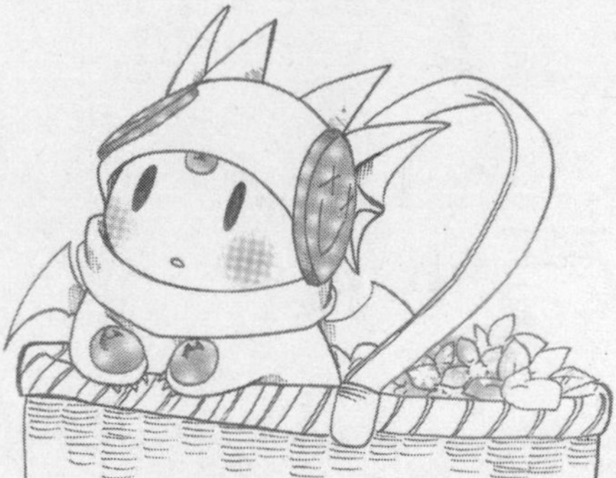
Classical medley...

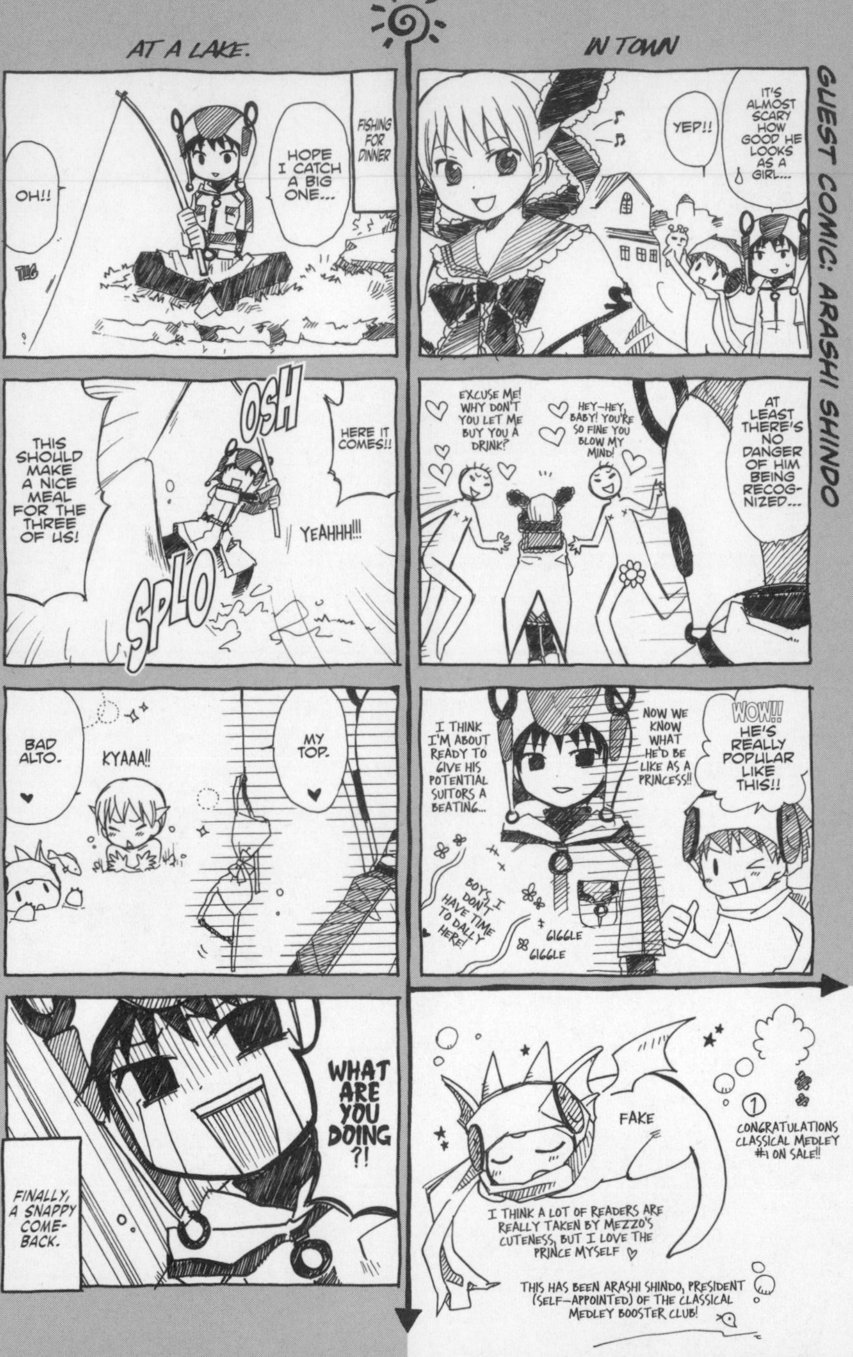
GUEST COMIC: ARASHI SHINDO
IN TOWN
IT'S ALMOST SCARY HOW GOOD HE LOOKS AS A GIRL...
YEP!!
AT LEAST THERE'S NO DANGER OF HIM BEING RECOGNIZED...
HEY-HEY, BABY! YOU'RE SO FINE YOU BLOW MY MIND!
EXCUSE ME! WHY DON'T YOU LET ME BUY YOU A DRINK?
WOW!! HE'S REALLY POPULAR LIKE THIS!!
NOW WE KNOW WHAT HE'D BE LIKE AS A PRINCESS!!
I THINK I'M ABOUT READY TO GIVE HIS POTENTIAL SUITORS A BEATING...
BOYS, I DON'T HAVE TIME TO DALLY HERE!
GIGGLE
GIGGLE
CONGRATULATIONS CLASSICAL MEDLEY #1 ON SALE!!
FAKE
I THINK A LOT OF READERS ARE REALLY TAKEN BY MEZZO'S CUTENESS, BUT I LOVE THE PRINCE MYSELF
THIS HAS BEEN ARASHI SHINDO, PRESIDENT (SELF-APPOINTED) OF THE CLASSICAL MEDLEY BOOSTER CLUB!
AT A LAKE.
FISHING FOR DINNER
HOPE I CATCH A BIG ONE...
OH!!
TUG
HERE IT COMES!!
OSH
YEAHHH!!!
THIS SHOULD MAKE A NICE MEAL FOR THE THREE OF US!
SPLO
MY TOP.
KYAAA!!
BAD ALTO.
WHAT ARE YOU DOING?!
FINALLY, A SNAPPY COME-BACK.

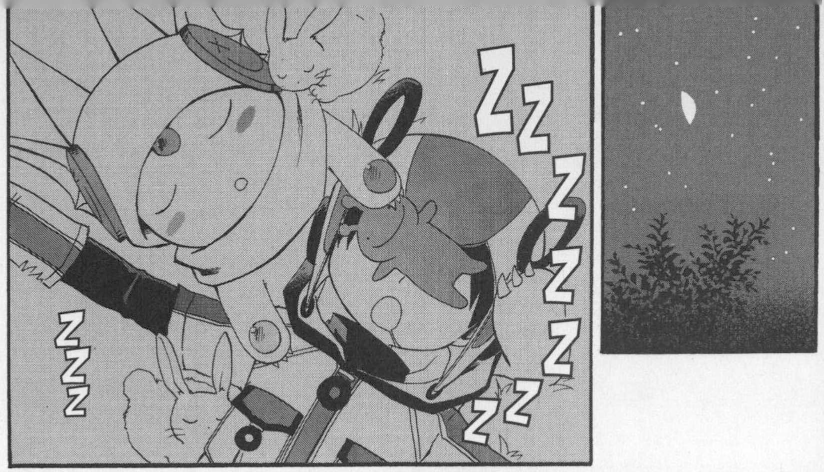
ZZZZZZZ
ZZZ

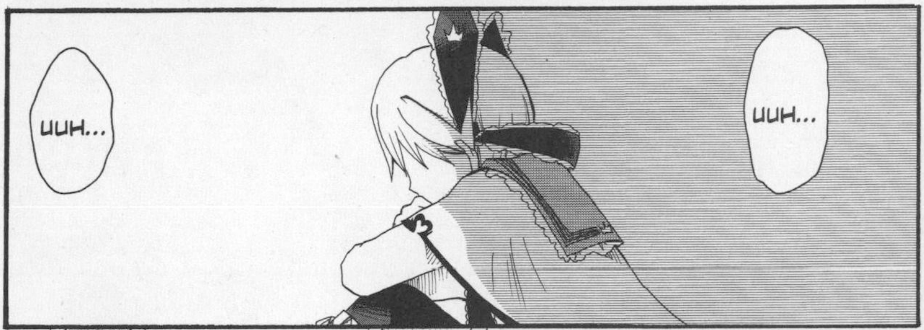
UUH...
UUH...

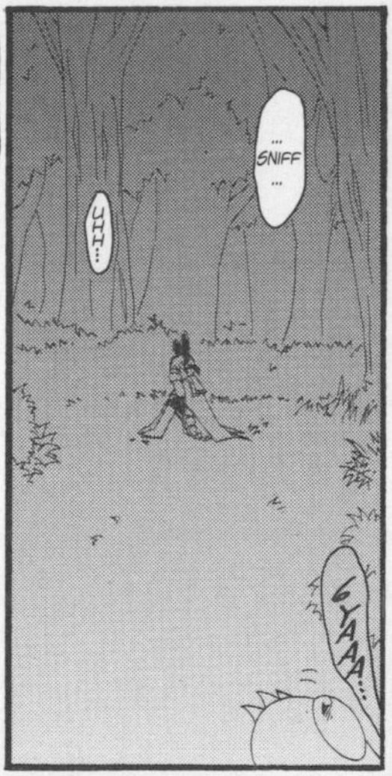
... SNIFF ...
UHH...
GYAAA...

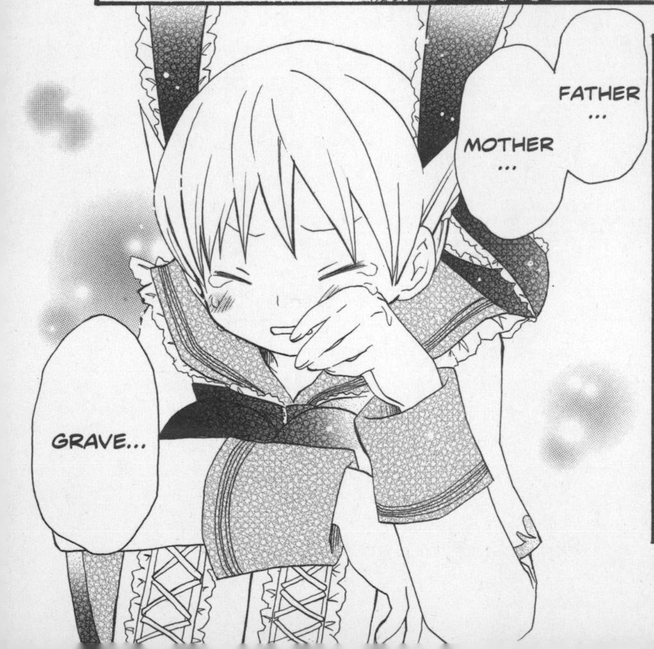
FATHER ...
MOTHER ...
GRAVE...

OP4: Amaze

OP4: Amaze

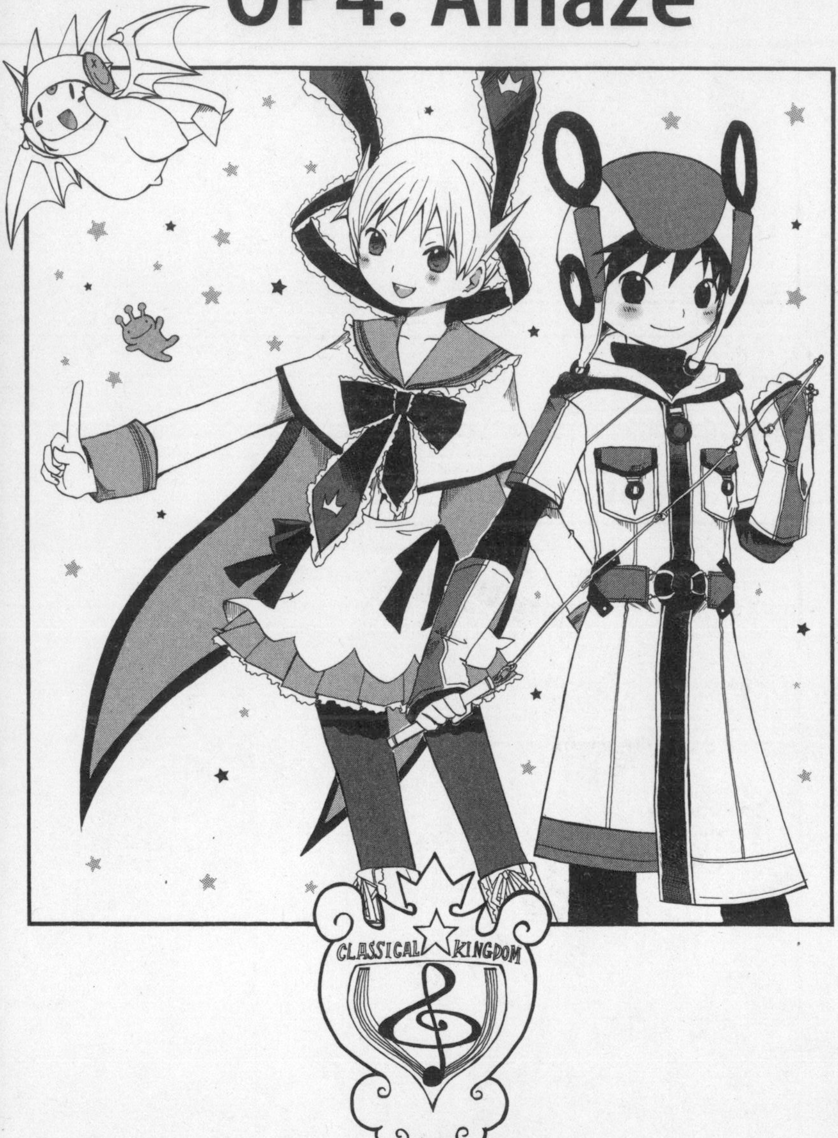
CLASSICAL KINGDOM

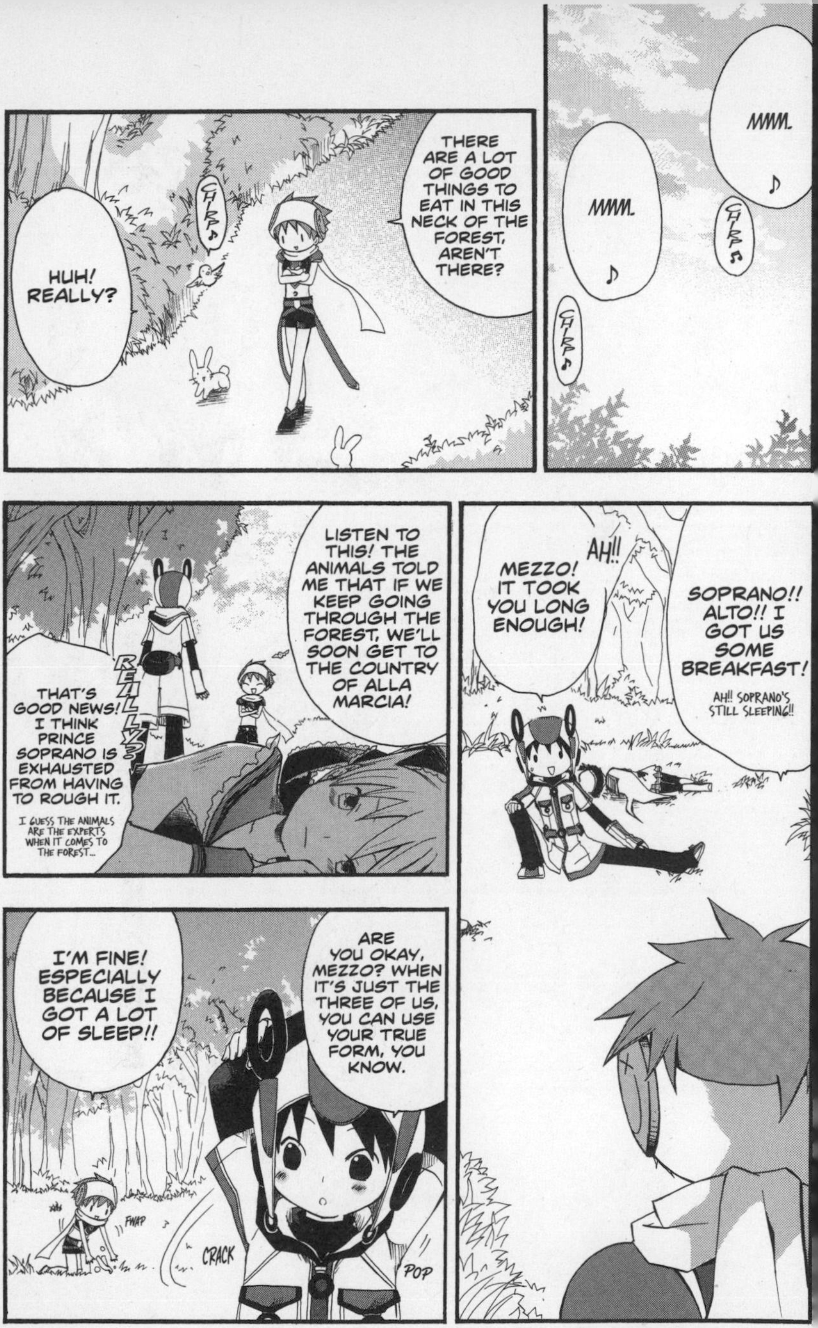
MMM. ♪
CHIRP♪
MMM. ♪
CHIRP♪
THERE ARE A LOT OF GOOD THINGS TO EAT IN THIS NECK OF THE FOREST, AREN'T THERE?
CHIRP♪
HUH! REALLY?
SOPRANO!! ALTO!! I GOT US SOME BREAKFAST!
AH!! SOPRANO'S STILL SLEEPING!!
AH!!
MEZZO! IT TOOK YOU LONG ENOUGH!
LISTEN TO THIS! THE ANIMALS TOLD ME THAT IF WE KEEP GOING THROUGH THE FOREST, WE'LL SOON GET TO THE COUNTRY OF ALLA MARCIA!
REALLY?
THAT'S GOOD NEWS! I THINK PRINCE SOPRANO IS EXHAUSTED FROM HAVING TO ROUGH IT.
I GUESS THE ANIMALS ARE THE EXPERTS WHEN IT COMES TO THE FOREST...
ARE YOU OKAY, MEZZO? WHEN IT'S JUST THE THREE OF US, YOU CAN USE YOUR TRUE FORM, YOU KNOW.
I'M FINE! ESPECIALLY BECAUSE I GOT A LOT OF SLEEP!!
POP
CRACK
FWAP

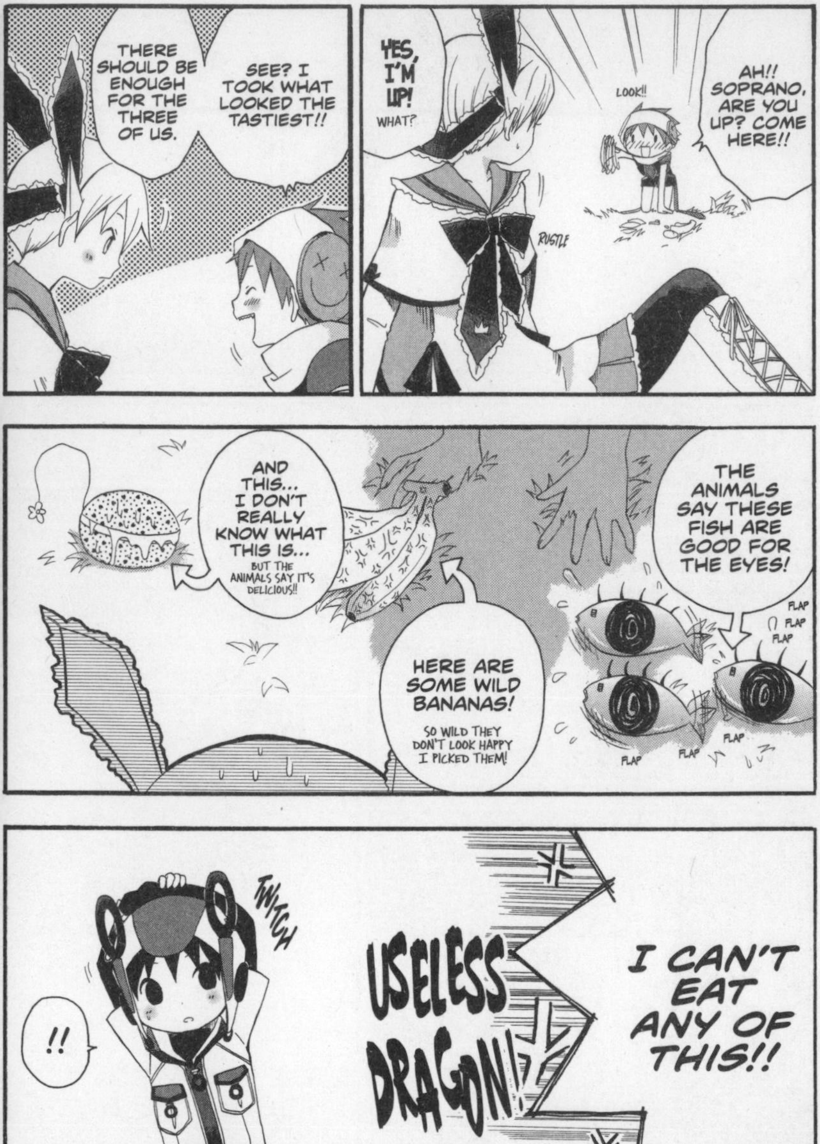
AH!! SOPRANO, ARE YOU UP? COME HERE!!
LOOK!!
RUSTLE
YES, I'M UP!
WHAT?
SEE? I TOOK WHAT LOOKED THE TASTIEST!!
THERE SHOULD BE ENOUGH FOR THE THREE OF US.
THE ANIMALS SAY THESE FISH ARE GOOD FOR THE EYES!
FLAP FLAP FLAP
FLAP FLAP FLAP
HERE ARE SOME WILD BANANAS!
SO WILD THEY DON'T LOOK HAPPY I PICKED THEM!
AND THIS... I DON'T REALLY KNOW WHAT THIS IS...
BUT THE ANIMALS SAY IT'S DELICIOUS!!
I CAN'T EAT ANY OF THIS!!
USELESS DRAGON!
TWITCH
!!

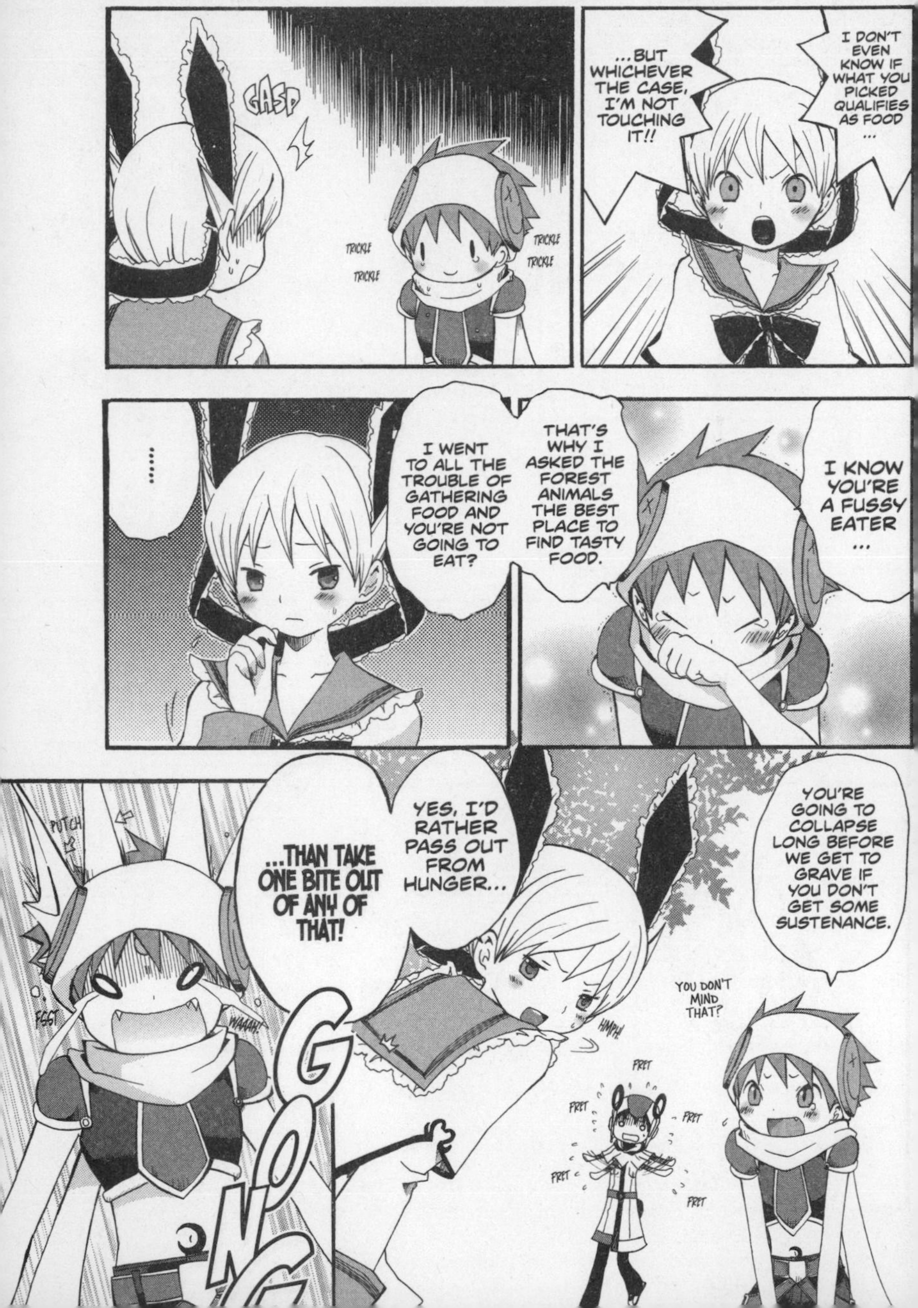
I DON'T EVEN KNOW IF WHAT YOU PICKED QUALIFIES AS FOOD ...
...BUT WHICHEVER THE CASE, I'M NOT TOUCHING IT!!
GASP
TRICKLE
TRICKLE
TRICKLE
TRICKLE
I KNOW YOU'RE A FUSSY EATER ...
THAT'S WHY I ASKED THE FOREST ANIMALS THE BEST PLACE TO FIND TASTY FOOD.
I WENT TO ALL THE TROUBLE OF GATHERING FOOD AND YOU'RE NOT GOING TO EAT?
......
YOU'RE GOING TO COLLAPSE LONG BEFORE WE GET TO GRAVE IF YOU DON'T GET SOME SUSTENANCE.
YOU DON'T MIND THAT?
FRET
FRET
FRET
FRET
YES, I'D RATHER PASS OUT FROM HUNGER...
...THAN TAKE ONE BITE OUT OF ANY OF THAT!
HMPH!
GONG
WAAAH!
FSST
PUTCH

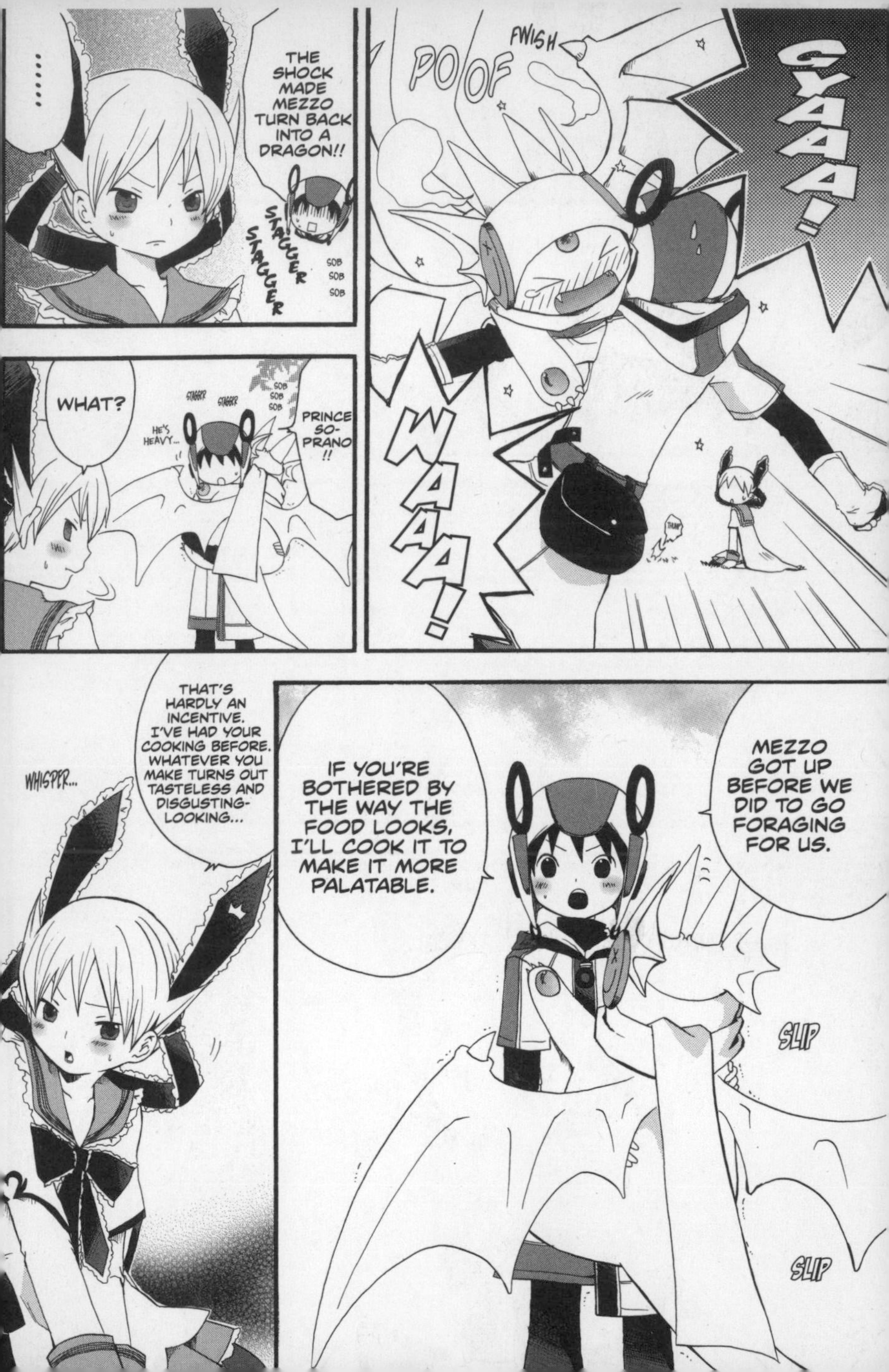
GYAAA!
FWISH
POOF
WAAA!
THE SHOCK MADE MEZZO TURN BACK INTO A DRAGON!!
STAGGER STAGGER
SOB SOB SOB
......
PRINCE SO-PRANO!!
SOB SOB SOB
STAGGER STAGGER
HE'S HEAVY...
WHAT?
MEZZO GOT UP BEFORE WE DID TO GO FORAGING FOR US.
IF YOU'RE BOTHERED BY THE WAY THE FOOD LOOKS, I'LL COOK IT TO MAKE IT MORE PALATABLE.
SLIP
SLIP
THAT'S HARDLY AN INCENTIVE. I'VE HAD YOUR COOKING BEFORE. WHATEVER YOU MAKE TURNS OUT TASTELESS AND DISGUSTING-LOOKING...
WHISPER...

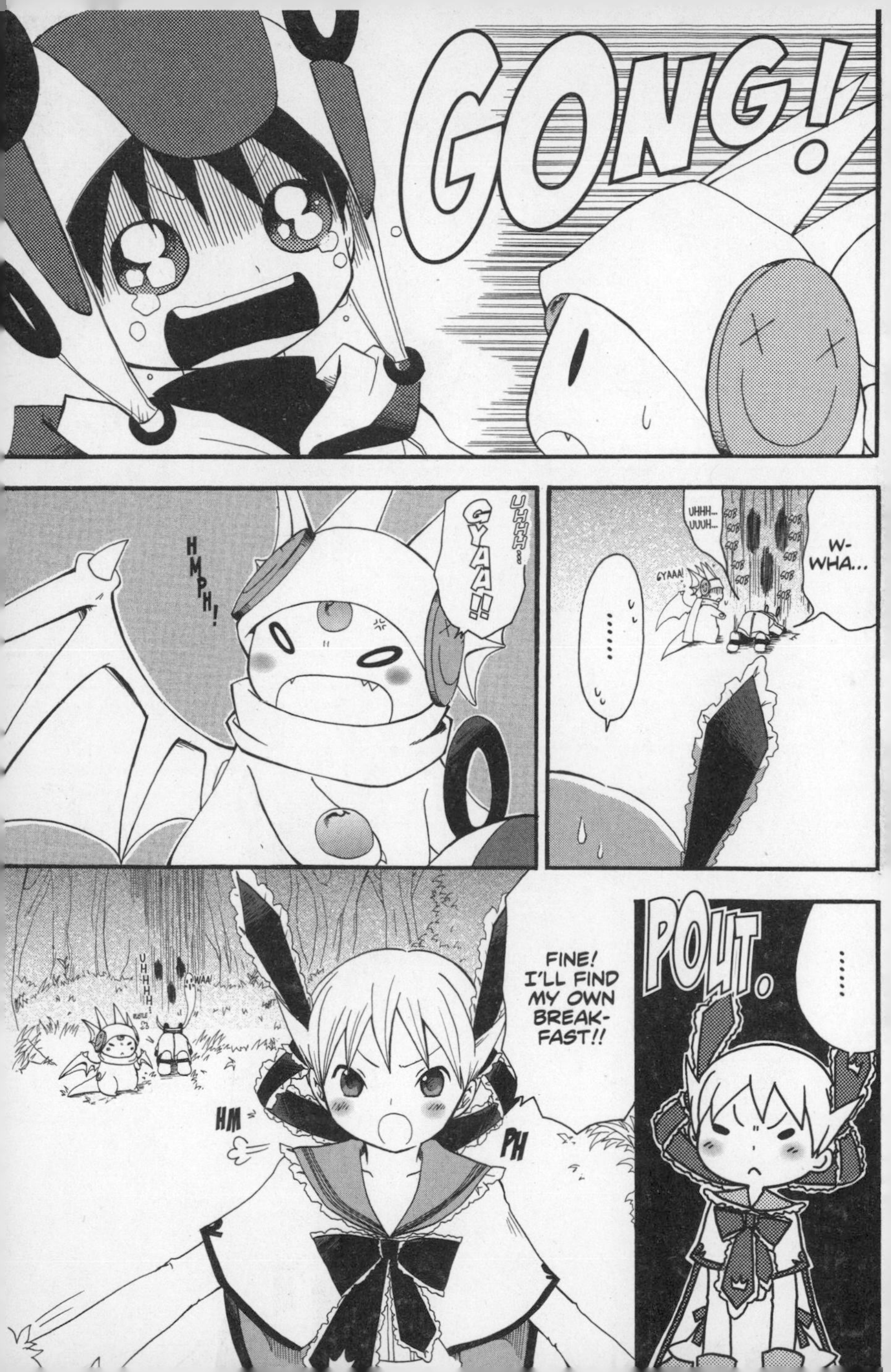
GONG!
W-WHA...
UHHH... UUUH...
SOB SOB SOB SOB SOB SOB SOB SOB SOB SOB SOB
GYAAA!
......
UHHHH...
GYAA!!
HMPH!
POUT.
......
FINE! I'LL FIND MY OWN BREAK-FAST!!
HMPH
UHHHH...
WAA!

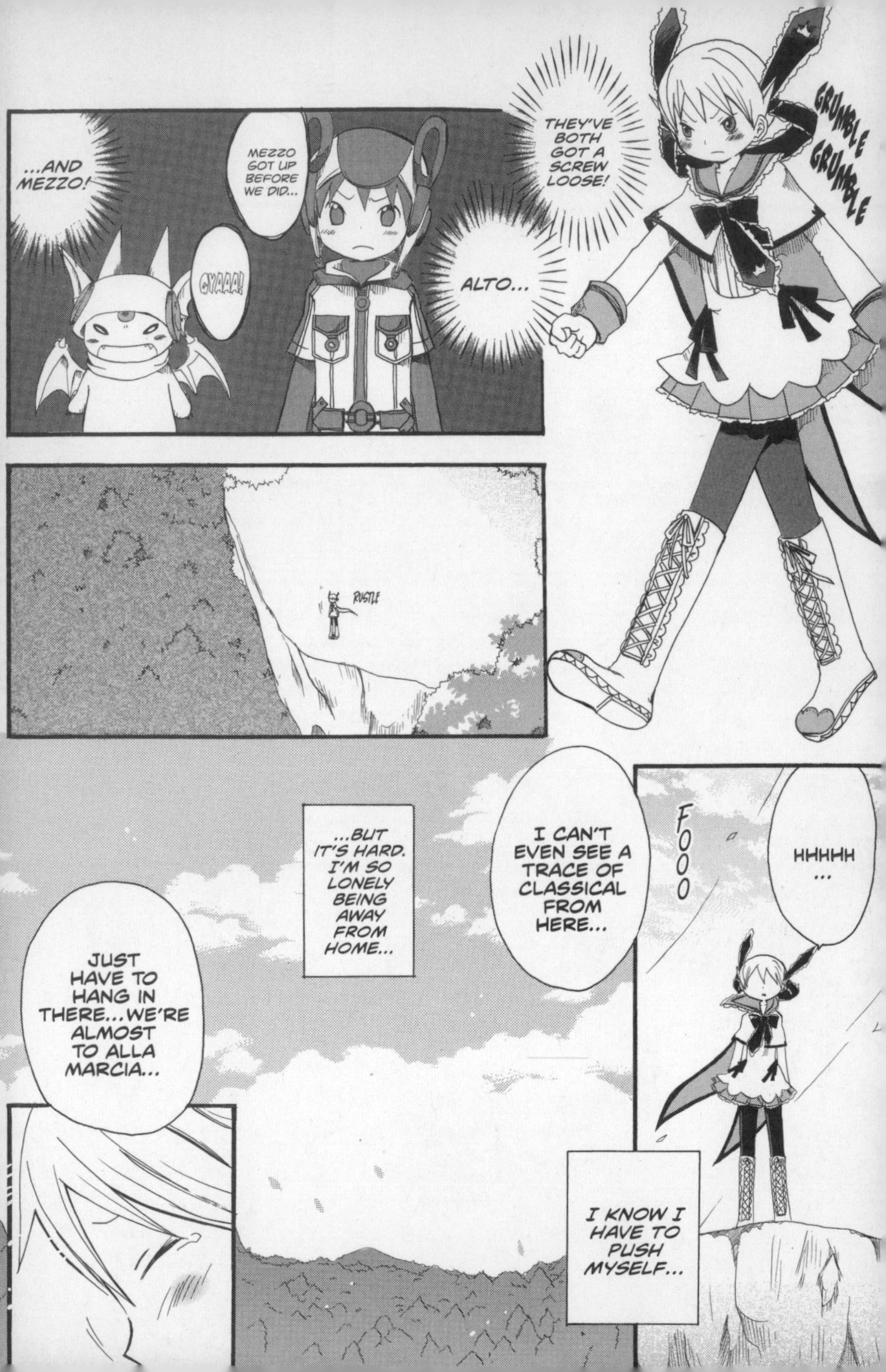
THEY'VE BOTH GOT A SCREW LOOSE!
GRUMBLE GRUMBLE
ALTO...
MEZZO GOT UP BEFORE WE DID...
GYAAA!
...AND MEZZO!
RUSTLE
HHHHH...
FOOO
I CAN'T EVEN SEE A TRACE OF CLASSICAL FROM HERE...
I KNOW I HAVE TO PUSH MYSELF...
...BUT IT'S HARD. I'M SO LONELY BEING AWAY FROM HOME...
JUST HAVE TO HANG IN THERE...WE'RE ALMOST TO ALLA MARCIA...

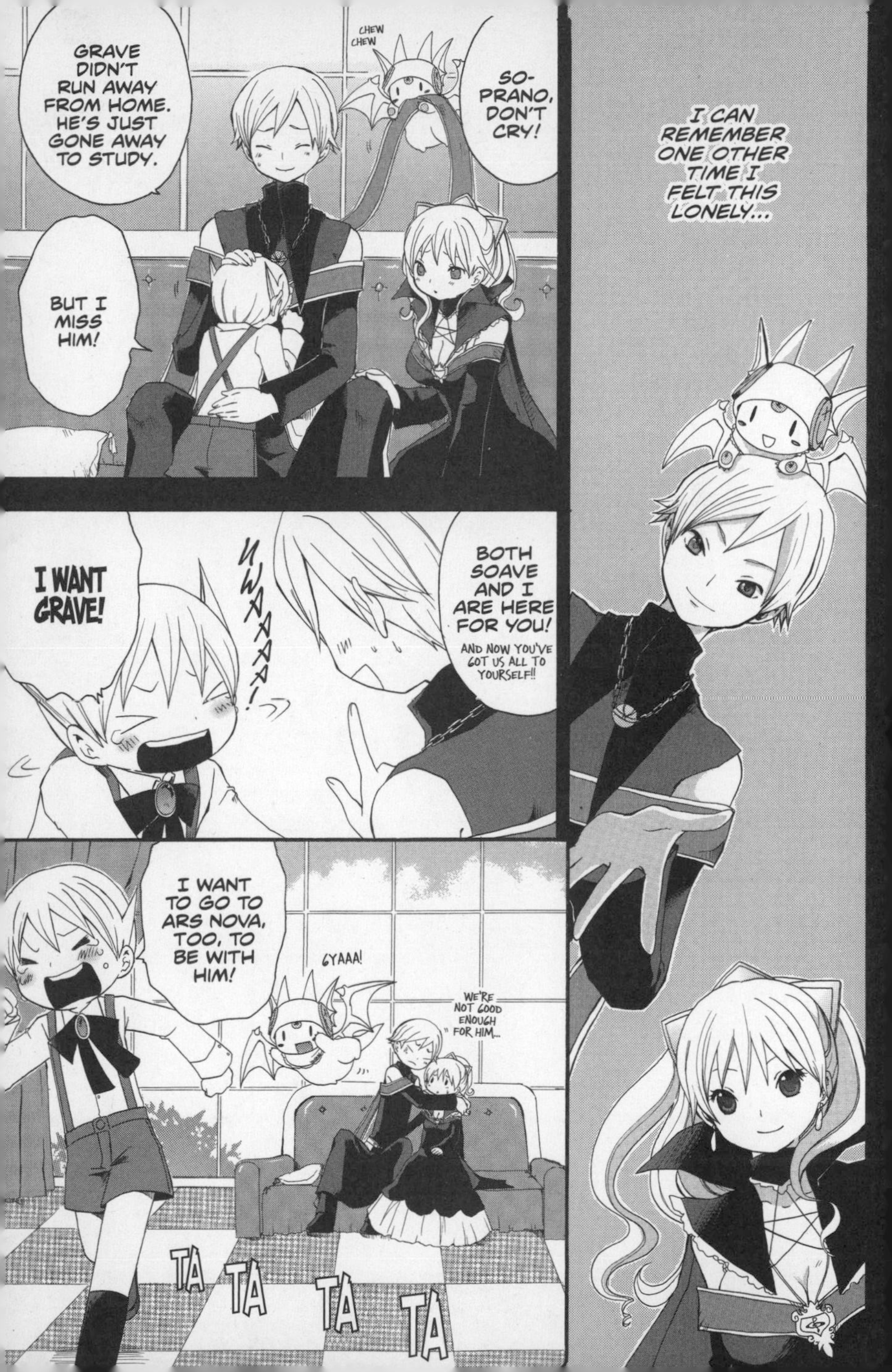

I CAN REMEMBER ONE OTHER TIME I FELT THIS LONELY...
SO-PRANO, DON'T CRY!
CHEW CHEW
GRAVE DIDN'T RUN AWAY FROM HOME. HE'S JUST GONE AWAY TO STUDY.
BUT I MISS HIM!
BOTH SOAVE AND I ARE HERE FOR YOU!
AND NOW YOU'VE GOT US ALL TO YOURSELF!!
UWAAAAA!
I WANT GRAVE!
WE'RE NOT GOOD ENOUGH FOR HIM...
GYAAA!
I WANT TO GO TO ARS NOVA, TOO, TO BE WITH HIM!
TA TA TA TA

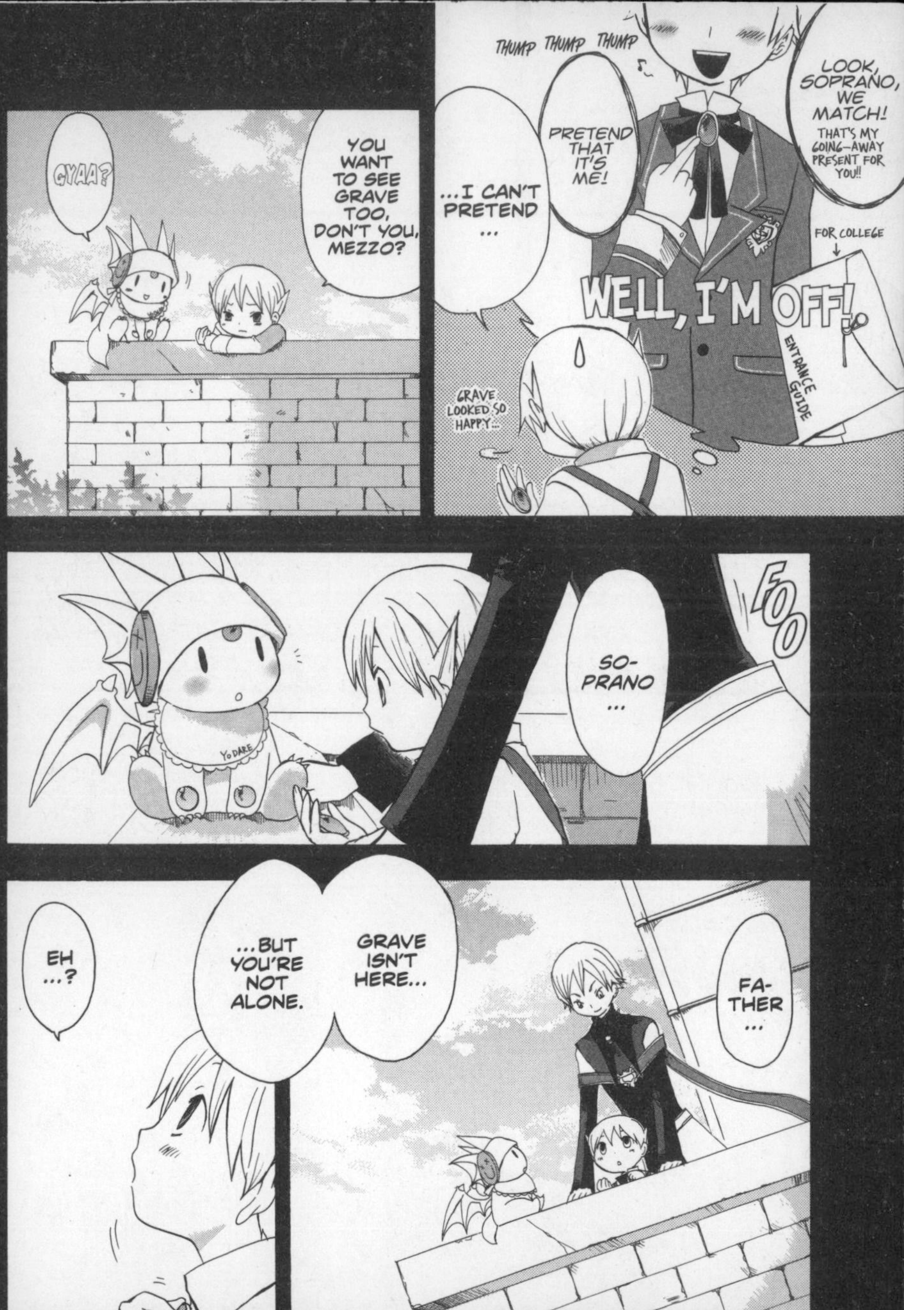
THUMP THUMP THUMP
LOOK, SOPRANO, WE MATCH!
THAT'S MY GOING-AWAY PRESENT FOR YOU!!
PRETEND THAT IT'S ME!
FOR COLLEGE
WELL, I'M OFF!
ENTRANCE GUIDE
...I CAN'T PRETEND...
GRAVE LOOKED SO HAPPY...
YOU WANT TO SEE GRAVE TOO, DON'T YOU, MEZZO?
GYAA?
FOO
SO-PRANO...
YODARE
FA-THER...
GRAVE ISN'T HERE...
...BUT YOU'RE NOT ALONE.
EH...?

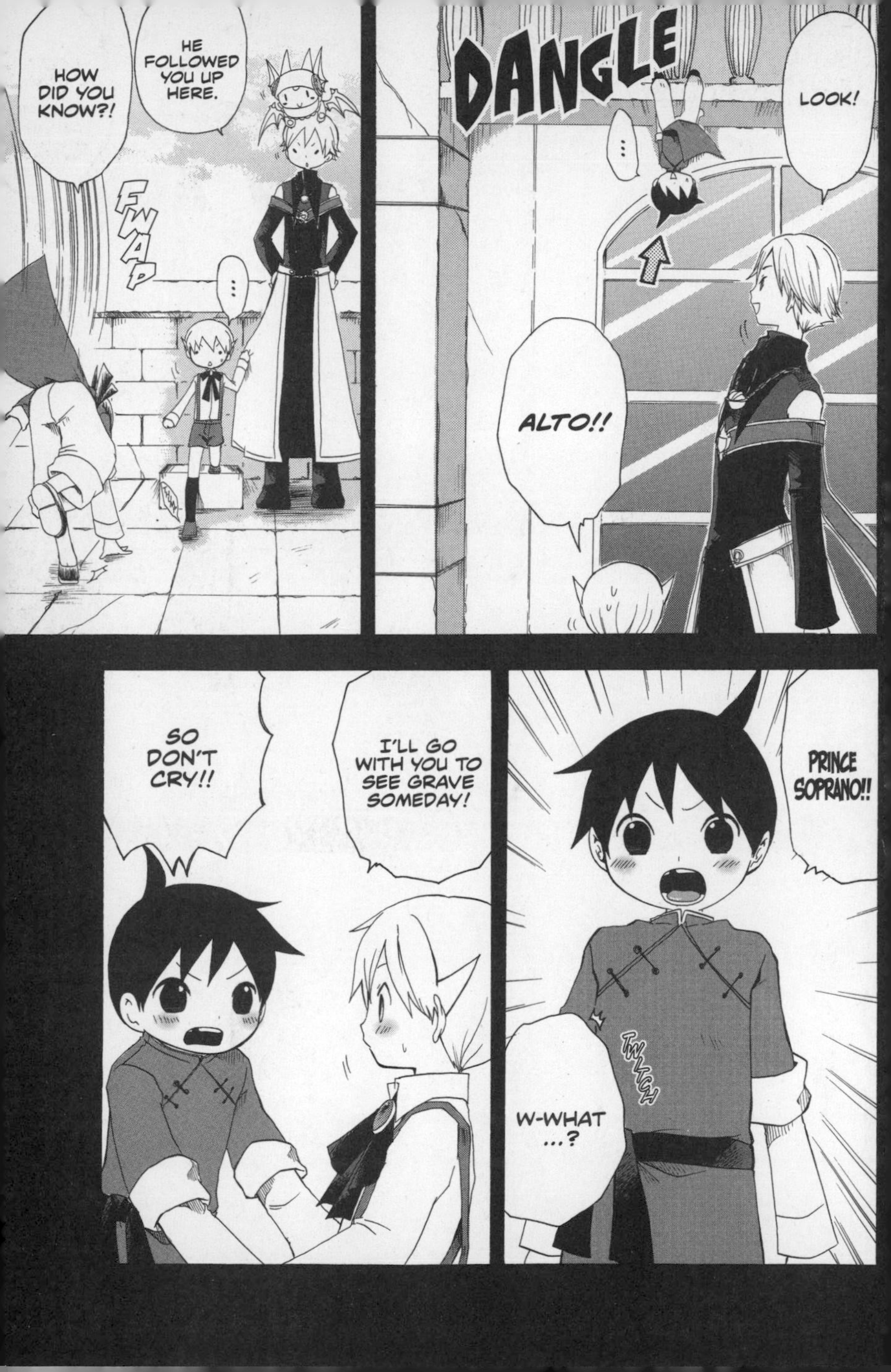
DANGLE
LOOK!
...
ALTO!!
HE FOLLOWED YOU UP HERE.
HOW DID YOU KNOW?!
FWAP
...
PRINCE SOPRANO!!
TWITCH
W-WHAT ...?
I'LL GO WITH YOU TO SEE GRAVE SOMEDAY!
SO DON'T CRY!!

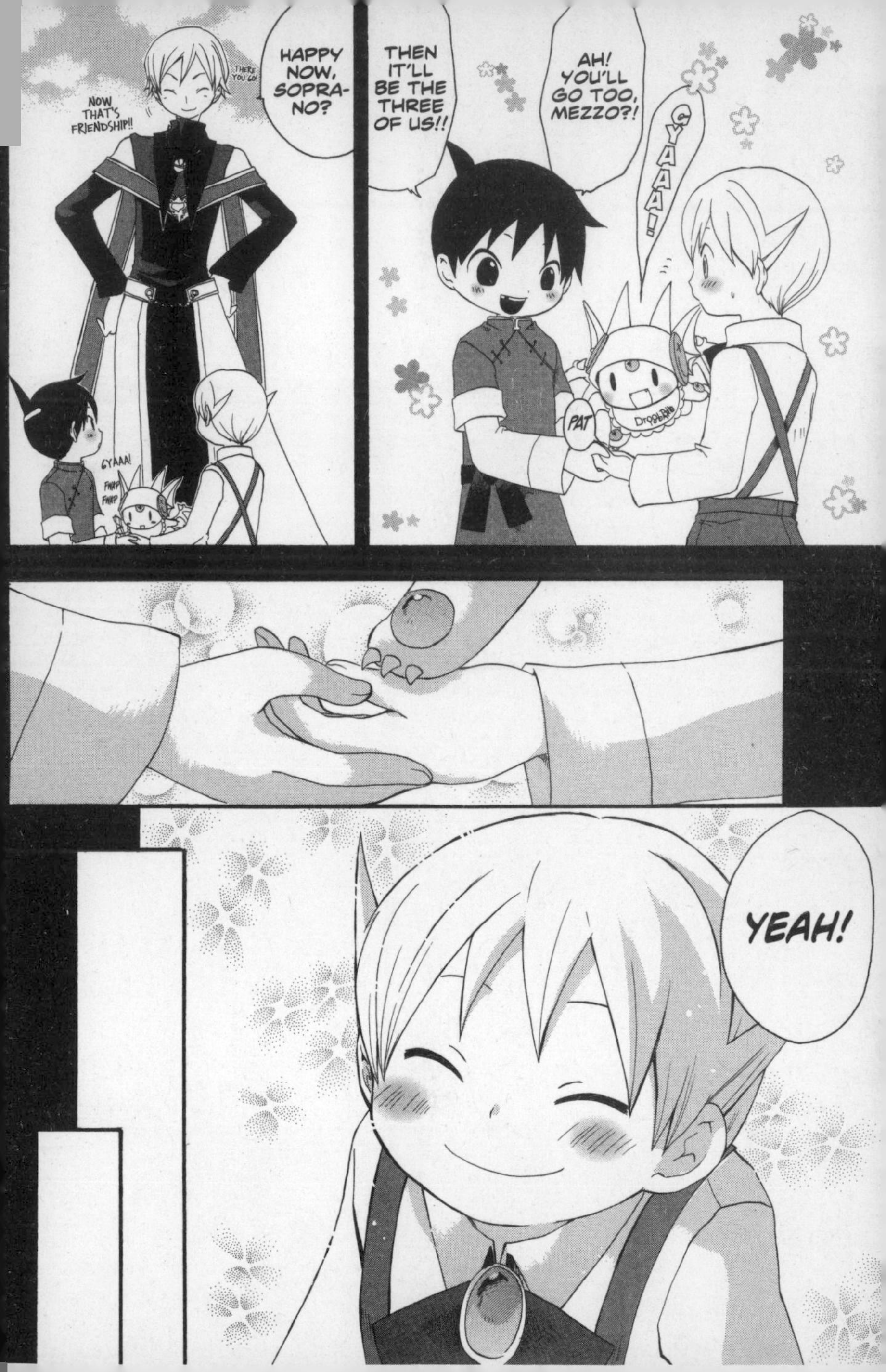

AH! YOU'LL GO TOO, MEZZO?!
GYAAAA!
PAT
THEN IT'LL BE THE THREE OF US!!
HAPPY NOW, SOPRA-NO?
THERE YOU GO!
NOW THAT'S FRIENDSHIP!!
GYAAA!
FWAP FWAP
YEAH!

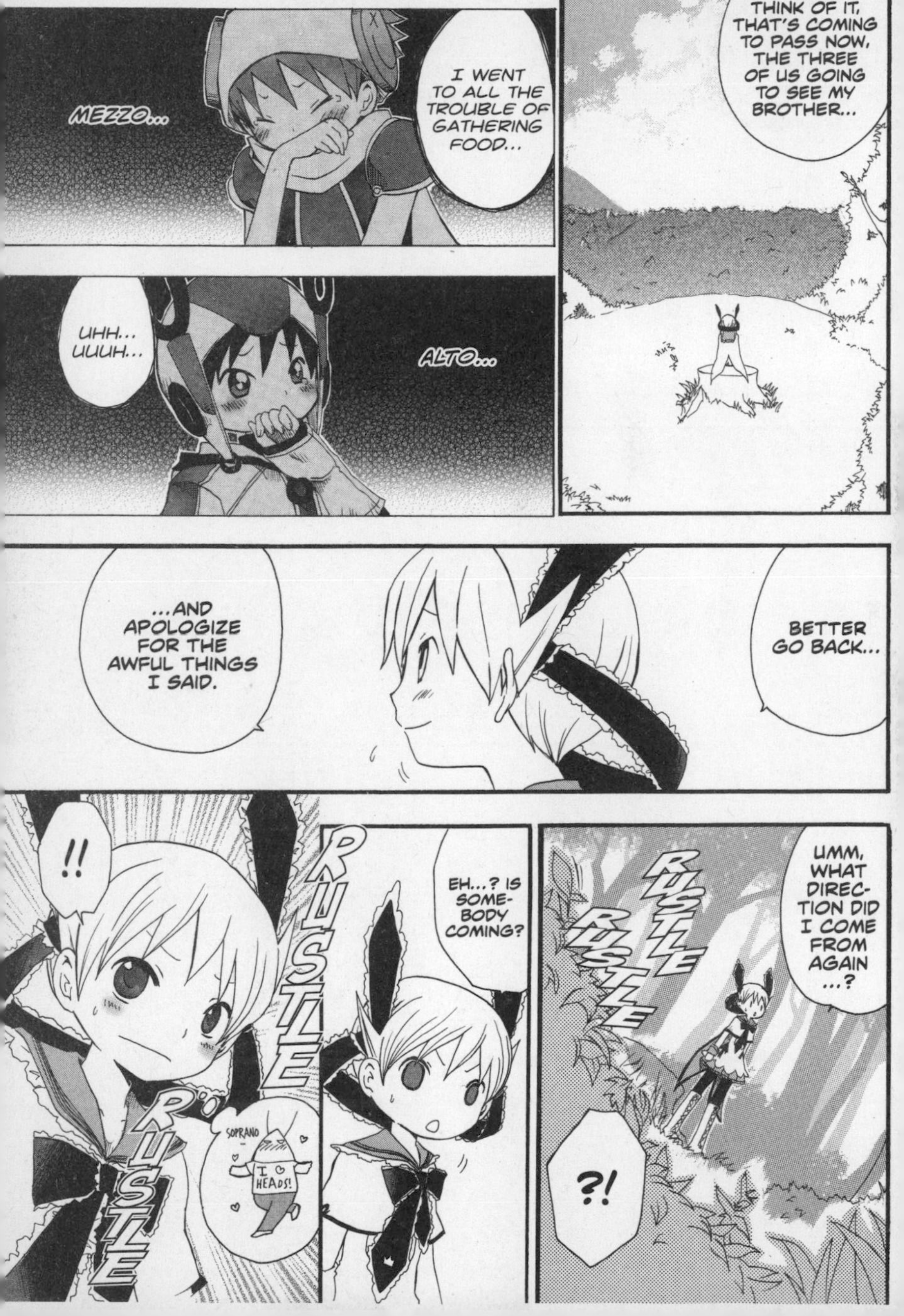
COME TO THINK OF IT, THAT'S COMING TO PASS NOW, THE THREE OF US GOING TO SEE MY BROTHER...
I WENT TO ALL THE TROUBLE OF GATHERING FOOD...
MEZZO...
ALTO...
UHH... UUUH...
BETTER GO BACK...
...AND APOLOGIZE FOR THE AWFUL THINGS I SAID.
UMM, WHAT DIRECTION DID I COME FROM AGAIN ...?
RUSTLE
RUSTLE
?!
EH...? IS SOME-BODY COMING?
RUSTLE
!!
RUSTLE
SOPRANO
I ♡ HEADS!

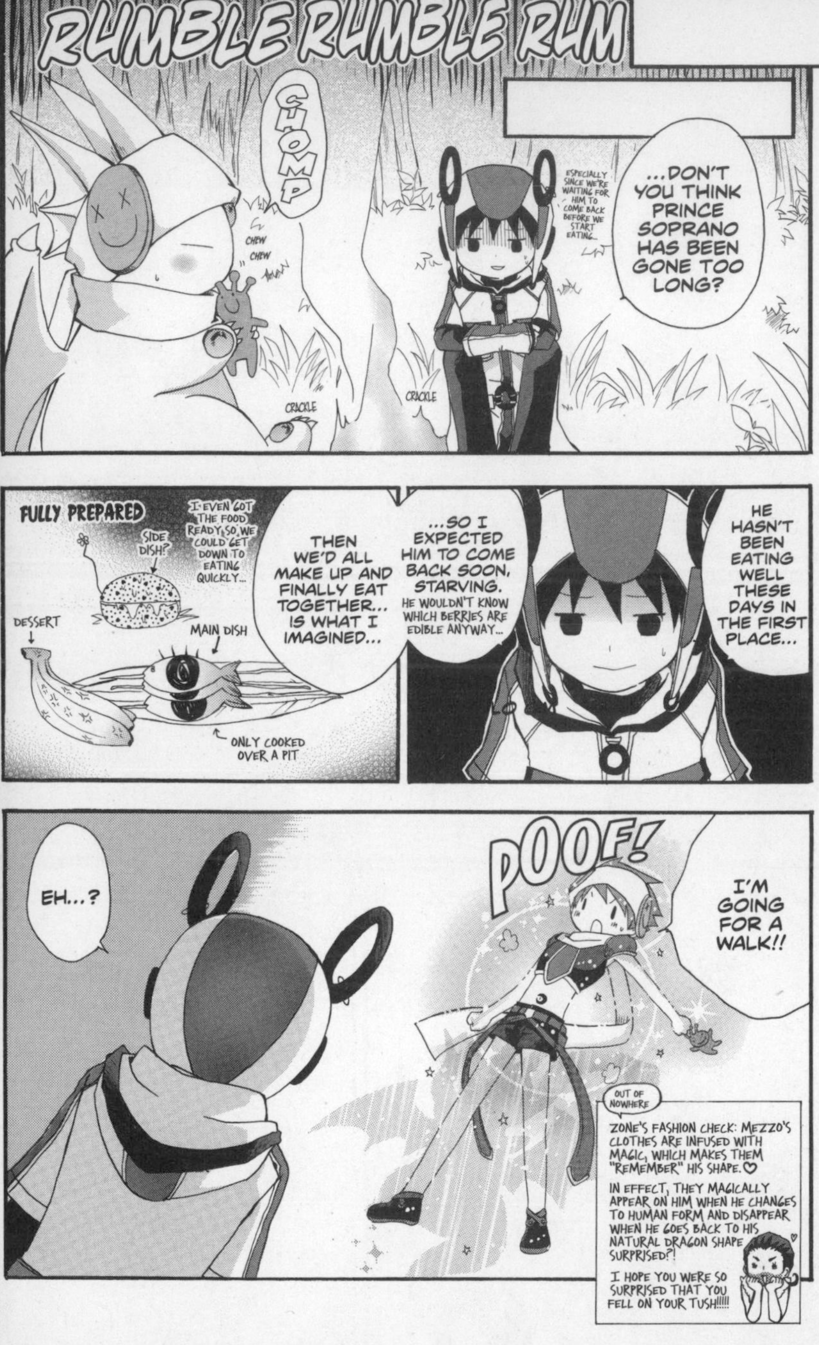
RUMBLE RUMBLE RUM
...DON'T YOU THINK PRINCE SOPRANO HAS BEEN GONE TOO LONG?
ESPECIALLY SINCE WE'RE WAITING FOR HIM TO COME BACK BEFORE WE START EATING
CHOMP
CHEW CHEW
CRACKLE
CRACKLE
HE HASN'T BEEN EATING WELL THESE DAYS IN THE FIRST PLACE...
...SO I EXPECTED HIM TO COME BACK SOON, STARVING.
HE WOULDN'T KNOW WHICH BERRIES ARE EDIBLE ANYWAY...
THEN WE'D ALL MAKE UP AND FINALLY EAT TOGETHER... IS WHAT I IMAGINED...
FULLY PREPARED
I EVEN GOT THE FOOD READY SO WE COULD GET DOWN TO EATING QUICKLY...
SIDE DISH?
MAIN DISH
DESSERT
ONLY COOKED OVER A PIT
POOF!
I'M GOING FOR A WALK!!
EH...?
OUT OF NOWHERE
ZONE'S FASHION CHECK: MEZZO'S CLOTHES ARE INFUSED WITH MAGIC, WHICH MAKES THEM "REMEMBER" HIS SHAPE.♡
IN EFFECT, THEY MAGICALLY APPEAR ON HIM WHEN HE CHANGES TO HUMAN FORM AND DISAPPEAR WHEN HE GOES BACK TO HIS NATURAL DRAGON SHAPE. SURPRISED?!
I HOPE YOU WERE SO SURPRISED THAT YOU FELL ON YOUR TUSH!!!!!

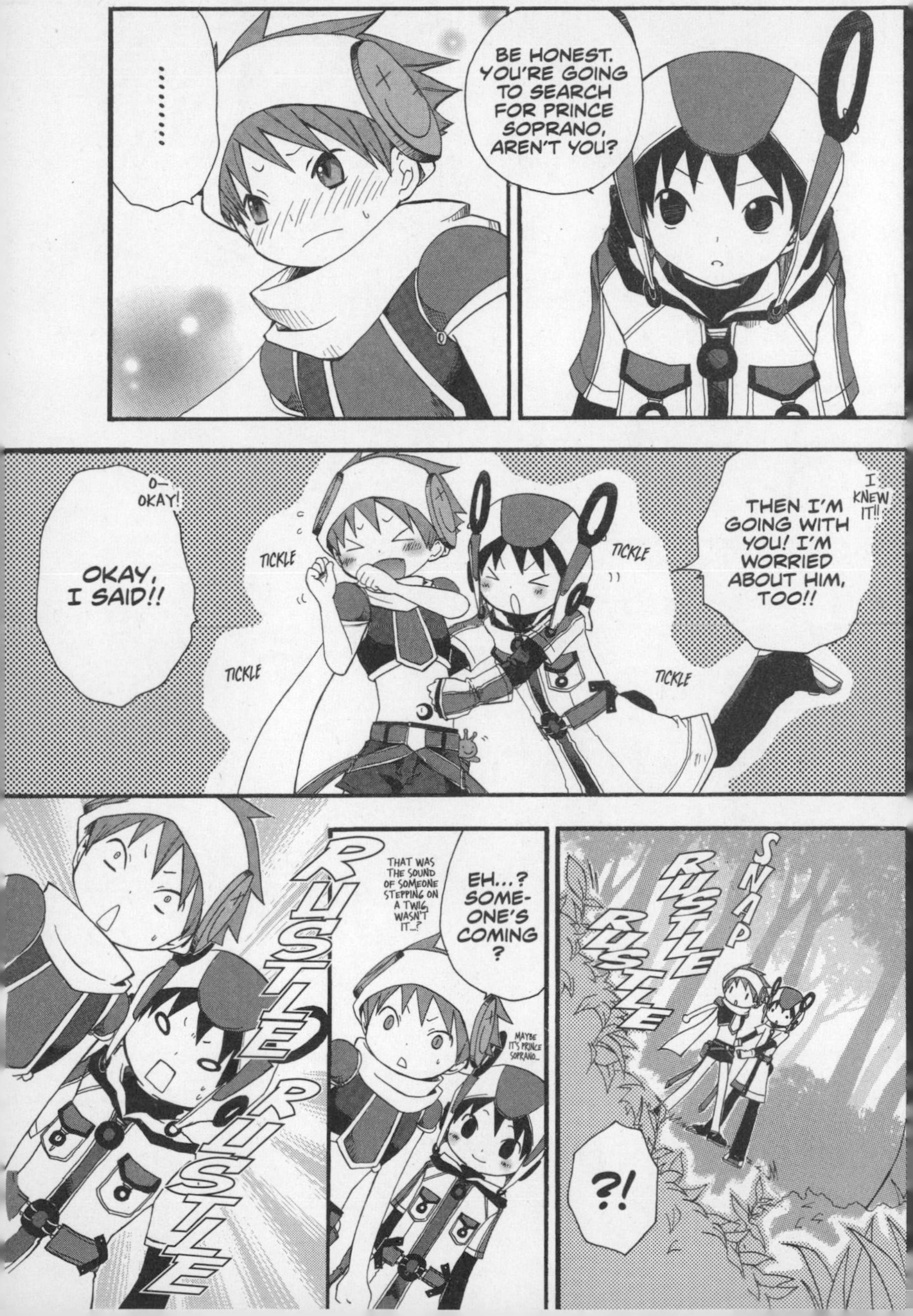
BE HONEST. YOU'RE GOING TO SEARCH FOR PRINCE SOPRANO, AREN'T YOU?
......
I KNEW IT!!
THEN I'M GOING WITH YOU! I'M WORRIED ABOUT HIM, TOO!!
TICKLE
TICKLE
TICKLE
TICKLE
O-OKAY!
OKAY, I SAID!!
SNAP
RUSTLE
RUSTLE
?!
EH...? SOME-ONE'S COMING?
THAT WAS THE SOUND OF SOMEONE STEPPING ON A TWIG, WASN'T IT...?
MAYBE IT'S PRINCE SOPRANO...
RUSTLE
RUSTLE

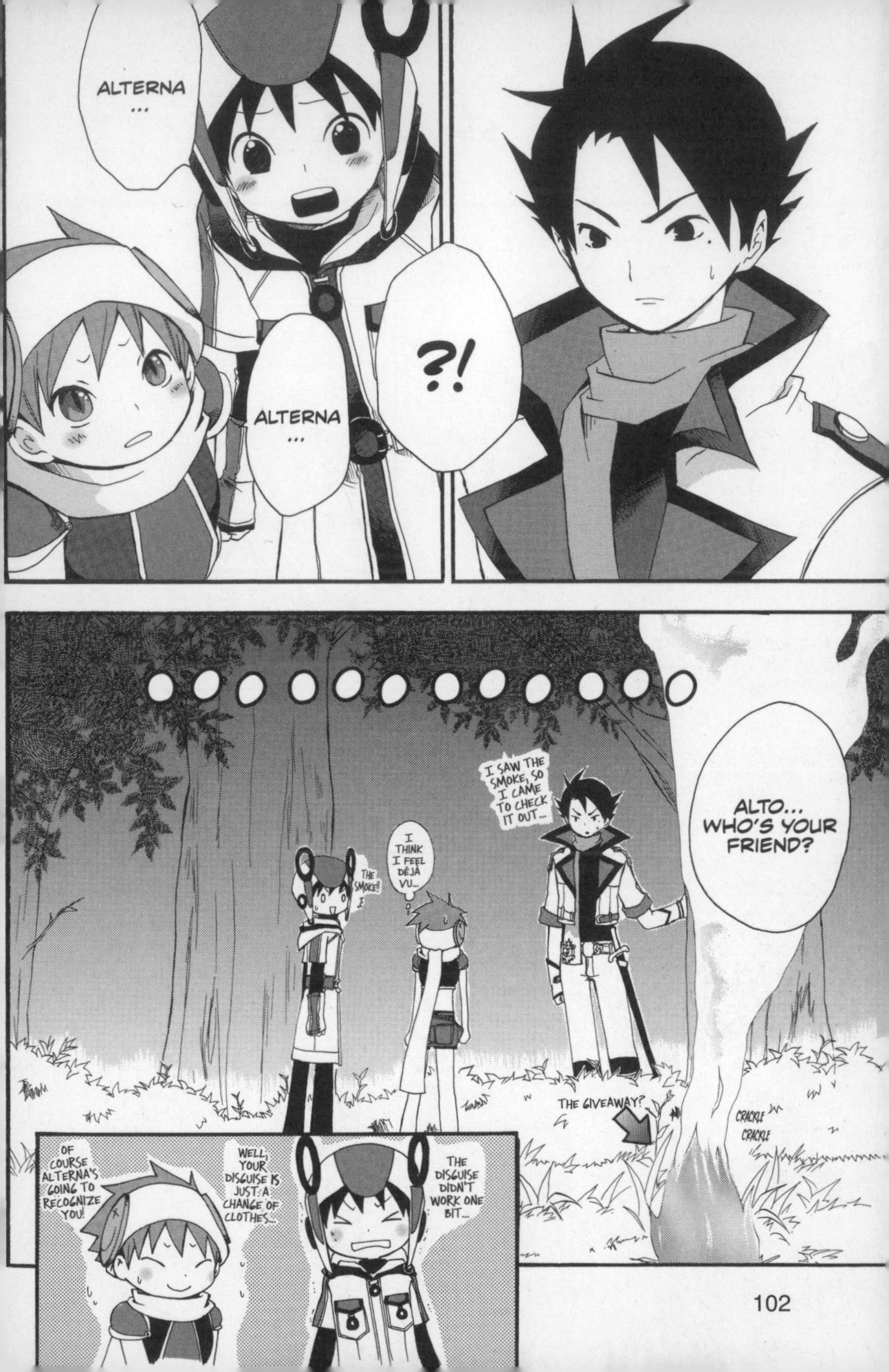
ALTERNA ...
?!
ALTERNA ...
ALTO... WHO'S YOUR FRIEND?
I SAW THE SMOKE, SO I CAME TO CHECK IT OUT...
I THINK I FEEL DÉJÀ VU...
THE SMOKE!!
THE GIVEAWAY?
CRACKLE CRACKLE
THE DISGUISE DIDN'T WORK ONE BIT...
WELL, YOUR DISGUISE IS JUST A CHANGE OF CLOTHES...
OF COURSE ALTERNA'S GOING TO RECOGNIZE YOU!

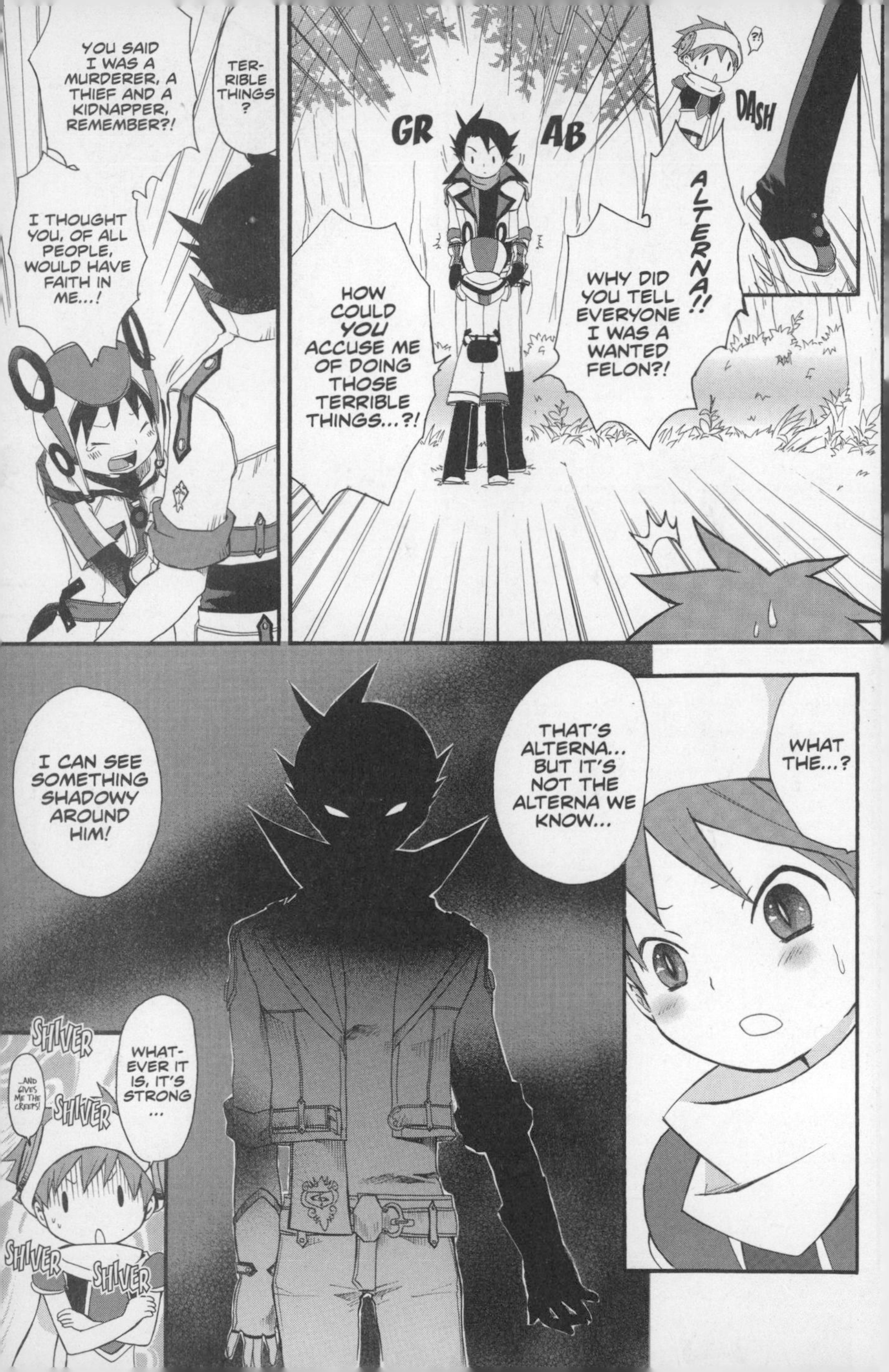
?!
DASH
ALTERNA!!
WHY DID YOU TELL EVERYONE I WAS A WANTED FELON?!
GR AB
HOW COULD YOU ACCUSE ME OF DOING THOSE TERRIBLE THINGS...?!
TER-RIBLE THINGS?
YOU SAID I WAS A MURDERER, A THIEF AND A KIDNAPPER, REMEMBER?!
I THOUGHT YOU, OF ALL PEOPLE, WOULD HAVE FAITH IN ME...!
WHAT THE...?
THAT'S ALTERNA... BUT IT'S NOT THE ALTERNA WE KNOW...
I CAN SEE SOMETHING SHADOWY AROUND HIM!
SHIVER
WHAT-EVER IT IS, IT'S STRONG...
SHIVER
...AND GIVES ME THE CREEPS!
SHIVER
SHIVER

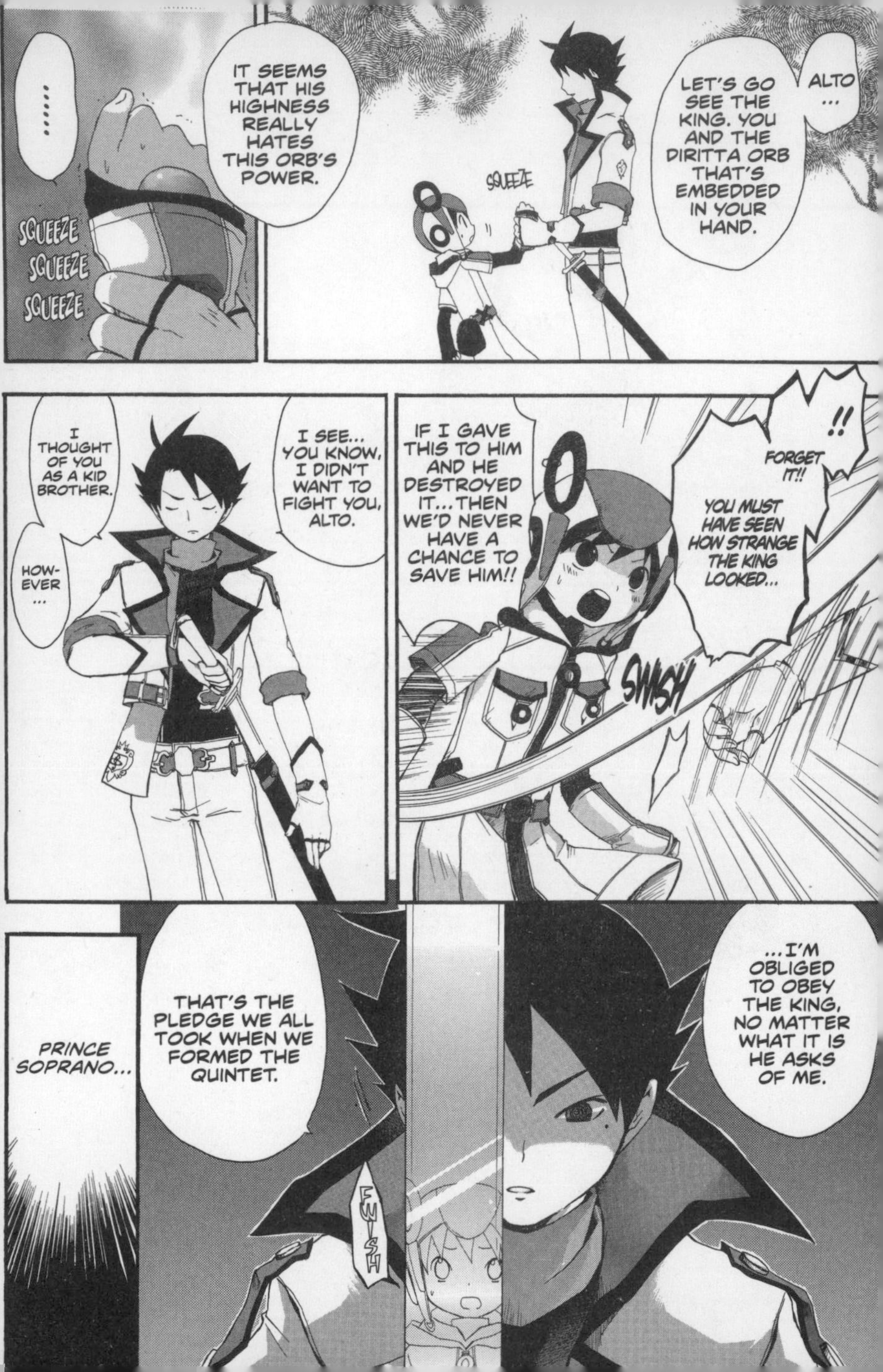
ALTO ...
LET'S GO SEE THE KING. YOU AND THE DIRITTA ORB THAT'S EMBEDDED IN YOUR HAND.
SQUEEZE
IT SEEMS THAT HIS HIGHNESS REALLY HATES THIS ORB'S POWER.
......
SQUEEZE
SQUEEZE
SQUEEZE
!!
FORGET IT!!
YOU MUST HAVE SEEN HOW STRANGE THE KING LOOKED...
IF I GAVE THIS TO HIM AND HE DESTROYED IT... THEN WE'D NEVER HAVE A CHANCE TO SAVE HIM!!
SWISH
I SEE... YOU KNOW, I DIDN'T WANT TO FIGHT YOU, ALTO.
I THOUGHT OF YOU AS A KID BROTHER.
HOW-EVER ...
...I'M OBLIGED TO OBEY THE KING, NO MATTER WHAT IT IS HE ASKS OF ME.
THAT'S THE PLEDGE WE ALL TOOK WHEN WE FORMED THE QUINTET.
FWISH
PRINCE SOPRANO...

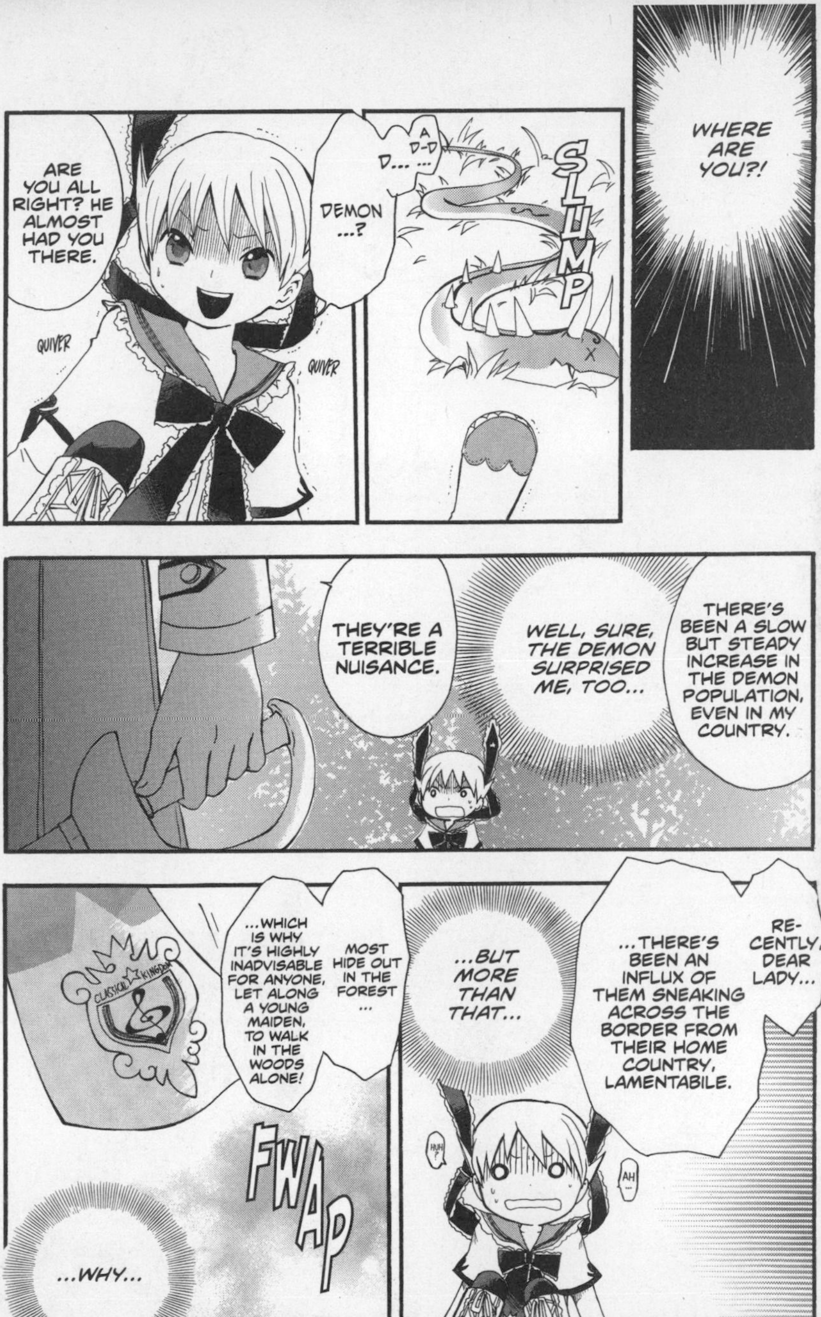

WHERE ARE YOU?!
A D-D D... ...
DEMON ...?
SLUMP
ARE YOU ALL RIGHT? HE ALMOST HAD YOU THERE.
QUIVER
QUIVER
THERE'S BEEN A SLOW BUT STEADY INCREASE IN THE DEMON POPULATION, EVEN IN MY COUNTRY.
WELL, SURE, THE DEMON SURPRISED ME, TOO...
THEY'RE A TERRIBLE NUISANCE.
RE-CENTLY, DEAR LADY...
...THERE'S BEEN AN INFLUX OF THEM SNEAKING ACROSS THE BORDER FROM THEIR HOME COUNTRY, LAMENTABILE.
...BUT MORE THAN THAT...
HUH?
AH ...
MOST HIDE OUT IN THE FOREST ...
...WHICH IS WHY IT'S HIGHLY INADVISABLE FOR ANYONE, LET ALONG A YOUNG MAIDEN, TO WALK IN THE WOODS ALONE!
CLASSICAL KINGDOM
FWAP
...WHY...

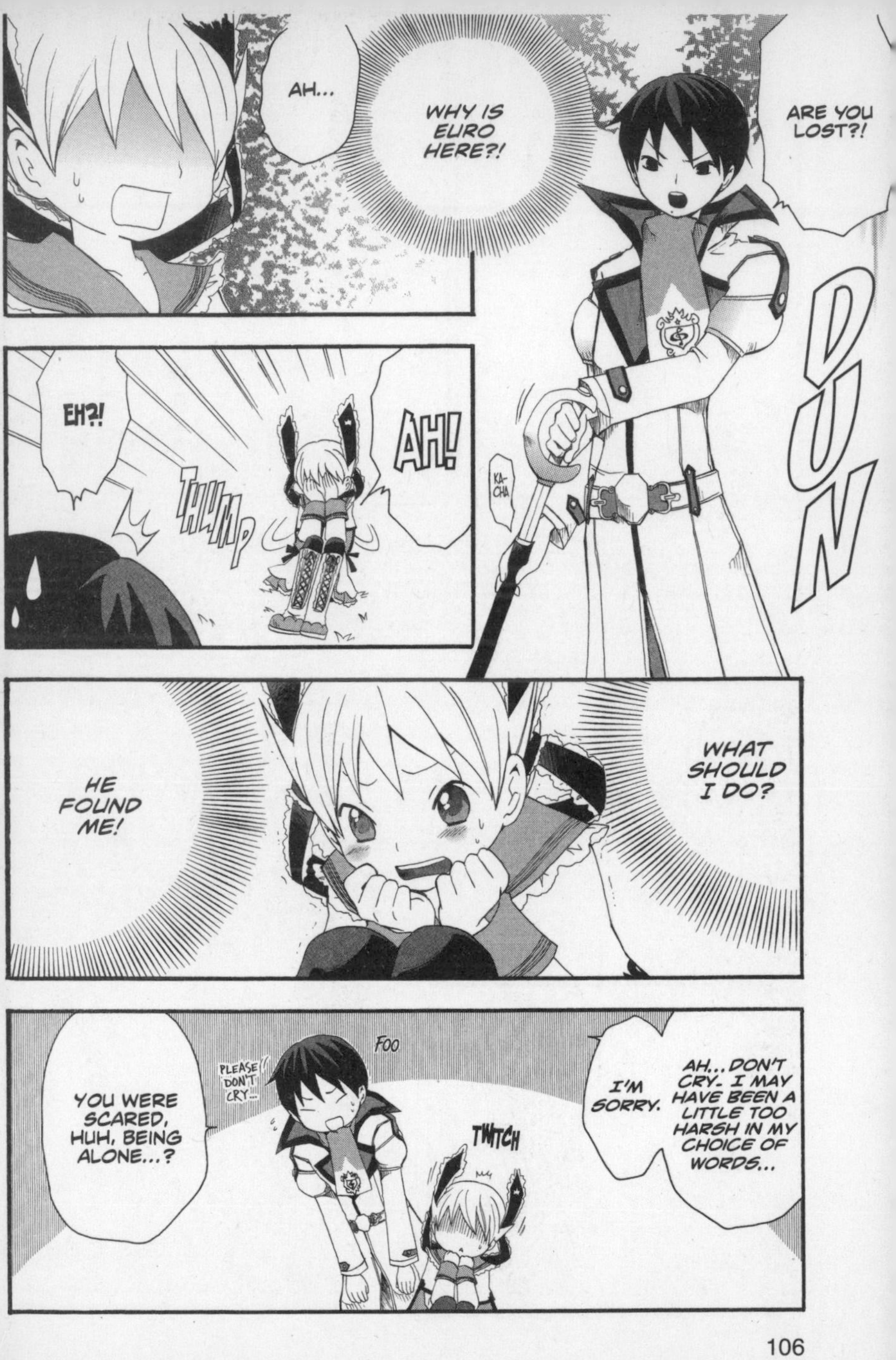
ARE YOU LOST?!
DUN
KA-CHA
WHY IS EURO HERE?!
AH...
AH!
THUMP
EH?!
WHAT SHOULD I DO?
HE FOUND ME!
AH... DON'T CRY. I MAY HAVE BEEN A LITTLE TOO HARSH IN MY CHOICE OF WORDS...
I'M SORRY.
TWITCH
FOO
PLEASE DON'T CRY...
YOU WERE SCARED, HUH, BEING ALONE...?

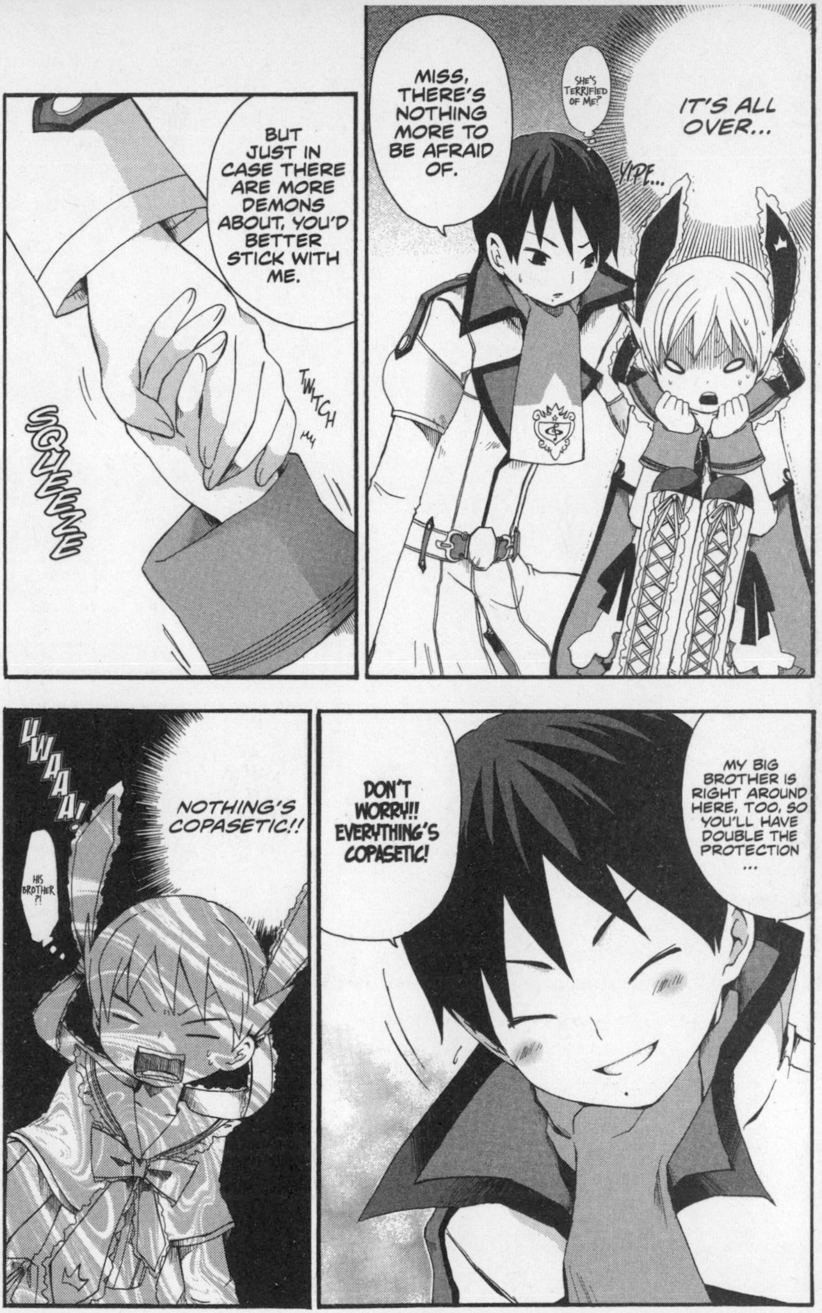

MISS, THERE'S NOTHING MORE TO BE AFRAID OF.
SHE'S TERRIFIED OF ME?
IT'S ALL OVER...
YIPE...
BUT JUST IN CASE THERE ARE MORE DEMONS ABOUT, YOU'D BETTER STICK WITH ME.
TWITCH
SQUEEZE
MY BIG BROTHER IS RIGHT AROUND HERE, TOO, SO YOU'LL HAVE DOUBLE THE PROTECTION ...
DON'T WORRY!! EVERYTHING'S COPASETIC!
NOTHING'S COPASETIC!!
HIS BROTHER ?!
UWAAA!

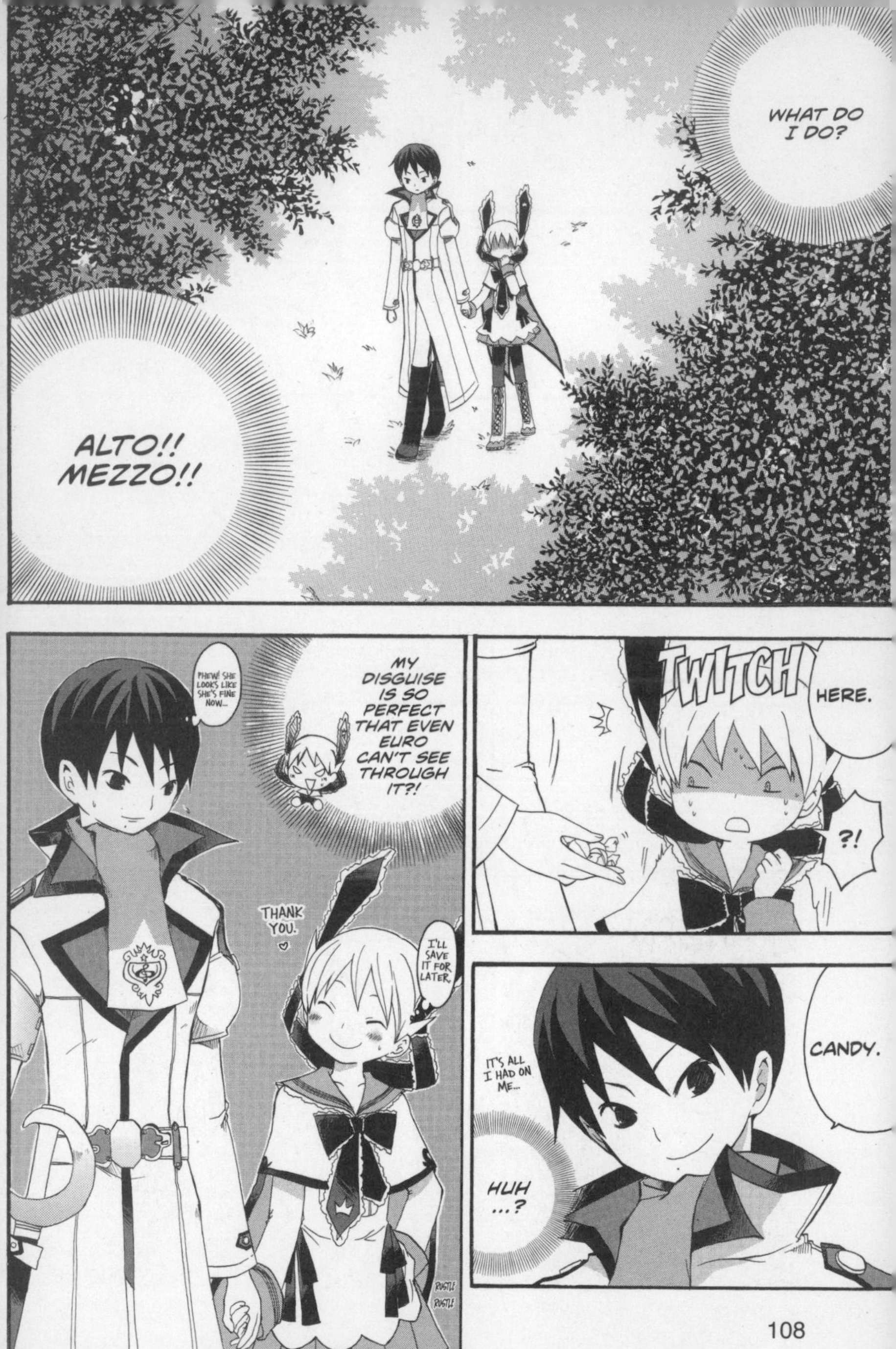
WHAT DO I DO?
ALTO!! MEZZO!!
TWITCH
HERE.
?!
CANDY.
IT'S ALL I HAD ON ME...
HUH ...?
MY DISGUISE IS SO PERFECT THAT EVEN EURO CAN'T SEE THROUGH IT?!
PHEW! SHE LOOKS LIKE SHE'S FINE NOW...
THANK YOU.
I'LL SAVE IT FOR LATER.
RUSTLE RUSTLE

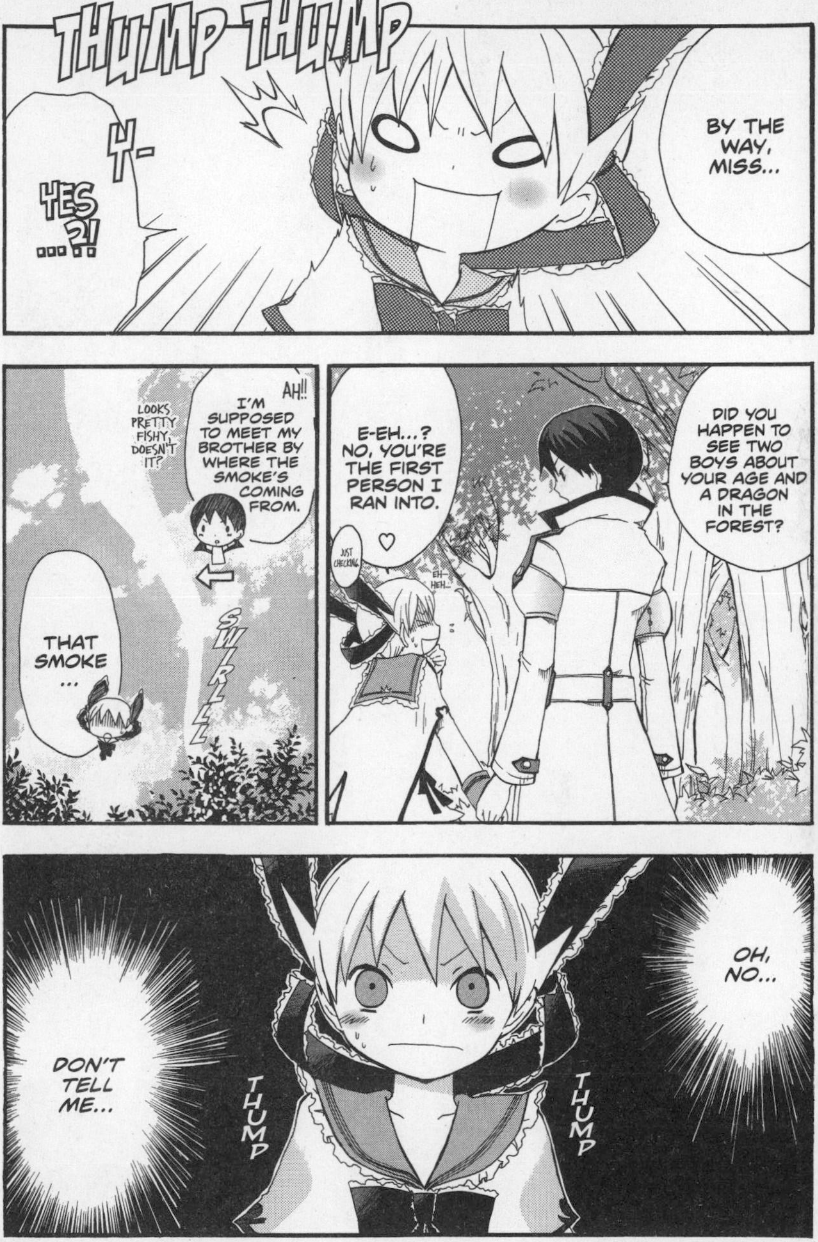
BY THE WAY, MISS...
THUMP THUMP
Y-YES...?!
DID YOU HAPPEN TO SEE TWO BOYS ABOUT YOUR AGE AND A DRAGON IN THE FOREST?
E-EH...? NO, YOU'RE THE FIRST PERSON I RAN INTO.
JUST CHECKING.
EH-HEH...
AH!! I'M SUPPOSED TO MEET MY BROTHER BY WHERE THE SMOKE'S COMING FROM.
LOOKS PRETTY FISHY, DOESN'T IT?
SWIRLLL
THAT SMOKE...
OH, NO...
THUMP
THUMP
DON'T TELL ME...

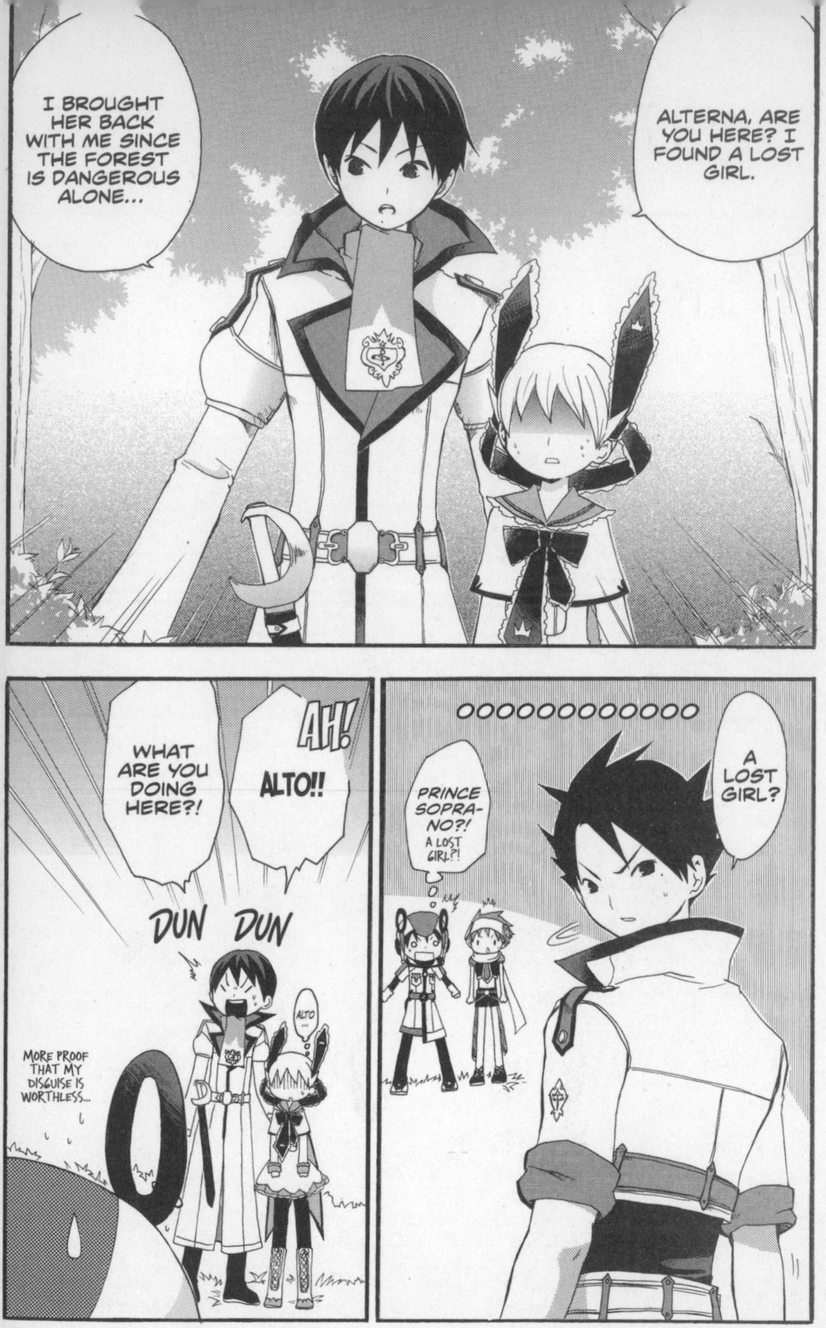
ALTERNA, ARE YOU HERE? I FOUND A LOST GIRL.
I BROUGHT HER BACK WITH ME SINCE THE FOREST IS DANGEROUS ALONE...
OOOOOOOOOOOO
A LOST GIRL?
PRINCE SOPRANO?! A LOST GIRL?!
AH!
ALTO!!
WHAT ARE YOU DOING HERE?!
DUN DUN
ALTO...
MORE PROOF THAT MY DISGUISE IS WORTHLESS...

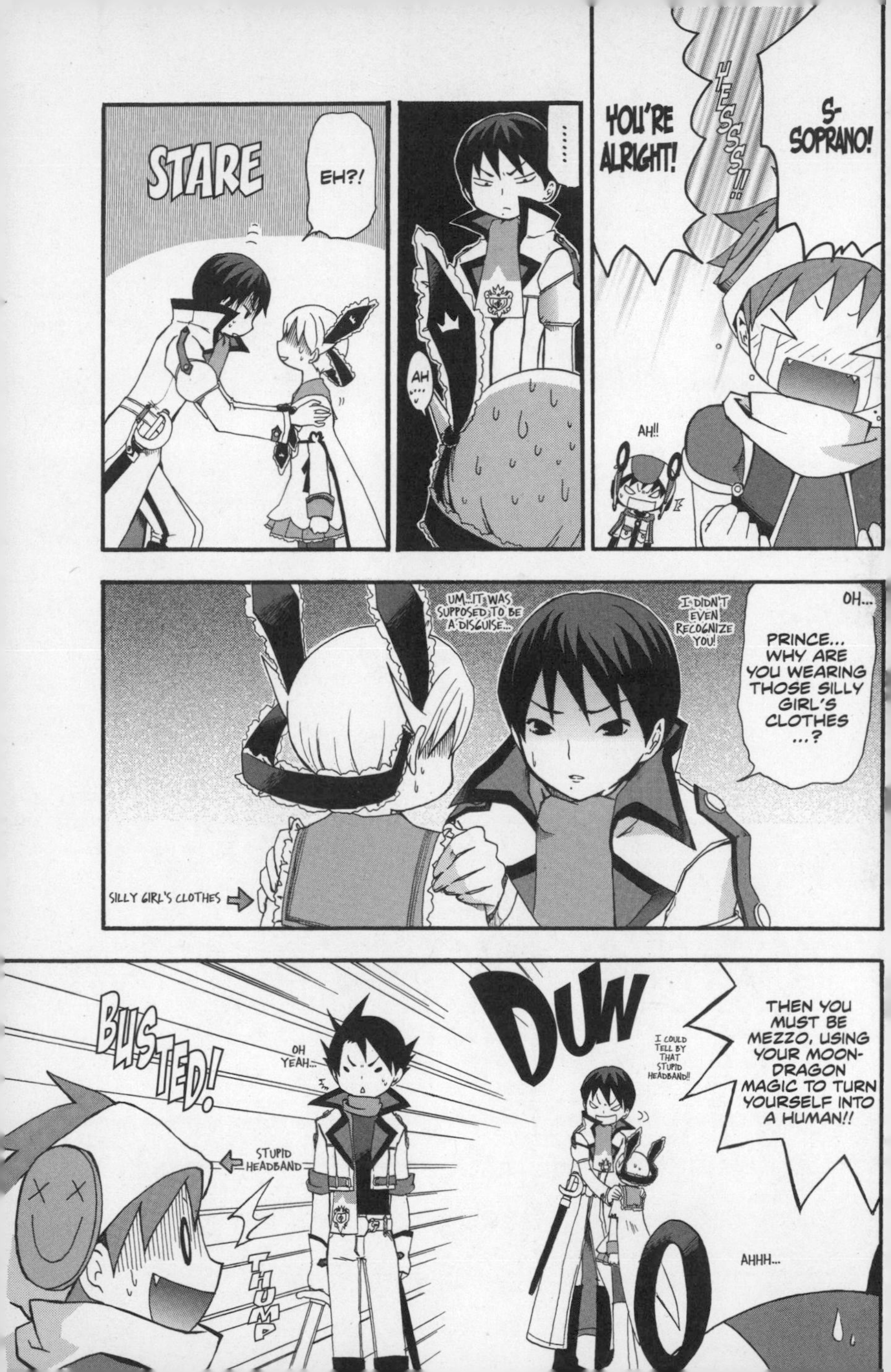
S-
SOPRANO!
HESSS!!
YOU'RE ALRIGHT!
AH!!
......
AH ...
EH?!
STARE
OH...
PRINCE... WHY ARE YOU WEARING THOSE SILLY GIRL'S CLOTHES ...?
I DIDN'T EVEN RECOGNIZE YOU!
UM...IT WAS SUPPOSED TO BE A DISGUISE...
SILLY GIRL'S CLOTHES
THEN YOU MUST BE MEZZO, USING YOUR MOON-DRAGON MAGIC TO TURN YOURSELF INTO A HUMAN!!
AHHH...
I COULD TELL BY THAT STUPID HEADBAND!!
DUN
OH YEAH...
BUSTED!
STUPID HEADBAND
THUMP

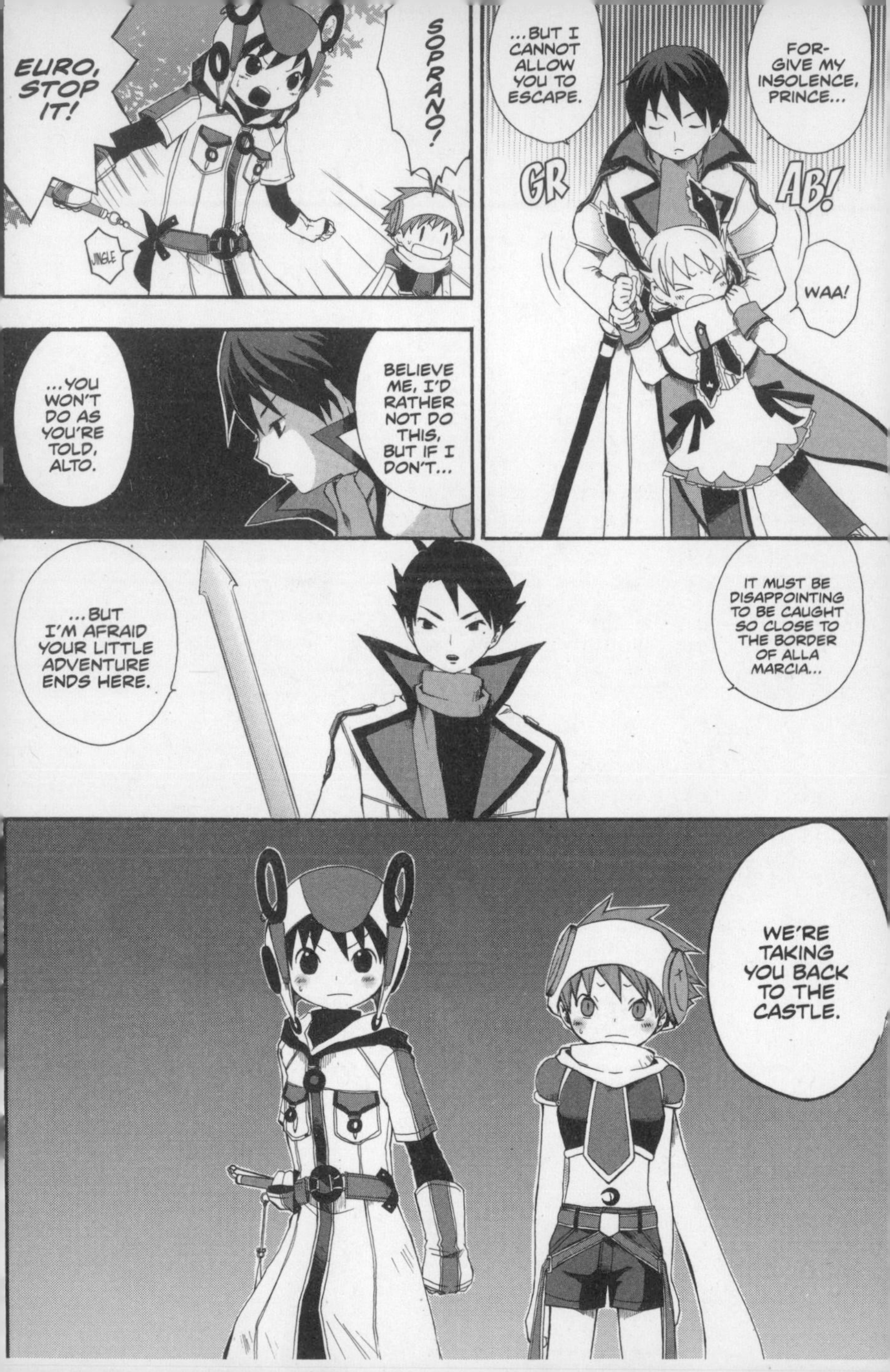
FOR-GIVE MY INSOLENCE, PRINCE...
...BUT I CANNOT ALLOW YOU TO ESCAPE.
GR
AB!
WAA!
SOPRANO!
EURO, STOP IT!
JINGLE
BELIEVE ME, I'D RATHER NOT DO THIS, BUT IF I DON'T...
...YOU WON'T DO AS YOU'RE TOLD, ALTO.
IT MUST BE DISAPPOINTING TO BE CAUGHT SO CLOSE TO THE BORDER OF ALLA MARCIA...
...BUT I'M AFRAID YOUR LITTLE ADVENTURE ENDS HERE.
WE'RE TAKING YOU BACK TO THE CASTLE.

OP5: Eurobeat Alternative

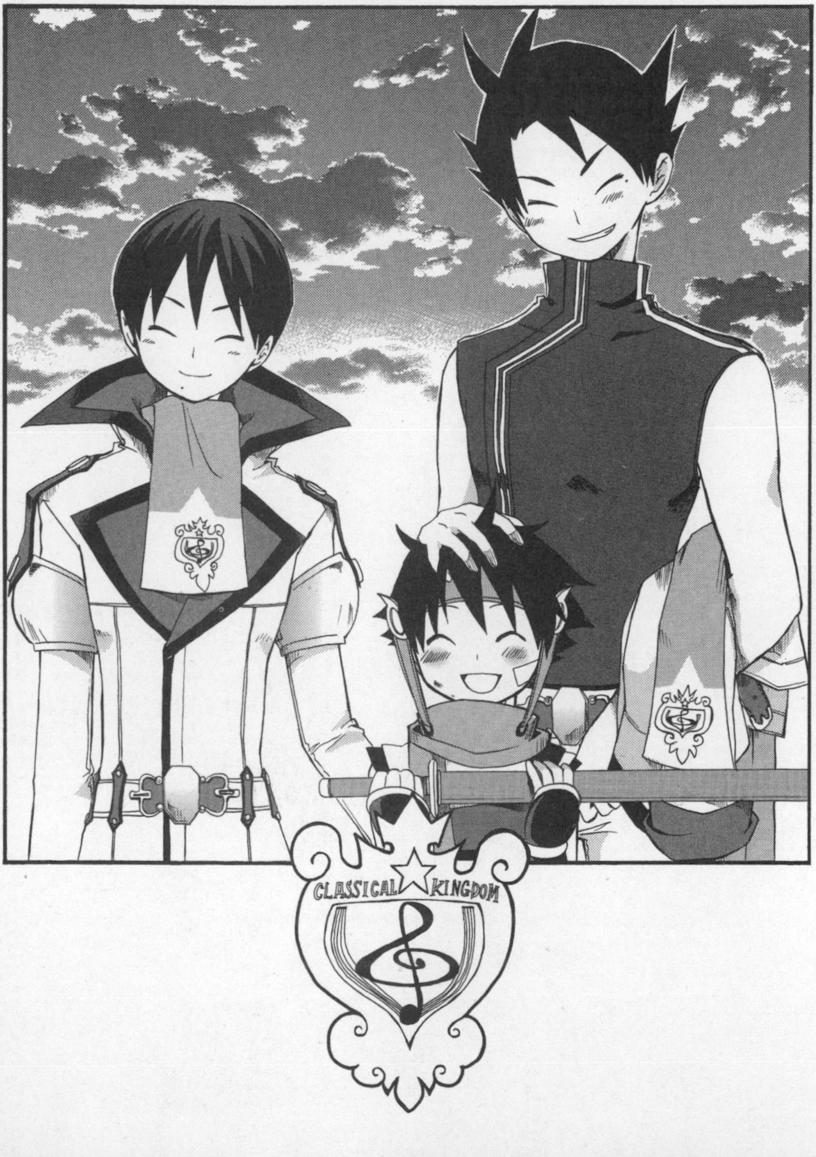
CLASSICAL KINGDOM

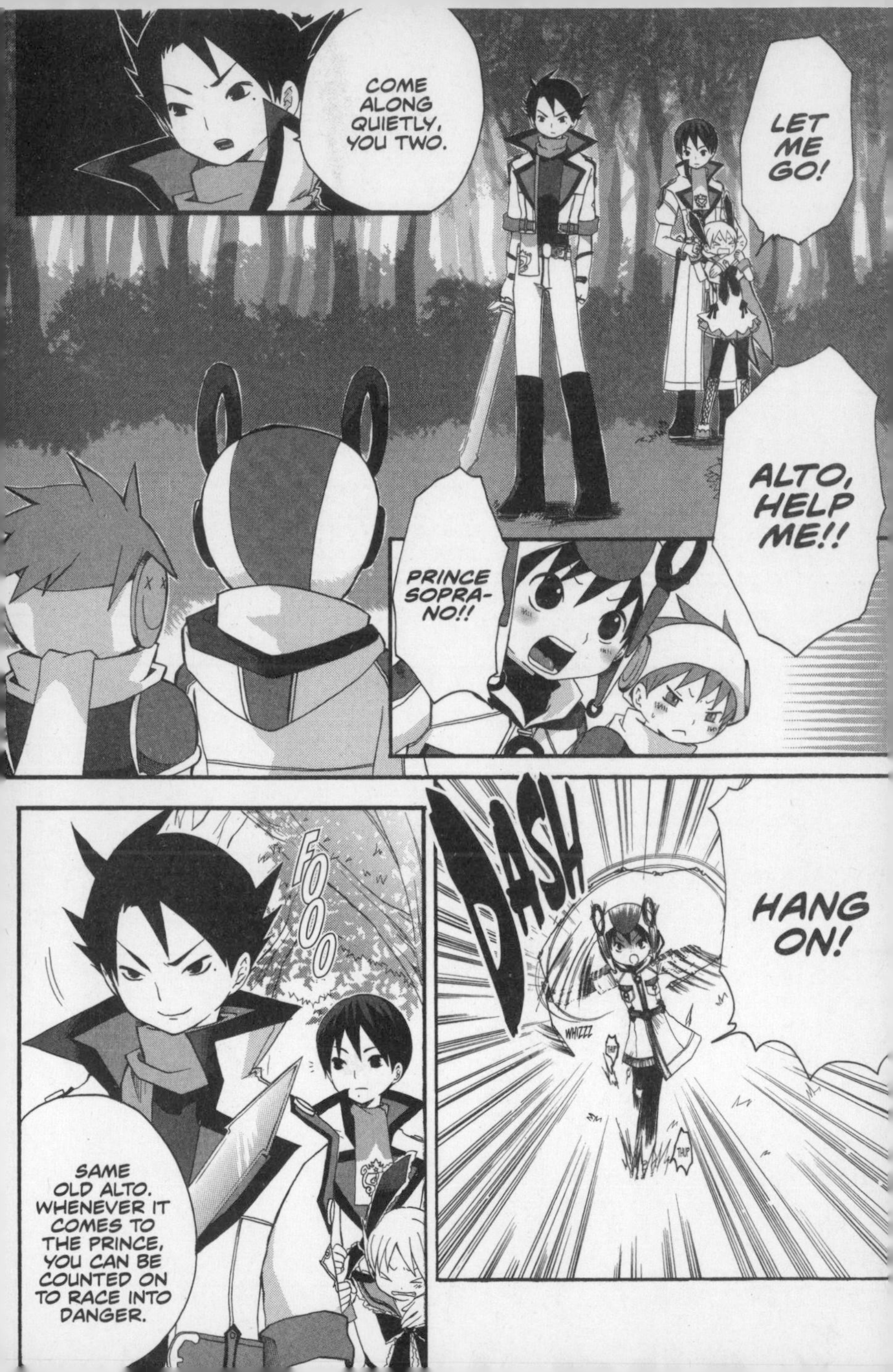
LET ME GO!
COME ALONG QUIETLY, YOU TWO.
ALTO, HELP ME!!
PRINCE SOPRANO!!
DASH
HANG ON!
WHIZZZ
THUP
THUP
FOOO
SAME OLD ALTO. WHENEVER IT COMES TO THE PRINCE, YOU CAN BE COUNTED ON TO RACE INTO DANGER.

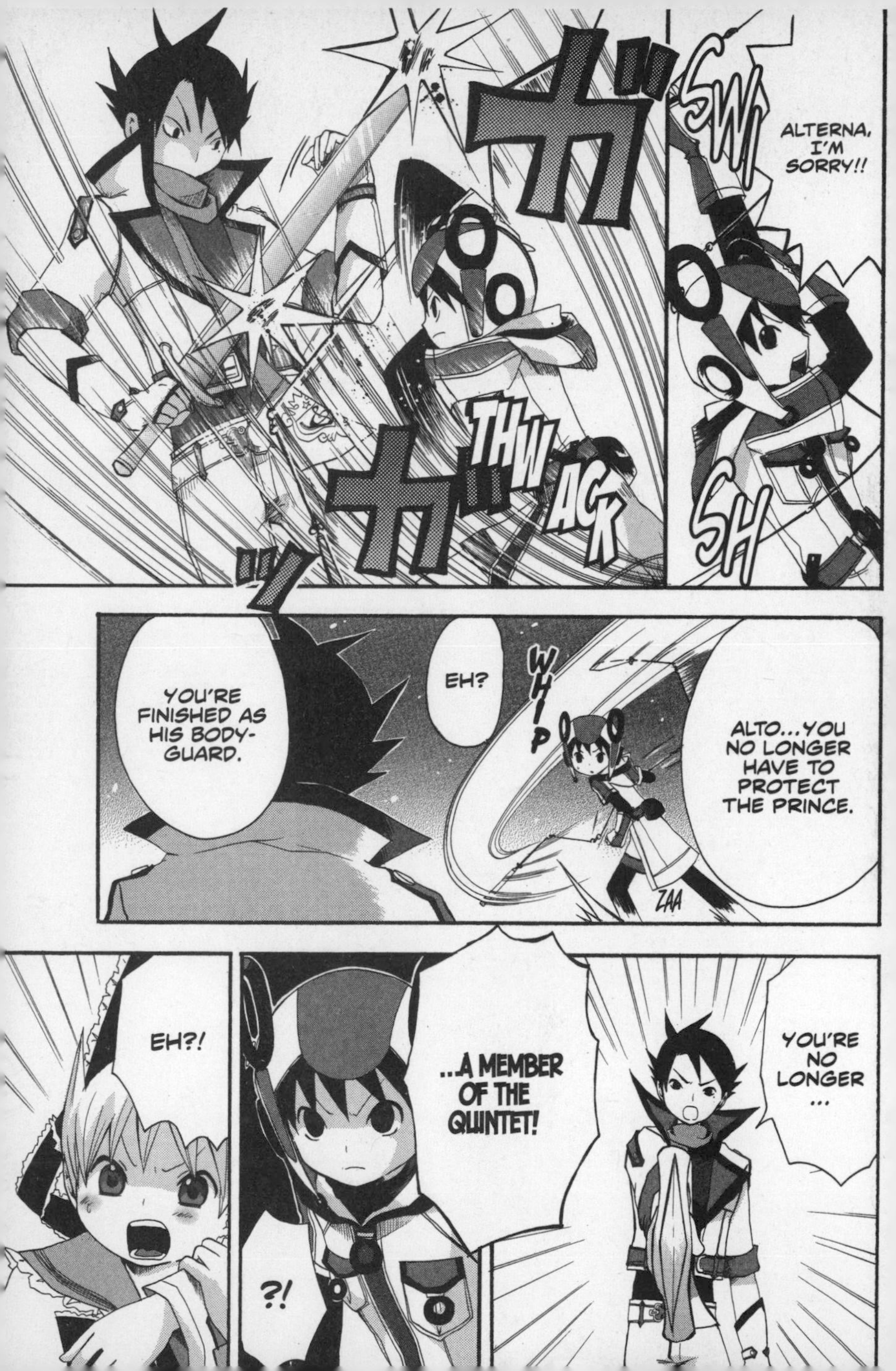
ALTERNA, I'M SORRY!!
SWISH
THWACK
ALTO...YOU NO LONGER HAVE TO PROTECT THE PRINCE.
WHIP
ZAA
EH?
YOU'RE FINISHED AS HIS BODY-GUARD.
YOU'RE NO LONGER ...
...A MEMBER OF THE QUINTET!
?!
EH?!

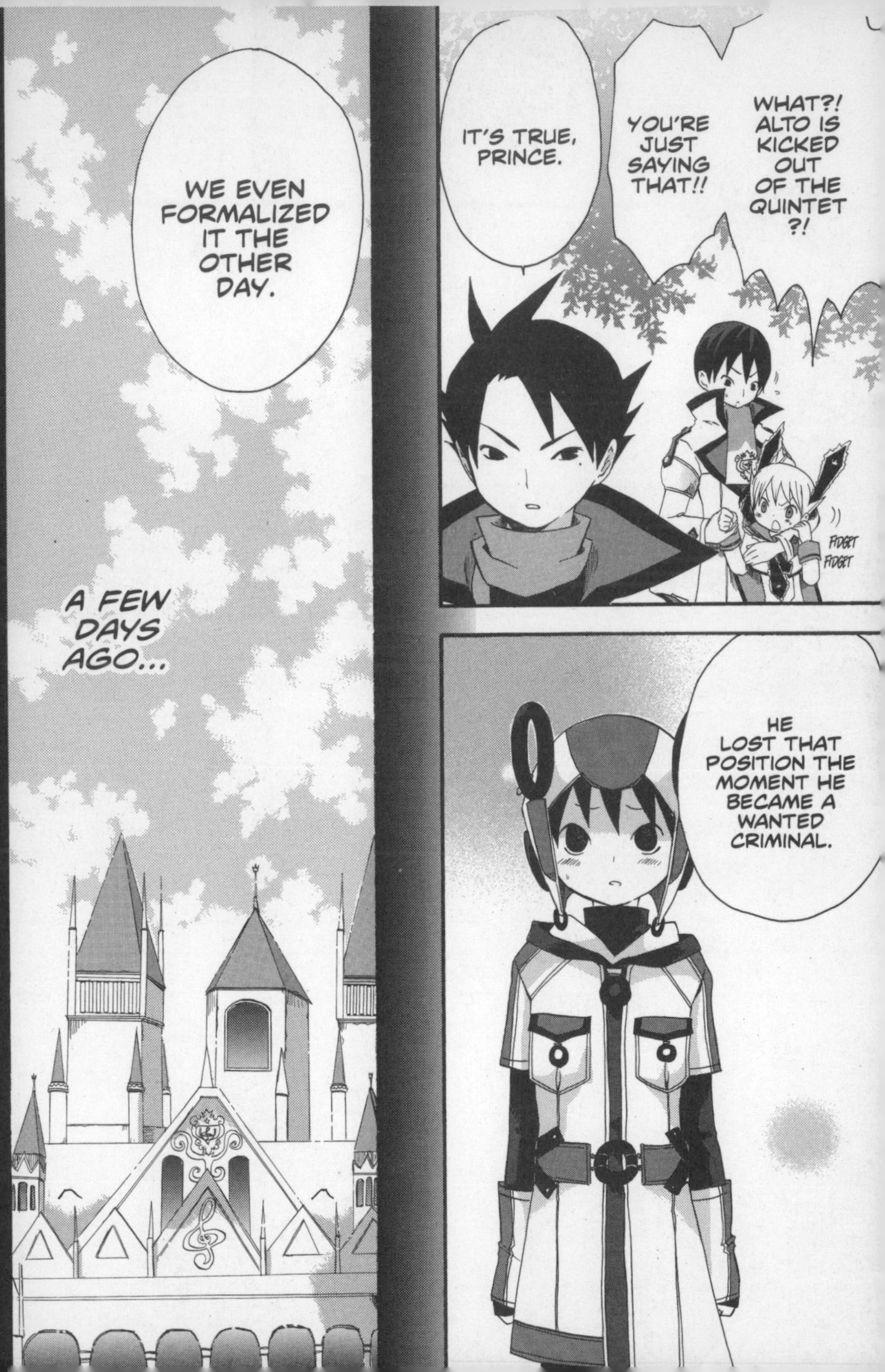
WHAT?! ALTO IS KICKED OUT OF THE QUINTET?!
YOU'RE JUST SAYING THAT!!
IT'S TRUE, PRINCE.
FIDGET FIDGET
HE LOST THAT POSITION THE MOMENT HE BECAME A WANTED CRIMINAL.
WE EVEN FORMALIZED IT THE OTHER DAY.
A FEW DAYS AGO...

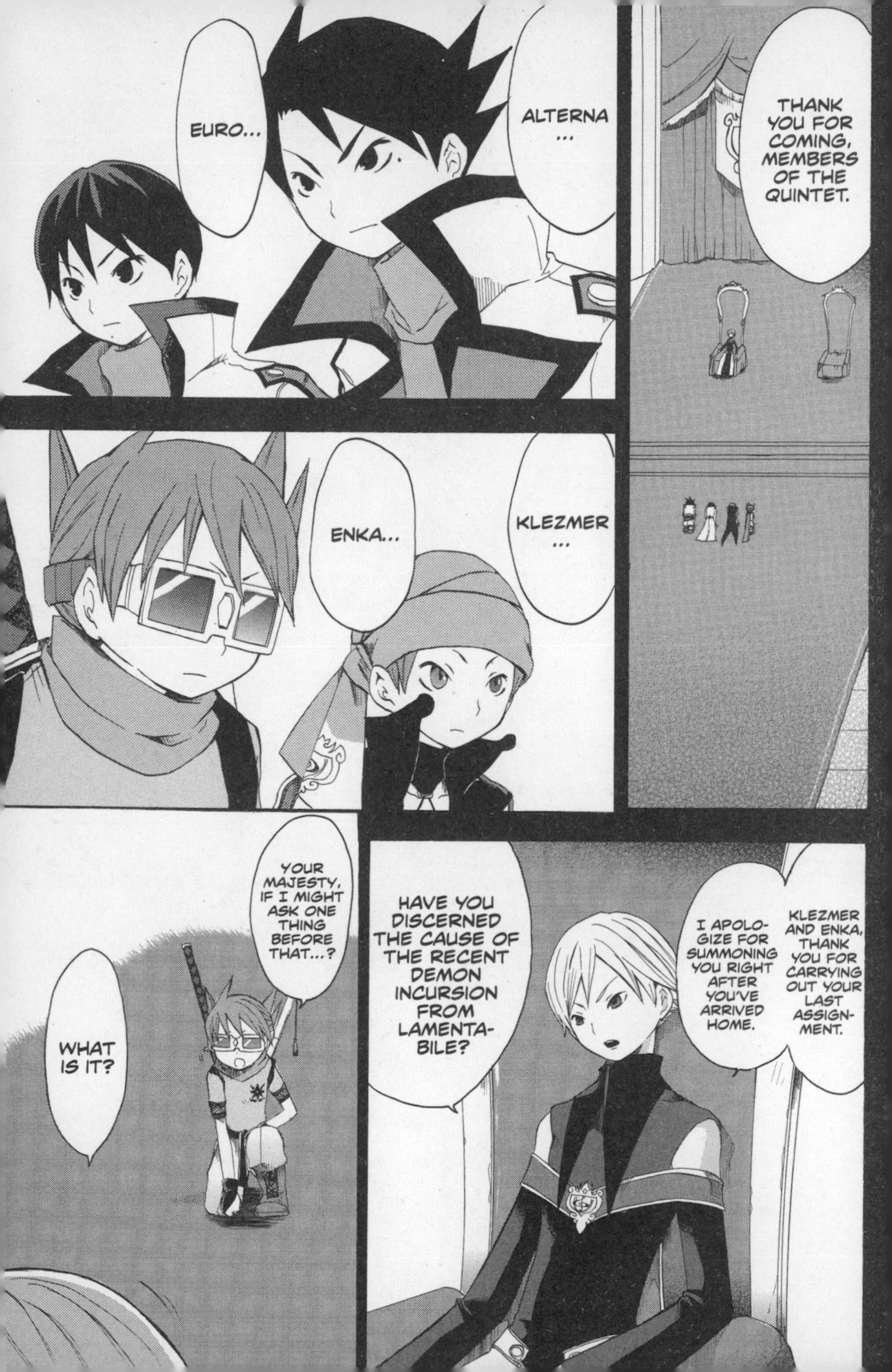
THANK YOU FOR COMING, MEMBERS OF THE QUINTET.
ALTERNA ...
EURO...
KLEZMER ...
ENKA...
KLEZMER AND ENKA, THANK YOU FOR CARRYING OUT YOUR LAST ASSIGNMENT.
I APOLOGIZE FOR SUMMONING YOU RIGHT AFTER YOU'VE ARRIVED HOME.
HAVE YOU DISCERNED THE CAUSE OF THE RECENT DEMON INCURSION FROM LAMENTABILE?
YOUR MAJESTY, IF I MIGHT ASK ONE THING BEFORE THAT...?
WHAT IS IT?

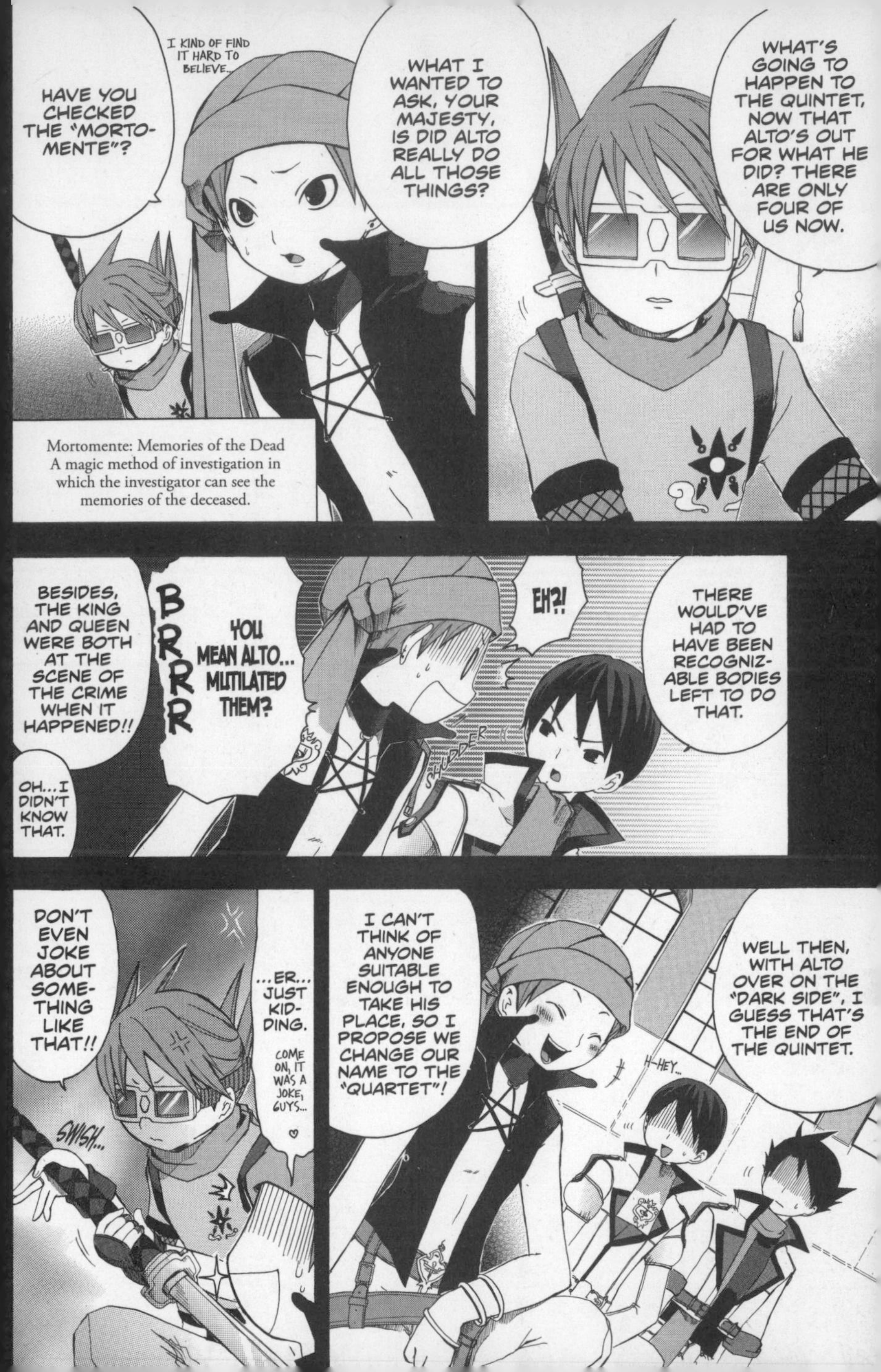
WHAT'S GOING TO HAPPEN TO THE QUINTET, NOW THAT ALTO'S OUT FOR WHAT HE DID? THERE ARE ONLY FOUR OF US NOW.
WHAT I WANTED TO ASK, YOUR MAJESTY, IS DID ALTO REALLY DO ALL THOSE THINGS?
I KIND OF FIND IT HARD TO BELIEVE...
HAVE YOU CHECKED THE "MORTOMENTE"?
Mortomente: Memories of the Dead A magic method of investigation in which the investigator can see the memories of the deceased.
THERE WOULD'VE HAD TO HAVE BEEN RECOGNIZABLE BODIES LEFT TO DO THAT.
EH?!
YOU MEAN ALTO... MUTILATED THEM?
BRRRR
SHUDDER
BESIDES, THE KING AND QUEEN WERE BOTH AT THE SCENE OF THE CRIME WHEN IT HAPPENED!!
OH... I DIDN'T KNOW THAT.
WELL THEN, WITH ALTO OVER ON THE "DARK SIDE", I GUESS THAT'S THE END OF THE QUINTET.
I CAN'T THINK OF ANYONE SUITABLE ENOUGH TO TAKE HIS PLACE, SO I PROPOSE WE CHANGE OUR NAME TO THE "QUARTET"!
H-HEY...
DON'T EVEN JOKE ABOUT SOMETHING LIKE THAT!!
...ER... JUST KIDDING.
COME ON, IT WAS A JOKE, GUYS...
SWISH...

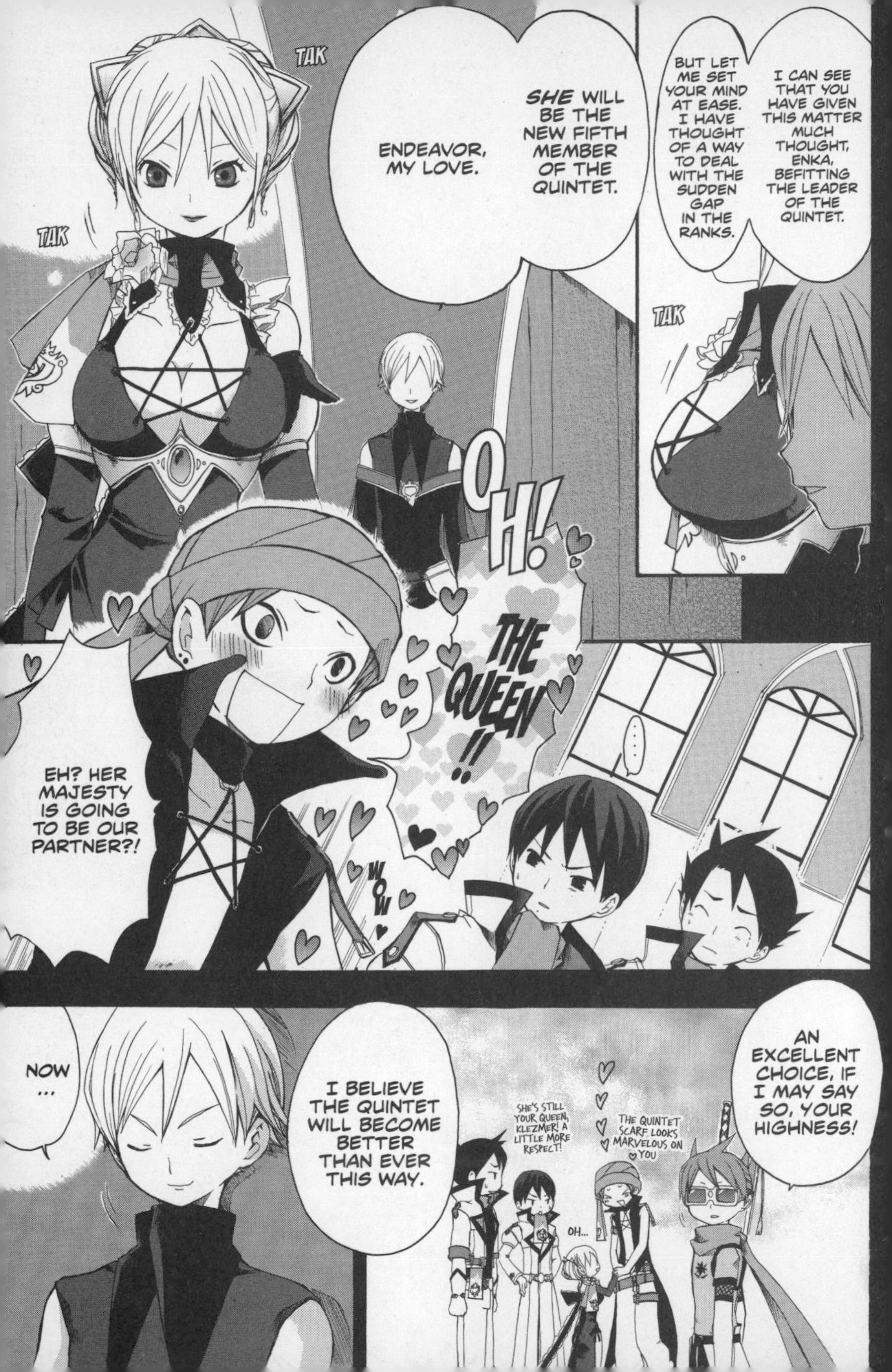
TAK
I CAN SEE THAT YOU HAVE GIVEN THIS MATTER MUCH THOUGHT, ENKA, BEFITTING THE LEADER OF THE QUINTET.
BUT LET ME SET YOUR MIND AT EASE. I HAVE THOUGHT OF A WAY TO DEAL WITH THE SUDDEN GAP IN THE RANKS.
TAK
TAK
SHE WILL BE THE NEW FIFTH MEMBER OF THE QUINTET.
ENDEAVOR, MY LOVE.
OH!
...
THE QUEEN!!
WOW
EH? HER MAJESTY IS GOING TO BE OUR PARTNER?!
AN EXCELLENT CHOICE, IF I MAY SAY SO, YOUR HIGHNESS!
THE QUINTET SCARF LOOKS MARVELOUS ON YOU
SHE'S STILL YOUR QUEEN, KLEZMER! A LITTLE MORE RESPECT!
OH...
I BELIEVE THE QUINTET WILL BECOME BETTER THAN EVER THIS WAY.
NOW ...

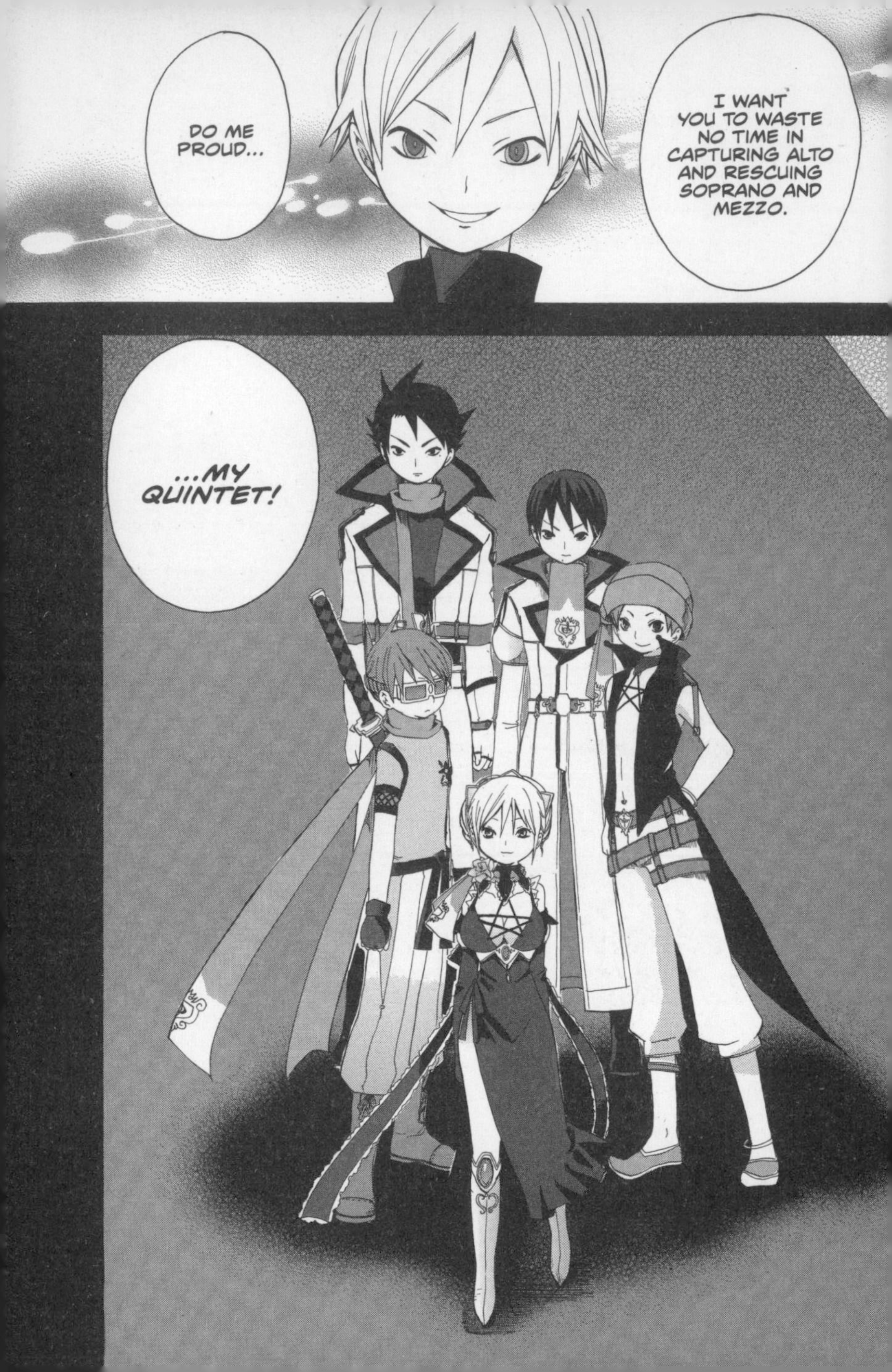
I WANT YOU TO WASTE NO TIME IN CAPTURING ALTO AND RESCUING SOPRANO AND MEZZO.
DO ME PROUD...
...MY QUINTET!

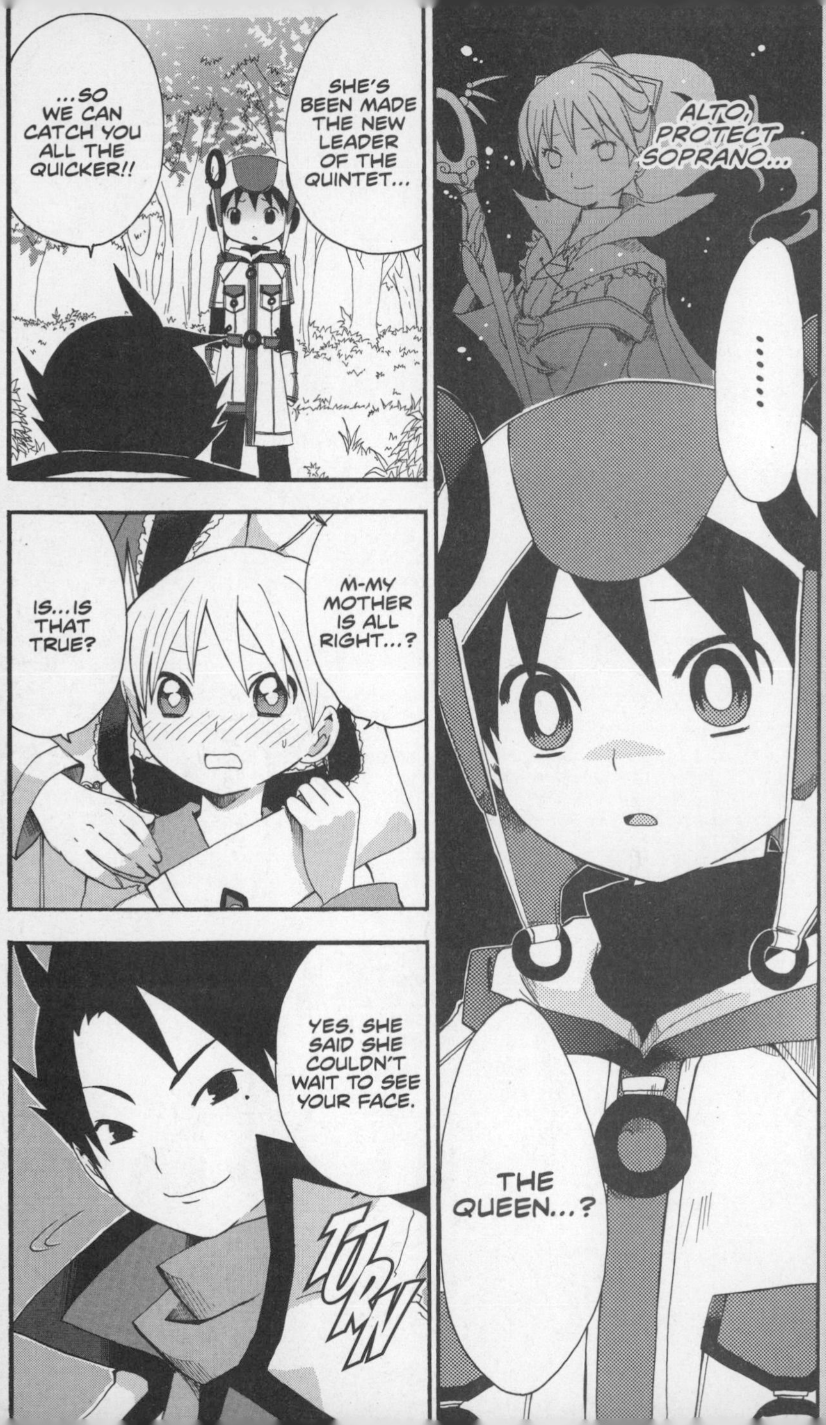
ALTO, PROTECT SOPRANO...
......
THE QUEEN...?
SHE'S BEEN MADE THE NEW LEADER OF THE QUINTET...
...SO WE CAN CATCH YOU ALL THE QUICKER!!
M-MY MOTHER IS ALL RIGHT...?
IS...IS THAT TRUE?
YES. SHE SAID SHE COULDN'T WAIT TO SEE YOUR FACE.
TURN

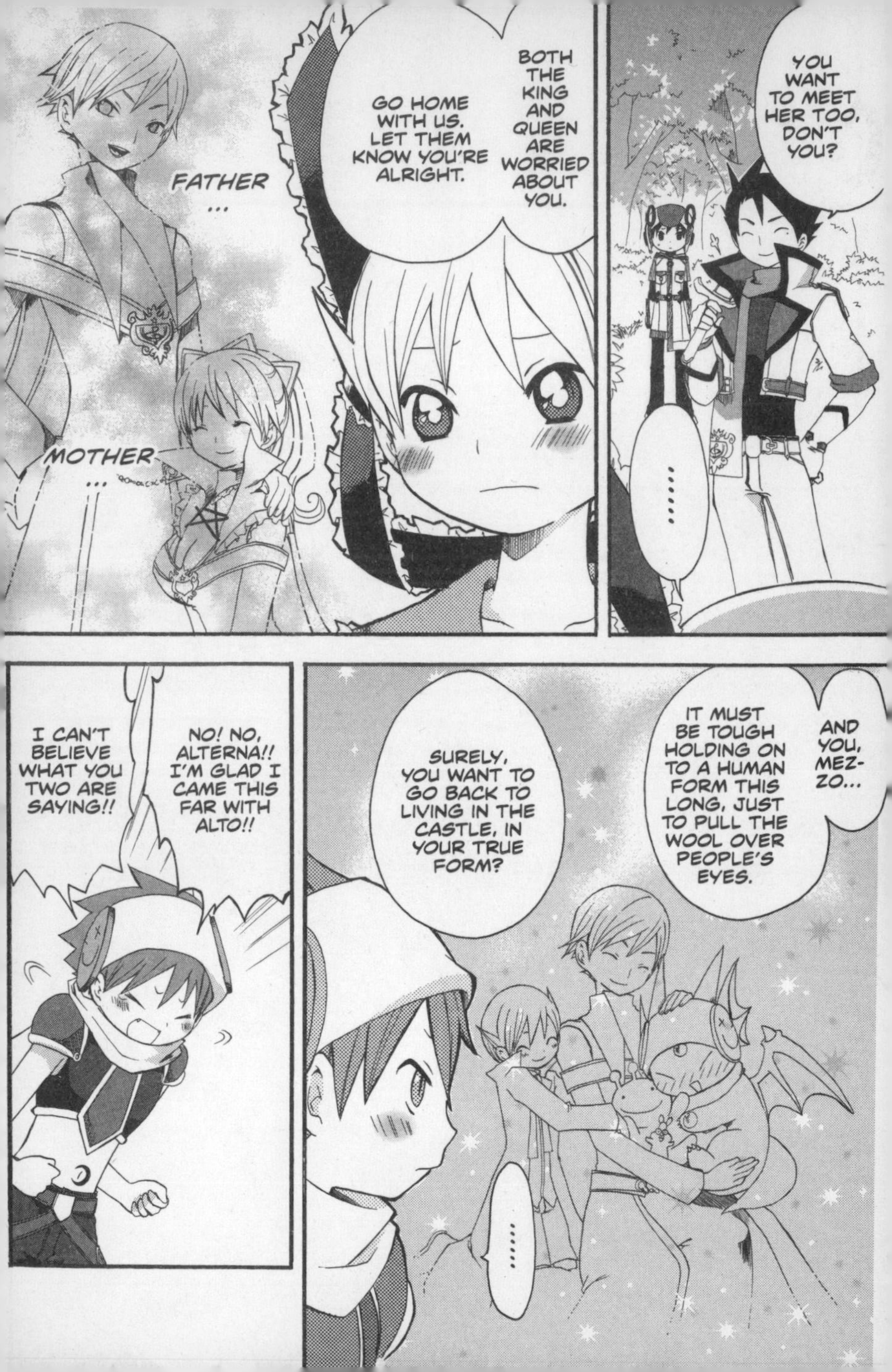
YOU WANT TO MEET HER TOO, DON'T YOU?
......
BOTH THE KING AND QUEEN ARE WORRIED ABOUT YOU.
GO HOME WITH US. LET THEM KNOW YOU'RE ALRIGHT.
FATHER ...
MOTHER ...
AND YOU, MEZ-ZO...
IT MUST BE TOUGH HOLDING ON TO A HUMAN FORM THIS LONG, JUST TO PULL THE WOOL OVER PEOPLE'S EYES.
SURELY, YOU WANT TO GO BACK TO LIVING IN THE CASTLE, IN YOUR TRUE FORM?
......
NO! NO, ALTERNA!! I'M GLAD I CAME THIS FAR WITH ALTO!!
I CAN'T BELIEVE WHAT YOU TWO ARE SAYING!!

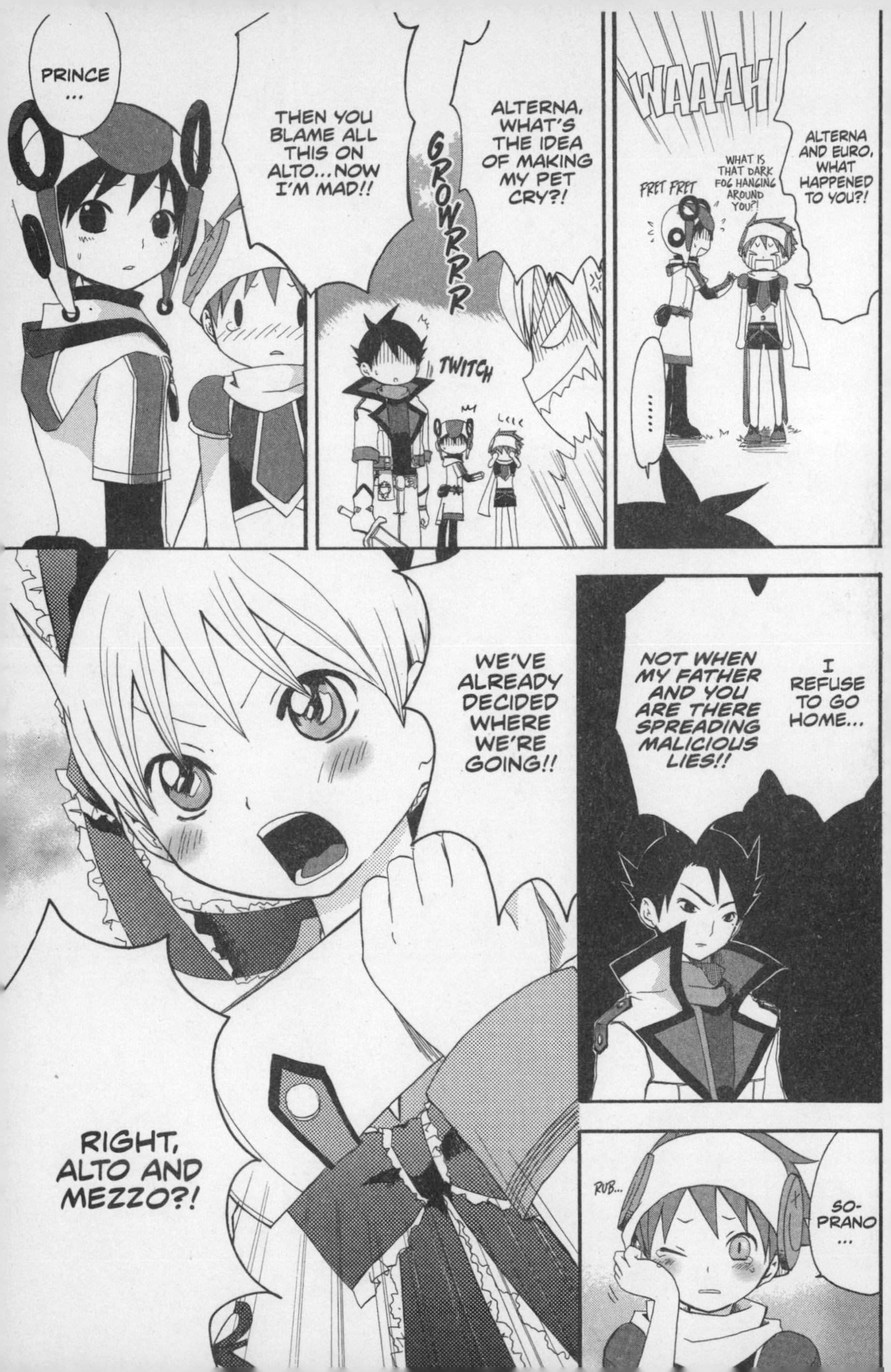
WAAAH
ALTERNA AND EURO, WHAT HAPPENED TO YOU?!
WHAT IS THAT DARK FOG HANGING AROUND YOU?!
FRET FRET
......
ALTERNA, WHAT'S THE IDEA OF MAKING MY PET CRY?!
GROWRRR
TWITCH
THEN YOU BLAME ALL THIS ON ALTO...NOW I'M MAD!!
PRINCE ...
I REFUSE TO GO HOME...
NOT WHEN MY FATHER AND YOU ARE THERE SPREADING MALICIOUS LIES!!
SO-PRANO ...
RUB...
WE'VE ALREADY DECIDED WHERE WE'RE GOING!!
RIGHT, ALTO AND MEZZO?!

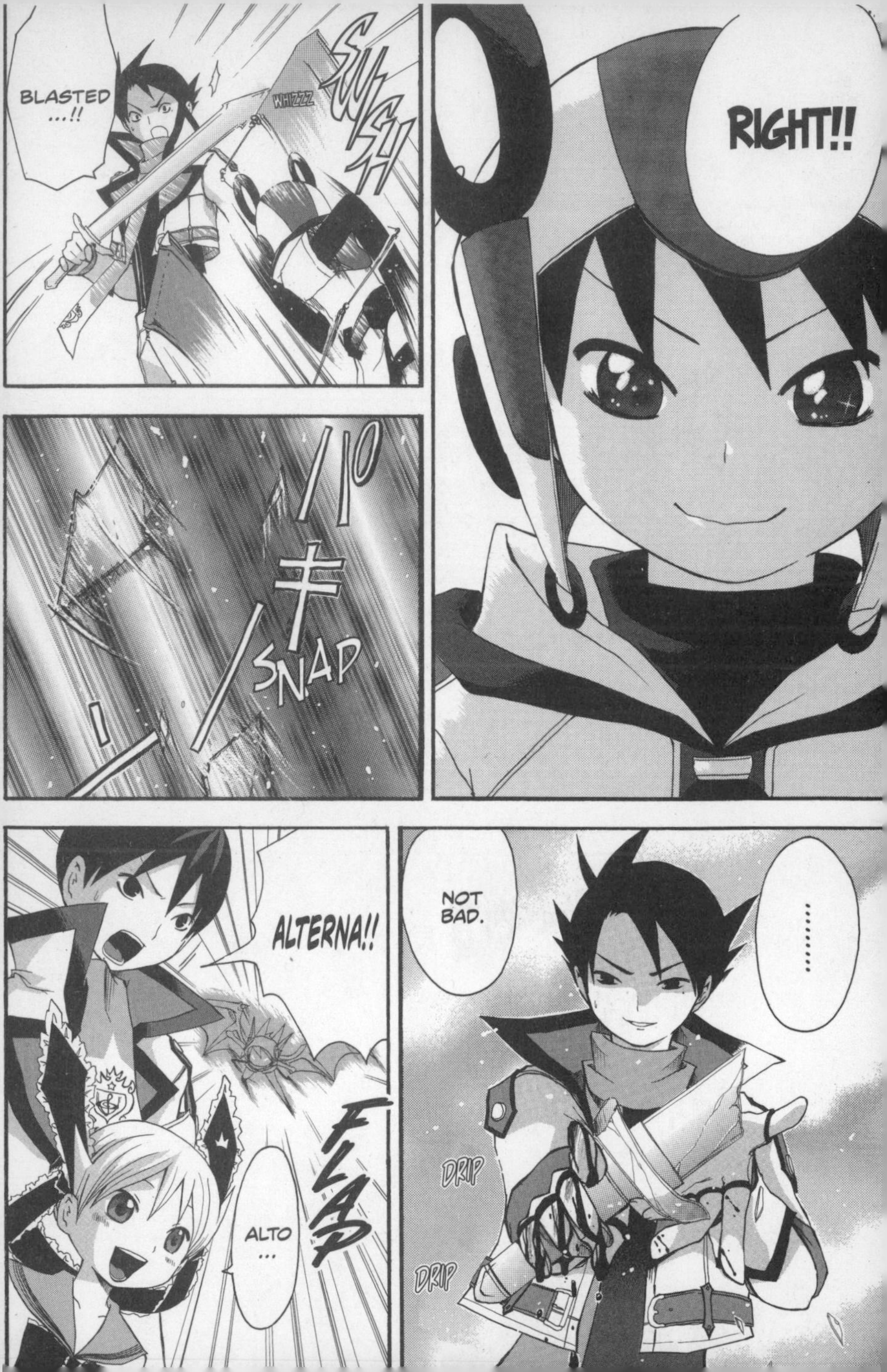

RIGHT!!
SWISH
WHIZZZ
BLASTED ...!!
SNAP
......
NOT BAD.
DRIP
DRIP
ALTERNA!!
FLAP
ALTO ...

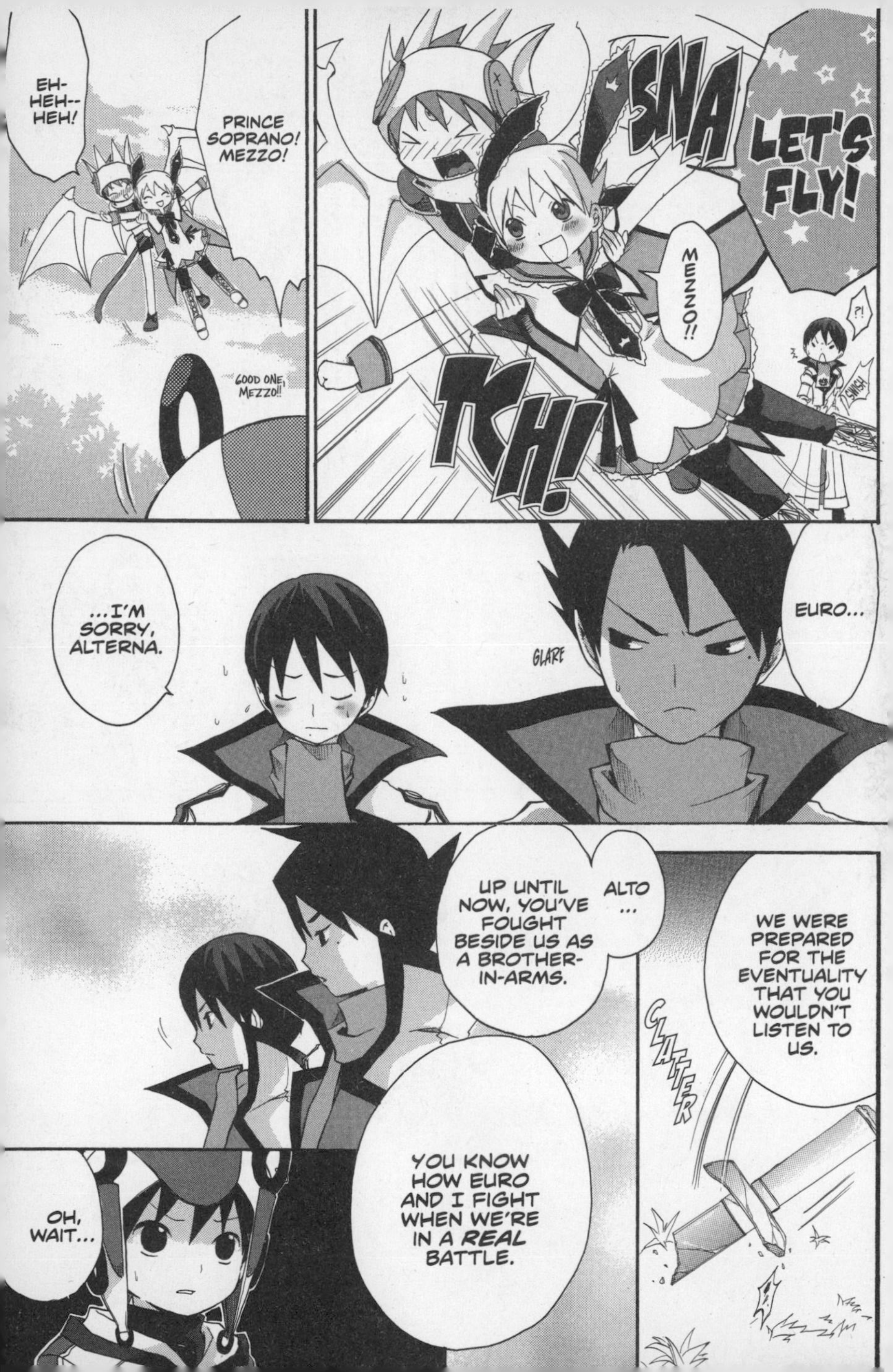
LET'S FLY!
SNA
MEZZO!!
?!
SWISH
KH!
PRINCE SOPRANO! MEZZO!
EH-HEH--HEH!
GOOD ONE, MEZZO!!
EURO...
GLARE
...I'M SORRY, ALTERNA.
WE WERE PREPARED FOR THE EVENTUALITY THAT YOU WOULDN'T LISTEN TO US.
CLATTER
ALTO ...
UP UNTIL NOW, YOU'VE FOUGHT BESIDE US AS A BROTHER-IN-ARMS.
YOU KNOW HOW EURO AND I FIGHT WHEN WE'RE IN A *REAL* BATTLE.
OH, WAIT...

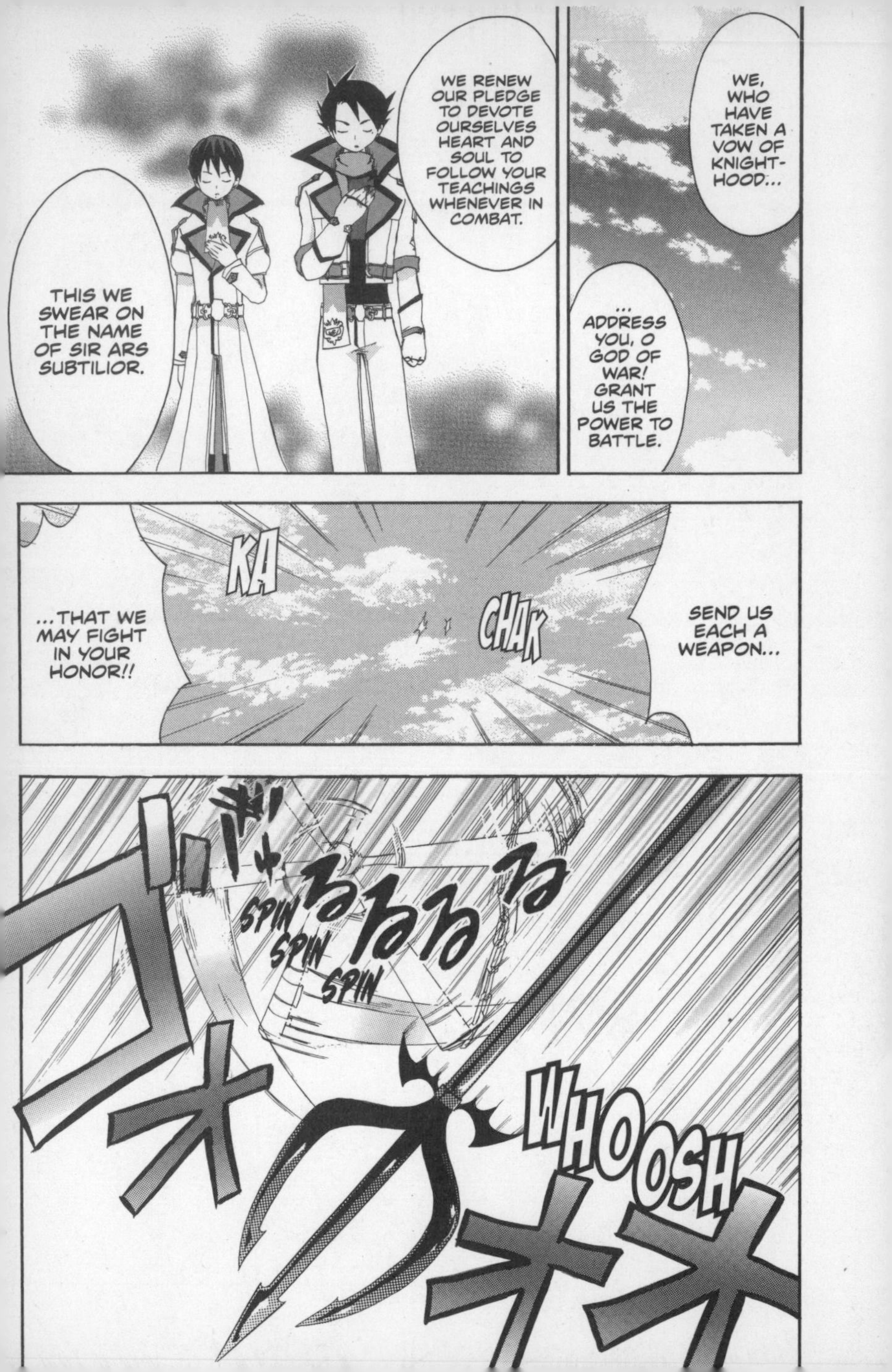
WE, WHO HAVE TAKEN A VOW OF KNIGHT-HOOD...
...ADDRESS YOU, O GOD OF WAR! GRANT US THE POWER TO BATTLE.
WE RENEW OUR PLEDGE TO DEVOTE OURSELVES HEART AND SOUL TO FOLLOW YOUR TEACHINGS WHENEVER IN COMBAT.
THIS WE SWEAR ON THE NAME OF SIR ARS SUBTILIOR.
SEND US EACH A WEAPON...
KA
CHAK
...THAT WE MAY FIGHT IN YOUR HONOR!!
SPIN
SPIN
SPIN
WHOOSH

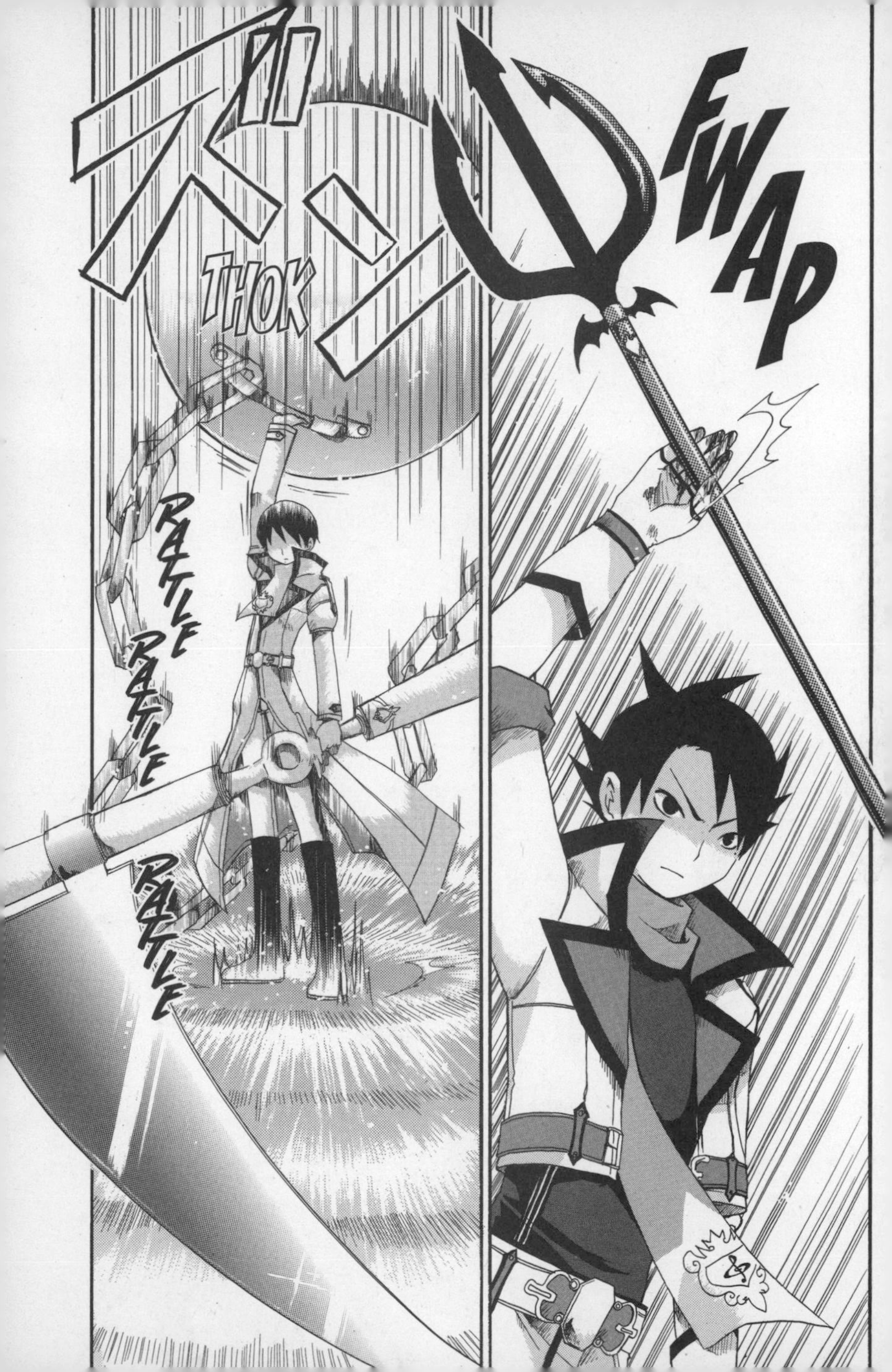
FWAP
THOK
RATTLE
RATTLE
RATTLE

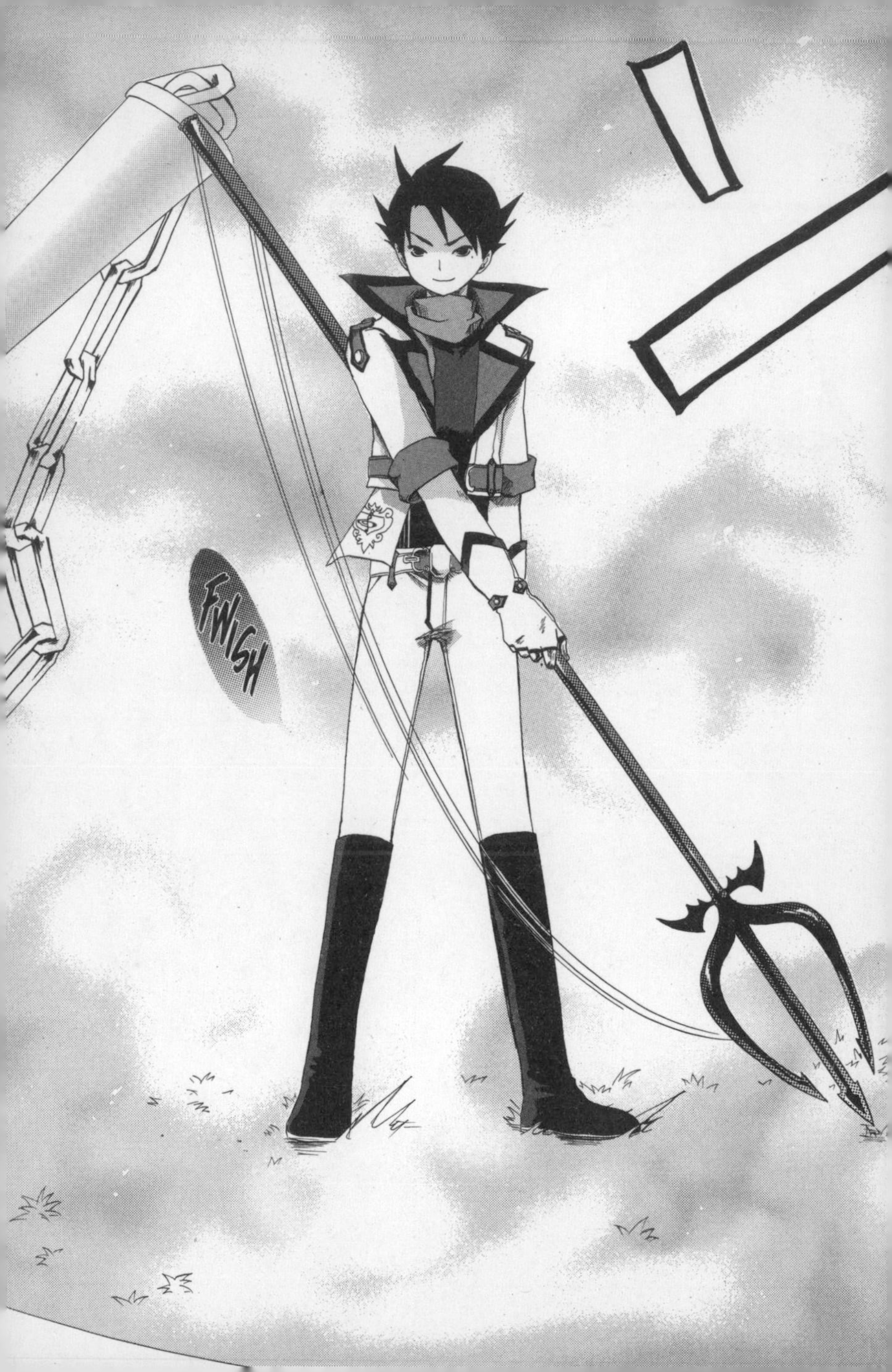
FWISH

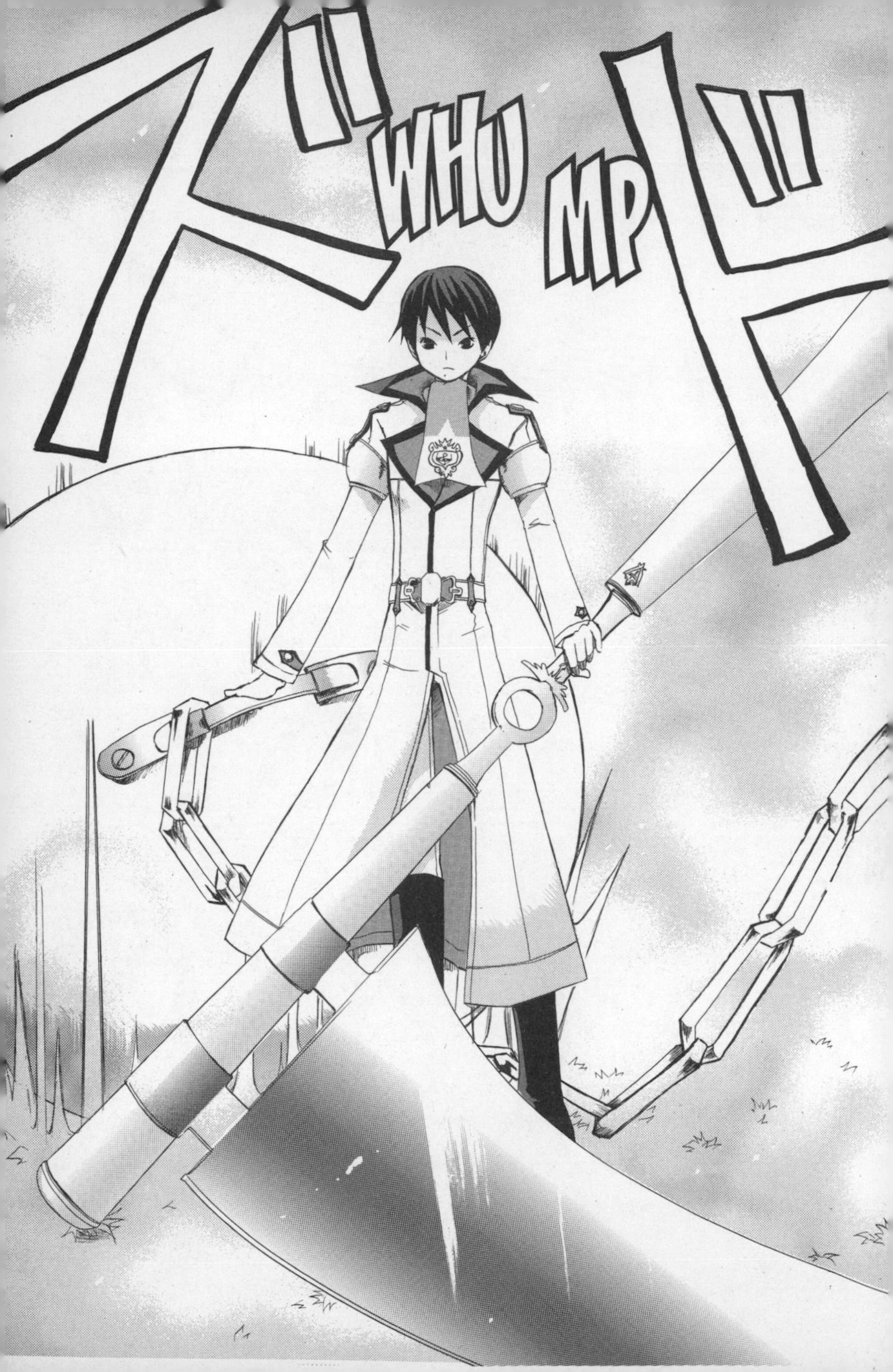
ズド
WHUMP

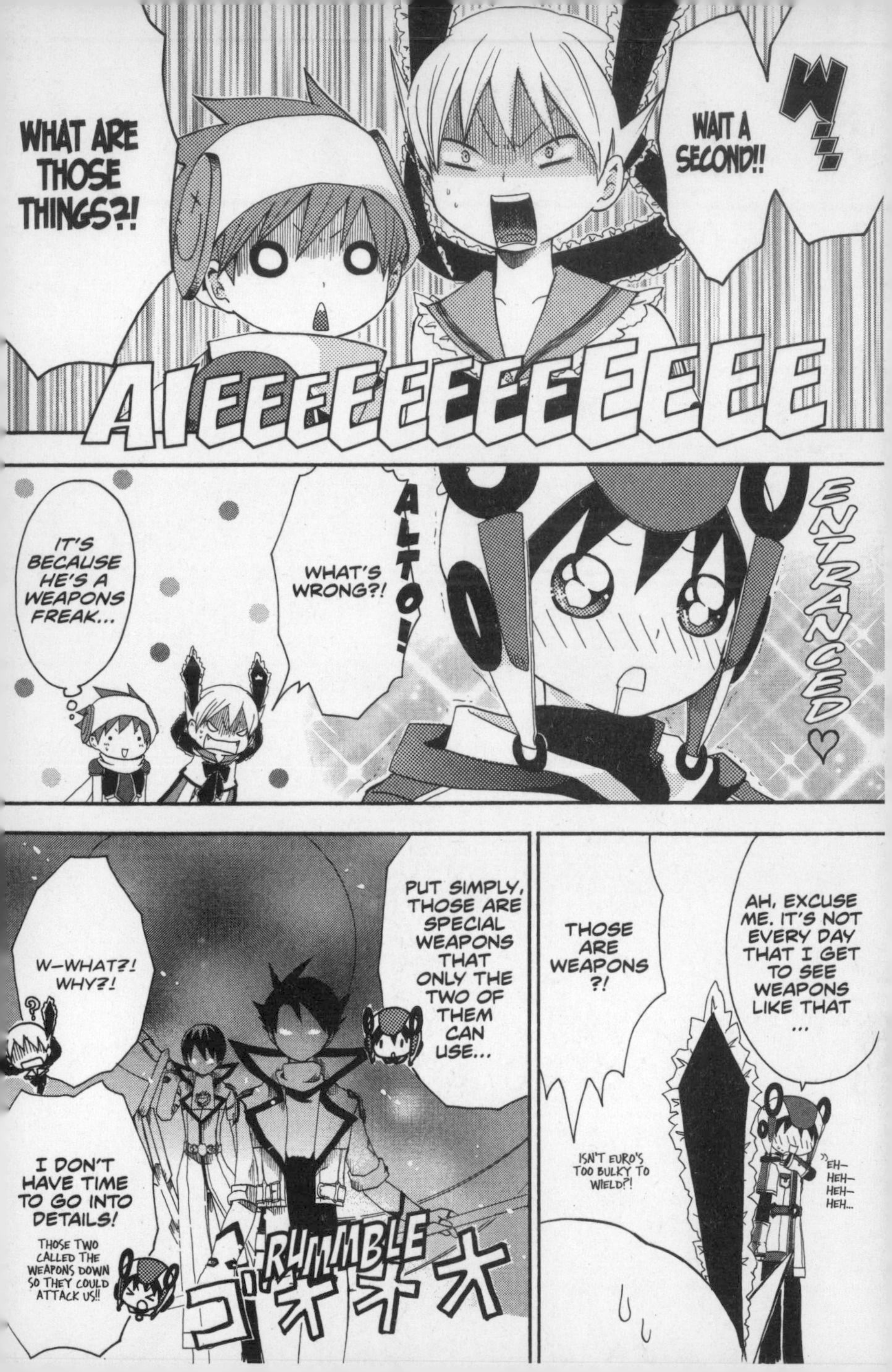
WAIT A SECOND!!
W...
WHAT ARE THOSE THINGS?!
AIEEEEEEEEEEEE
ENTRANCED♥
ALTO!
WHAT'S WRONG?!
IT'S BECAUSE HE'S A WEAPONS FREAK...
AH, EXCUSE ME. IT'S NOT EVERY DAY THAT I GET TO SEE WEAPONS LIKE THAT ...
THOSE ARE WEAPONS?!
EH-HEH-HEH-HEH...
ISN'T EURO'S TOO BULKY TO WIELD?!
PUT SIMPLY, THOSE ARE SPECIAL WEAPONS THAT ONLY THE TWO OF THEM CAN USE...
W-WHAT?! WHY?!
I DON'T HAVE TIME TO GO INTO DETAILS!
THOSE TWO CALLED THE WEAPONS DOWN SO THEY COULD ATTACK US!!
RUMMBLE
ゴオオオ

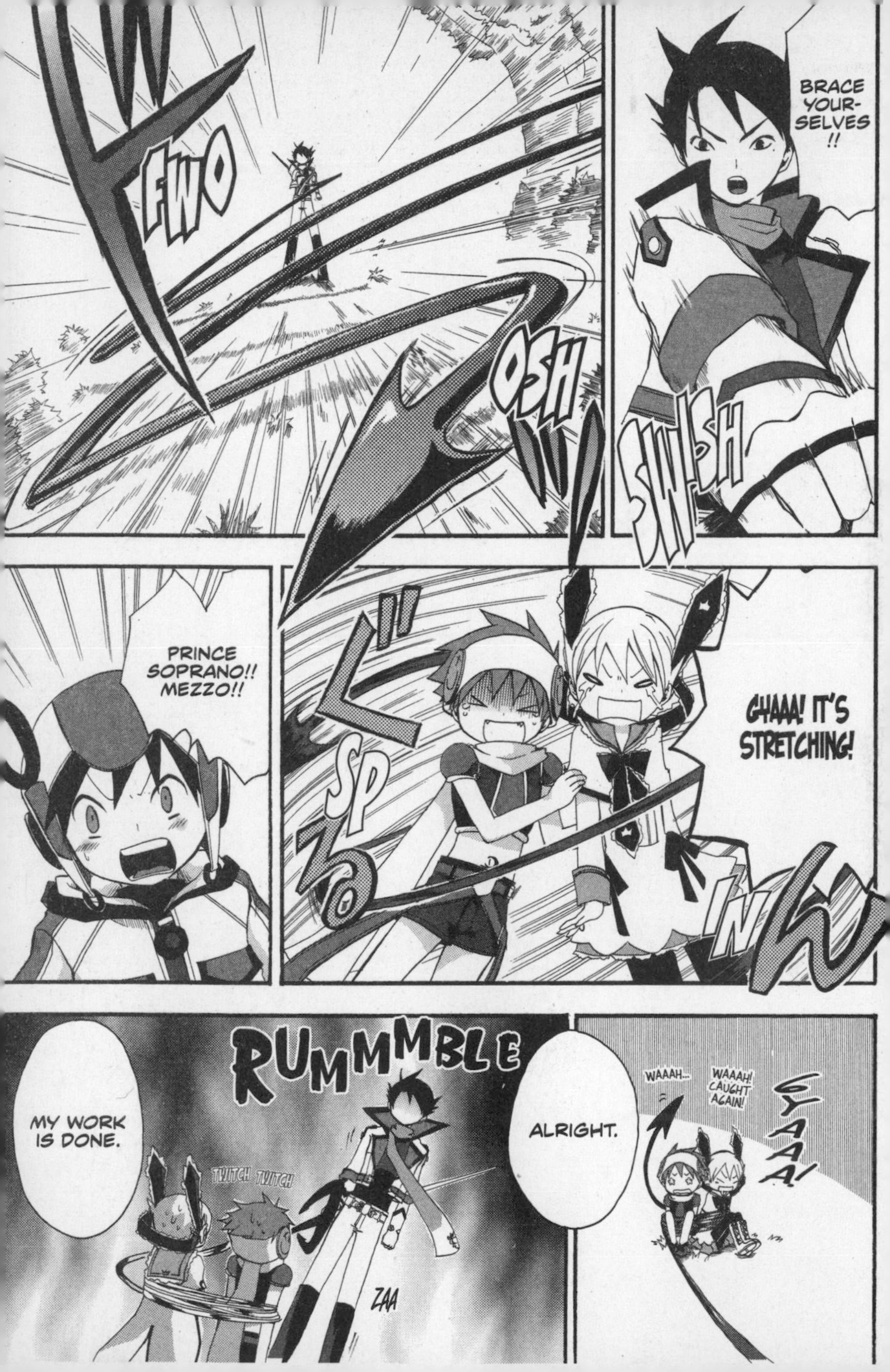
BRACE YOUR-SELVES !!
SWISH
FWO
OSH
GHAAA! IT'S STRETCHING!
PRINCE SOPRANO!! MEZZO!!
GYAAA!
WAAAH! CAUGHT AGAIN!
WAAAH...
ALRIGHT.
RUMMMBLE
MY WORK IS DONE.
TWITCH TWITCH
ZAA

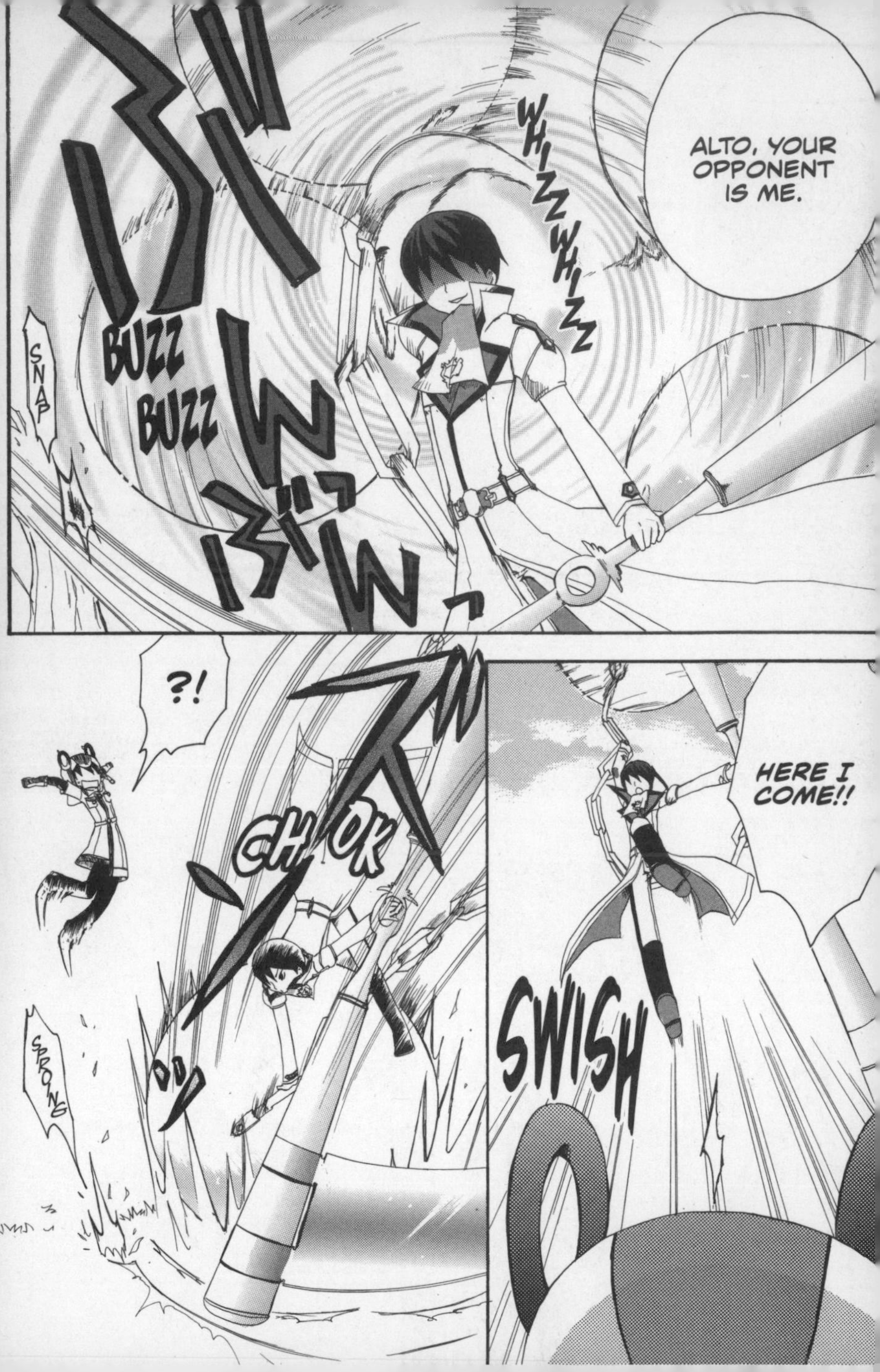

ALTO, YOUR OPPONENT IS ME.
WHIZZWHIZZZ
BUZZ BUZZ
SNAP
HERE I COME!!
SWISH
?!
CHOK
SPRONG

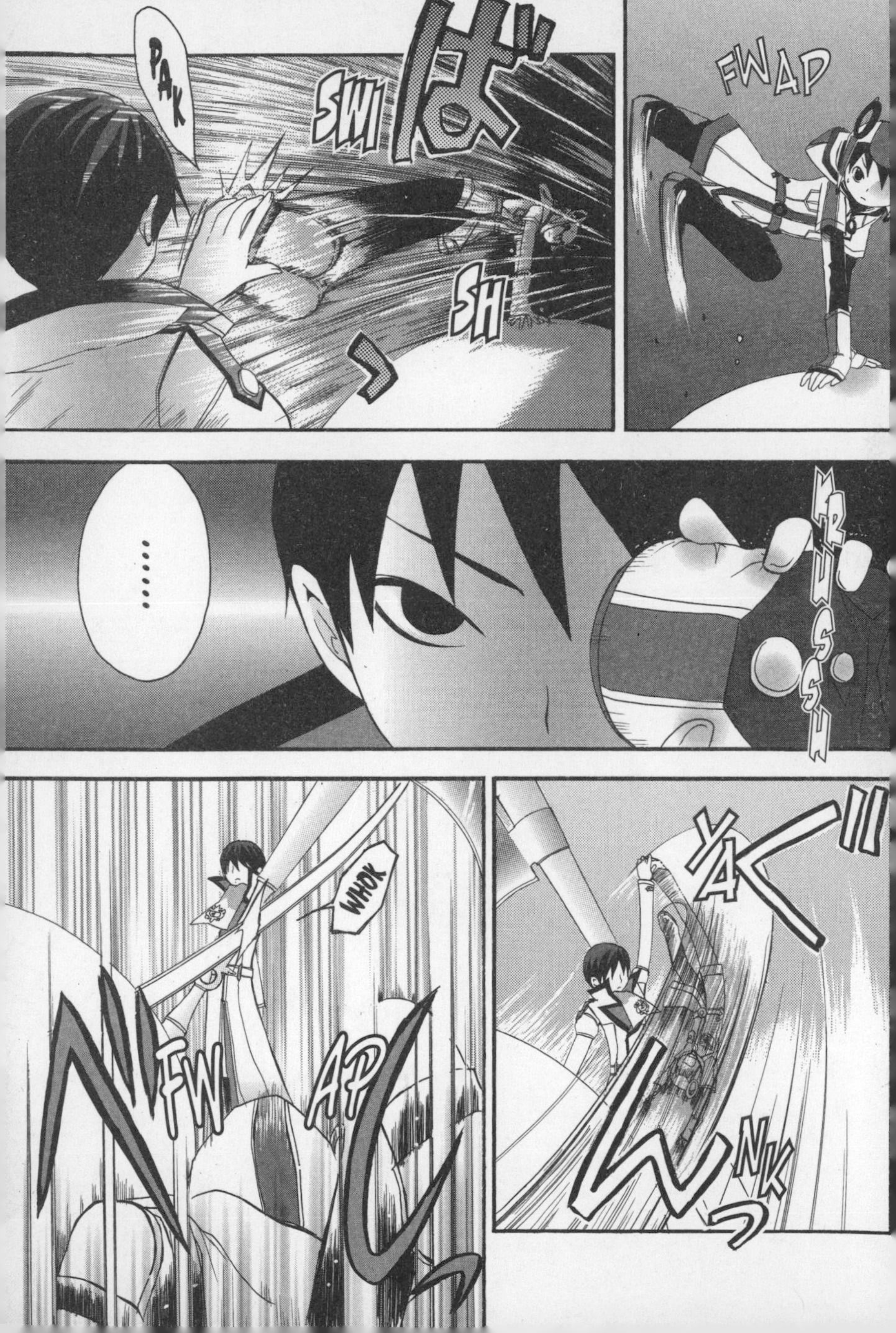
FWAP
PAK
SWI
ば
SH
KRUSSH
......
YAK
NNK
WHOK
FWAP

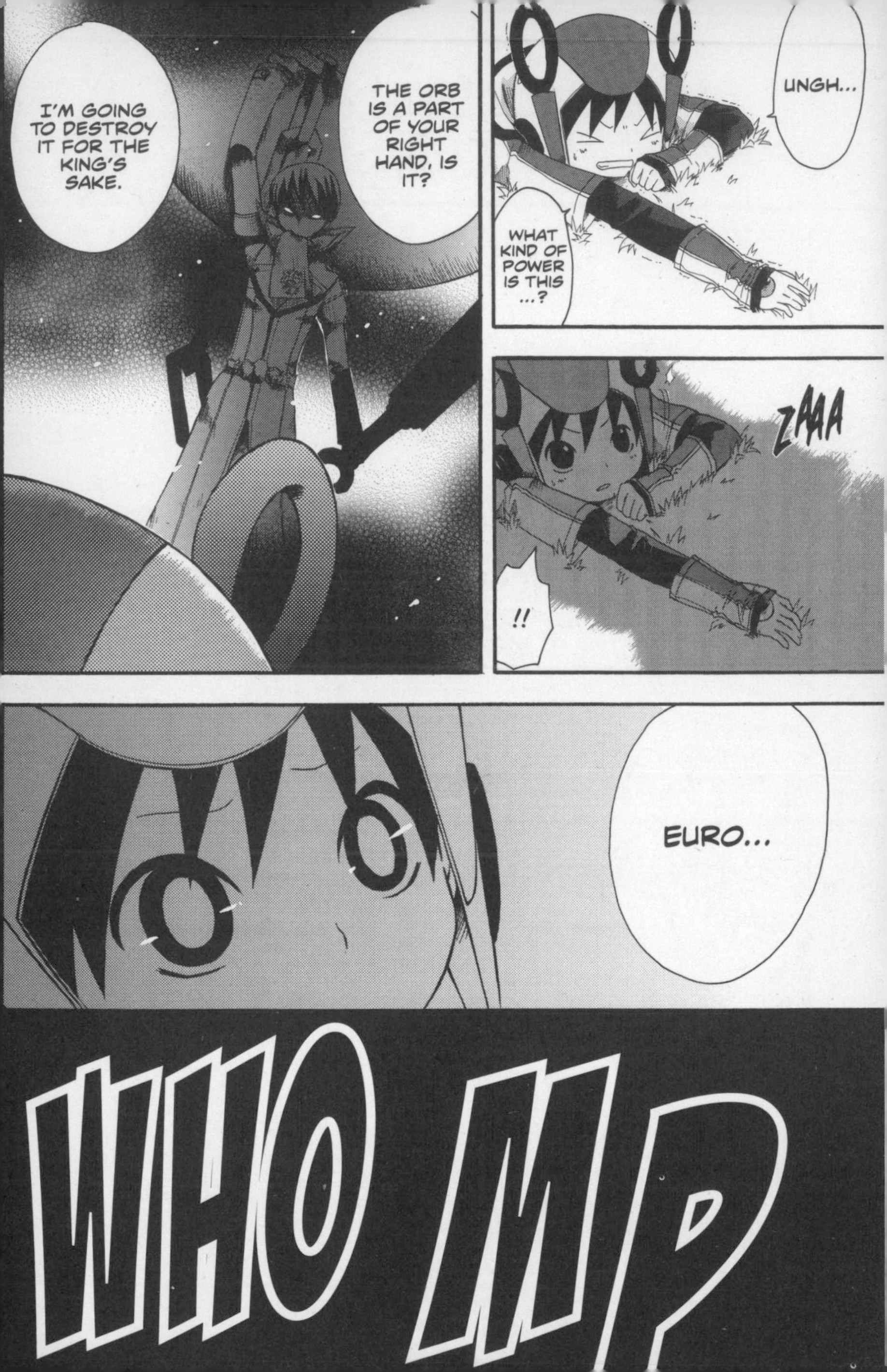
UNGH...
WHAT KIND OF POWER IS THIS ...?
ZAAA
!!
THE ORB IS A PART OF YOUR RIGHT HAND, IS IT?
I'M GOING TO DESTROY IT FOR THE KING'S SAKE.
EURO...
WHOMP

OP6: Not Looking Back on Classical

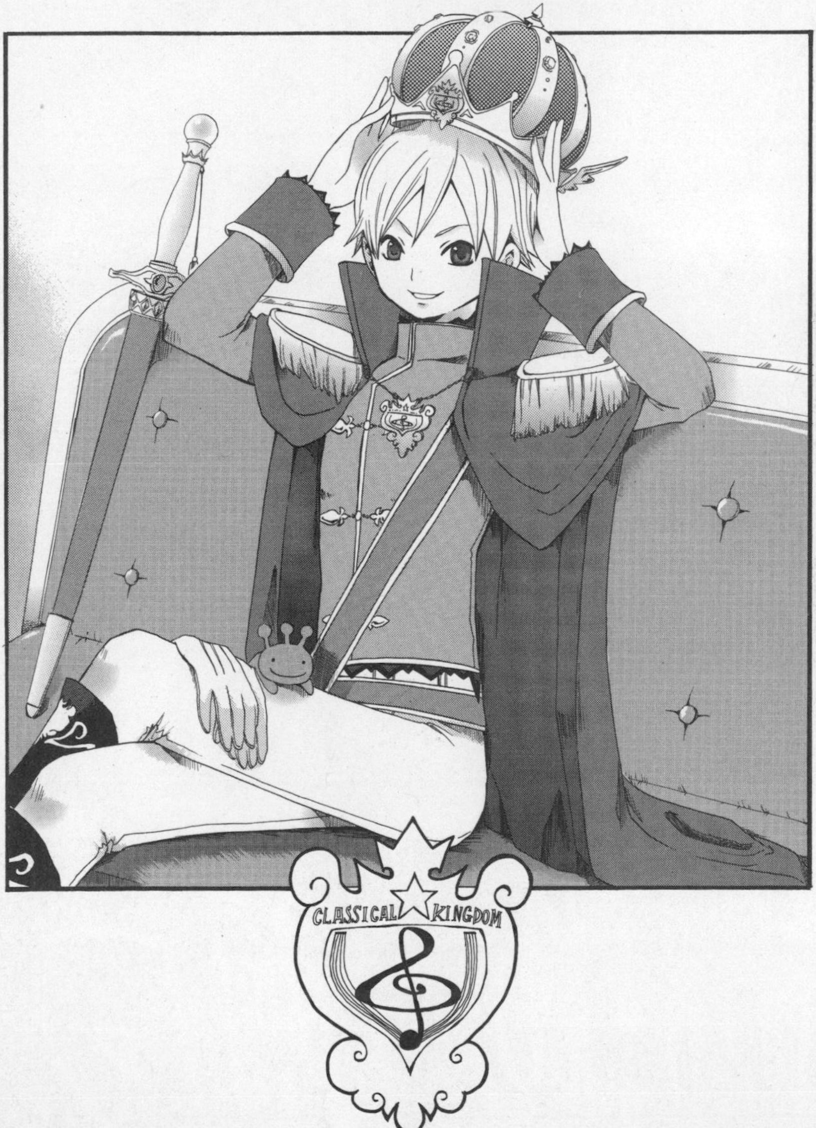
CLASSICAL KINGDOM

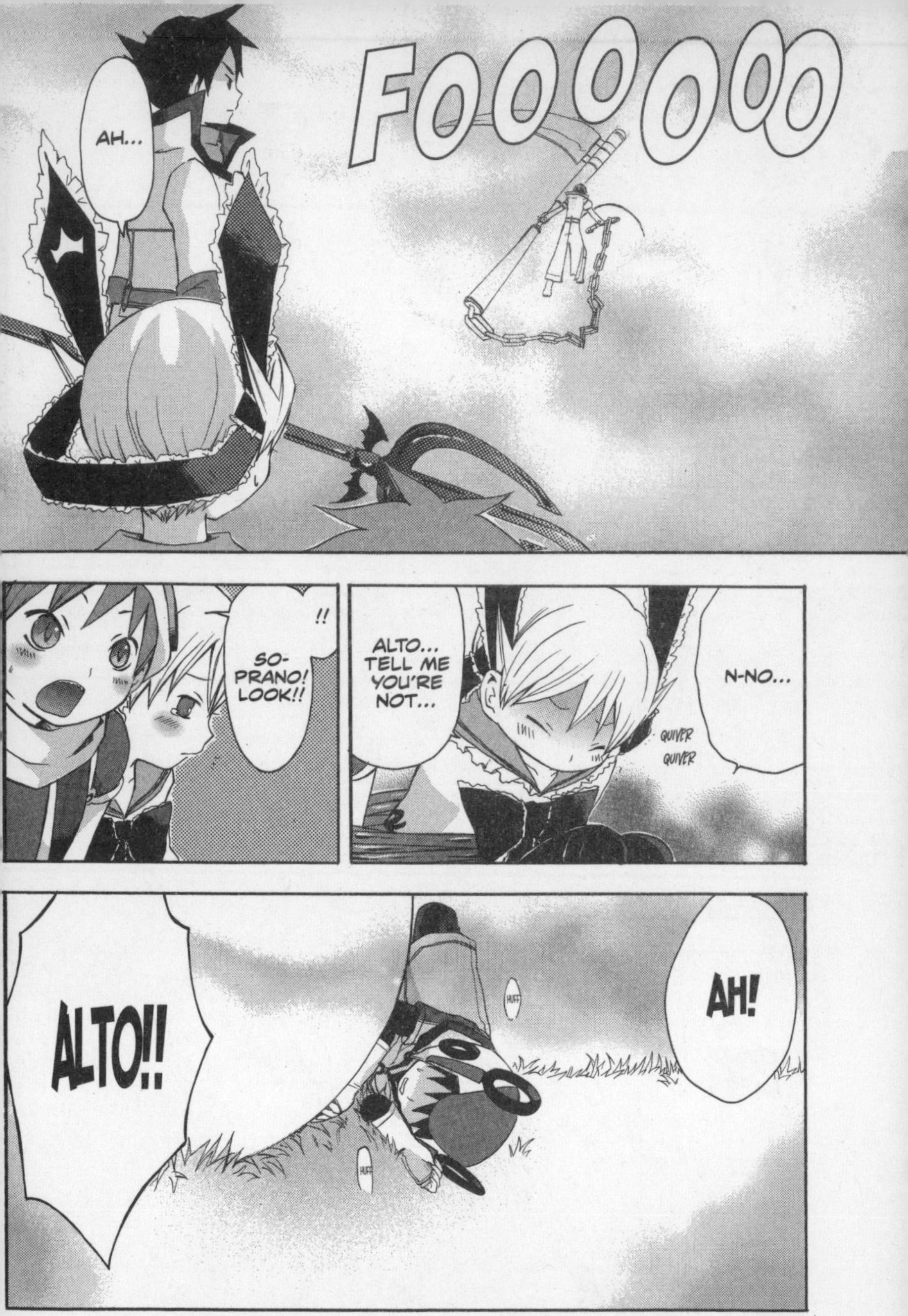
FOOOOOO
AH...
ALTO... TELL ME YOU'RE NOT...
QUIVER QUIVER
N-NO...
!!
SO-PRANO! LOOK!!
AH!
HUFF
HUFF
ALTO!!

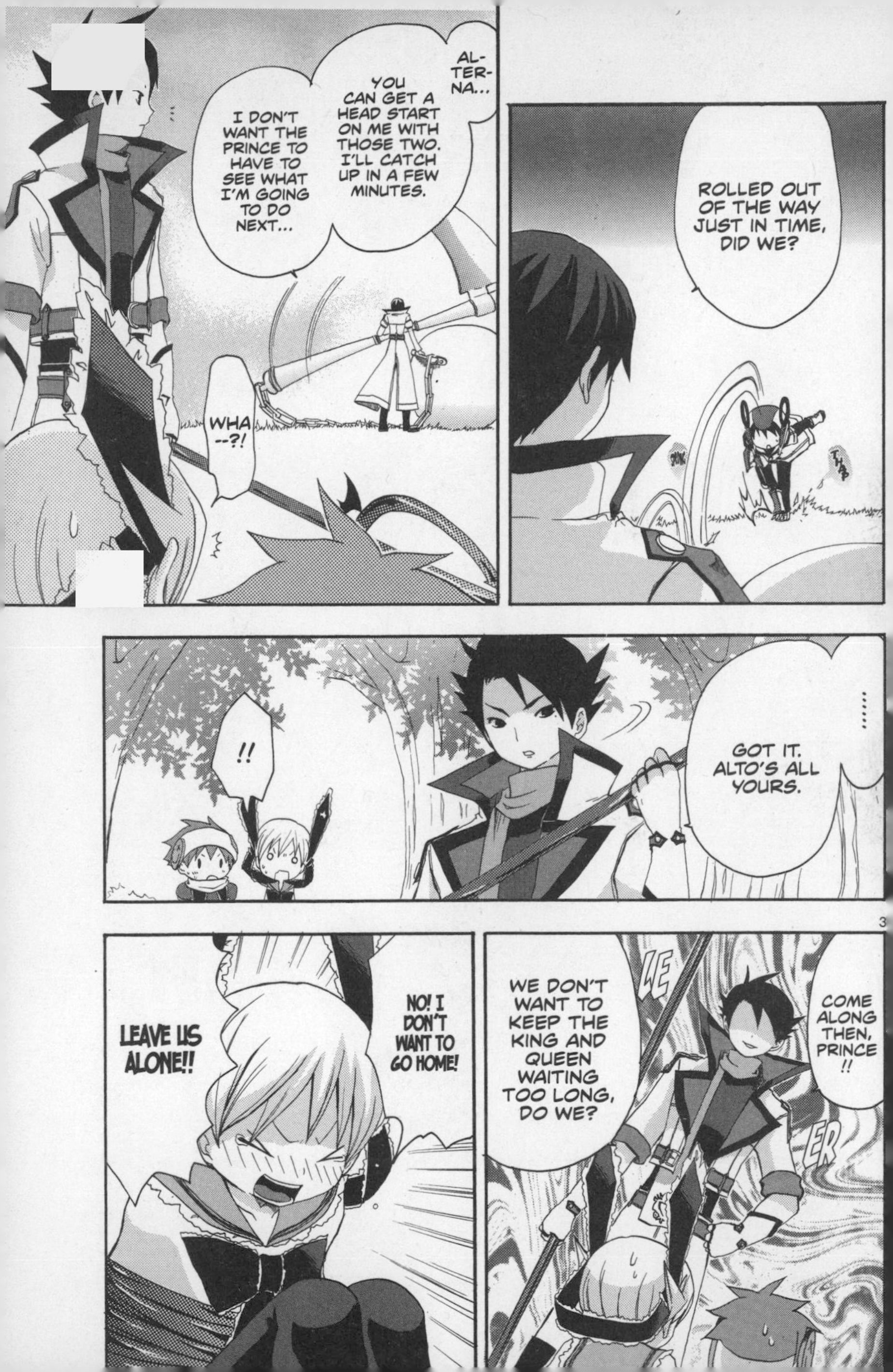
ROLLED OUT OF THE WAY JUST IN TIME, DID WE?
THMP
ALTERNA...
YOU CAN GET A HEAD START ON ME WITH THOSE TWO. I'LL CATCH UP IN A FEW MINUTES.
I DON'T WANT THE PRINCE TO HAVE TO SEE WHAT I'M GOING TO DO NEXT...
...
WHA--?!
......
GOT IT. ALTO'S ALL YOURS.
!!
COME ALONG THEN, PRINCE!!
WE DON'T WANT TO KEEP THE KING AND QUEEN WAITING TOO LONG, DO WE?
NO! I DON'T WANT TO GO HOME!
LEAVE US ALONE!!

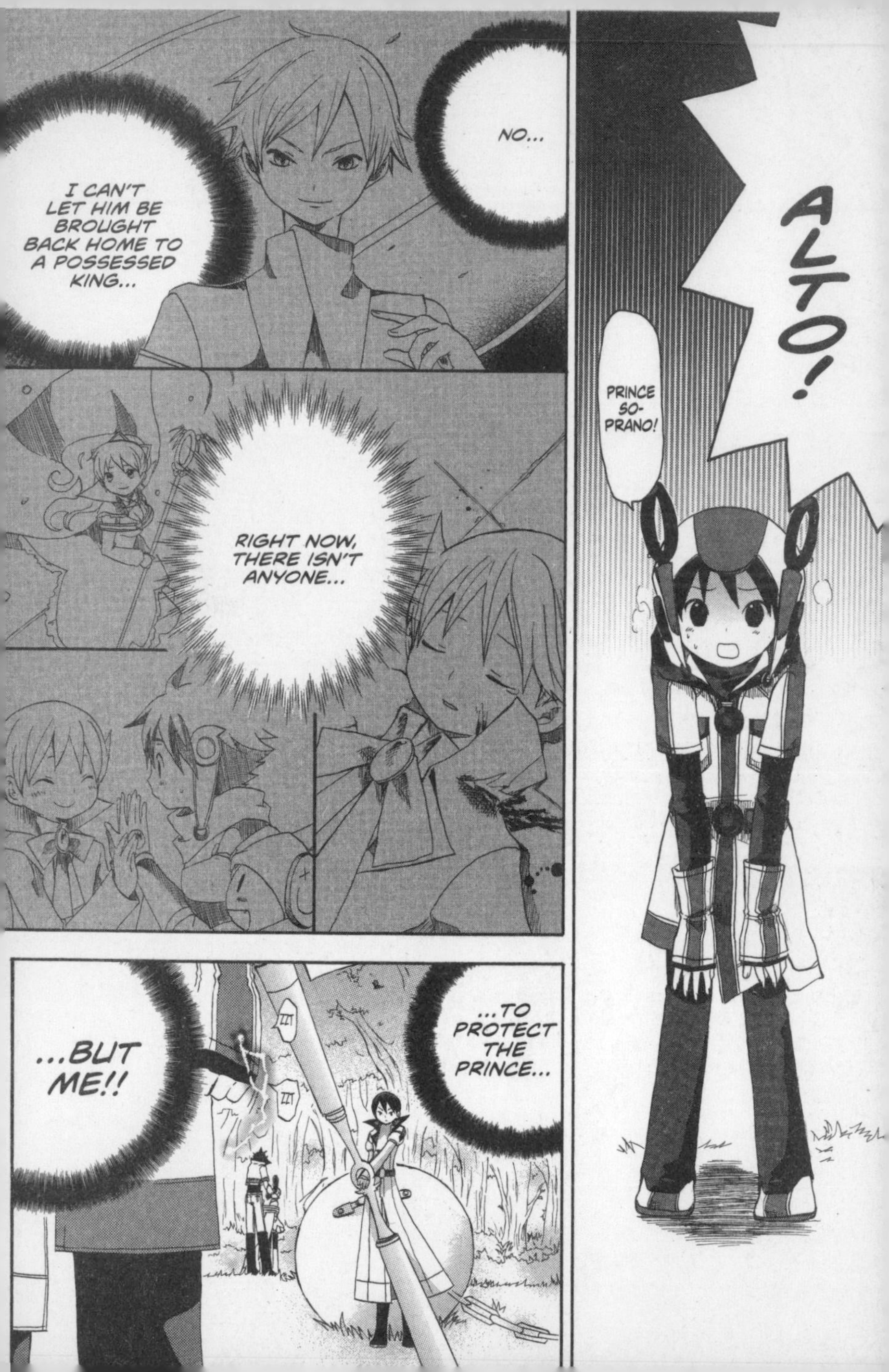
ALTO!
PRINCE SO-PRANO!
NO...
I CAN'T LET HIM BE BROUGHT BACK HOME TO A POSSESSED KING...
RIGHT NOW, THERE ISN'T ANYONE...
...TO PROTECT THE PRINCE...
ZZT
ZZT
...BUT ME!!

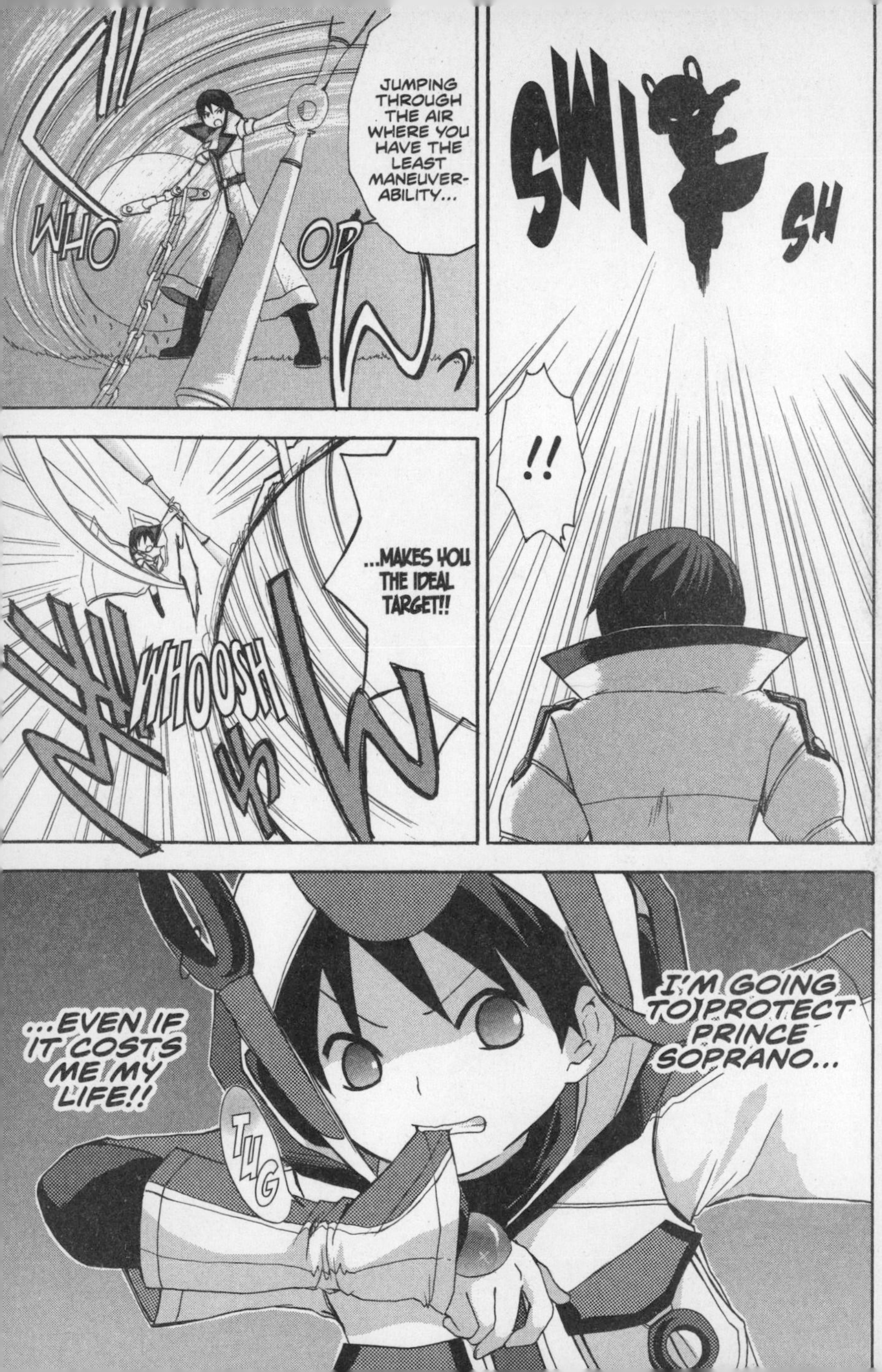
SWI
SH
!!
JUMPING THROUGH THE AIR WHERE YOU HAVE THE LEAST MANEUVER-ABILITY...
WHO
OP
...MAKES YOU THE IDEAL TARGET!!
WHOOSH
I'M GOING TO PROTECT PRINCE SOPRANO...
...EVEN IF IT COSTS ME MY LIFE!!
TUG

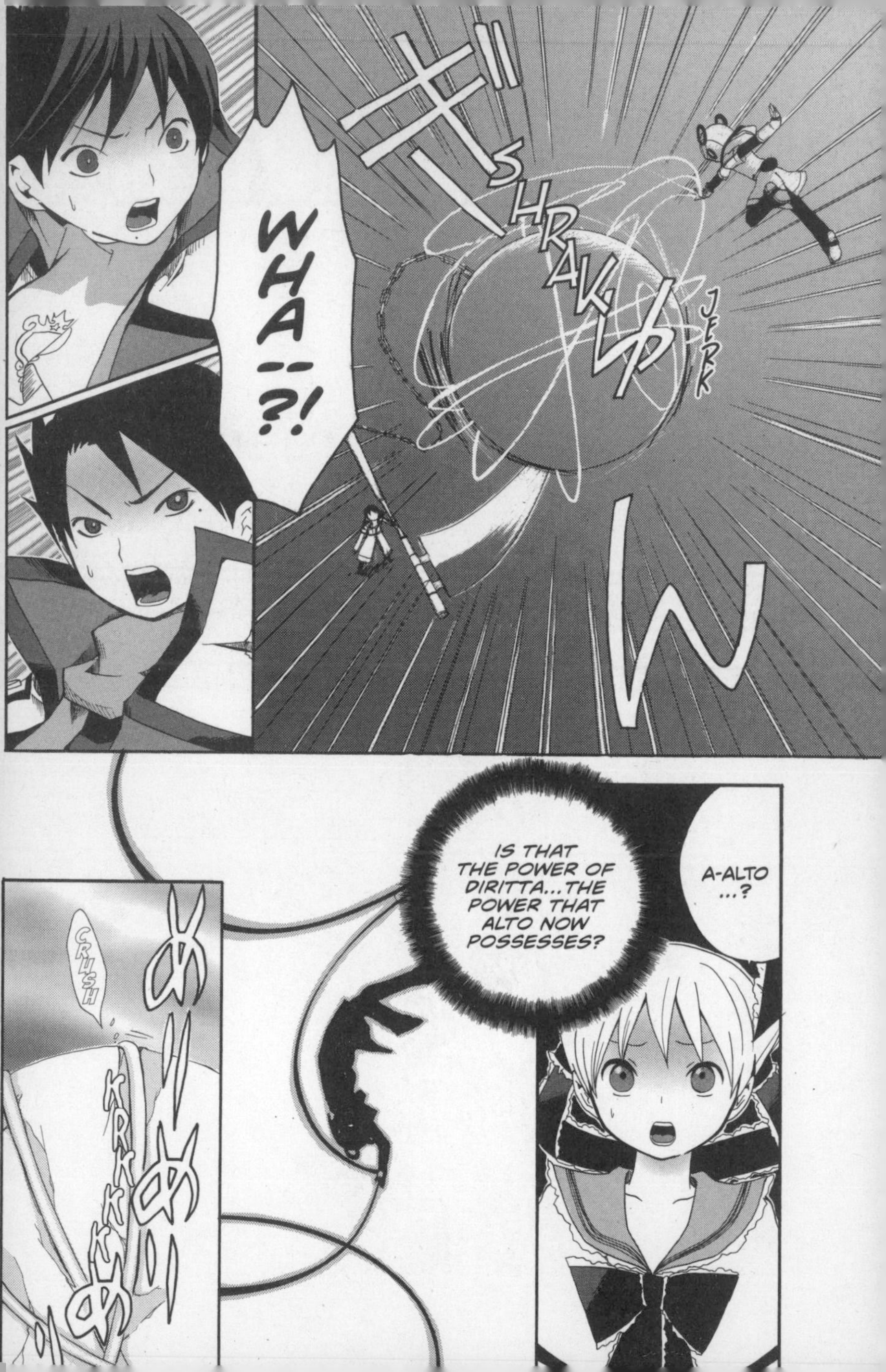
SHRAKK
JERK
WHA--?!
A-ALTO ...?
IS THAT THE POWER OF DIRITTA...THE POWER THAT ALTO NOW POSSESSES?
CRUSH
KRKKK

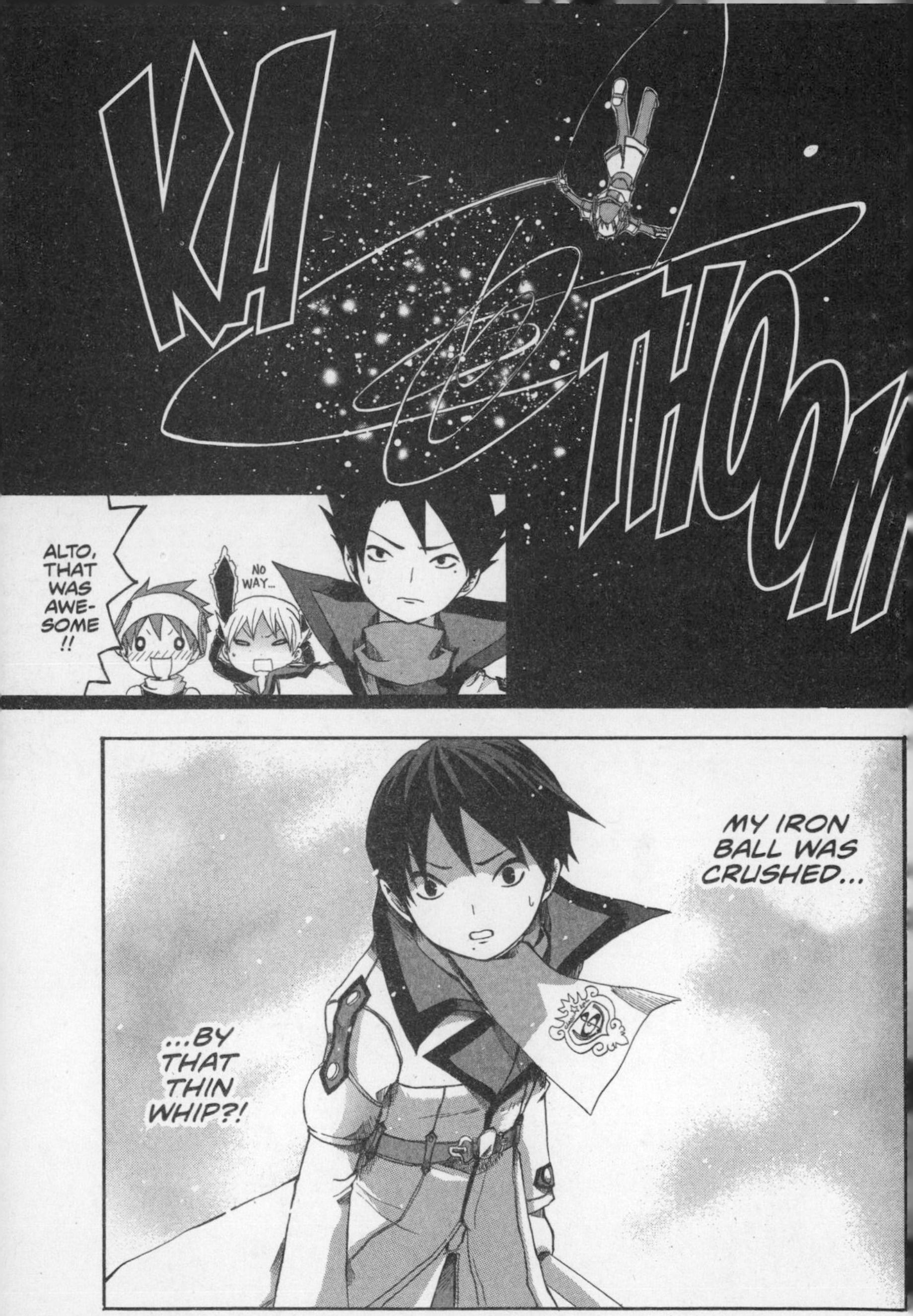
KA
THOOM
NO WAY...
ALTO, THAT WAS AWE-SOME!!
MY IRON BALL WAS CRUSHED...
...BY THAT THIN WHIP?!

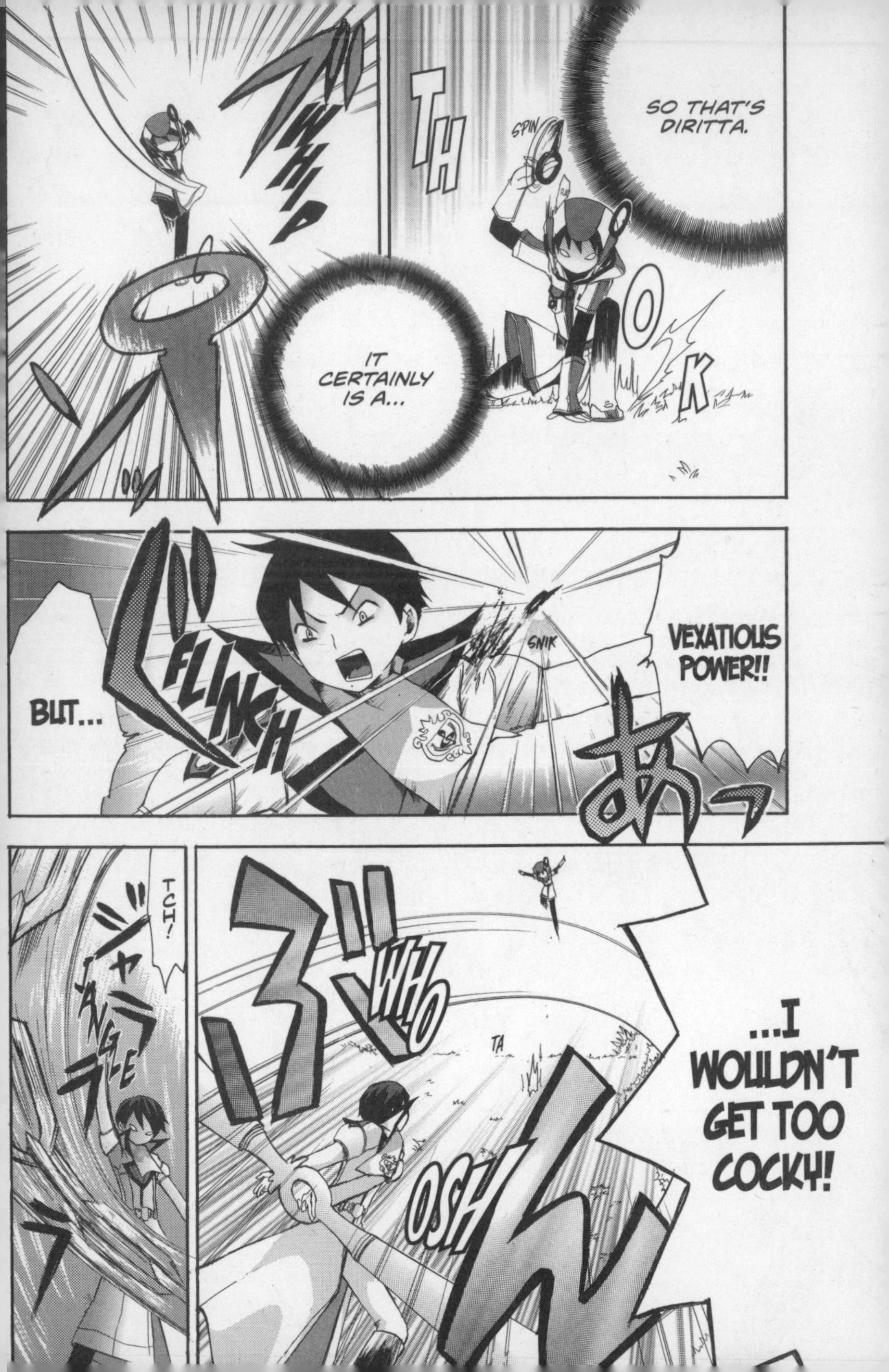

SO THAT'S DIRITTA.
SPIN
TH
O
K
WHIP
IT CERTAINLY IS A...
VEXATIOUS POWER!!
SNIK
FLINCH
BUT...
あっ
...I WOULDN'T GET TOO COCKY!
WHO
OSH
TA
TCH!
JANGLE

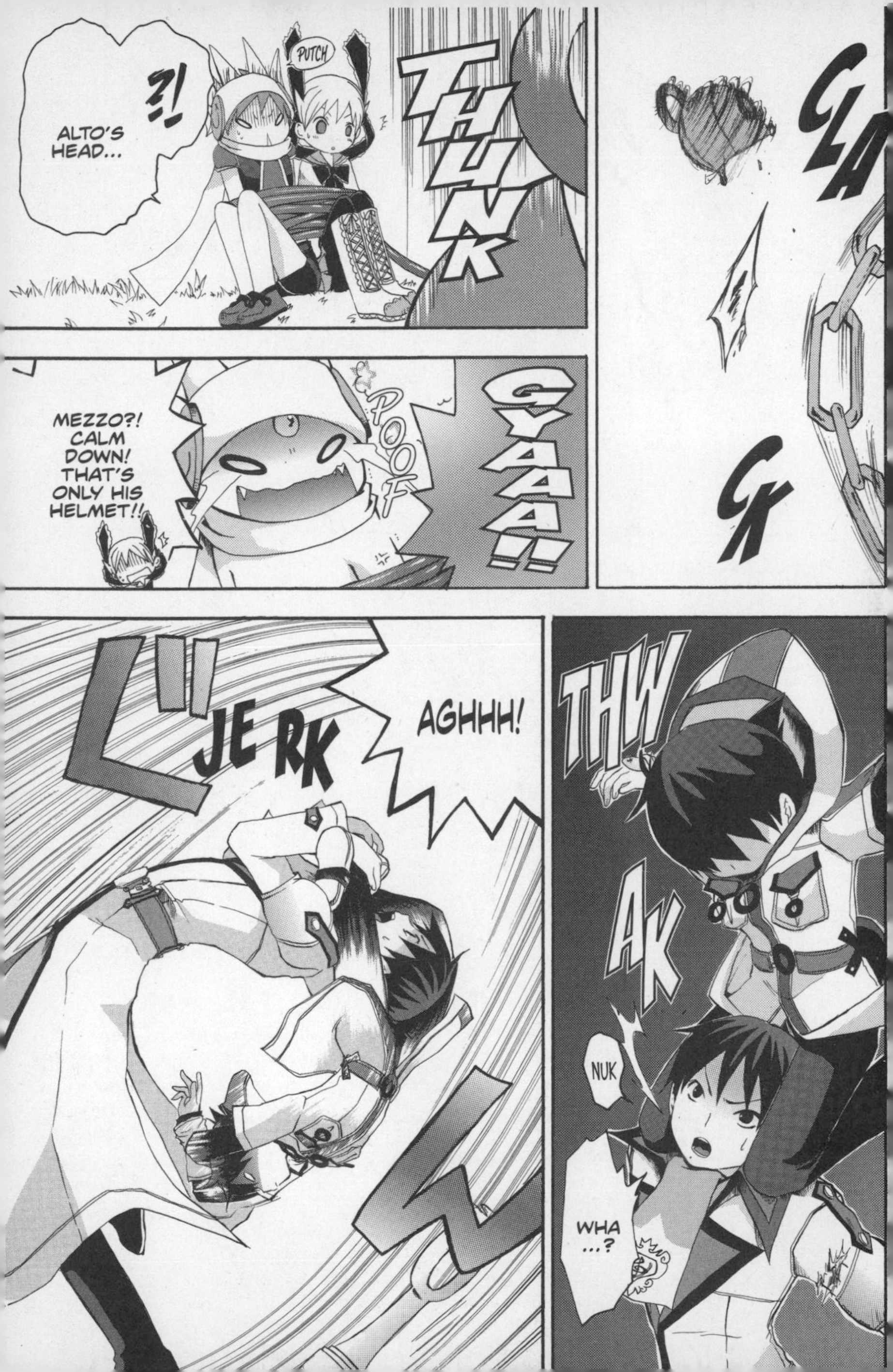

CLA
GK
THUNK
PUTCH
?!
ALTO'S HEAD...
GYAAA!!
POOF
MEZZO?! CALM DOWN! THAT'S ONLY HIS HELMET!!
THW
AK
NUK
WHA ...?
JERK
AGHHH!

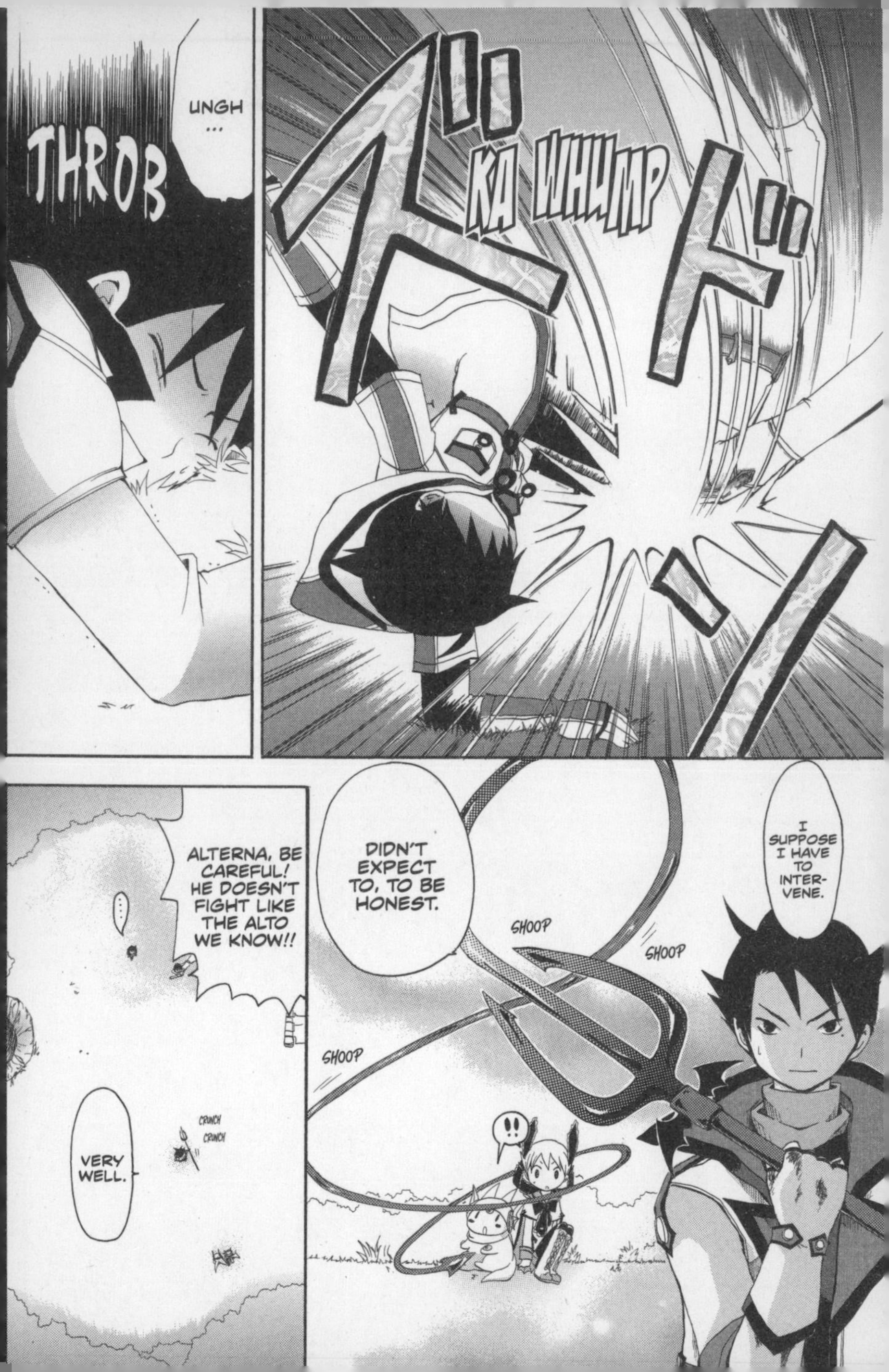
KA WHUMP
UNGH ...
THROB
I SUPPOSE I HAVE TO INTER-VENE.
SHOOP
SHOOP
DIDN'T EXPECT TO, TO BE HONEST.
SHOOP
!!
ALTERNA, BE CAREFUL! HE DOESN'T FIGHT LIKE THE ALTO WE KNOW!!
...
CRUNCH
CRUNCH
VERY WELL.

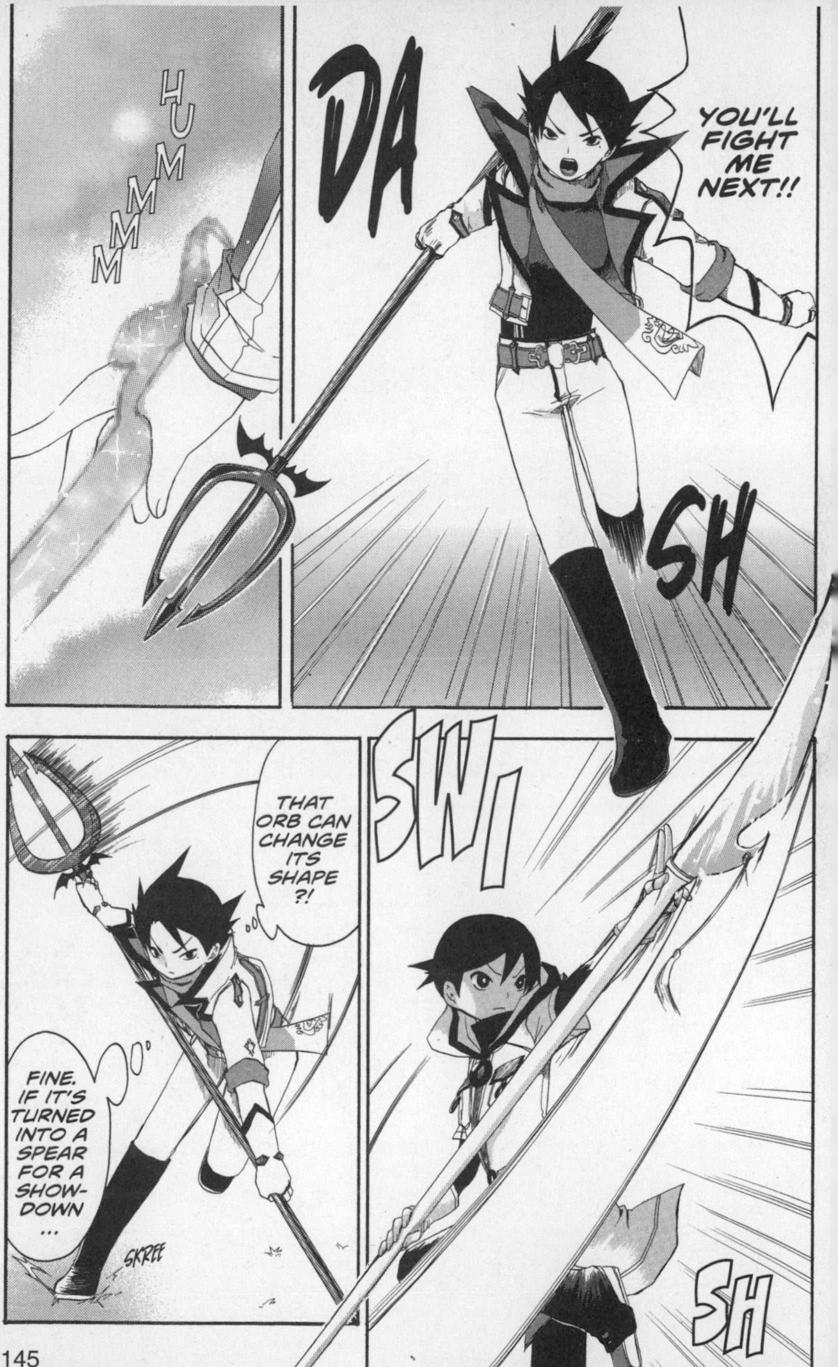
DA
YOU'LL FIGHT ME NEXT!!
SH
HUMMMM
SWI
SH
THAT ORB CAN CHANGE ITS SHAPE?!
FINE. IF IT'S TURNED INTO A SPEAR FOR A SHOW-DOWN...
SKREE

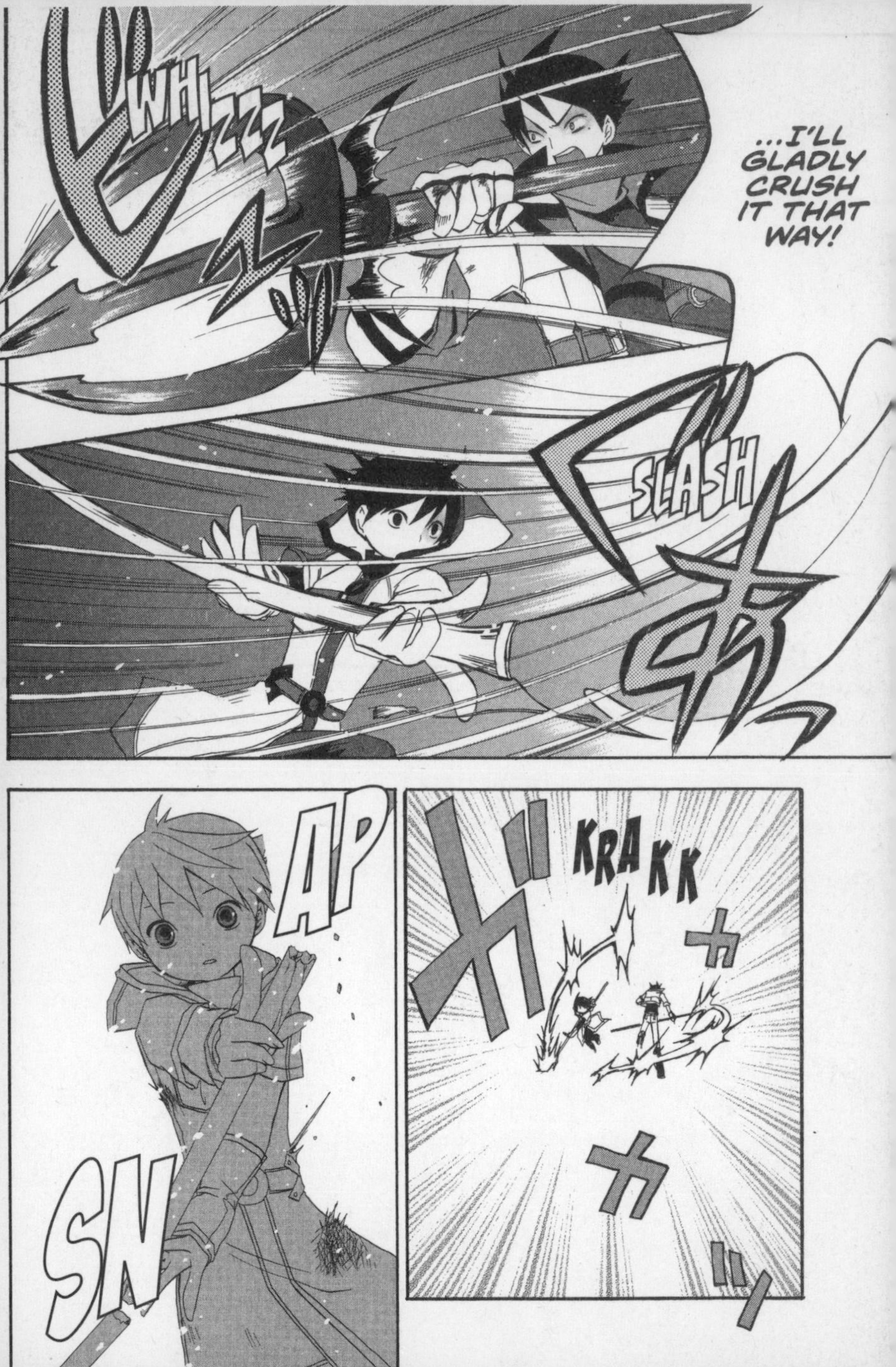
...I'LL GLADLY CRUSH IT THAT WAY!
WHIZZZ
SLASH
KRAKK
SNAP

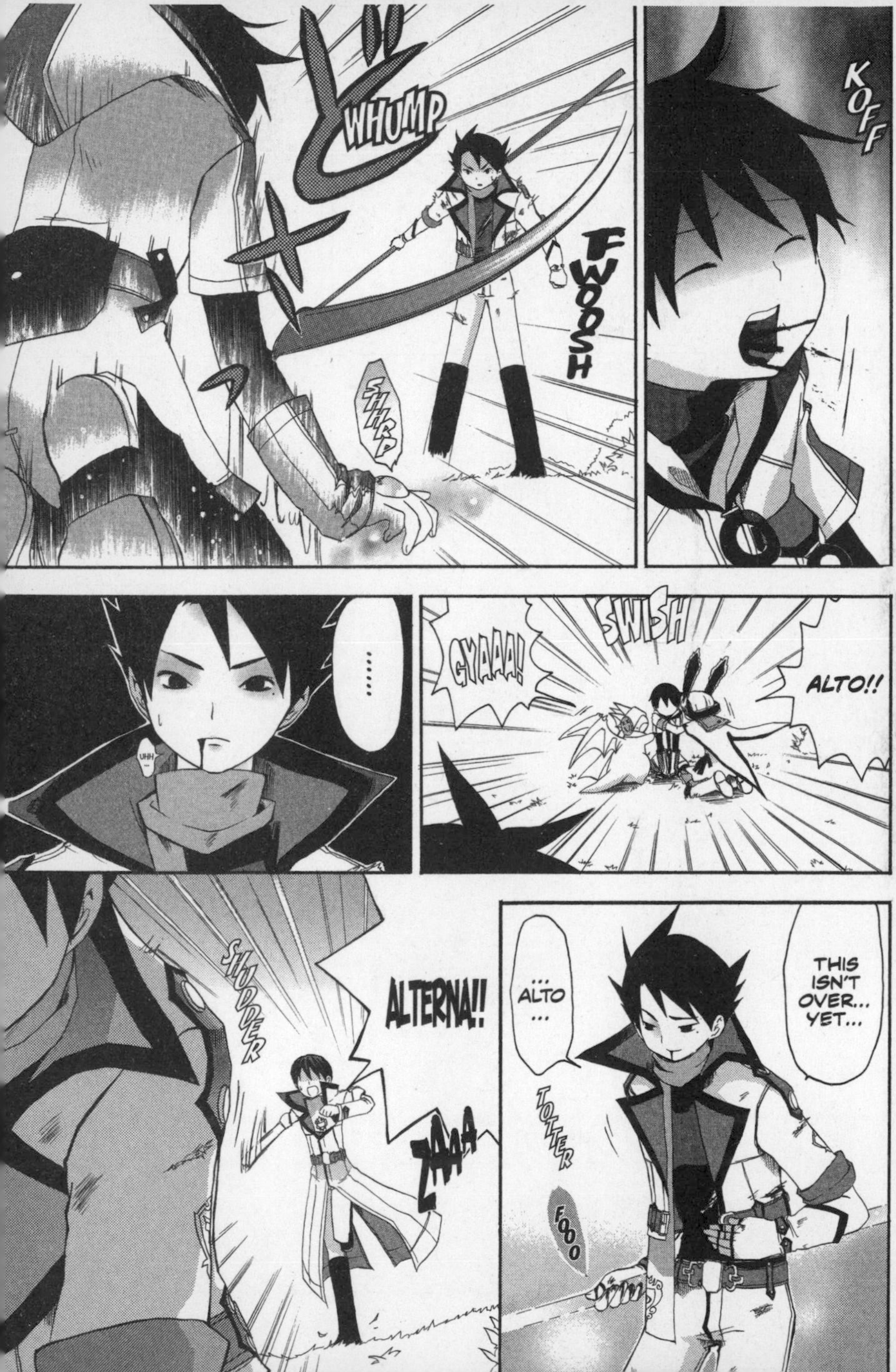
KOFF
WHUMP
FWOOSH
SHHRP
SWISH
ALTO!!
GYAAA!
......
UHH...
THIS ISN'T OVER... YET...
... ALTO ...
TOTTER
FOOO
ALTERNA!!
SHUDDER
ZAAA

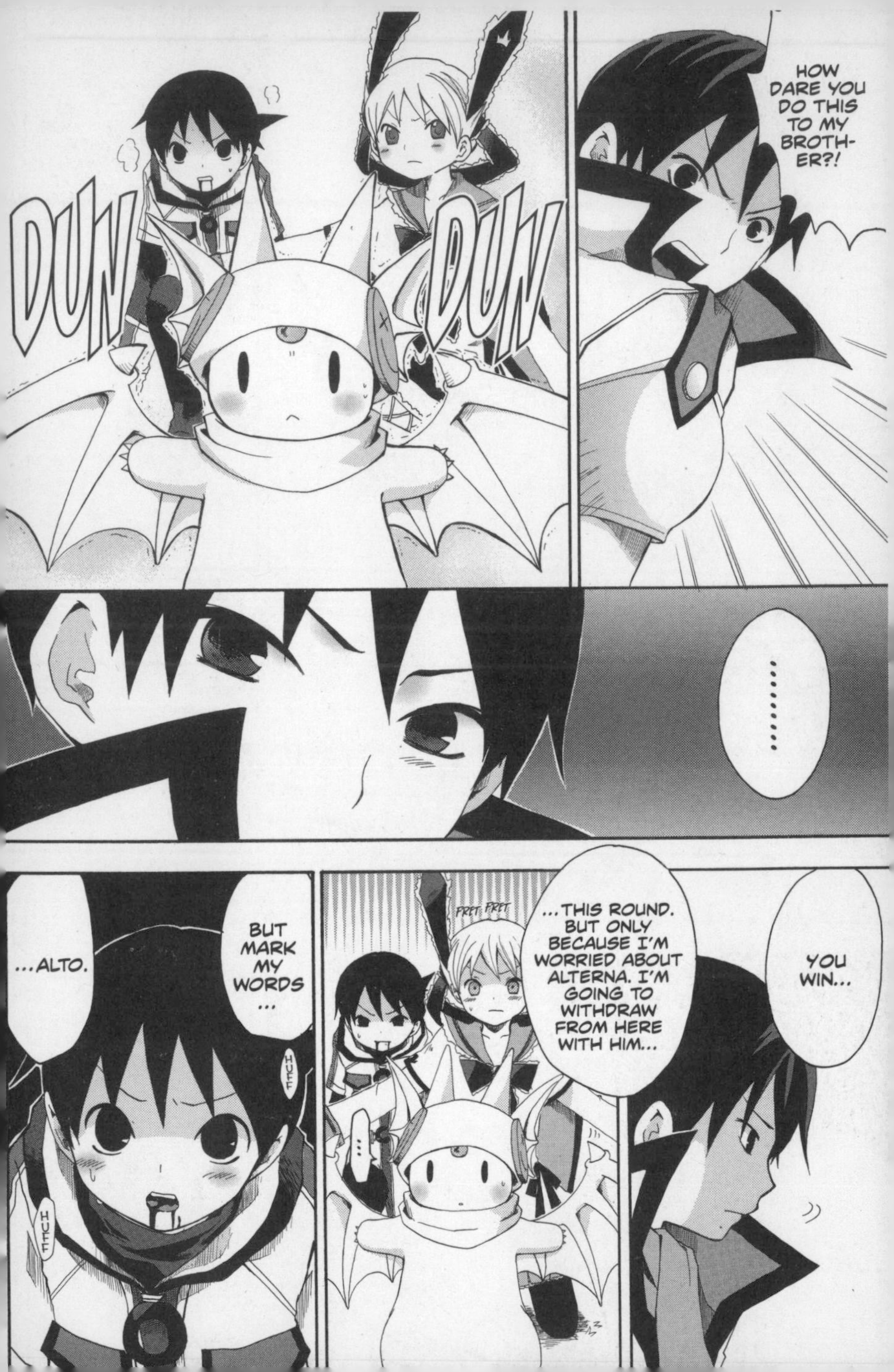
HOW DARE YOU DO THIS TO MY BROTHER?!
DUN
DUN
......
YOU WIN...
...THIS ROUND. BUT ONLY BECAUSE I'M WORRIED ABOUT ALTERNA. I'M GOING TO WITHDRAW FROM HERE WITH HIM...
FRET FRET
...
BUT MARK MY WORDS ...
...ALTO.
HUFF
HUFF

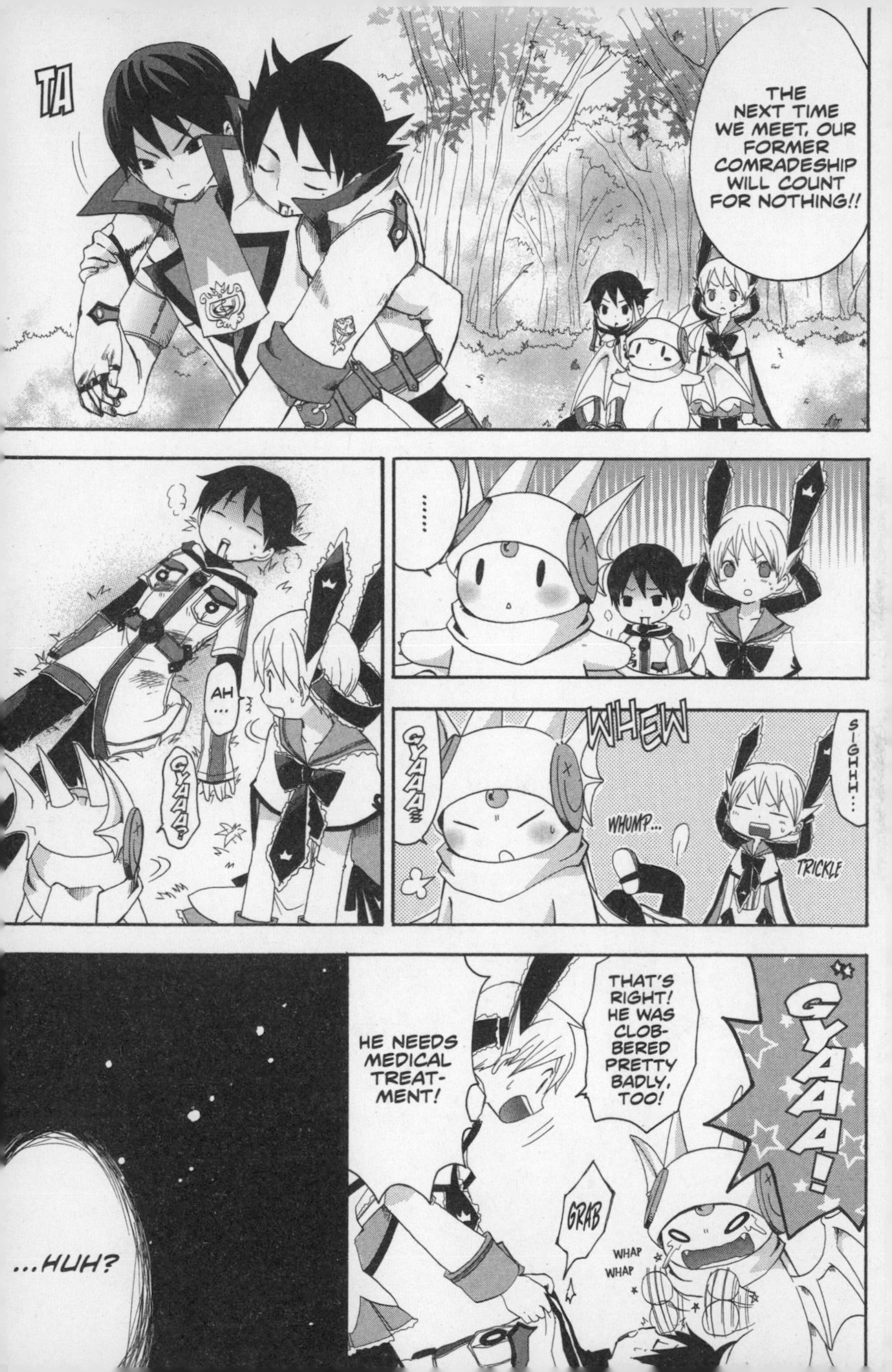
THE NEXT TIME WE MEET, OUR FORMER COMRADESHIP WILL COUNT FOR NOTHING!!
TA
......
SIGHHH...
WHEW
GYAAA
WHUMP...
TRICKLE
AH ...
GYAAA!
GYAAA!
THAT'S RIGHT! HE WAS CLOB-BERED PRETTY BADLY, TOO!
HE NEEDS MEDICAL TREAT-MENT!
GRAB
WHAP WHAP
...HUH?

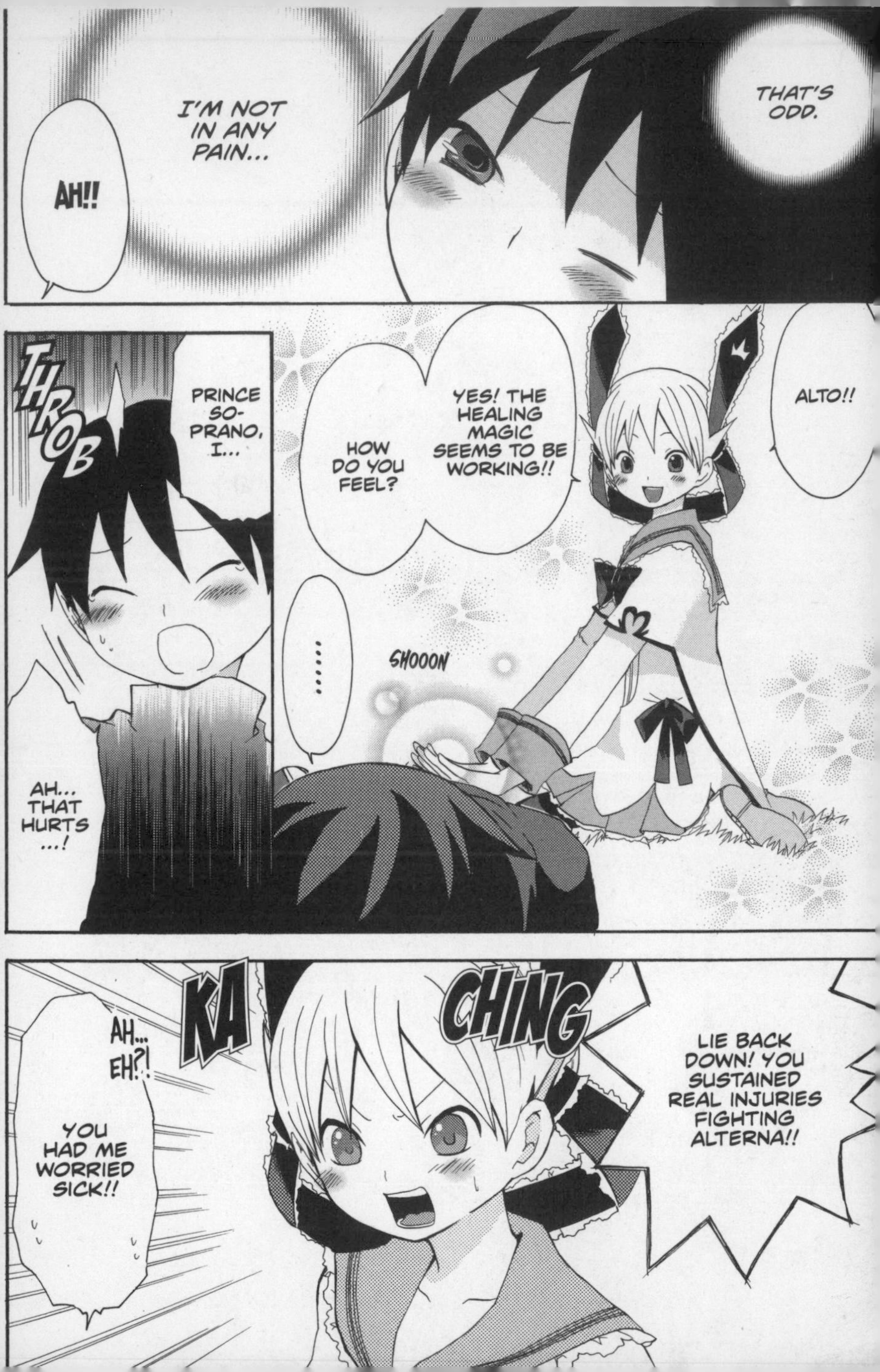
THAT'S ODD.
I'M NOT IN ANY PAIN...
AH!!
ALTO!!
YES! THE HEALING MAGIC SEEMS TO BE WORKING!!
HOW DO YOU FEEL?
......
SHOOON
THROB
PRINCE SO-PRANO, I...
AH... THAT HURTS ...!
KA
CHING
LIE BACK DOWN! YOU SUSTAINED REAL INJURIES FIGHTING ALTERNA!!
AH... EH?!
YOU HAD ME WORRIED SICK!!

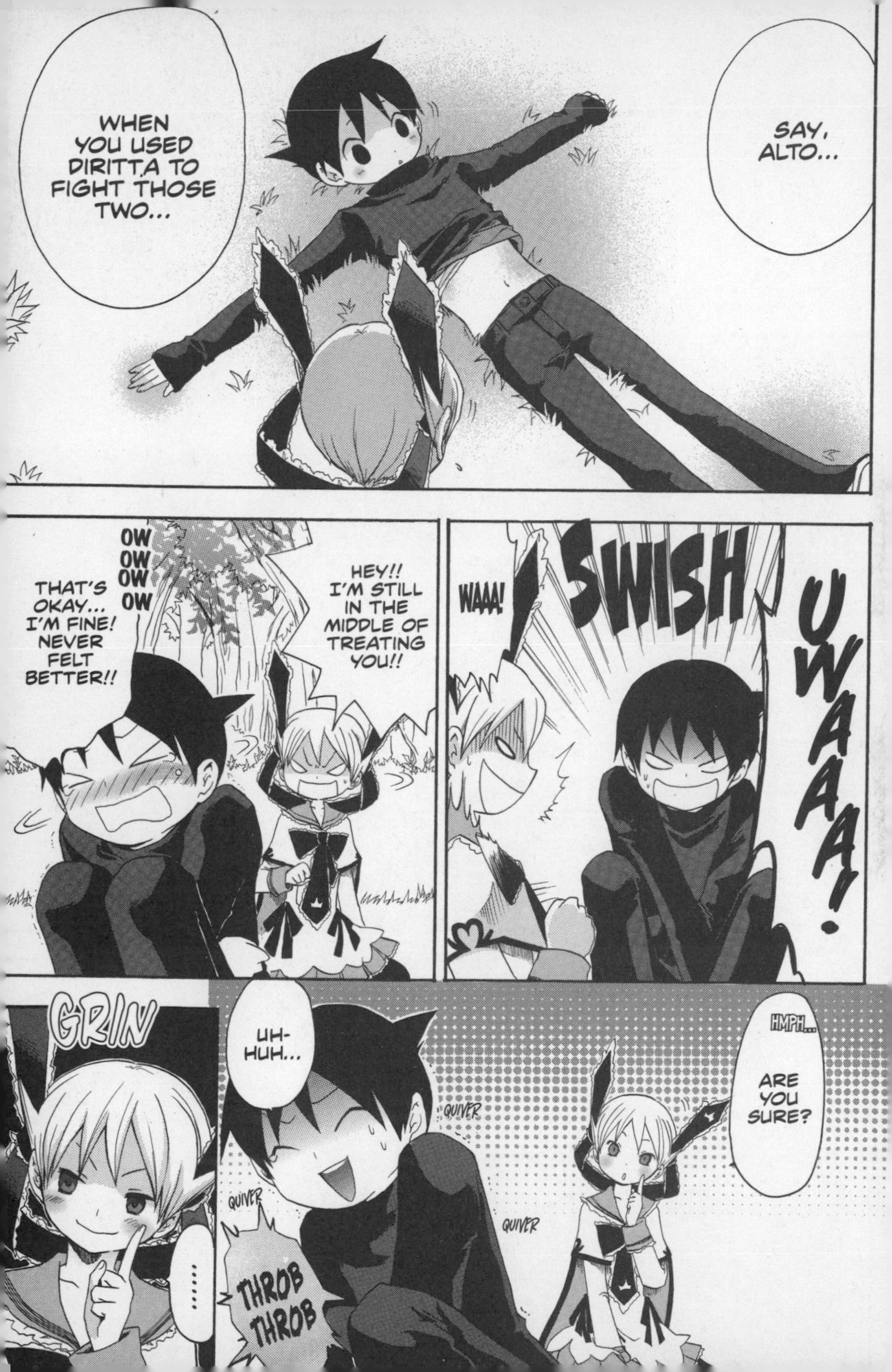
SAY, ALTO...
WHEN YOU USED DIRITTA TO FIGHT THOSE TWO...
SWISH
UWAAAA!
WAAA!
HEY!! I'M STILL IN THE MIDDLE OF TREATING YOU!!
OW OW OW OW
THAT'S OKAY... I'M FINE! NEVER FELT BETTER!!
HMPH...
ARE YOU SURE?
QUIVER
UH-HUH...
QUIVER
QUIVER
THROB THROB
GRIN
......

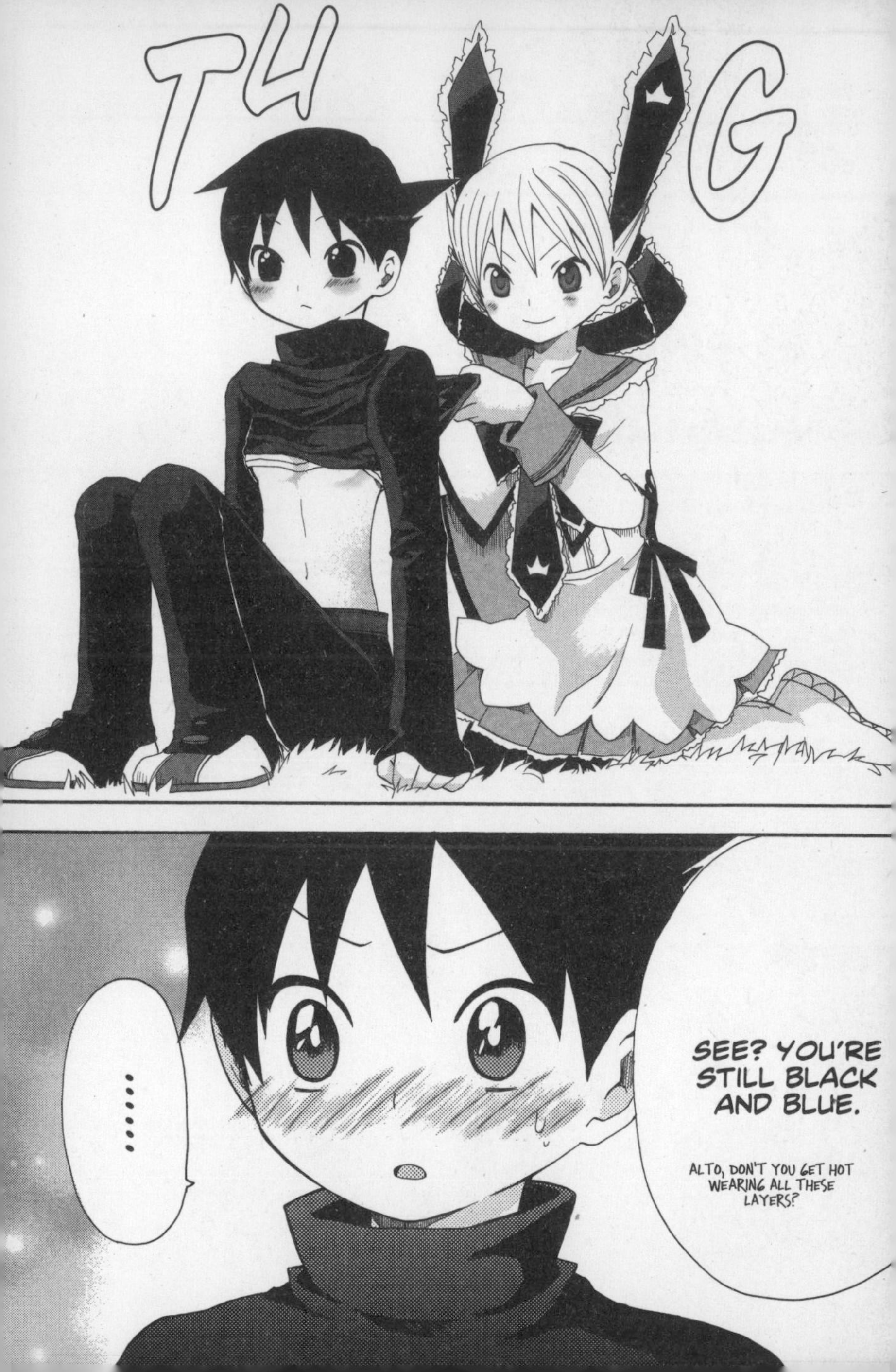
TUG
SEE? YOU'RE STILL BLACK AND BLUE.
ALTO, DON'T YOU GET HOT WEARING ALL THESE LAYERS?
......

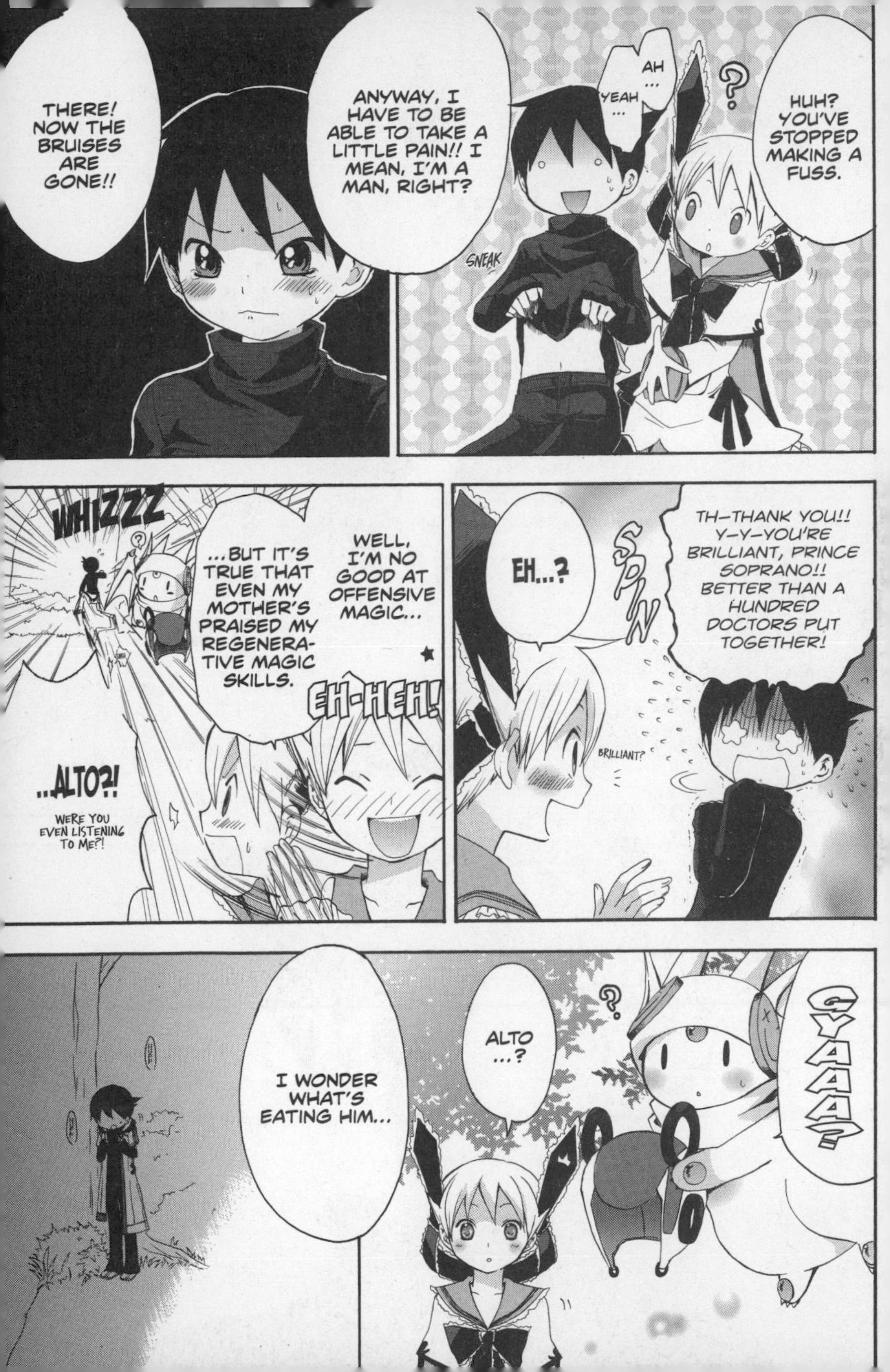
HUH? YOU'VE STOPPED MAKING A FUSS.
AH...
YEAH...
SNEAK
ANYWAY, I HAVE TO BE ABLE TO TAKE A LITTLE PAIN!! I MEAN, I'M A MAN, RIGHT?
THERE! NOW THE BRUISES ARE GONE!!
TH-THANK YOU!! Y-Y-YOU'RE BRILLIANT, PRINCE SOPRANO!! BETTER THAN A HUNDRED DOCTORS PUT TOGETHER!
SPIN
EH...?
BRILLIANT?
WELL, I'M NO GOOD AT OFFENSIVE MAGIC...
...BUT IT'S TRUE THAT EVEN MY MOTHER'S PRAISED MY REGENERATIVE MAGIC SKILLS.
EH-HEH!
WHIZZZ
...ALTO?!
WERE YOU EVEN LISTENING TO ME?!
GYAAA?
ALTO...?
I WONDER WHAT'S EATING HIM...

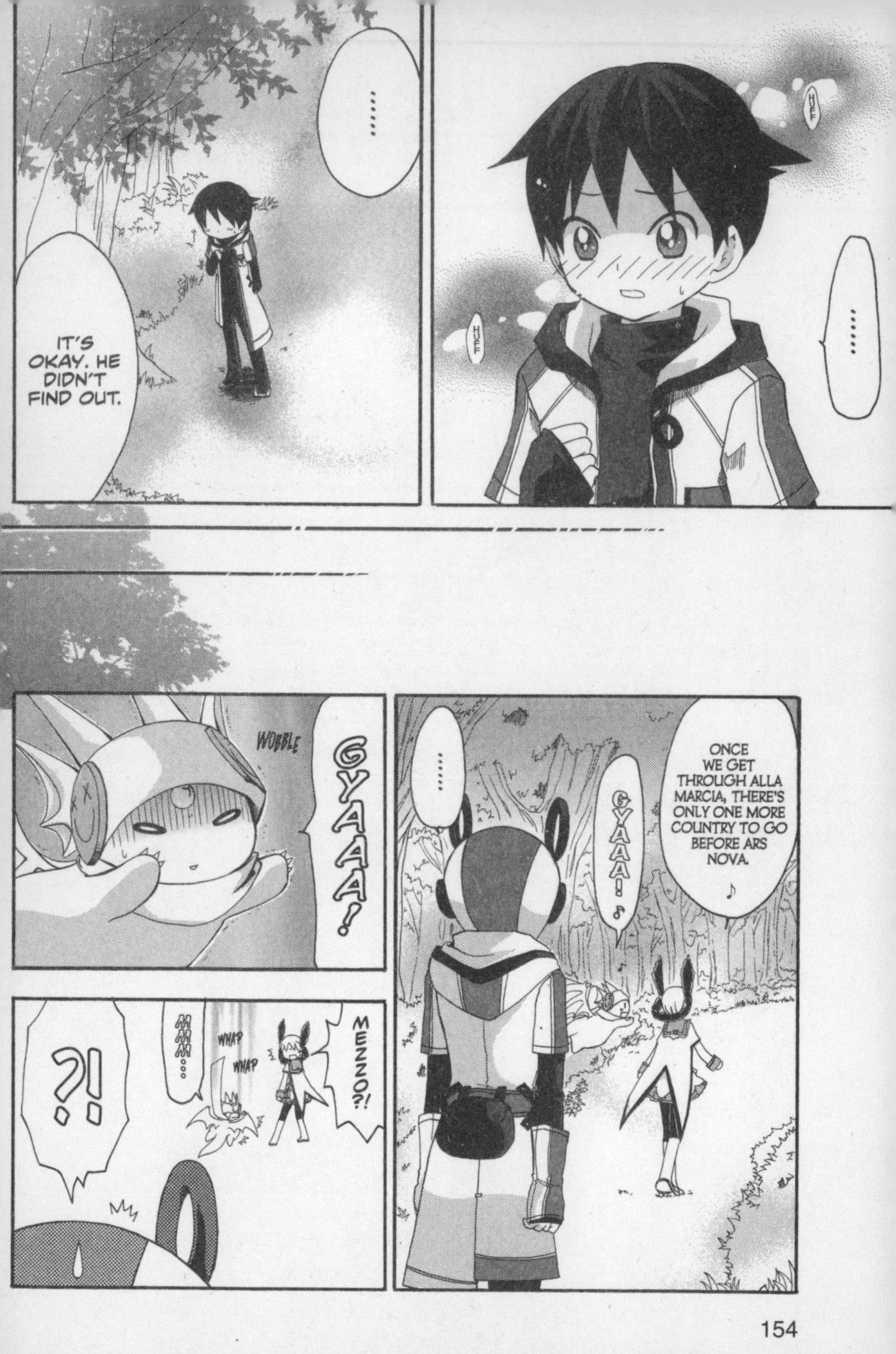
HUF
HUF
......
......
IT'S OKAY. HE DIDN'T FIND OUT.
ONCE WE GET THROUGH ALLA MARCIA, THERE'S ONLY ONE MORE COUNTRY TO GO BEFORE ARS NOVA. ♪
GYAAA! ♪
......
WOBBLE
GYAAA!
MEZZO?!
MMM...
WHAP
WHAP
?!

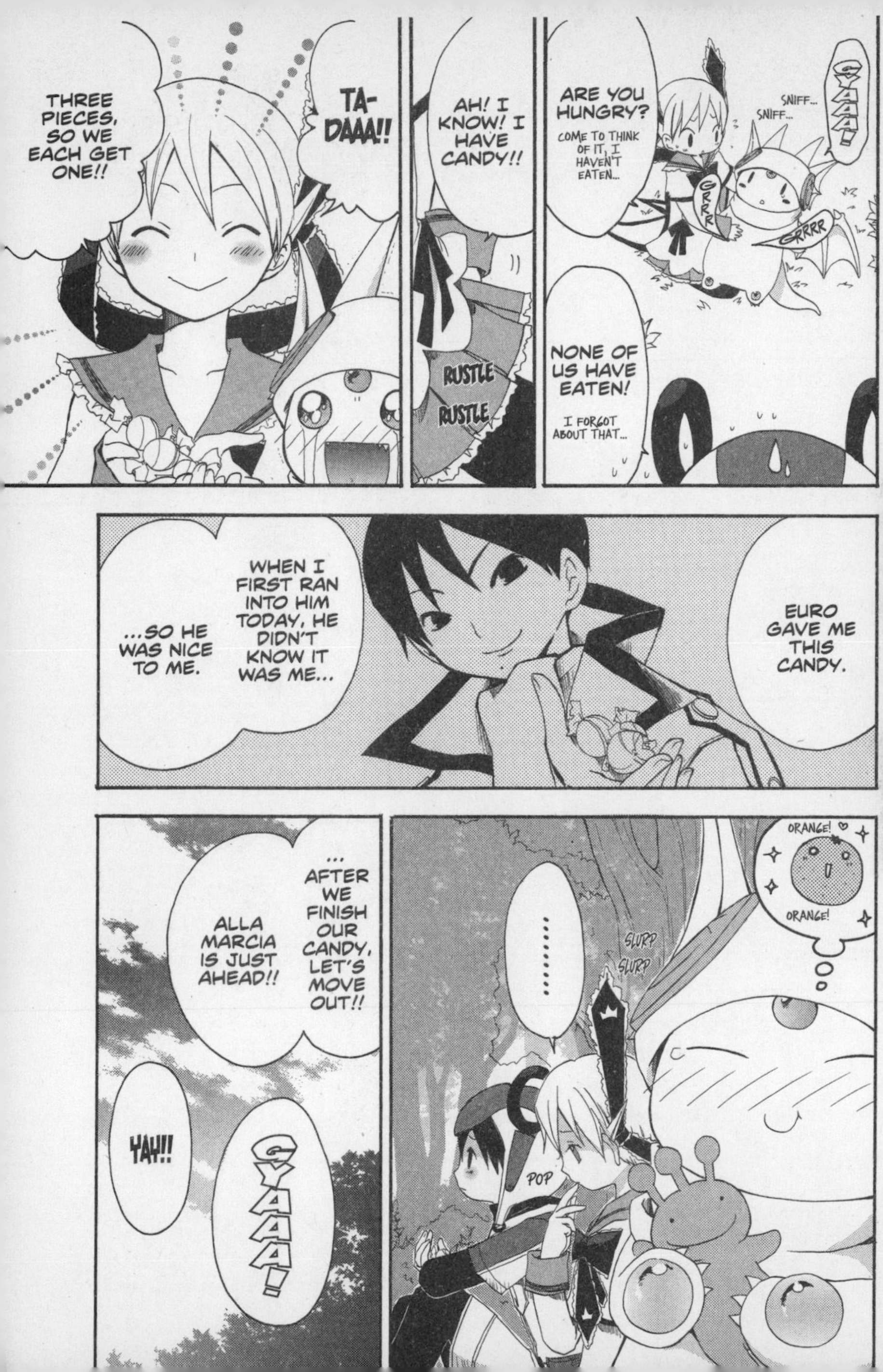
GYAAAA!
SNIFF... SNIFF...
ARE YOU HUNGRY?
COME TO THINK OF IT, I HAVEN'T EATEN...
GRRR
GRRRR
NONE OF US HAVE EATEN!
I FORGOT ABOUT THAT...
AH! I KNOW! I HAVE CANDY!!
RUSTLE
RUSTLE
TA-DAAA!!
THREE PIECES, SO WE EACH GET ONE!!
EURO GAVE ME THIS CANDY.
WHEN I FIRST RAN INTO HIM TODAY, HE DIDN'T KNOW IT WAS ME...
...SO HE WAS NICE TO ME.
ORANGE!
ORANGE!
......
SLURP
SLURP
POP
... AFTER WE FINISH OUR CANDY, LET'S MOVE OUT!!
ALLA MARCIA IS JUST AHEAD!!
GYAAAA!
YAY!!

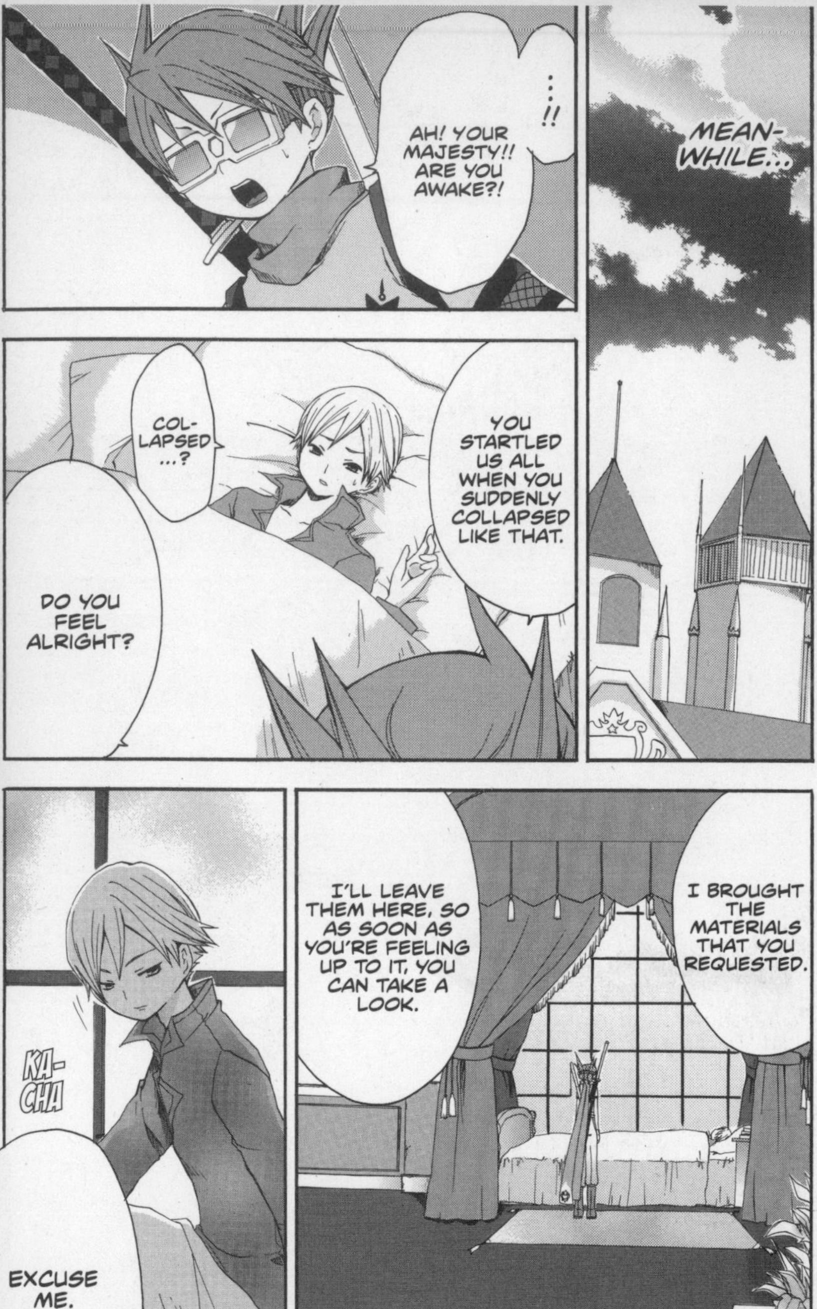
MEAN-WHILE...
...!!
AH! YOUR MAJESTY!! ARE YOU AWAKE?!
YOU STARTLED US ALL WHEN YOU SUDDENLY COLLAPSED LIKE THAT.
COL-LAPSED ...?
DO YOU FEEL ALRIGHT?
I BROUGHT THE MATERIALS THAT YOU REQUESTED.
I'LL LEAVE THEM HERE, SO AS SOON AS YOU'RE FEELING UP TO IT, YOU CAN TAKE A LOOK.
KA-CHA
EXCUSE ME.

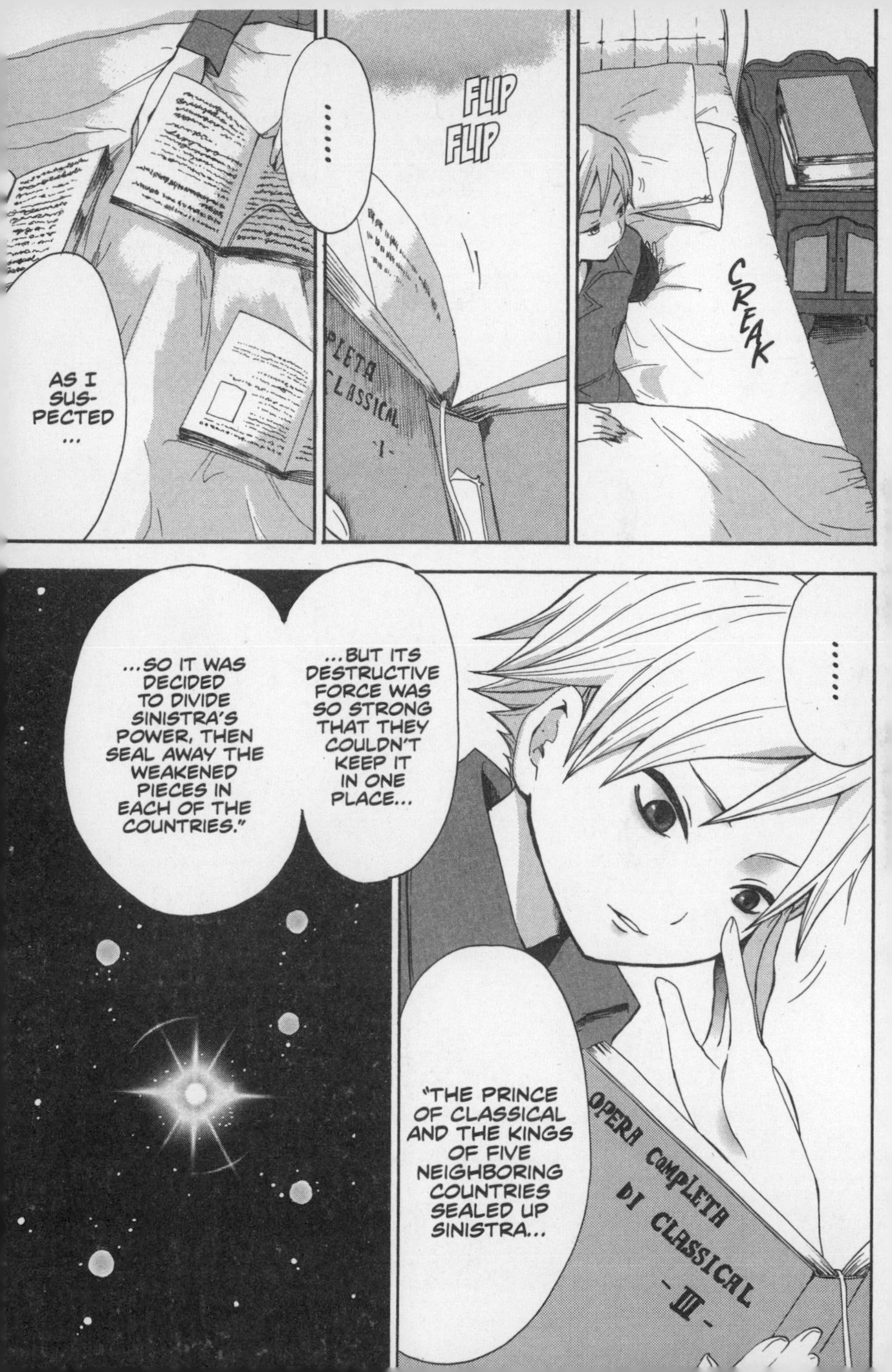
CREAK
FLIP FLIP
......
PLETA CLASSICAL -I-
AS I SUS-PECTED ...
......
"THE PRINCE OF CLASSICAL AND THE KINGS OF FIVE NEIGHBORING COUNTRIES SEALED UP SINISTRA...
OPERA COMPLETA DI CLASSICAL -III-
...BUT ITS DESTRUCTIVE FORCE WAS SO STRONG THAT THEY COULDN'T KEEP IT IN ONE PLACE...
...SO IT WAS DECIDED TO DIVIDE SINISTRA'S POWER, THEN SEAL AWAY THE WEAKENED PIECES IN EACH OF THE COUNTRIES."

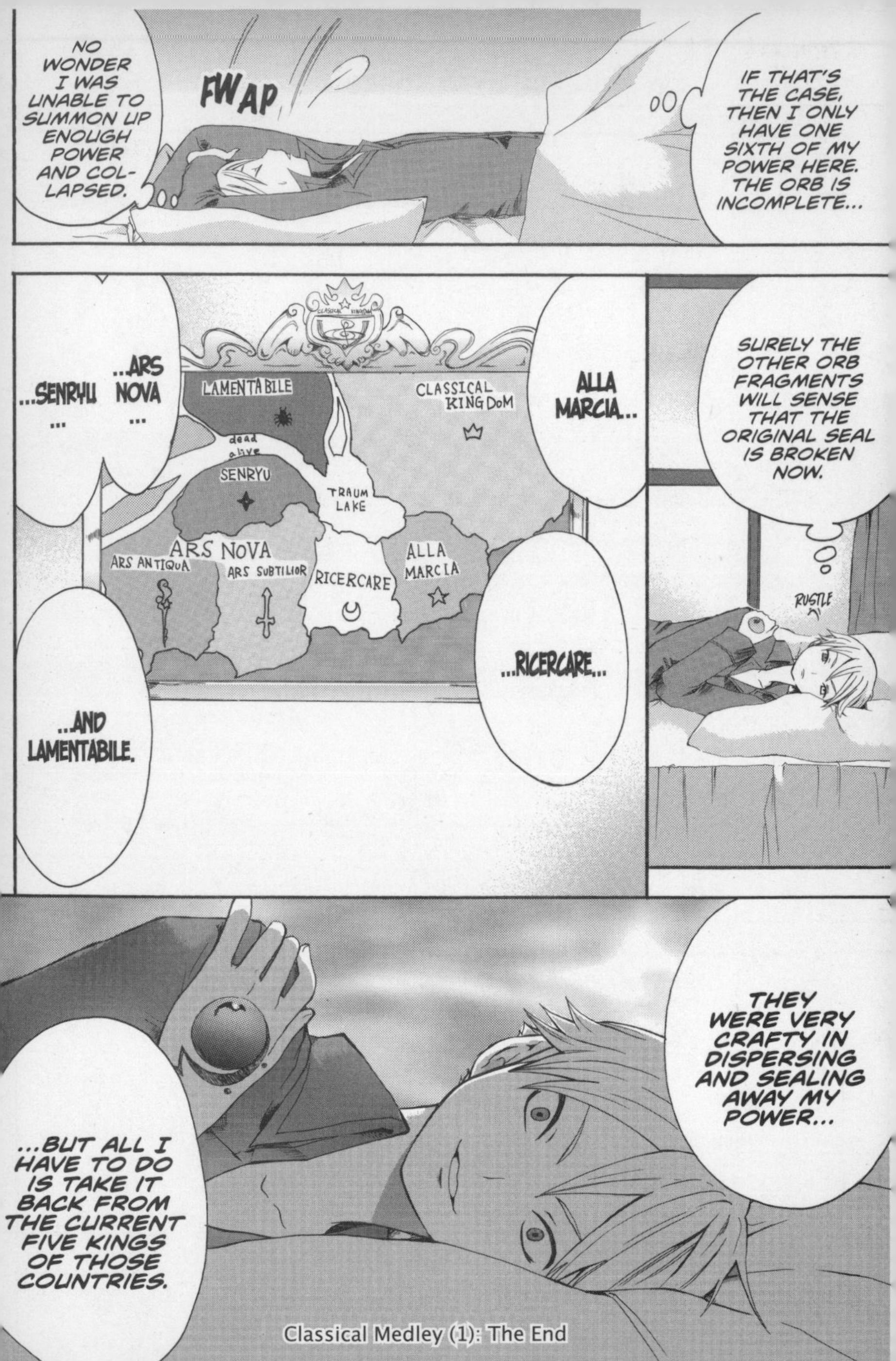
IF THAT'S THE CASE, THEN I ONLY HAVE ONE SIXTH OF MY POWER HERE. THE ORB IS INCOMPLETE...
FWAP
NO WONDER I WAS UNABLE TO SUMMON UP ENOUGH POWER AND COL-LAPSED.
SURELY THE OTHER ORB FRAGMENTS WILL SENSE THAT THE ORIGINAL SEAL IS BROKEN NOW.
RUSTLE
ALLA MARCIA...
...RICERCARE...
...ARS NOVA ...
...SENRYU ...
...AND LAMENTABILE.
CLASSICAL KINGDOM
LAMENTABILE
CLASSICAL KINGDOM
dead
alive
SENRYU
TRAUM LAKE
ARS NOVA
ARS ANTIQUA
ARS SUBTILIOR
RICERCARE
ALLA MARCIA
THEY WERE VERY CRAFTY IN DISPERSING AND SEALING AWAY MY POWER...
...BUT ALL I HAVE TO DO IS TAKE IT BACK FROM THE CURRENT FIVE KINGS OF THOSE COUNTRIES.
Classical Medley (1): The End

SPECIAL BONUS MANGA!!

★ Snacks with Mezzo

WITH THE QUINTET

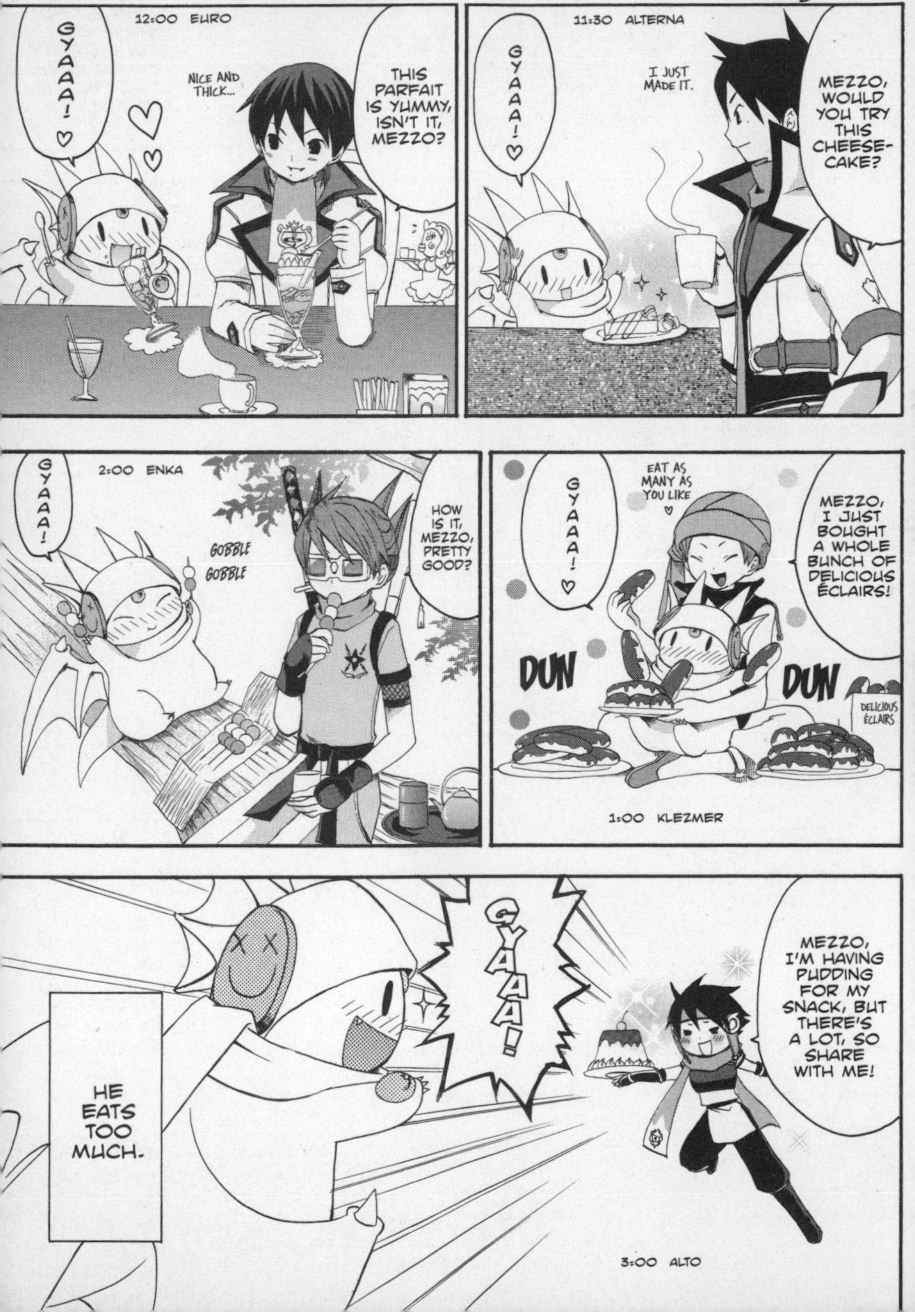

MEZZO, WOULD YOU TRY THIS CHEESECAKE?
11:30 ALTERNA
I JUST MADE IT.
GYAAAA! ♡
THIS PARFAIT IS YUMMY, ISN'T IT, MEZZO?
12:00 EURO
NICE AND THICK...
GYAAA! ♡
MEZZO, I JUST BOUGHT A WHOLE BUNCH OF DELICIOUS ÉCLAIRS!
EAT AS MANY AS YOU LIKE ♡
GYAAAA! ♡
DUN
DUN
DELICIOUS ÉCLAIRS
1:00 KLEZMER
HOW IS IT, MEZZO, PRETTY GOOD?
2:00 ENKA
GOBBLE GOBBLE
GYAAAA!
MEZZO, I'M HAVING PUDDING FOR MY SNACK, BUT THERE'S A LOT, SO SHARE WITH ME!
GYAAA!
3:00 ALTO
HE EATS TOO MUCH.

STORY AND ART BY SANAE KANA

THE DAY MEZZO WAS BORN

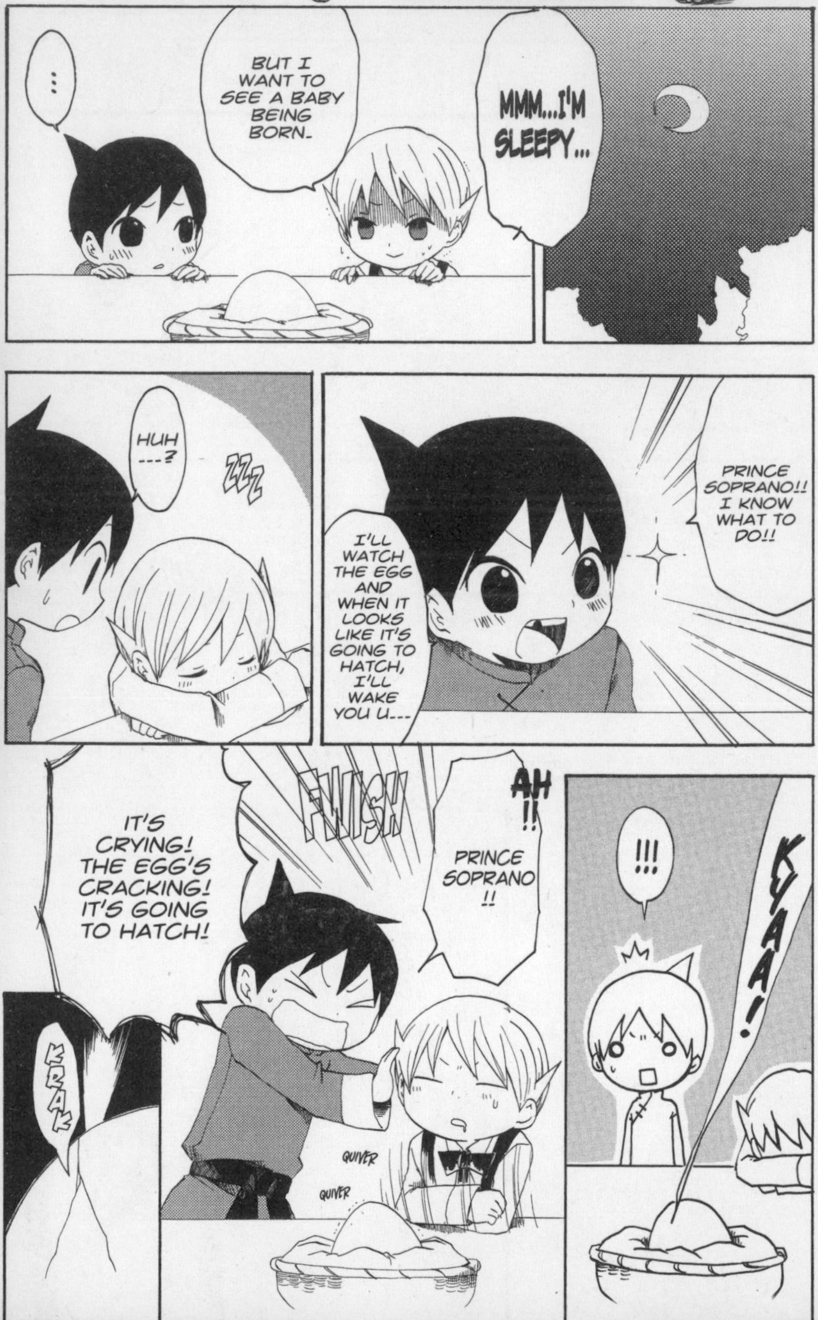
MMM...I'M SLEEPY...
BUT I WANT TO SEE A BABY BEING BORN.
...
PRINCE SOPRANO!! I KNOW WHAT TO DO!!
I'LL WATCH THE EGG AND WHEN IT LOOKS LIKE IT'S GOING TO HATCH, I'LL WAKE YOU U---
HUH ---?
ZZZ
!!!
KYAAA!
AH !!
PRINCE SOPRANO !!
FWISH
IT'S CRYING! THE EGG'S CRACKING! IT'S GOING TO HATCH!
QUIVER
QUIVER
KRAK

n Lee Editorial Director John Nee Senior VP—Business Development
nk Kanalz VP—General Manager, WildStorm Paul Levitz President & Publisher
org Brewer VP—Design & DC Direct Creative Richard Bruning Senior VP—Creative Director
trick Caldon Executive VP—Finance & Operations Chris Caramalis VP—Finance
hn Cunningham VP—Marketing Terri Cunningham VP—Managing Editor Alison Gill VP—Manufacturing
vid Hyde VP—Publicity Paula Lowitt Senior VP—Business & Legal Affairs
egory Noveck Senior VP—Creative Affairs Sue Pohja VP—Book Trade Sales
eve Rotterdam Senior VP—Sales & Marketing Cheryl Rubin Senior VP—Brand Management
ff Trojan VP—Business Development, DC Direct Bob Wayne VP—Sales

SSICAL MEDLEY Vol. 1 © 2007 Sanae Kana. All rights reserved. First published in Japan in 2007
lex Comix Inc., Tokyo.

ssical Medley Volume 1, published by WildStorm Productions, an imprint of DC Comics, 888
ospect St. #240, La Jolla, CA 92037. English Translation © 2008 DC Comics. All Rights Reserved.
lish translation rights arranged with FC Manga Seisaku Fund and Flex Comix Inc. CMX is a
emark of DC Comics. The stories, characters, and incidents mentioned in this magazine are
rely fictional. Printed on recyclable paper. WildStorm does not read or accept unsolicited
missions of ideas, stories or artwork. Printed in Canada.

Comics, a Warner Bros. Entertainment Company.

eldon Drzka – Translation and Adaptation
dWorld Design – Lettering & Retouching
rry Berry – Design
n Chadwick – Editors

cmx
FLEX
COMIX

ISBN: 978-1-4012-1898-0

WILL HARMONY RETURN TO CLASSICAL?
FIND OUT IN JANUARY 2009!

y **Sanae Kana.** Don't miss the dramatic conclusion as Soprano, Alto and Mezzo
ntinue to work together to return things to normal. Soprano's got the power now, but will
learn how to wield it? The possessed King is out to get the rest of his powers back from
e surrounding kingdoms, while Soprano still has to hold off his brothers Euro and Alterna.
ore thrills, more laughs and more adventure await!

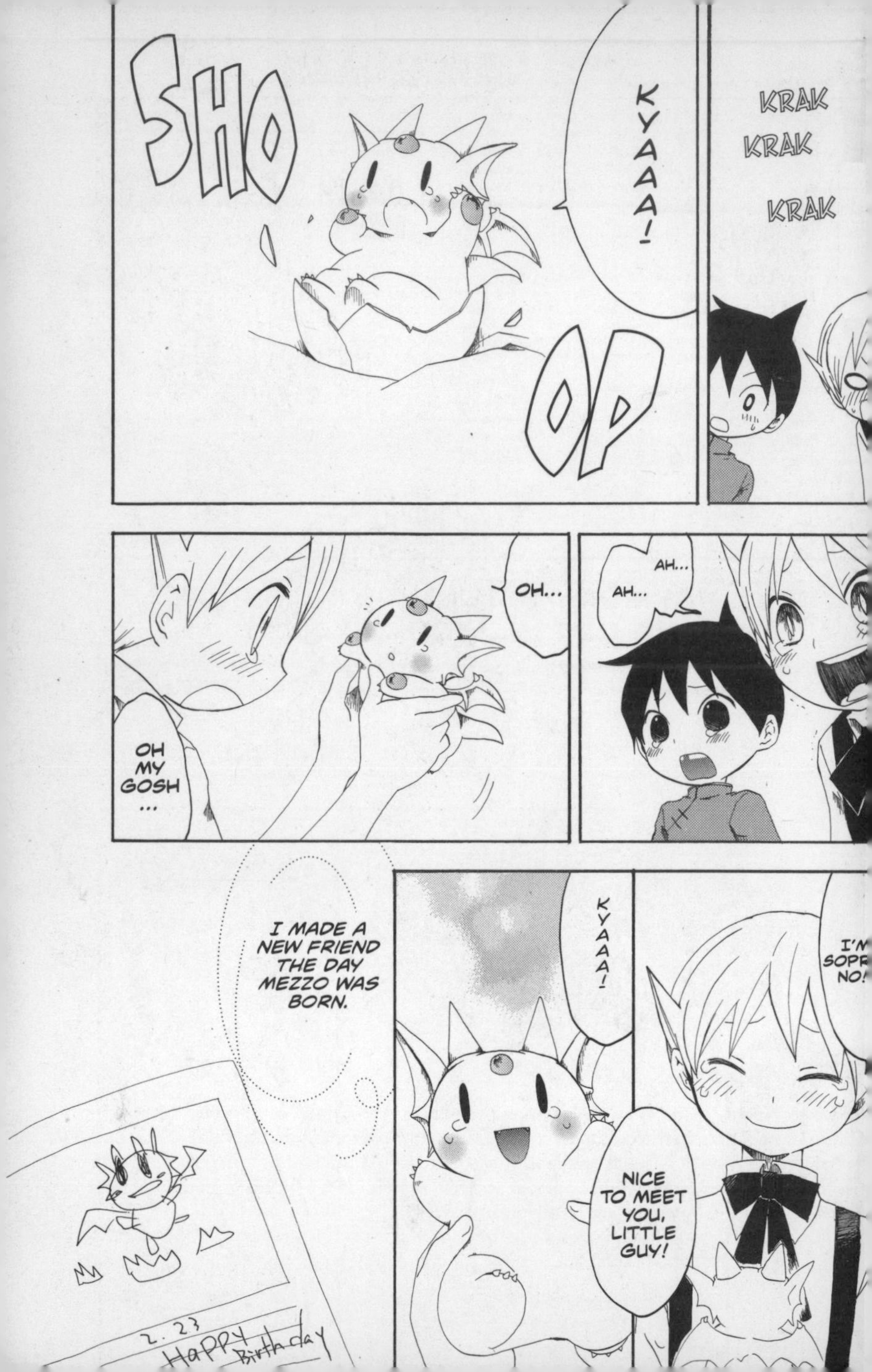
KRAK
KRAK
KRAK
KYAAAA!
SHO
OP
AH...
AH...
OH...
OH MY GOSH ...
I'M SOPR NO!
KYAAAA!
NICE TO MEET YOU, LITTLE GUY!
I MADE A NEW FRIEND THE DAY MEZZO WAS BORN.
2. 23
HAPPY Birthday